SCHOOL OF EUROPEANNESS

SCHOOL OF EUROPEANNESS

Tolerance and Other Lessons
in Political Liberalism in Latvia

Dace Dzenovska

CORNELL UNIVERSITY PRESS   **ITHACA AND LONDON**

First published 2018 by Cornell University Press

Printed in the United States of America

Library of Congress Cataloging-in-Publication Data

Names: Dzenovska, Dace, author.
Title: School of Europeanness : tolerance and other lessons in political liberalism in Latvia / Dace Dzenovska.
Description: Ithaca : Cornell University Press, 2018. | Includes bibliographical references and index.
Identifiers: LCCN 2017029176 (print) | LCCN 2017031204 (ebook) | ISBN 9781501716850 (epub/mobi) | ISBN 9781501716867 (pdf) | ISBN 9781501716836 | ISBN 9781501716836 (cloth : alk. paper) | ISBN 9781501711152 (pbk. : alk. paper)
Subjects: LCSH: Liberalism—Latvia. | Toleration—Political aspects—Latvia. | Minorities—Latvia. | Post-communism—Latvia. | Latvia—Politics and government—1991– | Latvia—Relations—Europe. | Europe—Relations—Latvia.
Classification: LCC JN6739.A15 (ebook) | LCC JN6739.A15 .D94 2018 (print) | DDC 320.51094796—dc23
LC record available at https://lccn.loc.gov/2017029176

Cornell University Press strives to use environmentally responsible suppliers and materials to the fullest extent possible in the publishing of its books. Such materials include vegetable-based, low-VOC inks and acid-free papers that are recycled, totally chlorine-free, or partly composed of nonwood fibers. For further information, visit our website at cornellpress.cornell.edu.

To Sofia

Contents

Preface   ix

Acknowledgments   xiii

Introduction: Paradox of Europeanness: The Need to
Exclude and the Virtue of Inclusion   1

1. Pride and Shame: The Moral and Political Landscape of
Europe's Colonial Past in the Present   19

2. The State People and Their Minorities: Rebirth of a
National State with a Minority Problem   44

3. Knowing Subjects and Partial Understandings:
Diagnosis of Intolerance and Other Knowledge
Practices after Socialism   81

4. Building Up and Tearing Down: Critical Thinking in the
Context of Tolerance Promotion   112

5. Language Sacred and Language Injurious: Ethical
Encounters with the Other   141

6. Repression and Redemption: The Tensions of
Rebordering Europe   174

Epilogue: Liberalism on the Fence   207

Notes   215

References   229

Index   249

Preface

I started researching and writing this book when the global victory of liberalism as the dominant rationality for organizing economic and political life seemed certain and ended it when it no longer does. For one of the main characters of the book—post–Cold War political liberalism—the shifts have been significant. In 1991, when the Soviet Union crumbled, liberalism seemed to be the light at the end of history (Fukuyama 1989). As most people and institutions grappled to find their bearings, a wide variety of economic and political liberalization projects were rolled out across the former socialist world. Neither entirely imposed, nor fully locally generated, they were the product of specific histories, shifts in the global distribution of power, and renewed faith in the efficiency of the market and the value of individual freedoms.

In 2005, when I began fieldwork in Latvia on attempts to embed the liberal political virtue of tolerance in public institutions and the hearts and minds of the public, the Latvian version of post-Soviet capitalism had produced a dizzying credit-based economic bubble. The Latvian economy seemed to be going full speed ahead, and Latvia's residents were urged to keep up—"put the pedal to the floor," as one politician put it at the time. The speed with which political liberalism was making its way into public institutions was much slower. This was often attributed to the difficulty of changing "socialist mentalities." Moreover, Latvians did not want to give up their collective sense of self and insisted on the importance of history and the nation alongside individual liberties and respect for diversity. Nevertheless, there was little doubt among the proponents of political liberalism that things were moving in the right direction. After all, Latvia had just joined the European Union. Geopolitics and the law were on their side.

In 2017, as this book goes to print, the position of political liberalism in Europe is no longer so confident. The 2008–10 financial crisis stopped the "pedal to the floor" politics, resulting in severe austerity measures that expelled large numbers of Latvia's residents from economic life and even from the country (Dzenovska 2018a, 2013b; Sassen 2014). This did not, however, weaken faith in the capitalist market, neither in Latvia nor globally. Neoliberalism, as Philip Mirowski (2011) has argued, has come out of the crisis stronger than ever. Instead, it is political liberalism that seems to be in crisis (Boyer 2016, Westbrook 2016).

Many scholars on the left link the crisis of political liberalism to the failure of liberal politics to address the grievances of those dispossessed by neoliberal forms of capitalism. As Ivan Krastev has put it, "In order to prevent anticapitalist mobilization, liberals successfully excluded anticapitalist discourse, but in doing so they opened up space for political mobilization around symbolic and identity issues, thus creating the conditions for their own destruction. The priority given to building capitalism over building democracy is at the heart of the current rise of democratic illiberalism in Central and Eastern Europe" (2007, 62).

Indeed, it is neoliberalism, rather than political liberalism, with its faith in the market as the most efficient and nonideological mechanism for resolving any disbalance in the system, that has come to be lodged in the hearts and minds of many ordinary people in Latvia and beyond (Mirowski 2011). Political liberalism has not taken such root. David Westbrook (2016) suggests that it may have served as an ideological layer that obscured the illiberalism at the foundation of the post–World War II supranational political economy: as a "house ideology" of Western liberal democracies, it was "a lingua franca or perhaps even a form of manners. It is the way civilized strangers address one another, the form of self-presentation that marks the better sort of people."

That said, both neoliberalism and liberalism are terms that should be used with care. Neoliberalism, as Sherry Ortner (2016) has recently pointed out, has become one of the dark forces in anthropological theory since the 1980s. As such, it often tends to be taken for granted as a foil against which to mount one's analytical and political interventions. Similarly, Lisa Hoffman, Monica DeHart, and Stephen Collier have argued that anthropology is concerned *with* neoliberalism, but that there are considerably fewer ethnographies *of* neoliberalism that "deconstitute neoliberalism," that is, "distinguish among, and focus attention upon, specific elements associated with neoliberalism—policies, forms of enterprising subjectivity, economic or political-economic theories, norms of accountability, transparency and efficiency, and mechanisms of quantification or calculative choice—to examine the actual configurations in which they are found" (2006, 10; see also Collier 2011).

My book sets out to deconstitute political liberalism as an actually existing post–Cold War formation in Latvia. My primary focus is not on political liberalism as a coherent system of thought and action, but rather on the contested projects of remaking people and institutions in the name of political liberalism that emerged in the context of democratization initiatives that, in turn, were part of the "postsocialist transition" in Latvia. The configuration of elements that made up actually existing political liberalism in Latvia in the 2000s is both trans-locally recognizable and locally specific. On the one hand, these elements can be discerned in various European Union accession documents that travel across the European political landscape and emphasize the norms of human rights, minority rights, tolerance, civil liberties, and the rule of law. On the other hand, the contours of actually existing political liberalism in Latvia emerge through encounters and arguments, as these norms were being introduced and implemented. They appear as explicit policy measures, political discourses, and as tacit understandings, sensibilities, and dispositions of those who promoted them, as well as those who contested them. These constitutive elements of actually existing political liberalism emerge most vividly at times and in places where political liberalism is thought to be absent—as, for example, in the context of the debates about Europe's "migration/refugee crisis," during which Eastern Europe was widely accused of lacking the sentiment and conduct of properly liberal Europeans (see the Introduction). It is such accusations of illiberalism that reveal the contours of political liberalism as an ideological and civilizing project located in historically specific fields of power.

I am not therefore suggesting that there is no need to think about how to talk with strangers or how to live with difference in Latvia and Eastern Europe more broadly. Rather, I am suggesting that in their confidence and moral superiority postsocialist liberalization projects may have missed the target. The confident adherents of post–Cold War political liberalism overlooked the role of geopolitics in the Latvian desire to join the "free world," as well as misrecognized the significance of historical and cultural embeddedness by taking it to be an impediment rather than a resource. Many Latvians did not necessarily believe in the idea of Europe promoted by the proponents of political liberalism, but wished to join Europe and other international alliances, such as NATO, because they were not convinced that history had really ended. The perpetual threat of Russia loomed large in the Latvian national imaginary. Moreover, there were many Soviet-era Russian speakers in Latvia, and many Latvians were convinced that their loyalties were directed eastward.

But there were also true believers among Latvia's residents, that is, individuals who were not only convinced that political liberalism offered the best model for living together across difference, but also tried in their capacity as professionals or activists to convince others that this was so. Many of my interlocutors—or "tolerance workers," as I refer to them in the book—belonged in this category. They were part of a network of civil servants, NGO workers, international consultants, and activists and were all engaged in efforts to promote tolerance as a public and political virtue. Some were returned second-generation diaspora Latvians who had grown up in the West during the Cold War; others were locals who had embraced liberal values as a result of education or life experience, or minorities who found a framework for their political struggles in liberalism. There were young people among them, individuals who were coming of age during the "postsocialist transition." Many developed their sense of self vis-à-vis liberal values, felt passionately about them, and were truly embarrassed and pained by their compatriots' reluctance to embrace liberal political virtues. They invested their hopes and futures in Europe as a liberal moral and political community. However, at the precise moment that my interlocutors were pushing full speed ahead toward the European present, which, they thought, was their future, Europe became unsure about itself, its present, and its future. Just as the young Latvian liberals thought that Latvia could finally approximate Europe, they found themselves amidst rising illiberalism across the European political landscape. Their well-intended efforts to find a way to live in a plural and interconnected world were undermined by institutionalized forms of political liberalism that failed to take seriously historical and cultural embeddedness and to address economic dispossession, thus alienating liberal political virtues from concerns of ordinary people not only in Latvia, but across Western liberal democracies.

This book puts forth a critique of institutionalized political liberalism from a moment in which it was still confident and from the perspective of a place and people that were welcomed into its orbit after the collapse of socialism while at the same time were considered to be in need of ever more lessons in political liberalism. It provides some insight about the unfolding of the current crisis of political liberalism before it had come into full view.

The cover art for this book—a tree with Latvian flags at the end of its branches—is taken from Agnese Bule's visual-conceptual series "The Latvian's Dream," which tells true and fantastic tales about the origins, mythology, and contemporary predicaments of Latvians. Becoming European is a contemporary predicament, during the course of which Latvians are invited to critically reflect upon themselves and their past. Agnese Bule does do ironically, and it is for this reason that I have selected her artwork for the book cover.

Acknowledgments

This book is a result of more than a decade of intensive learning, unlearning, and conversations in Latvia, the United States, and the United Kingdom. Of the conversation partners that I have encountered along the way, I am most indebted to my interlocutors in Latvia who will remain unnamed here for purposes of anonymity. I deeply appreciate their time and patience, as well as their willingness to share their stories and histories. I imagine our interpretations of some of the events described in this book will differ, and I look forward to further conversations.

In Berkeley, Alexei Yurchak showed me the analytical import of the familiar and encouraged me to conduct fieldwork "at home." Paul Rabinow questioned that very choice. Saba Mahmood helped to clarify what critique of liberalism from a postsocialist perspective might look like, Gillian Hart revealed the possibilities of the analytic of relationality, and Donald Moore made every place into space and back again. Charles Hirschkind stepped in with valuable advice during the last stages of writing. Yuri Slezkine had some reservations about contemporary anthropology, but nevertheless gave me the title of this book.

Iván Arenas and Katherine Lemons read multiple versions of every single line of the book. Guntra Aistara and Hadley Renkin shared fieldwork, political frustrations, and friendship. Many colleagues and friends read and commented on parts of the book, while others unwittingly participated in extremely useful conversations about it. I particularly thank Bridget Anderson, David Beecher, Alexandre Beliaev, Agnese Cimdiņa, Karīna Vasiļevska-Das, Nicholas De Genova, Brad Erickson, Zsuzsa Gille, Bruce Grant, Jessica Greenberg, Ricardo Hernandez, Benjamin Hickler, Cindy Huang, David Kangas, Mārtiņs Kaprāns, Michael Keith, Larisa Kurtović, Paolo Gaibazzi, Kristín Loftsdóttir, Adelaide Papazoglou, Olga Procevska, Patricia Purtschert, Inese Radziņš, Ieva Raubiško, Madeleine Reeves, Douglas Rogers, Peter Skafish, Vieda Skultāns, and Yves Winter.

The Berkeley Soviet and Post-Soviet Studies Program that subsequently became the Institute of Slavic, East European, and Eurasian Studies provided funding at crucial moments, as well as a multidisciplinary forum for discussing regional and theoretical matters. I am grateful to the University of California and the Wenner-Gren Foundation for funding research and writing. Several parts of the book have been tried out in the conferences of Soyuz: The Postsocialist Cultural Studies Network. The first chapter of the book benefited from conversations with the fellows of the residential research group "Imperial Legacies, Postsocialist Contexts" at the Humanities Research Institute, University of California, Irvine, as well as with participants of the "Colonialism Without Colonies" workshop at ETH Zurich. The Centre on Migration, Policy, and Society at the School of Anthropology and Museum Ethnography, University of Oxford, has been a supportive and stimulating place to work.

James Lance at Cornell University Press had faith in the book early on and patiently saw it through to publication. His support and professional integrity were exemplary, and I am very lucky to have been able to work with him and the wonderful team at Cornell University Press. I am also grateful to Kevin Platt and two anonymous readers for comments that significantly improved the manuscript. A big thanks goes to Agnese Bule, who kindly agreed to have her artwork used for the cover of the book.

My sisters Ilze and Līva, my father Uldis and Maija, and my mother Rūta and Valdis have suffered the most. I am very grateful for your unconditional love and for not asking how the book is going. I also thank the Arenas and Abrahamsen families in Seattle for support during different stages of research and writing.

Sofia Arenas and this book project are of the same age. At the very beginning, Sofia was the first two-month-old in Latvia to attend an embattled Pride parade. At the very end, our conversations about the hierarchical organization of wolf packs helped me to think about power and politics among humans. For that reason, this book is dedicated to you.

In the end, I am most grateful for the possibility of living another life of emotional and intellectual intensity. There is still a long, long road ahead, and the most complicated and difficult part of it is only just beginning.

An early version of chapter 1 was published as "Historical Agency and the Coloniality of Power in Postsocialist Europe" in *Anthropological Theory*. Fragments from chapters 2, 5 and 6 were published as part of articles in *Social Anthropology*, *Ethnos* and *Satori.lv*. All texts and fragments of texts are reproduced here with permission from Sage, Taylor and Francis, and John Wiley and Sons Publishers.

SCHOOL OF EUROPEANNESS

PARADOX OF EUROPEANNESS

The Need to Exclude and
the Virtue of Inclusion

Mid-morning, on a summer day in June 2006, my phone rang. "Dace, Dace, is this Dace?" The caller was Asad, one of the "seven Somalis" (*septiņi somālieši*), as he and his compatriots came to be known to the Latvian public. The "seven Somalis" had arrived in Latvia in August 2005. After a four-month journey, they had been left by a smuggler in the middle of the forest. Two days of wandering led them to the Red Cross offices in the center of Riga, where they were turned over to the Latvian State Border Guard and detained as illegal migrants. Four adults and three teenagers, they subsequently spent nine months in a detention facility administered by the Latvian State Border Guard, first as illegal migrants, then as asylum seekers awaiting decisions on their applications, and again, as illegal migrants after their applications were denied. On the day that Asad called me, the border guards had opened the doors of the detention facility and told them to go, because the legally permissible detention period had expired.

I first met the "seven Somalis" when an official of the Latvian State Border Guard, whom I interviewed, took me straight from the interview to the detention facility to translate to the Somalis the decisions on their asylum applications. By doing so, he did not comply with the procedure, for the decisions had to be delivered via a certified translator and in writing, but this enabled me to give the asylum seekers my phone number. On that day in June, they called me, because they had nowhere else to go. Failing in my attempt to contact the asylum seekers' reception center or find place for the Somalis in other state-run shelters, I

1

managed to reach a rural children's foster home run by a priest and his family, who graciously took them in.

"How can they disappear? Seven black people in the streets of Riga . . . ," said one border guard, when I later inquired about the circumstances of that day. The border guards had let the Somalis go, thinking that they could not possibly disappear in the largely homogenous—that is, white—Latvian society. They were right; the Somalis did not disappear. The border guards quickly found out where the "seven Somalis" had gone and paid visits to the rural foster home, occasionally intimidating its inhabitants. In between visits from state authorities, the foster home worked hard to integrate the Somalis into local life and local schools. In the meantime, human rights organizations examined the procedural aspects of the case in order to identify shortcomings in the Latvian asylum system, while a human rights lawyer worked pro bono to appeal the negative decisions on the Somalis' asylum applications. Civil servants of the Office of Migration and Citizenship Affairs, border guards, as well as members of the appeals board, struggled to establish the credibility (or the lack thereof) of the Somalis' stories, trying to determine whether they were indeed refugees or simply economic migrants.[1] After an arduous process, closely observed by Latvian and Russian-speaking publics, the Somalis were granted temporary protection, and things somewhat settled.

On November 16, 2006, days before I left after eighteen months of fieldwork on the politics of tolerance and other lessons in political liberalism in Latvia, I attended an event dedicated to the International Day of Tolerance on the premises of the Secretariat for the Integration of Society. I did not expect to see the "seven Somalis" there, but was not surprised when I did. Having been transformed from illegal migrants to asylum seekers to refugees and coresidents, they were objects of tolerance par excellence. Moreover, their case embodied some of the crucial tensions that characterized Latvia's road to Europe after the collapse of the Soviet Union, as well as arguments about tolerance, nationalism, and liberalism that I studied. Some of Latvia's residents believed that Latvia must and will become more open as a result of European integration, and that this openness meant more immigration, more refugees, and therefore the need for society to cultivate the virtue of tolerance. For them, the Somalis were a paradigmatic case of the kind of Europeanness that Latvians needed to embrace. Other residents of Latvia embraced a vision of Europeanness where a European people lead a life of national self-determination and thought that openness to difference and migration constituted a threat to the Latvian nation that had suffered under Soviet rule. For them, the Somalis were a paradigmatic case of misguided Europeanness that Latvians had to resist.

From the perspective of the liberal politics that were institutionalized as part of postsocialist democratization and European integration in Latvia, these were not different-but-equal visions of Europeanness. To the liberal eye, openness to difference was to intolerance what Europeanness was to not-yet-Europeanness. I show in this book, however, that both positions—that is, openness to difference and its refusal—share an underlying understanding of Europeanness as a civilizational space, and both enact and defend regimes of inclusion and exclusion. Their emergence as morally and politically opposed positions in the context of postsocialist democratization and European integration in Latvia, but also elsewhere in Eastern Europe, points to a tension that characterizes the contemporary European political and moral landscape, namely the imperative to profess and institutionalize the values of inclusion and openness while at the same time practicing—and also institutionalizing—exclusion and closure. This is to say that there are multiple modes of organizing inclusion and exclusion within the European political landscape, and that in particular historical moments some tend to be seen as more European than others. For Latvians, then, becoming European after socialism meant learning to live inclusion and exclusion the European way. It meant learning to live the paradox of Europeanness.

Lessons in (Neo)liberalism

In 2006, controversial as the case of the "seven Somalis" was, it was still only a case of seven Somalis. A decade later, Latvia found itself in the midst of Europe's "migration/refugee crisis."[2] In 2015, 1,046,599 people from Syria, Afghanistan, Iraq, and sub-Saharan Africa entered Europe by land and sea routes as migrants and asylum seekers, with many others dying en route.[3] In the middle of 2015, when it was recognized in public and political discourse across Europe that a crisis was afoot and that something had to be done to cope with the large number of migrants and refugees trying to enter Europe, the European Commission proposed refugee quotas to distribute the burden among European Union member states. Most Eastern European member states opposed refugee quotas. Lithuania, Latvia, and Estonia agreed to voluntarily take in small numbers of refugees. Slovakia, the Czech Republic, and Poland announced that they would only take Christian refugees, while Hungary mobilized troops, prisoners, and the unemployed to rapidly build a fence on its border with Serbia. After the quota plan, which envisaged resettling 120,000 refugees within a two-year period, was approved in the European Parliament in September 2015, the government of Slovakia threatened to contest the decision in court. Following terror attacks in Paris in November 2015, Poland, which had initially supported the plan, refused to carry it out. The president of Latvia, in turn, stated that Latvia would not accept any more refugees until Europe's border security could be assured.

In contrast with older European Union member states, Eastern European states did not have significant numbers of asylum applications or residents with Middle Eastern, African, or Asian backgrounds and were determined to keep it that way. The arguments against accepting refugees that came forth from Eastern European politicians and publics voiced concerns about cultural incompatibility, racial and religious difference, security threats, inability to distinguish genuine refugees from economic migrants, negative experiences with integration in other European Union member states and localities, lasting socialist legacies of population resettlement that continued to undermine postsocialist polities, poor economies, impoverished populations, and imposed solidarity by Europe that invoked memories of directives from Moscow. In response, commentaries in print and online media on both sides of the Atlantic and across Europe accused Eastern Europeans of moral failure. These commentaries suggested that Eastern Europeans lacked compassion and tolerance, and tried to shame Eastern Europe into moral maturity and, by extension, agreeable politics.[4] In one of the multiple seminars and discussions held on the topic in 2015 and 2016 at the University of Oxford where I teach, one Oxford academic summarized the emerging consensus on Eastern European conduct by saying that it is evident that Eastern Europe "has embraced lessons in neoliberalism, but has not received sufficient lessons in political liberalism."

Indeed, the "migrant/refugee crisis" came on the heels of the 2008–10 financial crisis, which brought hardship on Latvia's residents, but also provided an opportunity for Latvia and Latvians to boost their credentials as exemplary pupils of neoliberal economics. In response to one of the worst economic downturns in the world, the Latvian government implemented harsh austerity measures with little protest from Latvia's residents who either tightened their belts or left the country (Dzenovska 2018a, 2012). The financial crisis revealed an unexpected convergence between individual responsibility as an integral element of neoliberal subjectivity and the historically formed narratives of self and tactics of life prevalent in Latvia. For example, in the early post-Soviet years, learning to live in a market economy meant, among other things, learning to live on credit. Various small and large credit opportunities were aggressively promoted by transnational banks (Dzenovska 2018b). Across the former socialist world, taking credit, especially mortgage, came to be seen as a sign of maturity (Halawa 2015). When the economic bubble burst in 2008, many people in Latvia blamed individuals as much as they blamed the banks or the state. The prevailing view was that individuals agreed to take credit, and therefore it was their responsibility to get out of trouble. This stance was not necessarily—or not only—shaped by the neoliberal discourse of responsibility. It was a historically overdetermined stance, boosted by the imperative to overcome the Soviet past remembered as excessive reliance on the state, as well as by collective memory of suffering and the associated belief that resilience was the only reliable tactic of life in difficult moments. Moreover, moral frameworks that governed personal relations (for example, if I borrow money from you, I have to give it back to you) were transposed to measure individual conduct in the context of post-Soviet debt economy, as well as to evaluate the conduct of other people—for example, that of Greeks in the context of Greece's sovereign debt crisis.

Thus another way in which the Latvian government and the Latvian public asserted their exemplary economic conduct was by distinguishing themselves from those who did not quite behave as responsible economic subjects. In the midst of Greece's sovereign debt crisis in 2015, Latvia's minister of finance Jānis Reiris expressed a widely shared sentiment when he said: "Latvians do not understand the Greek people." In July 2015, in an episode of the weekly TV show *Sastrēgumstunda* (Hour of Congestion), financial consultant Gundars Kuļikovskis pointed out that "the EU is a club of countries based on rules. And now Greece says: we will not play by the rules."[5] Sitting next to Kuļikovskis, Ilmārs Rimšēvics, the president of the Bank of Latvia, emphasized that "the responsibility lies only with the government of Greece." He continued, "Latvia has positive experience with austerity measures. We did it in two years. You have to involve all sectors of society. We regained trust, and the economy recovered. All those who borrow money, know the rules. And if you do not follow the rules, there are consequences. One has to be very responsible on the large Euro ship." Furthermore, in an article published on the Internet site *Delfi.lv*, Inese Vaidere, a member of the European Parliament, suggested that Greeks have something to learn from Latvians. She pointed out that Latvians couldn't understand why Greeks refuse to be frugal, because "we are used to saving and living within our means. Germans, too, are used to spending as much money as is within their means. Similarly, if borrowing, the money has to be returned within a foreseeable period of time. But Greeks want it otherwise: they think they can borrow all the time and not repay."[6] Moreover, Vaidere continued, "Tightening of belts corresponds to European values. Why is it so difficult for Greeks to do it? Perhaps it is lack of information, perhaps it is tradition, perhaps it is the southern sun, which makes people more relaxed than in Latvia. But within Europe and within the European Union, all have to adhere to the same rules. . . . European rules stipulate that debt has to be repaid. Not repaying debt amounts to theft."

Evidently, lessons in neoliberal economics were also lessons in Europeanness. While Latvia seemed to succeed in obtaining Europeanness in the context of the financial crisis, Greece was failing according to fiscal measures of Europeanness and thus rapidly losing whatever Europeanness it may have accumulated over the years. However, Europeanness gained in the realm of neoliberal economics was quickly lost in the realm of liberal politics. In the context of the "migration/refu-gee crisis," Latvians, like other Eastern Europeans, did not wish to accept refugees and did not demonstrate the expected public sentiments, such as compassion, thus leading many liberals, the Oxford academic among them, to conclude that Eastern Europeans had not received sufficient lessons in political liberalism.

But that is an erroneous assumption. Eastern Europe, including Latvia, has been receiving lessons in political liberalism ever since setting on the road to rejoin Europe. For example, the tolerance that came to Latvia shortly before the seven Somalis was a post–Cold War liberal political virtue embraced by European political institutions and structures of governance. And it was precisely this mode of understanding and relating to difference that Latvians were to embrace in the process of European integration, even as the people inhabiting current-day Lat-via have both lived with difference and lived through various political regimes of difference, from religious toleration in the Russian Empire to the Soviet *druzhba narodov* (friendship of the peoples) (Platt 2015, Sahadeo 2007, Weeks 2013). In 2004, the same year that Latvia joined the European Union, the Cabinet of Min-isters approved the Latvian National Program for the Promotion of Tolerance, initiated by Nils Muižnieks, the special tasks minister for the Integration of Soci-ety.[7] But the question of tolerance had emerged on the policy agenda already in the late 1990s, when Muižnieks was still the director of a local NGO and around the time Latvia formally began its negotiations for membership in the European Union.[8] As part of the apparatus that produced a considerable flow of reports from Latvian government institutions and nongovernmental organizations to various European political and monitoring bodies, the NGO led by Muižnieks prepared reports on human rights and minority protection for the International Helsinki Federation for Human Rights (the federation was forced to close in 2000 due to financial fraud) and, later, the European Commission Against Racism and Intolerance. The reports were standardized, requiring a section on the problem of intolerance. "The category was ready," Muižnieks noted in a conversation we had in 2005.

The program, devised by a group of experts, which included minority repre-sentatives, civil servants, and human rights activists, posited tolerance as a lib-eral political virtue, that is, as a positive way of relating to politically recognized and equivalent categories of diversity, such as race, ethnicity, and religion, in public and political life (see chapter 3). Once the Latvian National Program for the Promotion of Tolerance was approved and its implementation began, a net-work of "tolerance workers" emerged who engaged in activities vaguely framed as "promoting tolerance" (*iecietības veicināšana*) in government offices, NGOs, policy think tanks, and academic institutions (see chapter 3). Some of the tol-erance workers claimed minority status—for example, they represented the

African Latvian Association, the Jewish Community Association, a number of Roma organizations, an LGBT organization, as well as minority cultural associations. Others insisted that they belonged to a "community of association" that adhered to liberal democratic principles and were adamant about not claiming minority status in public space. Some had grown up in Latvia, while others had moved to Latvia later in life, because they were born to Latvian parents abroad or had other family connections in Latvia. Others had come to Latvia during the Soviet period from other Soviet republics or from abroad either as students or workers and had remained in Latvia after independence in 1991. All lived and worked locally, but all also became tolerance workers through translocal relations insofar as they drew on collaborations with similar organizations in other countries, with transnational NGOs, and with universities. They often traveled to international conferences, as well as went on study and exchange visits to Western Europe or the United States. They also thought about the problem of intolerance by continuously comparing the situation in Latvia, usually unfavorably, to the situation in Western Europe, which they simply called Europe. Many of the tolerance workers were individuals who sincerely lived the values of openness and inclusion and who experienced what they saw as public instances of intolerance as politically maddening, personally painful, and all around embarrassing. At the same time, as I show in chapter 3, the tolerance workers also questioned each other's motivations and pointed to each other's failures to truly inhabit tolerance as a liberal political virtue.

However, even those who accepted tolerance as a liberal political virtue that values inclusion and diversity considered it necessary to defend Latvia's right to police the boundaries of Latvia's body of citizenry in ways that ensured the dominance of the cultural nation of Latvians in public and political space. As most Latvians saw it, this was necessary on the grounds that the Latvian nation had been endangered by Soviet rule, which required compensatory measures in the present (see chapter 2). Thus, as part of becoming European, Latvians were assembling their own historically specific paradox of Europeanness, that is, the coexistence of exclusion as a fundamental feature of European polities and the virtues of inclusion, openness, and tolerance.

A Map of Encounters

Rather than being articulated in a coherent ideological framework, the contours of the Latvian version of the paradox of Europeanness come into view through lessons in political liberalism that were extended to and contested in multiple sites. I came to these lessons by way of studying the promotion of tolerance, which, I found, served as an umbrella term for designating the virtues of open-ness and inclusion and, by extension, the moral and political goodness of Europeanness. In the process of studying tolerance promotion, I realized that lessons in political liberalism pertained to multiple spheres of life and exceeded the framework of tolerance. Thus, while tolerance remains a central theme in the book, its various chapters move through a variety of encounters that, taken together, illustrate both the contours of actually existing post–Cold War politi-cal liberalism and the paradox of Europeanness. Thus in chapter 1, I outline the moral landscape surrounding Europe's colonial history. On the basis of analysis of encounters between Latvians who take pride in appropriating colonial expe-ditions of a seventeenth-century duke into Latvian national history and their puzzled Western observers, I show that this moral landscape is characterized by an imperative to remember Europe's colonial history as a violent founda-tional moment that places ethical and political demands on the present. At the same time, this moral landscape is fraught with ambiguities and tensions. If mainstream liberals recognize European colonialism as shameful, but prefer to publicly talk about the values of democracy, human rights, and freedom as Euro-pean contribution to humanity, left-leaning postcolonial activists and scholars demand explicit recognition of colonialism's continued legacy—for example, racism—in European politics and institutions of governance. The proud Latvi-ans maneuver this moral landscape in ways that disturb both. They disturb the liberals by claiming Europeanness via colonial heritage rather than human rights, democracy, and freedom. While they thus recognize the role of colonialism in the making of Europeanness, as the left-leaning postcolonial scholars and activ-ists would have it, they misrecognize it as a source of pride rather than a sin that demands continuous expiation. These multiple failures therefore illuminate the tensions that underlie the European moral landscape that Latvians are expected to learn along with lessons in political liberalism.

In chapter 2, I consider whether and how Latvians took up lessons in politi-cal liberalism with regard to the most important issue at the foundation of the post-Soviet Latvian state, that is, how to handle the large number of Russians and Russian-speaking Soviet people in the making of a national state. This is one area where most Latvians—those who embraced tolerance and those who did not—converged in a belief that it is they who needed to teach rather than receive lessons. Namely, most Latvians believed that European institutions and publics did not understand Soviet history. For most Latvians, it was Soviet socialism rather than European colonialism—or even fascism—that placed moral and political demands on their present. It is this history that necessitated the implementation of restrictive citizenship and language policies in order to ensure the survival of the Latvian nation and the state. Shaped by Soviet history, yet claiming to also have a European one, Latvians tried to assemble a package of policies and attitudes that satisfied the historically particular form of exclusion at the foundation of the national Latvian state and the European imperative to profess and inhabit the values of inclusion and openness. It is at this juncture between Soviet and European histories, with their divergent political and moral demands on the present, that tolerance arrived in Latvia.

Chapter 3 analyzes attempts to introduce and institutionalize tolerance as a liberal political virtue defined primarily in terms of accepting inconsequential ethnic and racial diversity in a polity built on consequential ethno-national difference. The liberal political virtue of tolerance turned out to be quite useful for the task of advocating for inclusion within a polity based on an historically particular configuration of exclusion insofar it allowed for a focus on changing public attitudes and conduct rather than questioning the foundations of the state. Nevertheless, many Latvians refused this civilizational lesson, partly because they correctly recognized that it did not address the fundamental issues of concern to them. This, in turn, prompted the tolerance workers to redefine the problem of intolerance as a problem of not recognizing the problem of intolerance. Thereafter, tolerance workers engaged in extensive efforts to convince the Latvian public of the existence of the problem of intolerance through a variety of diagnostic exercises, which not only identified the problem of intolerance, but also its causes, such as lack of critical thinking among Latvia's residents.

Chapter 4 turns to critical thinking as the skill that tolerance workers understood to be crucial for cultivating tolerant selves and publics in Latvia. Tolerance workers' belief that critical thinking would inevitably lead to the correct conclusions about how to understand and live with ethnic, racial, and religious diversity coincided with extensive projects of promoting critical thinking in the former socialist world. From the liberal perspective, the former socialist world lacked critical thinking due to the legacies of an authoritarian political system and memorization-based education. This was thought to hinder the postsocialist subjects' ability to establish the kind of relationship to their collective past that the European moral and political landscape demanded. As a result, lessons in political liberalism overlooked the multiplicity and heterogeneity of critical practices of former socialist subjects and obfuscated the historical specificity and ideological underpinnings of "critical thinking" as the special truth-producing instrument of actually existing political liberalism.

Chapter 5 turns to language as the primary area of tolerance work. The use of words was an obvious object of analysis for tolerance workers who scrutinized public discourse for expressions of underlying sensibilities of speakers and discursive constructions of problematic forms of difference. The chapter shows that learning the liberal virtue of tolerance also required adapting new language ideologies, ones that viewed words as doing rather than expressing things. But just as language was the most obvious area of tolerance work, it was also the most sacred national attribute thought to have been abused by the Soviet nationalities policy and therefore the most contested political issue for the national state. Thus, while tolerance workers tried to convince Latvians to drop certain words, such as *žīds* (roughly equivalent to the English-language "yids") and *nēģeris* (negroes), Latvians resisted by suggesting that these words only appear as injurious from a foreign perspective. At the same time, the Latvian state tried to discipline unruly Russian speakers into learning and speaking Latvian. Struggles over language illustrate very well the intersection of multilayered histories and ethical-political claims in arguments about tolerance. The chapter shows which historical connections and thus ethical-political claims made sense to Latvians and which did not, thus further illuminating Europe's moral and political landscape.

Chapter 6 focuses on the site par excellence of exclusion, that is, borders. It is precisely here that the need to exclude that underlies European polities becomes most apparent. This, too, was part of the lessons that Latvians learned in the process of becoming European. But even bordering is shaped by the paradox of Europeanness insofar as it must adhere to the principles of human rights and the virtue of tolerance. Thus Latvian border guards found themselves struggling with the demand to both strengthen the border and to civilize it. Latvian migration officials and border guards were generally better at learning the repressive elements of Europe's migration regime (that is, securing the border and keeping barbarians at the gate) than embracing the redemptive ones (that is, tolerance and compassion). Or, rather, their compassion was differently directed—just like former European colonial empires police their boundaries to keep out former colonial subjects while at the same time fighting racism and cultivating tolerance toward them, Latvian border guards policed Latvia's boundaries to keep out former rulers (who were on occasion perceived as barbarians), while also exhibiting feelings of compassion and solidarity toward them. However, becoming European required that they turn their attention to Europe's former colonial subjects as well—both in terms of keeping barbarians at the gate and treating them right. Insofar as they failed to do so, they were deemed to lack Europeanness.

Europeanness and Its Logics of Difference

Lessons in political liberalism were consistently articulated as "catching up with Europe," where people were more democratic, politically mature, and also more tolerant (Böröcz 2006, Böröcz and Kovács 2001). In the process, the majority of Latvia's residents were often depicted as subjects mired in socialist legacies, as well as in ethno-territorial nationalist sensibilities that liberal Europe was thought to have left behind. There emerged a spatial and temporal configuration of goodness and Europeanness that was based on a recognizable logic of difference, variously referred to as racial or colonial by scholars of race and coloniality (e.g., Goldberg 2009, Hesse 2007, Mignolo 2007, Quijano 2007). This logic of difference sorts people and places into hierarchical relations marked by tropes of civilization, development, maturity, and Europeanness, which, in turn, inform a variety of projects of government, including tolerance promotion.

It is precisely for these reasons that the liberal politics of tolerance has come under criticism in political theory and anthropology (Brown 2006, Mehta 1999, Partridge 2012, Scott 2000). In addition to entrenching differences and establishing hierarchical relationships between those who extend tolerance and those who are to be tolerated, the liberal politics of tolerance is said to be a depoliticizing and civilizing project. First, it renders racism and other forms of marginalization as matters of attitude rather than structural injustice. Second, it sets out to civilize the not-yet-civilized margins—for example, Muslim Europeans who come to be seen as both objects of tolerance and subjects lacking the virtue of tolerance (e.g., Fassin 2010, Fernando 2014, Partridge 2012, chapter 3). Insofar as tolerance work in Latvia entailed educating a less-than-European population in public and political conduct appropriate for a liberal democratic European polity, tolerance promotion was a civilizational project.

This was not, however, the only vision of Europeanness mobilized in the context of postsocialist transformations in Latvia. In response to assertions of Europeanness as a marker of liberal freedoms, human rights, democracy, and tolerance, many Latvians mobilized Europeanness as a marker of politically self-determining cultural nations, Christianity, and civilization, while juxtaposing it to racialized visions of non-Europe. That is, while some Latvians were striving to convince others that becoming European meant becoming tolerant, others thought that post-Soviet independence enabled Latvians to take their rightful place among European nations, all part of a European civilization with a glorious (and colonial) history (see chapter 1). Latvians' Europeanness was nationalized insofar as it was articulated in the language of the nation rather than through universal values of freedom, democracy, and human rights, yet it was nonetheless informed by extranational conceptions of Europe as a cultural and political space within which a properly European people lead a national way of life.

In the chapters that follow, I analyze how Latvia's citizens and residents live the paradox of Europeanness—that is, the simultaneous demand for inclusion and exclusion, openness and closure, transcendence and erection of borders—through different sites where lessons in political liberalism were extended and Europeanness negotiated. I focus on the relationship between historically specific ways of being and becoming European and the trope of Europeanness that remains powerful even as it changes shape from one historical moment to another. I do not posit that there is a unified entity, such as Western Europe, or that there is a coherent European periphery. I take Europe to be a highly differentiated and multiple space. But I do argue that the trope of Europe as a normative and civilizing project remains powerful and continues to have material consequences for peoples and places inhabiting the political landscape vaguely defined as European, as well as for those striving to enter or remain in it. It is precisely because Europe is multiple and differentiated, fragmentary and incoherent, that the normative trope of Europe must continuously be reasserted.[9]

Moreover, my analysis of the liberal project of tolerance promotion in Latvia shows how the paradox of Europeanness is displaced spatially, that is, how certain spaces serve as "spatial fixes" that allow (Harvey 2010), if temporarily, the reassertion of the moral goodness of liberal Europe by dislocating Europe's vices, such as nationalism and intolerance, to marginal people and places, such as Eastern Europe or marginal members of Western European societies, such as the white working class and migrants.[10] Even as such fixes may be becoming less effective, especially in the context of the current rise of populism in Europe that defies the left-right distinction, the trope of a morally and politically superior Europe remains powerful across the political spectrum. A variety of peoples and states within and outside of the European Union's political, financial, and economic structures can become non-European or less European or, again, rejoin Europe depending on their conduct in particular circumstances. Thus, as I have shown, Europeanness came to be contested along the European Union's north-south axis in the context of the Greek sovereign debt crisis in 2015, when Greece and Greeks did not behave as "responsible economic subjects," but rather protested the austerity measures and privatization of public assets. And Europeanness was contested in the midst of Europe's "migration/refugee crisis," when Eastern Europeans, including Latvians, emerged as rogue subjects refusing to play by the rules. At the same time as Eastern Europe was losing Europeanness because of its refusal to accept refugees, Turkey was promised a ticket to Europe for its contribution to keeping migrants and refugees out of Europe.[11]

In deconstituting actually existing post–Cold War political liberalism and showing its entanglement with civilizational logics of difference, my aim is to reorient scholarly inquiry from the kind that laments lack of political liberalism in Eastern Europe to the kind that examines the nature of Europe's political and moral landscape and the contours of European polities. The need for such reorientation is derived from my analysis of arguments about tolerance in Latvia, which—in the last instance—pertain to the question of whether contemporary European polities should be open to difference and, if so, how much and what kind. As the Latvian case shows, tolerance is not only about attitudes toward neighbors, but also—if not more importantly—about whether a polity should or should not be open to difference, what kind of ethical or political justifications there are for one position or another, and what consequences openness or closure may have for the concrete polity, the European political landscape, and the lives of concrete people. The consequential question, then, is not so much about whether Latvians or Eastern Europeans are tolerant or not, but, rather, how limits to inclusion are drawn in contemporary European polities.

Nothing illustrates this better than the "migration/refugee crisis." Due to the politicians' and publics' reluctance and/or refusal to accept refugees, Eastern Europe emerged in the midst of this crisis as an ideal typical not-yet-European subject mired in racialized paranoia about foreigners, exaggerated concerns about self-determination and self-preservation, and timeworn claims of historical suffering. In a way, Eastern Europe was excluded from proper Europeanness in the name of the value of inclusion. Eastern European politicians, such as the Hungarian prime minister Victor Orbán, were widely depicted as rogue subjects, carriers of dangerous nationalism that risked contaminating Europe. And yet, it is more and more difficult to maintain the juxtaposition between liberal Europe and illiberal Eastern Europe amidst the closing of borders, building of fences, intensified policing, talk of states running out of the capacity to govern, heightened concerns about security, and widespread antimigration rhetoric and sentiment. Thus, in the face of the "threat of Islam," French republicanism begins to look more French than republican (Fernando 2014). In the face of Eastern European labor migration, certain parts of Britain begin to look more English than British (Green 2016). And, "even in Sweden" (Pred 2000), racial and cultural conceptions of the nation are as strong as the self-perception of a tolerant and cosmopolitan polity. Openness is only possible, it seems, if borders are properly guarded and if barbarians remain at the gate, while deserving foreigners and citizens are granted entrance and/or Europeanness.

The "migration/refugee crisis" illustrates particularly well that the question to be asked is not how to make illiberal people and places more liberal, but rather what are the multiple axes of inclusion and exclusion that organize the European political landscape. Which forms of inclusion and exclusion are visible and which remain invisible; which ones are legitimized and which demonized? It is noteworthy that in the context of the "migration/refugee crisis" there seemed to be one legitimate argument against accepting refugees—or more refugees—for the liberal side of the political spectrum, and that was the argument of "too many." For example, after an initial period of processing a record number of asylum claims, Sweden announced that its ability to cope with refugees had reached a limit: there was lack of housing, and the system could not cope with processing so many refugees (Kingsley 2015). As a result, Sweden introduced temporary border controls with Denmark.[12] The Swedish limits were thought to be legitimate, because they were not ideological (national or racial), but material—they were limits of infrastructure. The fact that the Swedish deputy prime minister cried when making the announcement boosted the legitimacy of the decision, suggesting that it was a forced and pragmatic decision that went against the ethical dispositions of the Swedish society.[13]

"Too many," an argument seemingly about numbers, can be measured in a variety of ways that are not necessarily numerical. For example, a local man in Boston, United Kingdom, told me that he had nothing against post-EU accession migrants from Eastern Europe, but that there were simply too many of them.[14] Although I did hear concerns from others about lack of doctors and nurses in Boston's medical establishments, for him it was not necessarily about infrastructure but rather about daily life. He said that he could no longer go to the shop in the morning, greet someone by saying "Good morning!" and expect to be greeted back in English. I heard a resonant argument from a Latvian woman living in Boston who was concerned about tensions between locals and newcomers. "There are too many of us," she said. On the basis of this perception of "too many," Boston's residents overwhelmingly voted to leave the European Union on June 23, 2016. In turn, the inhabitants of Mucenieki in Latvia—a locality where the asylum seeker reception center is located—have begun to convey discomfort about being a minority in their locality. "Our children are afraid to go to the stadium, because there are too many refugees there," inhabitants of Mucenieki wrote in a letter to Latvia's prime minister Laimdota Straujuma.[15]

The argument of "too many" assumes that a baseline form of life or quality of life must be retained, whether for the locals, incomers, or both. Some "too many" arguments can and do get easily dismissed as reactionary from within the liberal political frame. More often than not, those are the ones articulated through the trope of the nation or put forth by local communities, for they are thought to be manifestations of fear, prejudice, and a closed view of the world. The kinds of "too many" arguments that are taken seriously across the political spectrum pertain to the state's capacity to govern, such as shortages of infrastructure faced by Sweden.

It is worth considering, however, whether positing these different logics of "too many" as qualitatively different is entirely justified. Categories or logics of exclusion come to be mapped onto each other, reference each other, and in practice, tend to produce the same effects (M'charek et al. 2013). As I was told several years before the current crisis by a staff member of the Department of Citizenship and Immigration in Latvia, "Latvians are afraid because of the [Soviet] past, and Russians are afraid that they [refugees] will come and eat their *bulochka* [pastry, in Russian]." The effect is similar—both produce negative attitudes toward refugees. In other words, the "too many" arguments of the "unenlightened masses" or "not-quite-European" subjects are not radically different from the "too many" arguments of the liberal European state. Put another way, liberal and illiberal forms of exclusion may not be the same, but can and often do converge in keeping the same bodies out. Thus, in order to understand Europe's political landscape, it is necessary to undertake a relational analysis of the different configurations of the Europewide tension between inclusion and exclusion, as well as an analysis of the modes of power that differentiate between these configurations of inclusion and exclusion on moral grounds. Such critical analysis has been difficult to conduct from and within Eastern Europe. In the last section of the Introduction, I consider why that may be the case.

On Eastern Europe and the Limits of Critical Discourse

The collapse of the Soviet Union came with the pronouncement of the "end of history" (Fukuyama 1989). According to this perspective, free-market capitalism and liberal democracy had proven their superiority over socialism. All that was left to do was to implement a smooth transition. Eastern Europeans largely agreed. They readily embraced economic liberalization—in fact, Johanna Bockman (2011) has argued that neoliberal economics emerged through debates across the Iron Curtain rather than being forced on Eastern Europe as some critics of neoliberalism assume. Political liberalization, however, turned out to be a more contested process. Political elites seemed corrupt, the rule of law elusive, civil liberties curtailed, and attitudes toward minorities problematic. In 1997, Fareed Zakaria (1997) used the term *illiberal democracies* to describe the dilemma identified by American diplomat Richard Holbrook as he was observing the preparations for elections in Bosnia in 1996, namely that fascists and racists might be elected through free and fair elections. Establishment of democratic institutions did not guarantee that the electorate would support liberal candidates. While Zakaria used the term *illiberal democracies* to mark problems with democratic politics around the world, it is not an accident that it was Eastern Europe's seeming failure to follow the path of Western liberal democracy that gave the problem a name and thereafter instruments—such as the Freedom House index—through which to measure and diagnose polities.

It is also the collapse of Soviet and Eastern European socialisms that lent new life to Europe's self-ascribed moral superiority by opening new spaces to democratization and liberalization initiatives, much criticized in postcolonial literature. The collapse of Soviet and Eastern European socialisms produced a vast population actively engaged in becoming European even as what it meant to become European remained unclear. The liberalization, democratization, and Europeanization initiatives extended to Eastern Europe simultaneously posited Eastern Europe as having returned to Europe and as not-yet-European due to the continuous hold of both socialist legacies and backward nationalisms on the new Europeans. Put another way, the collapse of "Second World" socialisms provided a "spatial-temporal fix" for European—or Western—liberalism in the moment that it had begun to lose its moral and political superiority under the weight of postcolonial critique (e.g., Harvey 2010, Mehta 1999, Povinelli 2002, Said 1978, Spivak 1988). Importantly, the effectiveness of this spatial-temporal fix was aided by the fact that from within postsocialist contexts it seemed impossible to criticize Western liberalism in quite the same way as from within postcolonial contexts, or even from within the feminist, queer, or racialized margins of the West. Understanding this dynamic is crucial for outlining the critical contribution of postsocialist Eastern Europe as an analytical lens to the inquiry of contemporary modes of power in Europe.

In addition to setting into motion the postsocialist transition industry and the study of postsocialist transformations, the collapse of Second World socialisms also presented challenges to postcolonial thought. Anticolonial thought and activism had explicitly relied on actually existing socialisms, as well as abstract Marxist humanism, to craft visions of alternative futures (e.g., Chakrabarty 2000, Fanon 1967, Spivak 1988). Therefore, as David Scott (1999) notes, the collapse of actually existing socialisms in Eastern Europe and the former Soviet Union demanded a rethinking of postcolonial futures.[16] The collapse of socialism meant that imaginations of alternative futures came to rely on difference, that is, on concrete or imagined forms of life or "remainders of life" that could not be entirely subjugated by hegemonic Western power and knowledge regimes (Chakrabarty 2000, Tadiar 2011). This difference could not be made fully intelligible, however, for the process of rendering difference intelligible was thought to subject it to the violence of the hegemonic Western power and knowledge regime. And yet, even as the subaltern could not speak (Spivak 1988), imagining the possibility of the subaltern speaking gave rise to a critique of subjugation and to imaginations of alternative ways of living, of alternative futures. To put it another way, the possibility of referring to a space that could not be fully captured by hegemonic power and knowledge regimes, a space that was only partly intelligible to them or not intelligible to them at all, enabled and legitimated postcolonial critique (see Chakrabarty 2000; Mahmood 2005, 2009; Povinelli 2002).

"At home," that is, in Western liberal democracies, criticism of hegemonic power and knowledge regimes and attempts to excavate "subjugated knowledges" came from marginalized spaces and subjects such as racialized, queer, or feminist subjects (Foucault 1980). This criticism largely unfolded in gender studies, comparative literature, and ethnic studies departments in the United States and in the cultural studies milieu in the United Kingdom (El-Tayeb 2011, Ferreira Da Silva 2007, Gilroy 1993, Hong and Ferguson 2011, Tadiar 2011, Warner 2005). Importantly, here too, critique relied on the possibility of difference, only now arising from subjugated knowledges and forms of life within the West itself (see also Hage 2015). Scholars argued that even in Western contexts, where there were few coherent forms of life that could be traced to pre-Western or precolonial periods, there were subjugated knowledges and practices that could help to unsettle hegemonic ways of seeing, knowing, and doing (e.g., Bennett 2001, Hage 2015).

Formerly socialist Eastern Europe has been largely denied such spaces of difference that could be mined for alternative ways of organizing collective life or for alternative futures. Or, rather, former socialist Eastern Europe provided material for criticizing economic liberalization (e.g., Burawoy and Verdery 1999, Dunn 2004), but not political liberalization. For example, Nanette Funk (2004) suggested that feminist critique of the autonomous subject and individualism in Western liberalism is misguided in Eastern European contexts. In her view, it was more, rather than less, individual autonomy that was needed in Eastern Europe, for Eastern Europeans were mired in collectivist thinking. Given the strong criticism of Western liberalism and Western feminism as manifestations of universalizing and neocolonial power coming from postcolonial contexts (e.g., Mahmood 2005, Povinelli 2002), such insistence on more rather than less Western-style feminism in Eastern Europe is puzzling. It begins to make sense, however, when one realizes that the "other" of Western style-liberalism in Eastern Europe is not a subjugated postcolonial subject or a marginalized minority subject, but rather a not-yet-European subject exhibiting problematic nationalist attitudes and collectivist thinking.

Such an articulation of the Eastern European "other" has much to do with the perceived legacies of socialism that are thought to discourage individual thought in lieu of submission to authority (see chapter 4). However, it also derives from construing Eastern Europe as the site par excellence of the kind of understandings of collectivity that liberal Europe wishes to leave behind. Any attempt to assert an alternative to Western liberalism could not but be seen as dangerously close to backward nationalism or reactionary socialism of the Soviet kind. As a result, Eastern Europe becomes subject either to perpetual overcoming of the socialist past or perpetual criticism of problematic notions of culture not only in national politics, but also in the way that the "small peoples" of Eastern Europe understand themselves (see also Zelče 2000). Steeped in problematic pasts, Eastern Europe cannot produce insights about possibilities of alternative futures, but rather becomes a site through which to exorcise the past from the present.

This is a common understanding of Eastern Europe in politics and scholarship. This understanding is also one of the reasons why it is a challenge to criticize political liberalism from Eastern Europe in anthropological scholarship.[17] While Western liberalism seems to be immune to criticism from Eastern Europe, because such criticism lacks a legitimate space of difference, postcolonial critique of Western liberalism is effective precisely because the subject of this critique is thought of as innocent in its difference in relation to the violence that Western colonialism has brought on it. For example, in Elizabeth Povinelli's (2002) analysis of Australian multiculturalism's attempts to cleanse the Australian nation from the wrongs perpetuated by early settlers, the Aboriginal subject is innocent precisely because Australian multiculturalism finds it repulsive and thus wants to remake it, while nevertheless fixing it in place. In Scott Lauria Morgensen's (2011) critique of settler colonialism in the United States, Native American appeals to cultural tradition are not seen as complicit with problematic nationalism for they strive for the dismantling of hegemony, that is, the mode of political organization imposed by settler colonialism. Jasbir Puar (2011) criticizes the Israeli state's self-narrative as "gay friendly," an image used to brand Israel as democratic in relation to the Palestinian population depicted as homophobic. There is a tradition of postcolonial criticism of Western politics of sexuality (e.g., Massad 2007) that allows Puar to argue that the "gay friendliness" of the Israeli state and its depictions of "Muslim others" as homophobic converge with the racialization of South Asian, Muslim, and Middle Eastern states and peoples as less democratic and less white. That similar criticism cannot or has not come forth from postsocialist Eastern Europe is telling in relation to the prevailing moral and political imaginaries that shape the current historical conjuncture. These posit Eastern Europeans not as racialized non-European others, but as racializing and backward Europeans who could and should benefit from more rather than less Europeanization.[18]

And yet, engagement with this uncomfortable subject is crucial for understanding how power works in contemporary Europe. And thus my critical engagement with lessons in political liberalism is not animated by a desire to contribute to a long list of critical works on liberalism, which, similar to neoliberalism, is becoming a dark force in critical theory. Rather, I am suggesting that the "end of history" narrative and the perceived danger inherent in criticism of political liberalism from Eastern Europe have obscured the power hierarchies that shape the European present. My book is an attempt to render them visible.

PRIDE AND SHAME

The Moral and Political Landscape of Europe's Colonial Past in the Present

In a 2009 *Baltic Times* article titled "Tobacco? No, Tobago!" Portuguese journalist João Lopes Marques described how Inese, a "proud local Latvian," tried to counterbalance the bad press that Latvia was receiving in international media with regard to the 2008 financial crisis by saying: "But did you know that we once had a colonial empire? Did you know that Tobago Island was ours?" (Lopes Marques 2009; see also Merritt 2010, 500). Since Latvia had not previously registered on Lopes Marques's map of European colonialism, he reported a sense of surprise and disbelief at Inese's assertion of Latvia's colonial heritage and, moreover, at her evident pride in it. According to Lopes Marques's account, Inese proceeded to dispel Lopes Marques's disbelief by taking him on a tour of commemorative places—"Tobago Casino and other homonymous shops that mushroom in Old Riga"—during which Lopes Marques learned about the connections that Latvians make between the current-day Latvian nation and the seventeenth-century colonial pursuits of the Duchy of Courland.

The Duchy of Courland, a vassal state to the Grand Duchy of Lithuania and, subsequently, to the Polish-Lithuanian Commonwealth, existed between 1562 and 1726. It was the only independent state during the early modern period to exist in the territory of current-day Latvia. Its population is estimated at 200,000; it was ruled by Baltic Germans, and most of its subjects were indentured serfs—an ethnically distinct class of peasants who would later be mobilized to form the Latvian nation (Merritt 2010, 492). The reign of Duke Jacob Kettler between

1642 and 1682 is commonly thought of as the golden age of the duchy, a period when it prospered as a result of agricultural production, manufacture, and trade. Though primary historical research is scant, the few historical works that have researched the colonial history of the Duchy of Courland show that, in line with the colonial aspirations of seventeenth-century European maritime powers, Jacob Kettler attempted to obtain colonies on the Atlantic trade route (Andersons 1970a, 1970b; Berkis 1960; Jekabson-Lemanis 2000; Merritt 2010; Sooman et al. 2013; Spekke 2000).[1] As noted by Craig Koslofsky and Roberto Zaugg in their analysis of the connections between "German-speaking hinterlands and the early modern slave trade," despite the fact that few of these hinterlands possessed geopolitical prerequisites to partake in the Atlantic trade, its pull was too strong to resist (Koslofsky and Zaugg 2016, 27). As explained to me by Latvian historian Mārīte Jakovļeva when I sought her out to discuss the duchy's colonial pursuits, the duke wanted to "act on the global stage," for which having colonies was central at the time.[2]

Duke Jacob attempted to colonize the island of Tobago several times (Jekabson-Lemanis 2000, 28).[3] His first colonizing mission in 1639 was a failure, but he eventually established his reign on the island in 1654 via a tactic of "franchise colonialism," whereby, due to a shortage of manpower, he allowed the island to be settled by foreign colonists while retaining military control over it (Jekabson-Lemanis 2000, 35).[4] The duke also briefly held a trading station on the River Gambia in West Africa, which attests to his striving to participate in the Atlantic triangle trade—that is, bringing manufactured goods to West Africa, exchanging them for slaves, shipping the slaves to the Caribbean or the Americas, and then returning to Europe with sugar and other goods (Andersons 1970a, Merritt 2010, Sooman et. al. 2013). The duke spent much time trying to secure his colonial possessions in Tobago from encroachment by the Dutch and the British. Records indicate that coffee, pepper, and cinnamon were transported to Courland in the 1650s and from there sold to neighboring states (Sooman et al. 2013, 511). There is record of enslaved Africans on the island (Sooman et al. 2013, 511), though analyses of the duchy's ship records focus on the makeup of the crews rather than the content of shipments, and thus it is not clear whether and which ships carried slaves from West Africa to Tobago. There are, however, references to the use of slave labor in surviving documents, as well as indications that the conditions of life in colonial settlements were dismal for slaves and settlers both. The duke effectively controlled the island of Tobago and a fort on the River Gambia between 1651 and 1658, when he lost them to the British, but the duchy tried to assert its right to Tobago and reestablish settlements well into the 1680s, even after the duke's death (Sooman et al. 2013, 512).

The duchy's maritime achievements and colonial expeditions were glorified during the first independent Latvian republic from 1918 until 1940, especially in the 1930s when state-based efforts to build a history of the Latvian nation were particularly forceful. The glorification efforts resurfaced in the 1990s, when Latvia regained independence and continue to this day (Zalsters 2002). Contemporary Latvian writers, literary scholars, filmmakers, government institutions, history teachers, and ordinary Latvians routinely invoke the link between the colonial pursuits of the duchy and Latvian national history. At the time of research for this book, in the mid- to late 2000s, the website of the Latvian Institute—an institution charged with disseminating information about Latvia to an international audience—described the duchy's fleet and its colonial pursuits as noteworthy elements of Latvian history (see also Merritt 2010). In 2001, renowned Latvian poet Māra Zālīte wrote a musical titled *Tobago*, in which she depicted the travails of Courlanders, some of them allegedly Latvians, in Tobago. References to the duchy and its glories in public life tend to intensify around commemorative events, such as the duke's four hundredth birthday in 2010, which involved a range of celebrations across Latvia, the publication of books (e.g., Mirbahs 2010), as well as television shows on the relevance of the history of the duchy for contemporary Latvians. The glories of Duke Jacob are also embedded in popular consciousness insofar as some Latvians habitually invoke the duchy's colonial history when they feel compelled to boost Latvia's worldly credentials, as Inese did when speaking to Lopes Marques.

However, what is noteworthy about the encounter between Inese, a "proud local Latvian," and João Lopes Marques, a Portuguese journalist, is not only the Latvians' colonial aspirations, but also the reaction of Lopes Marques who himself hails from a former imperial power with more than its share of nostalgia for the glories of the past (Arenas 2006, Fikes 2009). Lopes Marques is surprised and considers that the Latvians' aspirations for colonial heritage require an explanation. He interprets these aspirations as an instance of "Baltic mini-megalomania," which he attributes to the Latvian "genetic code" and "the admirable effort to transcend smallness." Latvians' colonial aspirations seem puzzling to other outside observers as well. For example, in an article titled "The Colony of the Colonized: the Duchy of Courland's Tobago Colony and Contemporary Latvian National Identity," published in *Nationalities Papers*, Harry C. Merritt introduces the topic from the perspective of a "Western European and North American traveler" who, Merritt writes, may be "bemused" and "baffled" when encountering references to Tobago in Latvian public space, as well as in scholarly and political discourse (2010, 491). It is from the perspective of this bemused and baffled Western subject that the Latvians' aspirations for colonial heritage require an explanation. What follows is a thoughtful account of the duchy in

Latvian historiography and public consciousness. Merritt explains the Latvians' aspirations for colonial heritage with the help of Anthony D. Smith's "ethno-symbolist theory," which suggests that "though nations are themselves essentially modern creations, they draw upon the pre-existing history of a demographic group" (Merritt 2010, 501). Merritt's analysis is delimited within the frame of the currently existing Latvian nation, which is posited as the historical subject writing and rewriting its history. Moreover, Merritt construes the Latvian nation as a postcolonial subject that, after half a century of Soviet rule, needs to "mitigate negative postcolonial feelings in the present" (2010, 492). While Lopes Marques talks about smallness-induced megalomania, Merritt attributes Latvian aspirations for colonial heritage to their own recent past as a colonized nation at the hands of the Soviet state (Merritt 2010, 491, 501). Thus, in Merritt's and Lopes Marques's narratives, Latvian aspirations for colonial heritage are explained with the help of theories of nationalism and postcolonial trauma.

In putting forth these explanations, the baffled and bemused Western traveler and observer turns into a knowing and judging subject in relation to the peculiarities of Latvian nation-building efforts. The knowing and judging subject itself, however, remains outside the analytical frame and is not thought to require an explanation. And yet, it is precisely the relational constitution of the baffled observer-cum-knowing subject and the allegedly postcolonial Latvian nation writing its history that I find to be of analytical interest for the book's argument about the tensions that characterize Europe's political and moral landscape. Latvian assertions of a distant colonial heritage reemerge and are noticed at a time when the most contentious political issues in Europe—for example, migration—are explicitly linked to Europe's colonial past in the present, especially by left-leaning postcolonial activists and scholars who are critical of mainstream liberal politics (Böröcz 2006, Buck-Morss 2009, De Genova 2016, El-Tayeb 2011, Goldberg 2008, Mehta 1999, Ticktin 2011, Ticktin et al. 2007). In the mainstream liberal narrative of Europe as a civilizational space, colonialism is either a thing of the past that has been surpassed by values of freedom, democracy, and human rights or a historical aberration of an otherwise humanist and universalist ethics and politics (see also Povinelli 2002, Mehta 1999). Postcolonial scholars and activists, in turn, consider that such humanist and universalist ethics continue to reenact colonial logics of difference, as well as overlook colonialism as Europe's original sin.[5] They demand recognition that Europe is founded on the violence of colonialism, racism, and slavery. Thus, for example, writing on the relationship between the "migration question" and the "European question," Nicholas De Genova suggests that struggles around movement and migration displace and decenter hegemonic understandings of Europe and that today's "European question" "identifies Europeanness itself as a racial problem—as a problem of postcolonial whiteness" (2016, 79). Similarly, inspired by Aimé Césaire's view that "Europe is spiritually, morally indefensible," József Böröcz (2006) has criticized Hungarian liberals' idealization of French "goodness" in an attempt to denounce domestic racism by asking: "How is it possible to denounce racism by referring to Europe, especially western Europe, the main historic source and promoter of racism as we know it today?" (2006, 112).

Taken together, the mainstream liberal and leftist postcolonial perspectives on Europeanness and colonialism form the contested moral and political landscape of Europe's colonial past in the present that Latvians must grapple with as part of becoming European. Insofar as postsocialist Latvians seek to identify with Europe's colonial history by taking pride in the colonial endeavors of Duke Jacob, they maneuver the moral landscape of Europe's colonial past in the present in ways that disturb both the mainstream liberal narrative and the leftist postcolonial one. First, instead of asserting Europeanness via virtues of freedom, human rights, and democracy, some Latvians exhibit pride in colonialism. Second, while thus recognizing the role of colonialism in the making of Europe, as left postcolonial scholars would have it, they exhibit the wrong kind of affect and focus on the wrong aspects of Europe's colonial past: instead of shame or indignation they exhibit pride, and instead of slave trade and racism they focus on maritime achievements and potential Latvian presence in colonial settlements. These public and locally uncontested aspirations for colonial heritage therefore seem to suggest a failure or refusal to recognize how a properly European subject is to inhabit the moral and political landscape of Europe's colonial past in the present. The proud Latvians have not—or so it seems—absorbed lessons in how to liberalize historical narratives—their own and Europe's—in addition to economic and political institutions. And the Latvian public more generally has not taken up lessons in postcoloniality insofar as there are no publicly audible voices in Latvia that try to expose the colonial logics of difference that underlie Europeanness and that question public manifestations of Latvian colonial pride.

It is important to note that I do not suggest that describing Latvians' aspirations for colonial heritage as part of a nationalist myth, as Merritt does, is wrong. Rather, I suggest that such an explanation is partial. I therefore add another dimension to the analysis, namely an investigation of how the encounter between Latvians' aspirations for colonial heritage and the scholarly, political, and moral interpretations of these aspirations reveals the complex and contested dynamics of Europe's moral and political landscape in relation to colonialism. This allows me to show how the partial explanation provided by the liberal knowing and judging subject partakes in upholding a particular hegemonic version of Europe's colonial history, as well as protects Europe's goodness by refocusing attention on the peculiar practices of not-yet-European subjects. In the case of

Latvia, the liberal and knowing subject explains these peculiar practices by posit-ing Latvians as postcolonial subjects struggling to assert historical significance to compensate for their Soviet past. But the relationship between postcolonialism and postsocialism is not as straightforward as it may seem, and therefore in the following section I take some time to discuss the convergences and divergences between postsocialism and postcolonialism, as well as what they reveal about the modes of power that underlie the moral and political landscape of Europe's colonial past in the present.

The Postcolonial and the Postsocialist

Merritt's deployment of the language of postcolonialism in relation to Latvi-ans' aspirations for colonial heritage gestures toward a particular line of thinking about the relationship between postcolonialism and postsocialism. Over the last two and a half decades, it has become increasingly popular to consider whether postsocialism could benefit from a postcolonial perspective and vice versa. Early scholarship in this vein posed questions about the similarities and differences between the Soviet state and the British and French colonial empires, as well as the effects of the Soviet and colonial pasts on the post-Soviet and postcolonial presents (e.g., Chernetsky 2003, Collier et al. 2003, Edgar 2004, Hirsch 2005, Kel-ertas 2006, Khalid 2007, Northrop 2004, Račevskis 2002). Some scholars used postcolonial analytical tools to make sense of Soviet administrative practices in peripheral territories, such as in Central Asia (e.g., Northrop 2004), while oth-ers claimed a colonial past and therefore postcolonial mentality and status for post-Soviet nations in order to obtain political recognition for the historical injury inflicted on them by the Soviet regime, such as in the Baltics (e.g., Kelertas 2006). Merritt's suggestion that the Latvian national identity project, especially the appropriation of the Duchy of Courland's history into the national narrative, is haunted by Latvians' Soviet past as a colonial history, falls within this com-parative framework. However, scholars of early and late Soviet socialism have cautioned against a hasty equation of the Soviet state with colonial empires, as it obscures important differences of political rationality, organization, and admin-istration, as well as social ideology, aesthetic taste, and moral intention (see Yur-chak 2005; also Slezkine 1994).

A more generative line of thinking considers postsocialist and postcolonial states, subjects, and knowledge practices in relation to contemporary hierarchies of power. For example, the Russian gender studies scholar Elena Gapova has suggested that debates about the colonial nature of the Soviet state in Russia are not so much interested in history as they are animated by postsocialist scholars' attempts to obtain recognition in Western academia (Edgar et al. 2008). Gapova argues that the "appropriation of the postcolonial agenda" by Russian scholars is inspired by "the intellectual curtain," which prevents them from becoming players in the global intellectual field. In Gapova's view, postcolonial scholars' relationship with the West provides postsocialist intellectuals with a recognizable platform from which to assert their voice in relation to Western academia. Zsuzsa Gille (2010), in turn, argues for a relational approach in making sense of the prevailing national(ist) discourses in Central Eastern Europe, specifically Hungary, through which right-wing politicians articulate political grievances and claims. Drawing on Stuart Hall, Gille writes that understanding the ways in which the Eastern European political terrain is constituted in a dialectical relationship with the West leads one to conclude that the national(ist) subject positions are comparable to the first stages of postcolonial politics where "post" is primarily "anti," that is, an essentialist move necessary for becoming a political subject. The "anti" of the postsocialist "post," however, is not directed toward the socialist past, but rather toward the global present (2010, 22; see also Kideckel 2009, Rogers 2010).

Heonik Kwon (2010), in turn, has pointed out how postcolonial theory and critique could benefit from an engagement with histories of the Cold War and its aftermath in Europe, thus complicating the unified image of Europe assumed and produced by postcolonial critique. Similarly, but with a critical lens turned toward "post-Soviet criticism," Neil Lazarus has accused "post-Soviet criticism" for reproducing Eurocentrism by seeking "to install oneself at the very heart of 'Europe'—as 'core European'—by way of emphasizing not only one's *modernity* (despite one's belatedness on the scene, so to speak), but also, and however paradoxical this may sound, one's *postcoloniality*" (2012, 126). I read Lazarus as arguing that assuming a postcolonial positionality reproduces the centrality of a particular conception of Europe, since Lazarus criticizes postcolonial theory for reifying the idea of homogenous Europe and not recognizing internal differentiation within Europe (see also Kwon 2010). While the point is well taken, it should also be recognized that Europe serves as a normative trope in relation to its internal others, whether at the core or at its margins, and that it has enormous discursive force even in conditions when there is no unified space called Europe. At the same time, one might agree with Lazarus that it is indeed worth investigating how Europe and its internal differentiations appear in particular historical conjunctures and especially in relation to postsocialist spaces and subjects. Deployment of postcolonial theory may indeed be of limited use here because it does tend to invoke the dichotomy of the West and the Rest, thus the difference that a European postsocialist perspective might introduce gets subsumed in this dichotomy.

In their seminal 2009 article, Sharad Chari and Katherine Verdery observe that the collapse of the Soviet Union and the disintegration of the "Second World" have not led to a reconfiguration of the Cold War terrain of knowledge production. Rather, it has resulted in the sense that one side—and its way of knowing the world—has won, and therefore its analytical tools are appropriate for making sense of the post–Cold War world (see also Kwon 2010). This is also reflected in critical scholarship, where there is still an overwhelming presence of the "West and the Rest" approach. For example, the equation of the Soviet state with colonial empires and the differentiation of former Soviet subjects into colonizers and the colonized simply treats the former socialist world as freshly available for interpretation with existing analytical tools, such as postcolonial theory. This overlooks how these tools were themselves shaped by Cold War dynamics, as experienced in left-leaning Western scholarly and political circles (Kwon 2010, Scott 2004).[6] To move beyond this Eurocentric, if leftist, Cold War trap, Chari and Verdery suggest that a conversation between the two "posts"—postcolonialism and postsocialism—could be generative on three accounts: as a critique of contemporary imperialism and neoliberalism; a reworking of Cold War geopolitics, including knowledge practices; and as a critique of state racisms, that is, of "institutional and biopolitical mechanisms, which differentiate populations into subgroups having varied access to means of life and death" (2009, 12). The suggested analytical trajectories are oriented toward a critique of contemporary forms of power—imperialism, capitalism, state-based racism, and knowledge production. It is important, in my view, to take Chari and Verdery's argument seriously, while at the same time taking care not to consider postsocialism and postcolonialism as companion projects in producing a metacritique of contemporary forms of power. This may overcome the risk of homogenizing Europe, but entails a new risk of homogenizing power. Instead, I suggest conducting a relational comparison, that is, the kind of comparison that acknowledges how both postsocialist and postcolonial formations and perspectives are constituted in relation to each other and vis-à-vis past and present power configurations that reach beyond particular localities. To put it another way, I suggest using one as a critical perspective on the other and vice versa with a view to larger power formations.

For example, the Eastern European postsocialist perspective can help to critically consider the dynamics of knowledge production within the West and the Rest frame. Within the juxtaposition between the West and the postcolony, the West gains its mastery by attempting to render the postcolonial subject knowable and governable, whereas the postcolonial subject exceeds this frame vis-à-vis her incommensurable difference (e.g., Chakrabarty 2000). While not entirely outside the Western sphere of knowledge, the postcolonial subject nevertheless has access to a space of otherness, which can be a location of critical enunciations. As I argued in the Introduction, European postsocialist spaces and subjects are not quite legible from within this framework, because they are neither one nor the other. They are not quite the West, as it is continuously illustrated in both scholarly and public discourse; and they are also not quite the Rest, for while they are subjected to similar techniques of government as postcolonial spaces and subjects, the critical space of radical otherness, so familiar from postcolonial contexts, seems elusive, if not entirely absent, in European postsocialism. As Madina Tlostanova and Walter Mignolo have pointed out with the help of a quotation from Victor Yerofeyev, "From Moscow I can go to Asia, if I want, or to Europe. It is clear where I am going to. It is not clear where I am coming from" (Tlostanova and Mignolo 2012, 36). The discursive location of postsocialist Europe is analytically generative precisely because it is elusive.

Importantly, it comes into view not by abstraction, but by grounded and relational comparison. Thus the specificity of the encounter between Latvians' colonial aspirations and the Western traveler's interpretations of them cannot be accessed by resorting to a new metaspace of analysis. Such a metaspace does not exist. Instead, there are different relational configurations—for example, the relation between Latvians with aspirations for colonial heritage and Western observers, or the relation between Latvians with aspirations for colonial heritage and the inhabitants of those places that Latvians claim as their colonial heritage. They bring out different understandings of the situation because of their different positioning in relation to them. Let me illustrate with an example.

I met Abdi while I was working with the African Latvian Association, an organization that was initially established in 2005 as a support group for people of African descent residing in Latvia. The group was established in response to a racist anti–European Union political advertisement that used images of some of the group's founding members while misleading them to think that the advertisement would be part of a pro-European Union campaign with an emphasis on cultural diversity. Shortly after its establishment, the association acquired a public presence as some of its more active members spoke out against racism. Its most outspoken members were part of Latvia's network of tolerance workers that I discussed in the Introduction, but also the assumed beneficiaries of tolerance promotion efforts. They were also my interlocutors. Abdi, a member of the association, was an East African cinematographer who graduated from the All-Soviet State Cinematographic Institute in Moscow, ended up living in Latvia, and in 2007 accompanied a group of Latvian businessmen and adventure-seekers on a road trip from Morocco to South Africa, which took them through Gambia, the location of Duke Jacob's briefly held colonial possessions. I first heard about the expedition during communications training for the association's members on how to better communicate their concerns to the public. As part of the first round of introductions, the participants were invited to speak about the kind of problems they thought were important to address publicly. Abdi spoke about the expedition. He told workshop participants about an incident that occurred during a dinner the expedition members had with their Gambian hosts. As an attempt to tell the hosts about the country he came from, Māris, one of the expedition's members, asked the hosts whether they knew that Latvia once had colonial possessions in Gambia. As recounted by Abdi, Māris's question was met by polite silence, and the conversation moved on. Abdi explained Māris's behavior as stemming from a preoccupation with placing Latvians on the world map, while at the same time lacking awareness that the invocation of such a colonial relationship might seem strange, if not offensive, to his Gambian hosts.

During the break, I talked with Abdi about the trip, and he offered more reflections: "He [Māris] was seeing Africa, well, in a racist way, pointing his camera to poverty, exotic nature, everything like that. But not to normal things, like people in city streets or shops." Abdi, whose own life path had led him from East Africa to Soviet Moscow with its own peculiar configuration of official antiracist discourse and institutional and everyday racism (Matusevich 2007), sounded recognizably postcolonial. He commented on Māris's way of seeing as exoticizing and racially coded, his camera turning to scenes of extreme poverty and nature, while ignoring scenes that looked too familiar—for example, scenes of modern urban life. I cannot comment here how Abdi's own way of seeing was formed, to what extent it was his experiences as an African in Moscow that shaped the way he saw Māris, and to what extent it was his resocialization as a black person in post-Soviet Latvia striving to become European. But in the context of our conversation, Abdi's comments diverged from those of the knowing and judging liberal subject insofar as he spoke from the position of a subject that could become the target of Māris's exoticizing gaze. The difference lay in the fact that Abdi did not depict Māris as a racist individual or explain Māris's racial and racist way of seeing by attributing it to an unenlightened and therefore not-yet-European worldview shaped by Māris's Soviet past. Rather, he pointed out how Māris inadvertently reenacted a racialized and racist way of seeing that was common within European modernity. In other words, Abdi did not attribute this to the collective past of Latvians or to Māris's moral failure, but rather to the ways in which Māris's post-Soviet vision was shaped by the prevailing racialized hierarchies and epistemologies—first, in the form of boasting about Latvia's colonies as a way to place Latvia on the world map, and second, when seeing Africa through the racialized logic of colonial modernity.

Viewing the encounter with Abdi alongside that between the Western observer and proud Latvians shifts focus from Latvian postcolonial trauma to the broader framework of (post)socialist and (post)colonial modernity within which Latvians are both racialized and racializing subjects. If Abdi's reading of the situation opens analysis onto modes of power that organize relations between everyone involved, the Western traveler's reading removes the Western traveler as the object of reflection and concentrates attention to specific instances of Latvian history that can account for Latvians' misguided aspirations for colonial heritage and nudge Latvians toward proper Europeanness, that is, the embracing of Europe's virtues and distancing from Europe's vices.

What baffles the Western traveler, but not the East African cinematographer, is that the proud Latvians do not identify with the normative vision of Europe as the source of universal values of freedom, democracy, and human rights, but rather with European colonialism. The Western traveler is baffled, and even though he tries to contain Latvians' colonial aspirations within the framework of national identity, it does not quite work. The Western traveler cannot explain or does not wish to consider how it is that colonial history is an especially desirable aspect of Europeanness. Abdi, in turn, views Māris's attempts to place Latvia on the map within the repertoire of racial ways of seeing that postcolonial scholars consider as formative of Europeanness. Indeed, Latvian colonial pride is not a national pathology, but the product of historically shaped ways of partaking in European modernity. In what follows, therefore, I turn to early Latvian nation-building efforts to suggest that colonial pride derives from attempts to write a counterhistory within hegemonic historical frames.

The Nation's Struggle for History

In late nineteenth and early twentieth centuries, intellectuals of the Latvian "national awakening," such as Jānis Krodznieks (1851–1924) who was educated in Moscow and acknowledged as the first Latvian historian, called for the writing of Latvian history against the grain of Baltic German historiography (Plakans 1999, 294). Baltic German historiography was an ethnically and socially undifferentiated account of urban and territorial development, of trade routes, and of political regimes. Latvians did not appear in this historical narrative, because they were not agents of history, but rather, as the nineteenth-century Baltic German ethnographer August Bielenstein put it, "a laboring mass" (Grāvere n.d.). Jānis Krodznieks argued that "our *tauta* [Volk] has not had a phase during which it has been a notable leader, a bearer of culture, and a purveyor of enlightenment; it has had to act as others have wanted and others have commanded. . . . Nonetheless Latvians have carried a certain weight in the Baltic past, which, though passive, has turned the course of this land in certain directions. To research and to understand the passive role of Latvians in Baltic history is our assignment and obligation" (quoted in Plakans 1999, 295). As a result of this effort to reinterpret the existing historical data, new themes were introduced in the historiography of the Baltic provinces of the Russian Empire, such as legal regulation of serfdom, peasant rebellions, and agrarian reforms (Plakans 1999, 300). Latvian history was excavated and built from sources published by Baltic German historians in an effort to constitute Latvians as a historical subject.

At the time of the first "national awakening" in the late nineteenth and early twentieth centuries, the current-day Latvian territory was part of the Russian Empire—of Vidzeme, Kurzeme, Vitebsk, and Pskov provinces. The territorial consolidation of the nation unfolded on the heels of the Russian revolution through attempts to repartition Russian imperial provinces according to the ethnic principle. With the empire crumbling and Russia weakened by World War I and its own civil war, territorial and ethnic consolidation of Latvian-speaking territories resulted in the proclamation of an independent Latvian state in November 1918.

In contemporary political discourse, this event is seen as the realization of a cultural nation's will for political self-determination. Moreover, it has become a lens for interpreting historical events, especially the ones covered by the writing of this counterhistory, as leading up to the declaration of independence, the highest expression of the nation's spirit and political maturity. However, the writing of counterhistory that began in the late nineteenth century should not be viewed only through the prism of a politically realized cultural nationalism. As a project of social and cultural emancipation, the writing of counterhistory did not have a necessary relationship with ethno-political nationalism. As noted by Andrejs Plakans, "There is no doubt whatever that this 'history from below' inserted into existing Baltic historical knowledge themes and descriptions that had not been prominent—in fact had been nearly absent—in the writings of Baltic German historians. An outsider asked to fill in the 'blank pages' of Baltic history would have chosen precisely the same foci" (1999, 301). It's relationship with ethno-political nationalism was forged after the establishment of the Latvian state and solidified during the authoritarian rule of Kārlis Ulmanis (1934–40), when most spheres of life came under concerted efforts of "Latvianization" (Plakans 1999, 301; Sooman et al. 2013; see also Purs 2002). In 1936, the state founded the Latvian Institute of History with the explicit goal to write the history of the Latvian nation. As stated by the institute's first journal, "Latvian historians will read these sources [of Baltic German historians] not only to study them, but also to analyze them and to draw from them information about Latvians so as to build a history of Latvia" (Plakans 1999, 293, quoted in Merritt 2010, 494).

Latvian interwar history, both formal historiography and popular historical writings, of which there were many, produced a historical subject—the cultural nation of Latvians—who had suffered under "700 years of German rule." This suffering subject was cultivated throughout the Soviet period and survived into the post-Soviet period with an added burden of suffering, namely the Soviet occupation. Moreover, the suffering subject was now said to exhibit a "mentality of servitude" formed over centuries of foreign domination and transmitted across generations (Dribins 1997, Dzenovska 2013a, Jirgens 2006, Plakans 1999, Račevskis 2002, Zake 2007b). Given this history of domination, it becomes particularly important for Latvian national historiography to identify moments when Latvians as a nation can be said to have had a history. The Duchy of Courland played an important role in this project in the 1930s, continued to play this rule during the Soviet period among Latvians in exile, and has been mobilized in the post-Soviet period as well (Merritt 2010; Sooman et al. 2013, 515).

What makes the duchy a particularly fruitful figure for the writing of Latvian history is that it was the only independent political entity to have existed on the current-day Latvian territory (Sooman et al. 2013). This enables the insertion of imaginaries of autonomy into a history of domination, Baltic German rule of the duchy and the indentured status of peasants-cum-Latvians notwithstanding. But it is also the duchy's attempts to partake in the European project of colonialism that aids the writing of Latvian history. Participation in European colonial expeditions enabled the duchy to approximate the status of the most advanced European powers. Similarly, asserting colonial heritage for the Latvian nation in the present seems to boost the nation's historical presence and agency.

It should be noted that such civilizational aspirations permeated not only the writing of counterhistory and history, but also the broader field of emancipatory struggles that unfolded in the Baltic provinces of the Russian Empire from the mid-nineteenth century onward. These struggles were contradictory and diverse and thus much more nuanced than the hegemonic narrative of ethno-political nationalism would have it. Ivars Ijabs illuminates the obscuring effect of this narrative in his article on the political thought of Miķelis Valters, who is often presented as the author of the idea of an independent Latvian state, especially since he partook in the founding of the state in 1918 and later became its ideologue. Contemporary readings fold Valters into the ethno-nationalist narrative, whereas Ijabs shows how Valters's intellectual trajectory was influenced by Russian *narodnichestvo* (populism) and liberal legal theory. The former influenced his support for the dismantling of the Russian Empire, whereas the latter led him to diverge from narodnichestvo insofar as Valters argued for political self-determination of national communities in the form of democratic states rather than for a federation of peasant communes (Ijabs 2012, 251). Valters thought that the national project had to become a project of emancipation from national elites—that is, the recently formed Latvian bourgeoisie represented by the Riga Latvian Association (*Rīgas Latviešu biedrība*), as well as from the Russian autocracy (Ijabs 2012, 452).[7] While it is not entirely invalid to connect Valters's thought to the national state, Valters's case illustrates the internal tensions of Latvian political thought. It is these tensions, that is, the interplay between different emancipatory logics guiding historical struggles and the imaginations of political frameworks for their realization, that should be viewed as the tradition of Latvian political thought. Latvian political thought, then, is a tradition of argument developed in relation to multiple traditions of thought, such as German Romanticism and Russian narodnichestvo, rather than an autonomous and purposeful movement toward ethno-nationalist political thought and practice.[8]

If Valters understood national communities as units for self-governance that could ensure individual liberties, other strands of Latvian political thought understood the object of emancipation as a cultural subject built around the figure of the native peasant, who was governed by German landowners and Russian imperial administration (Zake 2007b, 18). Partisans of the Young Latvian (*Jaunlatvieši*) movement in particular saw themselves as the vanguard of the peasant-cum-Latvian subject, which had to be freed socially in order to be cultivated culturally. For them, "national awakening" was primarily a project that aimed to counter the cultural hegemony of Baltic Germans by proving Latvians' capacity for culture and thus establishing their historical and civilizational presence (Ijabs 2014, Zake 2007b; see also Bula 2000, 2005; Dribins 1997). Most of the nineteenth-century Latvian nation builders, such as Krišjānis Valdemārs, Juris Alunāns, Atis Kronvalds, Fricis Brīvzemnieks, and Krišjānis Barons, were sons of rural families who were educated at what is now Tartu University in current-day Estonia and who subsequently worked as teachers or civil servants in Russia's imperial centers, such as St. Petersburg or Moscow (Zake 2007b). While the Russian imperial government supported the education of Latvian peasants in hopes that they would ally with the Russian imperial administration against the German landlords and eventually would merge into the greater Russian people, the new Latvian intellectuals, influenced by German Romanticism and the Russian Slavophile movement, set out to construct a specifically Latvian identity by selectively cultivating aspects of peasant culture, such as folk songs and the vernacular language and, subsequently, by educating peasants about their newly constituted Latvianness (Dribins 1997, Zake 2007b). The Young Latvians did not aspire for political independence, but rather for equality among German and Russian intellectual elites.[9]

The writing of the Duchy of Courland into Latvian national history was a similar project of seeking equality among nations as agents of history. It required the use of the tactics of counterhistory insofar as the historical record contained scant traces of Latvian presence in Duke Jacob's colonial endeavors. The majority of the labor force of the duchy consisted of Latvians recognized at that time as a linguistically marked class of indentured serfs (Merķelis 2005 [1797]). While Baltic German records depict Latvians as unskilled peasant labor, Latvian historians, such as Edgars Andersons, argue that Latvian serfs were also involved in craftsmanship and manufacturing (Andersons 1970a). Moreover, Andersons suggests that Latvians participated in the duke's colonial expeditions. Andersons, who wrote from exile in the United States, defended a doctoral dissertation at the University of Chicago in 1956 on the seventeenth-century colonial exploits of the Duchy of Courland in Tobago and Gambia. Like many other Latvians whose families left Latvia at the end of World War II to escape Soviet power, Andersons spent much of his personal and professional life furthering the goal of Latvian nation building from exile. In his book *Tur plīvoja Kurzemes karogi* (1970a), published by a Latvian publishing company in New York, Andersons analyses ship records of the duchy's fleet that traversed the Atlantic. Andersons describes the gruesome conditions under which the duchy's colonial expeditions took place—shortages of food and water, conflicts with other colonial powers en route, rebellions of the ships' crews, foul weather, and disease. On numerous occasions Andersons suggests that historical records might contain traces of Latvian presence in these colonial expeditions. Describing the crew of the Di Mullen expedition which left Courland for Gambia in September 1652 on a ship called *Patientia* (Patience), Andersons writes: "The majority of crew members were Germans, Danes, Swedes, and, one should think, also some Latvians. Warkell might be Varkalis. Virwarr could be Visvars, quite a popular family name in Courland" (1970a, 77). Some pages later, when describing the hardships encountered by the crew, Andersons writes: "The following days were dark, with snow and rain. The storm was throwing the ship back and forth. Jākobs Pētersens Vārna (Waarn) died on February 25. Was he a Latvian? Let the linguists answer that" (1970a, 90).

Indeed, Andersons continuously engaged in examining historical data for possible Latvian connections (see also Merritt 2010, 496). Andersons does not suggest that Tobago and Gambia were colonized by Latvians or that the duchy's colonial pursuits should be claimed as Latvian national heritage, but rather that the duke might have recruited Latvian serfs to man the ships and to settle the colonies, and that Latvians thus might have sailed as far as Tobago and Gambia. In doing so, Andersons tries to establish a Latvian presence in Europe's colonial history, which, he feels, has been denied to them by dominant historical narratives (Andersons 1970a, Merritt 2010). Like other exile Latvian historians, such as Aleksandrs Berķis, Edgars Dunsdorfs, and Arnolds Spekke, Andersons writes against works such as that of Otto von Mattiesen (1940)—a historian of German heritage—which suggest that the colonization efforts were organized solely by Baltic Germans and that there were no Latvians in Tobago at all, while at the same time recognizing that the colonies and the crews were multinational (Andersons 1970a, Merritt 2010, 497). Aleksandrs Berķis also provides a rationale for how Latvian peasants may have ended up in Tobago (for example, they had an interest to go to the colonies, because the duke would have freed them in that case), but goes further by including slaves in the Latvian national imaginary. He suggests that "the former serfs of the ducal domains not only became freemen, but also the owners of Negro slaves" (quoted in Merritt 2010, 496). Whether that is the case or not, the important point here is that it was not just the courage of setting out on dangerous seas and settling a colony that was meant to boost Latvians' historical credentials, but also ownership of slaves.

Following Ancestors' Footsteps

Edgars Andersons died in 1989, but until then he organized biannual commemorative get-togethers on the island of Tobago that were attended mostly by émigré Latvians from South and North America.[10] These gatherings served to remind the Latvian diaspora living outside Soviet Latvia that even though Latvia's statehood was short lived—Latvia lost independence to the Soviet Union in 1940, Latvians had a world historical presence long before that. It is here that Jānis, a Latvian living in California, met Professor Andersons and, as Jānis told me when I met him in Los Angeles in 2010, came up with his "crazy idea" to visit the former "Latvian colony in Gambia." Jānis's visit was enabled by the flourishing of African American heritage tourism that emerged in the United States following the publication of Alex Haley's book *Roots* in the 1970s and the production of a TV series with the same title. American travel agencies organized tours to a village in Gambia that was allegedly the home of Kunta Kinte—Alex Haley's slave ancestor (Bellagamba 2005). In 2004, Jānis went on such a roots tour to Gambia along with about thirty African Americans. He justified his presence to the group and to the tour group leader, who was visibly surprised at his whiteness at the airport, by saying that he was simply interested in history. When I asked Jānis how he had become interested in the history of the duchy, he replied: "Every Latvian must seek out his ancestors' footprints." Jānis had learned from Andersons how to read the historical record and material evidence for traces of Latvian presence. That afternoon back in November 2010, Jānis told me about some paintings he saw in a museum in Gambia, which depicted shocks of rye—a sight characteristic of the Latvian countryside. "Who could have painted those, and how did they get there?" Jānis asked suggestively, implying some Latvian connection.

As we continued our conversation, I found out that Jānis had pursued his ancestors' footprints not only in Gambia, but also in Siberia where many Latvians had been sent by the Soviet state during the deportations of the 1940s and 1950s. It appeared that Jānis was interested in the traces of people he understood to be his tribe, while not necessarily enfolding them into a politically delimited historical subjectivity. For example, when visiting the old fort on James Island in Gambia, Jānis pulled out the flag of the Duchy of Courland—a black crab on a red background—that he had made before the trip.[11] He presented the flag to the Gambian Minister of Culture and Tourism saying that the flag of the duchy deserves to fly on the fort alongside other colonial flags, including that of the contemporary Latvian state.[12] The flag of the duchy was as important to Jānis, if not more, than the flag of the Latvian state, for it was a more accurate symbol for the possible presence of Latvian serfs than the flag of the nation.

However, this was not the first time the flag of the duchy had appeared on the island. Moreover, its relationship with the nation has not always been as loose as in Jānis's story. About the same time that Jānis was on his tour, a film-crew from Latvia was visiting Gambia and filming material for what was to be a three-part documentary following Latvian footsteps in Gambia and Tobago. The filmmakers—seasoned Latvian TV producer Pēteris and amateur American Latvian filmmaker Inga—wanted to make the film "to raise the self-confidence of Latvians" which, they thought, was significantly lacking. "If you don't know why you are Latvian," said Pēteris in a conversation over dinner, "if you cannot fill that with positive content, then we are in big trouble." "The main message of the film," he continued, "is that we have a history, and that each nation needs its self-confidence." For Pēteris, then, it was important for Latvians to realize that they "had a history" insofar as they were present in trade and commerce at the foundation of Europe's prosperity. It was this presence in events of world historical significance that was to be the source of the contemporary self-confidence of Latvians not only as a tribe but, importantly, as a nation.

Similar to Harry C. Merritt, Pēteris thought that the self-confidence of Latvians as a nation had been crushed by Soviet rule and that Latvians now exhibited a postcolonial mentality, that is, a submissive attitude toward more powerful historical actors. This is a theme that is common in Latvian intellectual and literary circles (see Jirgens 2006); it also runs through several important works in Latvian literature—for example, Alberts Bels's 1987 novel *Cilvēki laivās* (People in Boats), which takes place in a nineteenth-century fishing village in Courland that is about to be swallowed by a large sand dune. As interpreted by Kārlis Račevskis (2002) in an article that argues for Latvia's postcoloniality, "as the narrative unfolds, the dune becomes a multilayered symbol for the novel's principal themes: it represents, by turns, the flow of time, the march of history, the force of nature, the oppression of state despotism, the discord that tears communities apart, as well as the self-destructive urges individuals harbor within themselves. Above all else, it stands for the force of destiny: just as the dune finally engulfs the hamlet, history eventually swallowed up the once prosperous nation of Courland." Račevskis further suggests that "what gives the narrative its tragic resonance is the evocation of the inexorable force of geopolitical circumstances to which small nations are subject. In a world in which small countries have naturally fallen prey to the predatory designs of the larger ones, the fate of the colonized is made all the more bitter by the lack of concern the more powerful nations have often manifested for the lot of the small ones." In the filmmakers' view, since nobody else can be relied on to recognize Latvians' historical presence, it is up to Latvians themselves to rebuild their self-confidence. The glories of Duke Jacob seemed like a good place to start.

As the visual images shot from a boat pan across the coast of Gambia, the film's narration suggests that contemporary Latvians could find reason for self-confidence in the memory of their ancestors who sailed dangerous seas and constructed colonial forts. In another scene, the filmmakers and their team present the flag of the Duchy of Courland to their Gambian guides. The film shows Gambian hosts raising the flag above the former colonial fort. "We need to learn the history of slavery," says the Gambian guide, "and that's why we need to learn the history of Courland."[13] In response, an ethnologist accompanying the film crew adds: "Knowing history can make us take our place in history." Whereas the Gambian guide emphasizes that learning the history of Courland is necessary for learning about the "darker side" of modernity, the Latvian ethnologist emphasizes that learning the history of Courland is necessary for finding a place for Latvia in History.

In her essay on alternative universal history, Susan Buck-Morss shows that more often than not historical facts cannot be contained within the exclusionary conceptual frames of the nation and the state, yet hegemonic historical narratives continuously posit nations and states as primary agents of history (2009, 110). The history of the Duchy of Courland as written by Edgars Andersons and as lived by Jānis, as well as Inga, Pēteris, and their team, illustrates this tension. While all are trying to establish the presence of Latvians on the world historical stage, that is, to write the history of underdogs, they do so within the discursive frame provided by the winners. If late nineteenth- and early twentieth-century Latvian historians, not unlike scholars of subaltern studies (e.g., Guha 1988), read between the lines of historical records in order to excavate alternative historical problem-spaces, Anderson's work reiterates hegemonic understandings of historical agency as primarily national by ignoring the wide variety of people on the duke's ships and focusing on the link between the political and economic history of the duchy and the presence of ethnic Latvians in it. Latvian serfs may or may not have been on the duke's ships. Either way, there is no necessary connection between identifying a Latvian presence amidst the sailors and settlers and folding this presence into a narrative of national historical presence.

Anderson's concern with Latvians on the duke's ships stems from the subsequent link made between ethnic groups and national states, thus enabling establishment of the nation's past and continuity in time. It also stems from a historical imagination that privileges the bounded historical subject of the nation or the state and evaluates its historicity in accordance with various Enlightenment and counter-Enlightenment conceptions of historical agency. To conjure up an imagination of a different historical space, Susan Buck-Morss (2009) draws on Peter Linebaugh and Mark Rediker's analysis of the seventeenth- and eighteenth-century Atlantic slave trade from the perspective of the "dispossessed commoners, transported felons, indentured servants, religious radicals, pirates, urban laborers, soldiers, sailors, and African slaves,"—that is, the "motley crew" or the proletariat of the Atlantic (Linebaugh and Rediker 2000, 4; see also Clifford 1994, Gilroy 1993). Linebaugh and Rediker argue that as much as the English and Dutch colonial rulers strove to impose order on their "global labor force," the "motley crew" of the Atlantic developed practices of cooperation that often led to rebellions, strikes, or mutinies, thus claiming their own specific historical agency (2000, 5). The authors aim to recover "the lost history of a multiethnic class that was essential to the rise of capitalism and the modern global economy," whose historical invisibility is the effect of the "violence of abstraction in the writing of history," which takes the nation-state as an unquestioned framework of analysis.

Linebaugh and Rediker's work also inspired Paul Gilroy (1993) in his quest for a "transnational counterhistory" to nationalist orientations that animate not only the history of modernity but also the history of black resistance. Critical of the centrality of essentialist national identities in black resistance narratives, Gilroy emphasizes the slave ship and the mobile scene of the Atlantic as formative of black resistance to colonial displacement. As noted by James Clifford, the writing of such a transnational counterhistory is a politically and analytically ambitious, even a utopian, project (Clifford 1994, 205), yet it forcefully argues for a different vision of historical space, one based on connections and solidarities formed between those subject to history's violent displacement. Theirs is a vision that goes beyond the demand to recognize the colonial past in the present, inviting a rethinking of global history.

In the context of the juxtaposition between the hegemonic historical space of European modernity and the subjugated historical agency of the Atlantic motley crew or black diaspora, the Latvian case is noteworthy. In his historical writings,

Edgars Andersons describes the multiethnic crews of the duke's ships and the rebellions that broke out on the ships due to food and water shortages. He writes of the drunkards and criminals, of disease and hardship, which required that crew members form solidarities across linguistic and other boundaries. And yet, despite the violence that connected this "motley crew" and imbued it with agency that on occasion made the expeditions change course, Andersons uses his interpretive energies to conjure up and emphasize a Latvian national presence. In asserting this national historical presence, Andersons and Latvian intellectuals and their publics do join the European story of modernity within which colonial expansion and slave trade are important building blocks.[14] Yet, as I argue in the next section, rather than embrace colonial injuries—such as slave trade—as a necessary downside to the colonial glories, Latvians identify themselves with colonial glories while distancing themselves from colonial injuries. This is not unique to Latvians. Other European nations engage in similar projects that parse out colonial glories from colonial injuries. What is noteworthy, however, is the ways in which Latvians achieve the simultaneous identification and distancing in relation to both European colonial powers and non-European colonial subjects. This dynamic is telling about how colonial history continues to shape Europe's political landscape and how postsocialist Europe is recruited in this project.

Identification with and Distancing from Europe's Colonial History

Contrary to liberals who wish to emphasize human rights, democracy, and freedom as Europe's contribution to humanity, left-leaning postcolonial theorists and activists point out that contemporary Europe is postcolonial insofar as colonial logics of difference inform distinctions between Europeans and non-Europeans (or not-yet-Europeans), citizens and migrants, and majorities and minorities (El-Tayeb 2011, Huggan 2008, Huggan and Law 2009). In the self-narrative of European liberal democracies, colonialism is a thing of the past or, in some cases, a thing of somebody else's past (Goldberg 2009). For example, Nordic nations often claim to have had nothing to do with colonialism (Fur 2015; Keskinen et al. 2009; Loftsdóttir and Jensen 2012; Purtschert 2011, 2015; Vuorela 2009). In response, scholars working from within the postcolonial framework, such as Barbara Lüthi, Francesca Falk, and Patricia Purtschert (2016), call this phenomenon "colonialism without colonies" and use it as a lens for reexamining the contours of Europeanness as a political and cultural formation. Purtschert, Lüthi, and Falk write against the mainstream public and political discourse across Europe, suggesting that colonialism tends to be reduced to the political and legal fact of colonial possessions, thus compartmentalizing Europe's colonial legacy. This, they argue, enables national publics whose states did not have direct colonial relationships to claim innocence with regard to colonialism. Their aim is to render the European states and publics "without colonies" complicit with the violence of colonialism. They suggest that distancing from colonialism vis-à-vis the argument that states, such as Switzerland, did not have colonies overlooks how they participated in and benefited from cultural forms of colonialism, as well as the ways in which their national publics' sense of self is formed within the frame of Europeanness produced through colonial encounters (Gullestad 2005, Purtschert 2011).

For example, Patricia Purtschert analyzes a statement made by a Swiss government official during the 2001 Durban antiracism conference in South Africa that "Switzerland has nothing to do with slavery, slave trade, and colonialism" (2011, 173). Since its utterance, the phrase has taken on a life of its own—it has been cited, critiqued, and contested. While the phrase has outraged a narrow circle of activists, Purtschert suggests that it resonates with broad segments of the Swiss public who also believe that Switzerland has nothing to do with colonialism. Purtschert points out that by claiming innocence with regard to colonialism on the basis that Switzerland did not have colonies, the Swiss overlook the fact that Swiss companies traded with and profited from colonial regimes, circulated colonial images, used colonial rhetoric, and sold and marketed colonial goods (Purtschert 2011, 122).

Marianne Gullestad (2005) has put forth a similar argument with regard to the Norwegian debates about the use of the word *neger*. Gullestad shows that the Norwegian public maintains that Norwegians cannot possibly be racist, because they did not possess colonies and thus did not participate in the direct implementation of oppressive racial regimes. Similar to the Swiss, Norwegians cleanse their modernity from colonialism by arguing that they did not politically and legally participate in the European colonial project, thus, in Gullestad's view, overlooking how colonialism remains constitutive of Norwegians as modern political subjects. Kesha Fikes shows that even states that did have colonies engage in absolution from colonial guilt. As described by Fikes, the Portuguese public holds that Portuguese colonizers were not racists due to their affective relationships with colonial subjects, thus defining racism as "the colonizer's absence of human compassion toward differently raced others abroad" (2009, 39; see also Stoler 2002). In turn, as illustrated by Elizabeth Povinelli, the Australian nation-state, as a state that aspires to membership in the global community of liberal democracies, that is, the West, cleanses its liberal present from the stains of the colonial past by positing colonial violence as an aberration of the social and political system at the basis of the contemporary state rather than as its constitutive element (2002, 7). The authors of these works argue that European colonialism has shaped many, if not most, places and people around the world, albeit in different ways. Most important, asserting Europeanness, in their view, is an act complicit with colonial violence and its legacies—a stance that those Latvians who take pride in the duchy's brief colonial past do not embrace, instead engaging in simultaneous identification with and distancing from Europe's colonial history shaped by their perceptions of the history of Latvian nation as a history of domination.

Throughout Pēteris's film, an emphasis on the duchy's colonial presence, such as raising the colonial flag on Jacob's Fort in Gambia, intermingles with moments of solidarity with the once enslaved Gambians. The slave trade that was part of the trade route that Courlanders wished to join is noted and condemned, yet Latvians as a people are cleansed from association with it through an emphasis on their own indentured status within the Duchy of Courland.[15] When I prompted Pēteris to reflect on how pride in colonial glory went together with the slave trade, he responded as follows:

> You have to separate two things here. One, there is the thing you speak of, that is, the slave trade. Two, there is the building of national self-confidence, even as the nation might actually be in demise. But there is another thing here: Latvians themselves were not free people. They were indentured serfs and between indentured servitude and slavery . . . well, those are just different phases. Then there is the question to what extent they [slave traders] were Latvians and to what extent they were Germans.

Pēteris's response is typical of how many Latvians I spoke with related to the fact that Duke Jacob's colonial aspirations were linked with the slave trade. The distancing tactics described above, as well as the Latvians' ability to both identify with the colonial project and absolve themselves from its undersides, reflects the ways in which colonialism is compartmentalized in Europe.[16] The compartmentalization of colonialism into good and bad elements that can be separated from each other and the associated reduction of "bad colonialism" to the political and legal fact of having colonies or, within that, to oppressive and compassionless ways of relating to colonial subjects, has created the possibility to posit other elements of colonial projects and their legacies, such as exploration, trading, and traffic in racialized and exoticized images, outside the mainstream story of shameful colonial history. It has created the conditions within which it becomes possible to glorify colonialism as an integral element of the history of European modernity; something that has been done not only by Latvians, but also by other ambiguously positioned eastern Europeans.

For example, historian Lenny A. Urena (2010) describes how nineteenth-century Polish explorers wanted to compete with European scientific explorers. Since Poland was not a state at the time, they were ridiculed at home. Yet, they argued that in order to be part of European modernity, Poles did not have to have a nation-state that possessed colonies. Being part of European modernity meant participating in the European project of knowledge production through exploration, which was possible from within other political structures.[17] Once in Africa, Polish explorers attempted to distinguish their pursuit of the higher good—that is, knowledge—from the pursuit of profit in which European colonial powers were engaged. This episode is interesting precisely because it illustrates that identification with the project of European modernity was profoundly colonial even in the absence of colonial possessions. It should not therefore come as a surprise—nor cause bafflement—that for many in Latvia being part of European history means partaking in the colonial project. And yet, it seems to generate precisely that—bafflement and bemusement, as well as ridicule, as I observed in a conference where I heard another paper on Polish colonial fantasies. The presenter exhibited an openly mocking attitude toward the colonial fantasies she described; her presentation took the form of an exposé. She expected everyone in the audience to understand intuitively how ridiculous these fantasies were without her doing the work of outlining what precisely was so ridiculous about them. The audience responded as expected—by chuckling in moments marked by the presenter with a change in the tone of voice.

Yet neither the absurdity of colonial claims and fantasies, nor their ability to produce laughter or discomfort, are necessarily evident to those who make them. More often than not, those Latvians who perform the historical appropriation of the duchy's colonial pursuits do so without much awareness of the possible effects of their utterances in European public and political space. And it is precisely this—the affective relationship of Latvians to Europe's colonial history—that seems to suggest to the Western traveler that, indeed, Latvians are not yet European. In the eyes of the Western traveler, Latvians seem to lack the skill to correctly identify those elements of the European past that liberal Europe wants to strategically forget rather than proudly remember. Thus the Latvians' and other not-quite-Europeans' colonial aspirations become yet another site through which the Western traveler or scholar can assert moral superiority, as well as authority to affectively and discursively interpret the situation—by bafflement, bemusement, or laughter and thereafter by explanations that locate the source of these colonial aspirations in the national histories of the not-quite-Europeans.

Complicities of Europeanness

The project of writing Latvian history as a countermove to being overrun by history cannot but fail in the sense that it must take up the categories of European modernity in making a claim to historical presence. In other words, counterhistory amounts to writing oneself into recognizable narratives rather than changing the frame. These were, in fact, the conditions within which Latvian history was construed as a history of the Latvian cultural community in the late nineteenth and early twentieth centuries and subsequently as a history of the Latvian political community following 1918. And these are the conditions within which Latvian historians, intellectuals, and ordinary people assert Latvian historical presence vis-à-vis Duke Jacob's colonial expeditions. And yet, while articulated through the categories of European modernity, Latvian colonial aspirations also unsettle it.[18]

Latvian identification with the European colonial project cannot be completely appropriated and contained by dominant discourses. It is the bafflement and ridicule that identification with the European colonial project produces that serve as markers of the impossibility of containment. Enthusiastic references to Gambia and Tobago in public spaces and discourses in Latvia baffle the Western scholar and traveler because identification with Europe's colonial past is legible, yet unintelligible for those wishing to bring Latvians into political maturity vis-à-vis lessons in political liberalism.[19] On the one hand, Latvians speak a recognizable language of national history. On the other hand, they earnestly articulate claims to a colonial past from which liberal Europe wants to distance itself (e.g., Gullestad 2005, Purtschert 2011). On the one hand, socialist-cum-European Latvians facilitate the erasure of colonialism from Western Europe's self-narrative by occupying the "not-yet-European" slot, thus enabling the Western knowing and judging subject to focus on democratization and liberalization projects rather than his or her own shameful past. On the other hand, socialist-cum-European Latvians throw that project into disarray when, in order to overcome their seemingly permanent "not-quite-European" position, they strive to identify with colonialism, thus challenging the criteria of "goodness" in Western Europe's self-narrative (Böröcz 2006).

From the postcolonial perspective, the proud Latvians' colonial aspirations bring into focus the fact that colonial history is fundamentally constitutive of European modernity and that attempts to emphasize political virtues of freedom, democracy, and human rights as Europe's defining contribution to humanity are contestable. The scene of bafflement, whereby a Western traveler encounters Latvians' colonial pride, may therefore seem like an opportunity for postcolonial analysis of Europe's colonial legacies in the present, one that emphasizes Europe's continued coloniality rather than the Latvians' postcoloniality in relation to the Soviet past. However, here too, socialist-cum-European Latvians fail insofar as they do not recognize that becoming European entails learning to inhabit Europe's colonial past in the present critically—for example, through continued reflection on contemporary racisms, their histories, and their legacies. However, by pointing this out, postcolonial scholars and activists risk complicity with their liberal counterparts' civilizational project. That is, they risk complicity with what József Böröcz, drawing on Partha Chatterjee's notion of "the rule of colonial difference" has called the "rule of European difference," namely a set of cognitive operations that posit that goodness in Europe is distributed unevenly, that the uneven distribution of goodness maps onto the east-west and north-south axes with the east and the south marred in insufficiencies, and that goodness is to be found in its "highest empirical density" in Western Europe (2006, 130). The socialist-cum-European Latvian subject is well positioned to illuminate this potential complicity. At the same time, as I pointed out in the Introduction, this entails the risk of being relegated to the space of parochial nationalism or reactionary Soviet socialism within both liberal and postcolonial narratives due to lack of other recognizably legitimate discursive spaces from which to mount a critique of the moral and political landscape of Europe's colonial past in the present.

It is precisely this predicament that also makes many Latvians cautious when they are summoned to reevaluate their collective past and present vis-à-vis the dominant imperatives of Europe's moral and political landscape, such as recognition of the stains of colonialism and fascism in European history or recognition of racism as a foundational problem that needs to be continuously expelled from a properly European moral and political community. Many suspect that by embracing the problems of intolerance and racism as their own they risk being marked as a paradigmatic site of Europe's vices and thus in need of continuous civilization. To put it another way, they are wary that recognizing the problem of intolerance or the problem of racism will be interpreted via the cognitive operations of "the rule of European difference." Western Europeans can critically reflect on the problem of racism or intolerance in their midst without tainting their civilizational credentials, because, in part, they are able to claim this critique itself as their civilizational achievement that can be extended to non-Europeans or not-yet-Europeans in various democratizing contexts. At the same time, Latvia and Latvians can claim neither colonialism nor its critique as their own. In both cases, Latvia and Latvians can only strive to become European.

THE STATE PEOPLE AND THEIR MINORITIES

Rebirth of a National State with a Minority Problem

While the Latvian state's legislative frameworks, such as the citizenship law, are not exclusively ethnic, Latvia defines itself as a national state. The 2014 preamble to the Constitution stipulates that the Latvian state was established in 1918 as a result of the political will of the cultural nation of Latvians and for the purpose of ensuring its continuity and flourishing.[1] As a state that explicitly emphasizes the cultural identity at its foundations, the Latvian state is significantly different from states, such as France (Fernando 2014), where it is republicanism that defines the nation, or Sweden, which defines itself vis-à-vis Olaf Palme's cosmopolitan legacy (Levitt 2015). As a state that is not based on exclusively ethnic citizenship, Latvia is also different from Israel (or, until recently, Germany), where citizenship and migration politics are exclusively ethno-religious (Aktürk 2012, 2011).

Within the European political landscape and normative political theory, such differences tend to be arranged on a developmental scale from illiberal to liberal polities. There is a rich body of scholarship on the question of whether and how liberalism as respect for personal autonomy can be reconciled with nationalism with its emphasis on collective belonging, and moreover, what to do when individual rights valued by liberal regimes are understood as rights to practice cultural and collective difference publicly (e.g., Kymlicka 1996, Kymlicka and Opalski 2002, Tamir 1995). Within these debates, it is generally assumed that those states whose citizenship, migration, language, and minority policies are not based on ethnicity and who recognize the rights of groups and individuals to live their ethnic difference publicly are more inclusive and liberal. Eastern European states, including Latvia, are commonly thought to be more nationalistic than liberal. In the very least, their liberal credentials are in question and must be continuously asserted (Aktürk 2012, Brubaker 2004, Kymlicka and Opalski 2002, Ijabs 2016).[2]

In his analysis of "regimes of ethnicity" in the Soviet Union, Russia, Turkey, and Germany, Sener Aktürk (2012, 2011) claims to propose a more objective system of classification of how states govern the relationship between ethnicity and citizenship. Instead of the imprecise and moralizing categories of "civic" and "ethnic"—or liberal and illiberal—nationalism, Aktürk classifies ways of governing ethnic difference as monoethnic, multiethnic, or antiethnic (2012, 7). Monoethnic regimes restrict membership in the nation to one ethnic category through discriminatory immigration and naturalization policies, antiethnic regimes accept "people from ethnically diverse backgrounds as citizens, but discourage or even prohibit the legal, institutional, and public expression of ethnic diversity," and multiethnic regimes "accept people from ethnically diverse backgrounds as its citizens . . . , and allow, encourage, or even participate in the legal and institutional expression of ethnic diversity" (Aktürk 2012, 6–7). Aktürk argues that Germany before 1999 (when the ethnicity principle was removed from citizenship legislation) is a good example of a monoethnic state, Turkey before 2004 and France are ideal-typical examples of antiethnic states, and the Soviet Union and the post-Soviet Russian Federation approximate "the ideal-type of a state with a multiethnic regime" (2012, 6–7).

Aktürk's analysis of "regimes of ethnicity" provides useful insights within a convincing conceptual framework that strives to go beyond the moralizing liberal/illiberal divide. However, it is still not sufficient for understanding what makes Latvia a national state, even as its citizenship regime could be classified as multiethnic. Emphasis on differences with regard to treatment of ethnicity in policy instruments overlooks the historically specific ways in which nation-states engage in efforts to cultivate coherent "communities of value" (Anderson 2013), as well as how these come to define citizenship. If viewed through the prism of the relationship between ethnicity and citizenship, the Latvian state can hardly be said to be a monoethnic state, insofar as the body of citizenry of the first independent Latvian state (1918–40), which the post-Soviet Latvian state claimed as the basis for the post-Soviet body of citizenry, was not ethnic. The interwar Latvian state granted citizenship to all individuals who had resided in the territory of Latvia prior to the beginning of World War I. Many, including current-day political leaders critical of the national state, argue that interwar citizenship and minority politics in Latvia were among the most inclusive in Europe. For example, granting citizenship to some of the Jewish residents was initially problematic, because they were not formally registered in the Baltic provinces of the Russian Empire and thus could not prove their residency. However, in 1927, despite discontent within the most nationalistic segments of the population and within emerging fascist organizations, the Latvian government enabled pre–World War I Jewish residents to become citizens of Latvia on the basis of witness testimony of their resident status.[3] Moreover, representatives of the new minorities—Baltic Germans, Jews, and Russians—were part of the government apparatus and were granted considerable educational and cultural autonomy (Pabriks 2003, Silova 2006).[4]

And yet, it is precisely in the name of this multiethnic interwar body of citizenry that the post-Soviet Latvian state disenfranchised the equally multiethnic, but Russian-speaking former Soviet citizens who had come to reside in Latvia during the Soviet period. Instead of citizenship, they were granted resident noncitizen status, which provided social, but not political rights. They were also allowed to naturalize after passing naturalization exams or, in the case of young people, after graduating from high school in independent Latvia and applying for citizenship. Since it was first adopted in 1994, the Law of Citizenship has undergone several changes, gradually liberalizing access to naturalization and access to citizenship for children born in Latvia to noncitizen parents.[5] Nevertheless, in 2016, about 12 percent of Latvia's multiethnic Russian speakers were still noncitizens (compared to 29 percent in 1995).[6]

The seemingly strange formulation "Russian speakers" (krievvalodīgie)—in addition to or instead of Russians—is a post-Soviet marker of Latvia's residents who may or may not recognize themselves or be recognized by others as ethnically Russian, but who use Russian as their first language of communication. This multiethnic population of Russian speakers emerged during the Soviet period as pre–World War II Russians living in Latvia mixed with people of different ethnic backgrounds, but mostly Russians, Ukrainians, and Belorussians, who came to live and work in Latvia from other parts of the Soviet Union.[7] They were both ethnic and Soviet insofar as the multiethnic Soviet state recorded its citizens' ethnicity in internal passports—a mechanism of governance that was initially meant to facilitate affirmative action, but ended up also facilitating ethnically based repressions, such as deportations (Aktürk 2012, Arel 2001, Martin 2001).[8] In the 1950s, when most of the Soviet ethnics came to Latvia, ethnicity was deemphasized in favor of building a Soviet nation or people (Sovetskii narod), though ethnicity remained written in Soviet passports until after the dissolution of the Soviet Union (Aktürk 2012). Russian language played a central role in the making of the Soviet people in Latvia, where Soviet citizens of various ethnic backgrounds adopted the Russian language as their primary means of private and public communication. Latvians, in turn, fought for public relevance of the Latvian language as a marker of their nationality.

During the late 1980s, many of the Russian speakers supported Latvian independence (Dzenovska and Arenas 2012). However, Latvians did not trust them to endorse the Latvian state as a national state. They suspected that some Russian speakers wished for a binational or non-national state with equal status for Russian and Latvian languages, while others harbored sympathies toward Russia as the successor state of the Soviet Union, or had simply forgotten about their nationality and thus could not be expected to understand the Latvian will for a national state.[9] It is for that reason that the Latvian state did not give them automatic citizenship and required that all Soviet-era incomers without descent-based links to the interwar body of citizenry undergo naturalization regardless of the length of their residence in Soviet Latvia. As part of the naturalization process, they were expected to demonstrate their commitment to the national state and the "community of value" at its foundation. As a result of the contested role of language in the making of the Soviet people, language became the most important marker of the "community of value" at the foundation of the Soviet Socialist Republic of Latvia and the most sacred attribute of the post-Soviet national state. Soviet-era Russian speakers were required to demonstrate Latvian language skills in order to become citizens of the new polity. The Latvian language did not have an imperial history and could not lay claims to consolidating a multiethnic community of speakers into an antiethnic "new historical community of people," as Nikita Khrushchev had claimed Russian could (Aktürk 2012). Thus the language requirement of the national Latvian state was perceived as a manifestation of ethnic nationalism. It was that indeed, but it was also an attempt to build a "community of value" out of a multiethnic population.

Insofar as language was and continues to be mobilized not only as an ethnic marker, but also as an integral feature of the "community of value" at the foundation of the Latvian national state, the difference between Latvia and states that deemphasize the role of cultural identity within their polities begins to blur. It is increasingly common for Europe's self-defined liberal democracies to grant citizenship on the basis of demonstrated ability to adhere to the principles of tolerance, equality, civil liberties, or sexual freedom valued by national communities. For example, Christine Jacobsen (2018) argues that values of gender and sexual equality have become part of Norwegian national identity. When such values come to define the boundaries of a national community as a "community of value," they also function as grounds for exclusion of those who are deemed as failing to adhere to such values—for example, Muslims. Similarly, non-EU citizens wishing to reside in the Netherlands are required to take a civic integration exam, which tests the would-be residents' or citizens' tolerance for female nudity among other things (Fassin 2010). The overlap between boundaries of value and boundaries of ethnicity, race, or religion may be historically contingent, but it is not insignificant. It suggests that when not explicitly acknowledged, or even when actively denied, the racial and cultural contours of national communities form the "deep story," that is, the story that is more felt than stated, but that powerfully shapes the way citizens of a particular state orient in public and political life (Hochschild 2017). Thus analysis of regimes of ethnicity must be supplemented with analysis of *regimes of value*, that is, the ways in which particular values get deployed in granting residence or citizenship and the ways in which such values overlap with markers of ethnicity, race, or religion in governing difference through the liberal frameworks of citizenship and majority-minority relations.

Analysis of the Latvian national "regime of value" alongside its "regime of ethnicity" shows that the Latvian state governs difference through regulating *conduct* in addition to governing difference through political and legal categories of belonging. Thus, for example, in an attempt to remake some of the Russians and Russian speakers into the kind of subjects that value cultural belonging and understand the Latvian national project, the independence movement of the late 1980s, led by the Popular Front (*Tautas fronte*), attempted to "awaken" proper national sentiments among ethnic Russians and Russified ethnics. In doing so, independence-era politicians drew on: (1) selected aspects of Latvia's interwar minority politics where minorities, such as Baltic Germans, Russians, and Jews, were granted cultural autonomy and political representation (Pabriks 2003); (2) the Soviet nationalities policy, which emphasized national difference as both basis for political organization and a matter of ethnographic culture (Hirsch 2005, Slezkine 1994); and (3) contemporary European legislative instruments, such as the Framework Convention for the Protection of National Minorities. As stated by Baiba Pētersone, an independence-era politician who subsequently became a high-level civil servant in the Ministry of Education:

> The idea of restoring cultural autonomy for minority education . . . was a strategic move. I can openly say now that the politics were geared toward splitting the opposition and distinguishing among the Russified minorities—Lithuanians, Estonians, Ukrainians, Belarusians, Jews—all of whom were studying in Russian schools and did not even think of their own identity. There was no tradition to openly talk about ethnic identity during Soviet times. Therefore, it was necessary to use education, particularly minority education and culture, as an instrument of returning minorities to their ethnic identity and reversing the effects of Russification. This was the primary motive why the minority education issue was raised at the time. (Silova 2006, 53)

As I show further in this chapter, some Russian speakers did take up the national minority identification, others lived public lives through the minority category while otherwise exhibiting divergent ethical and political orientations, and others yet lived resentfully and defiantly within the framework of the national state that they did not consider to be theirs. Their resentment was linked to the post-Soviet state's exclusive citizenship policies, which were particularly offensive, because many Russian speakers had supported independence on the basis of a deceitful promise on the part of the Popular Front politicians that all of Soviet Latvia's residents would receive citizenship in the restored national state. As reported by Iveta Silova, years later one of the Popular Front leaders admitted that,

> theoretically, Latvians had the possibility to honestly fight for their independence with arms in their hands. And this would have led to bloodshed. The other option seemed more meaningful—to use legal means to enter the government structures at the time. This option required votes—at that time, all of Latvia's residents voted. And we were consciously saying that our goal was the so-called zero-option [of citizenship]. Yes, these were *conscious lies*, which helped to avoid human casualties. (Panteļejevs in Silova 2006, 57)

Despite the new state's deceitful politics, the Latvian state and the Latvian public consider that those Russian-speaking residents who continue to harbor resentment with regard to the Latvian state fail to behave as "good minorities."[10] From the perspective of the state, behaving like a good minority subject means recognizing the Latvian nature of public and political space and entering the public sphere either as a liberal citizen-subject or as a subordinate member of a cultural minority practicing its difference ethnographically (through food, tradition, etc.). Behaving like a bad minority subject means not recognizing the Latvian nature of public and political space either by remaining defiantly and politically Russian and not learning Latvian or by mobilizing politically in ways that threaten the Latvian nature of the state (for example, by calling for a referendum on whether to recognize Russian as the second state language, which did take place in 2012, see Ijabs 2016). Importantly, citizenship status does not determine whether one behaves as a good or a bad minority subject. In institutions of governance, the language of groups and numbers—for example, the number of Russian speakers or the number of noncitizens—provides a footing on which to construe the minority problem as a tangible policy matter. Rogers Brubaker (2004) has named such a mode of governance "groupism." "Groupism" runs into limits in Latvia, where minority status does not map onto sociologically or legally defined groups, but is most salient in relation to public and political conduct. All of Latvia's residents are expected to subscribe to the vision of *virtuous life as a national life*. From the perspective of the Latvian national state, Latvia's minorities can live this virtuous life if they recognize that being part of a cultural community is a fundamental aspect of human life and, moreover, that they live in someone else's state, that is, in a state that belongs to the Latvian cultural nation. They can reside in this state, but it can never be truly theirs.

This chapter examines how and to what effect the post-Soviet Latvian state struggled to become a national state in an international community of self-described liberal democratic states. In what follows, I first discuss how the minority question was historically constituted at the time of nation-state formation in Eastern Europe following World War I. I then move on to discuss the disjuncture between contemporary minority politics and the self-perception of Latvia's citizens and residents, which defies the majority/minority distinction. I focus in particular on the formation of Soviet people as a distinct identification that does not fit the majority/minority framework. Thereafter, I show how some of the former Soviet subjects did become national minority subjects, yet how this becoming was unstable insofar as people could both publicly inhabit the national minority category while simultaneously feeling marginalized as Russian-speaking former Soviets or even occupiers. Finally, I provide an example of how the Latvian state attempts to discipline the conduct of Russian speakers through enforcement of the Latvian State Language Law, which stipulates Latvian language proficiency levels necessary for various professions.

Importantly, language and minority politics that pertained to Latvia's Russian speakers was one area where most Latvians—nationalists and liberals alike—converged in a belief that they did not need to take lessons in political liberalism, but rather give lessons in history. To be sure, there were arguments about how strict language and minority policies should be and whether the right policy tools were being used to achieve the desired ends, but the ends themselves—a national Latvian state and a Latvian-language public sphere—were not in question. Most Latvians considered that European institutions and publics did not understand Soviet history. For Latvians, it was Soviet socialism rather than European colonialism—or even fascism—that placed the most urgent moral and political demands on their present. It is this history that necessitated the implementation of strict language and citizenship policies in order to ensure the survival of the post-Soviet Latvian nation and the state. And it is this history that European liberals seemed reluctant to learn. And thus between Soviet history and the European present, Latvia was attempting to assemble its own package of policies that satisfied the historically particular form of exclusion at the foundation of the national Latvian state and the European imperative to profess and inhabit the values of inclusion and openness. That is, Latvia was assembling its own paradox of Europeanness.

Statism and Nationalism

After restoring the state in 1991, the celebrated Latvian counterstate nationalism that contributed to the dissolution of the Soviet Union throughout the late 1980s and early 1990s quickly turned into the kind of state-framed—that is, exclusionary—nationalism that Europe considers to be one of its most vicious internal threats (Brubaker 2004, McDonald 2006). The prevailing, though not uncontested (Zake 2007b), frame of intelligibility through which Latvian and other Eastern European nationalisms were read at the time juxtaposed Western European civic nationalism with Eastern European ethnic nationalism (e.g., Kohn 2008 [1944]; see also Aktürk 2012; Brubaker 2004; Zake 2007a, 2007b,). However, the emphasis on imaginations of the nation as decisive for postsocialist Eastern European politics overlooks the role of statism in the formation of political nationalism and thus also of the minority question in Eastern Europe and in Latvia (Brubaker 2004; Zake 2007a, 2007b). As Ieva Zake (2007a, 2007b) has argued, it is the development of statism as belief in a strong and centralized state that provides a crucial missing lens for analyzing postsocialist nationalisms, including their historical conditions of possibility in the late nineteenth and early twentieth centuries. In current-day Latvia, early twentieth-century nation formation and state building were fraught democratic processes, characterized by arguments about whether it was cultural self-determination that should be sought within other political structures, such as the Russian Empire, or whether it was political self-determination that should be sought in the name of socioeconomic self-determination against the domination of Baltic German elites, Latvian bourgeois nationalists, and the Tsarist regime (Ijabs 2009, 2012, 2014; Zake 2007a, 2007b; see also chapter 1). Political scientist Ivars Ijabs (2012) has also illustrated the diverging and dynamic views and arguments that formed the early tradition of nation and state formation in Latvia. When retrospectively evaluating events that led up to the establishment of the People's Council (*Tautas padome*) and proclamation of the Latvian Republic in 1918, contemporary historians, politicians, and intellectuals claim that the Latvian political elites and a large part of the population exhibited a strong and clear will to establish the state, and that the proclamation of the republic in 1918 was its final manifestation (Ijabs 2012). However, Latvian statehood was brought about as much by the crumbling of empires, international interests, and historical contingency as by something that might be called "the will of the people" (Ijabs 2009). Rather than being a logical conclusion to a political process, the foundational moment of the state was the beginning of its domestic and international becoming. The suddenly existing state had to be legitimated, defended, strengthened, and reproduced.

Thus, for example, even prior to the authoritarian regime of Kārlis Ulmanis in the late 1930s, which undertook a massive effort to nationalize the multiethnic polity, the Latvian government thought that concerted efforts were needed to ensure the national nature of the multiethnic state. This is brilliantly shown by historian Aldis Purs (2002) who analyzes the workings of a secret government committee established in the 1920s for the purpose of unifying the national state and securing its nationally ambivalent frontiers. During the 1920s, minorities had considerable state-supported autonomy in the sphere of education and culture—for example, the Latvian state supported minority schools in municipalities with at least thirty minority children (Pabriks 2003, 27). Thus, 28.1 percent of all schools open during the 1930–31 school year were minority schools (Pabriks 2003, 27). Purs (2002) shows, however, that within the bureaucratic corridors of the government, a number of civil servants, with the support of politicians, were planning the Latvianization of the nationally ambivalent Eastern frontier. Capitalizing on war-induced poverty, the bureaucrats of the new national state came up with the idea to secretly channel money to Latvian schools in the area to enable them to provide free lunches, which would attract non-Latvian children to Latvian schools and away from minority schools.

It should be noted again, however, that working out the relationship between "state people" and minorities in a newly constituted state was not a distinctly Latvian problem. It was a problem faced by most Eastern European nation-states formed in the aftermath of World War I. The creation of new states in Eastern Europe following the collapse of empires crafted "state people" and "minorities" out of a multitude of peoples that populated the former imperial territories.[11] Since in many cases the proportion of "minorities" in relation to the "state people" was quite large, the new states came to be known as minority states and were placed in—or pushed into, as some would argue—a supervisory relationship with the League of Nations, which also oversaw mandate relationships between "mature" Western European states and the "less mature" African colonies and Middle Eastern territories of the former Ottoman Empire (Cowan 2007, Weitz 2008).[12] As anthropologist Jane Cowan (2007) has argued, these asymmetrical relationships rendered the new Eastern European states not only "minority states," but also "supervised states," that is, states that had to report on minority politics to an overseeing supranational body. Similarly, minorities could submit complaints about their states to the League of Nations. The category of minority thus marked a problem that was built into the constitution of Eastern European states, something that they would have to tackle continuously as part of statecraft.

Indeed, the initial years of Latvian interwar statehood were characterized by chaotic negotiations about the relationship between the "state people" and minorities in the Latvian Parliament. However, the chaos of the "democratic marketplace" that was the Latvian Parliament gradually gave way to the belief that a strong state and leadership were needed to govern the chaos, as well as that a strong state needed a strong and unified nation (Zake 2007a, 2007b). This eventually led to a coup by Kārlis Ulmanis, then prime minister of the Republic of Latvia, and the establishment of an authoritarian regime under his presidency (1934–40). Ulmanis's regime was supported by nationalist intellectuals who had grown weary of the "impure," that is, businesslike, parliamentary dealings and wished for a stronger idealist orientation of the state (Zake 2007a). Nationalist intellectuals glorified the authoritarian regime, created the cult of Ulmanis as the father of the nation and great leader, and consolidated a strong state-based nationalism as the dominant form of imagined community (Hanovs and Tēraudkalns 2011; Zake 2013, 2007b). Within this imaginary, the state and the nation became one: a strong state required a unified nation consolidated on the basis of Latvian cultural identity and the nation needed a strong state for its survival. In the name of national unity, Ulmanis closed minority schools, thus paving the way for minority support of socialist forces, as well as carving out historical grooves for the strictly national orientation of the post-Soviet state.[13]

It is this understanding of the relationship between the nation and the state that informed both anti-Soviet nationalism and post-Soviet state building. During the Soviet period, nationalist intellectuals, many of them in exile, continued to fuel nationalist dissent. In the late 1980s, people looked to the old and the new generation of national intellectuals to give shape to the nation struggling for independence. These intellectuals drew on pre–World War II ideas of nationhood solidified during Ulmanis's authoritarian rule and thus reinstated the hegemony of state-based nationalism in the popular imaginary. However, contrary to the widely held views that the Soviet state worked against this imaginary, the Soviet nationalities policies also reinforced the relationship between culturally defined nations and territories—for example, Latvians were the "titular nation" of the Soviet Socialist Republic of Latvia. Moreover, as I show in the next section, national communists tried to secure the public relevance of the Latvian language in Soviet Latvia. Thus the nation was solidified as the primary collective identification for the purposes of living Soviet socialism and for resisting it. The nation was also needed for post-Soviet state building, because in the liberal post–Cold War era establishment of new states still required nations. Most Latvians were thus concerned that diminishing numbers of ethnically Latvian citizens could seriously endanger the existence of the state. The following episode, where a managing director of a Latvian news portal criticizes tolerance promotion efforts because they do not address the fundamental issues of concern to the Latvian state and the nation, exemplifies this well.

In late 2006, I interviewed Kārlis, the managing director of a popular Latvian language online news portal. We met to discuss the "Internet without Hatred" project launched by a nongovernmental organization called Dialogi. The project aimed to fight hate speech on the Internet. Kārlis was invited to participate in the project along with directors, managers, and editors of other portals. All project participants were invited to publicly express commitment to Internet without hatred and to increase monitoring of user commentaries for statements that constituted hate speech. During our conversation, we discussed the challenges of determining which statements amounted to hate speech and should therefore be subject to censorship and which, while perhaps unacceptable to some groups or individuals, did not merit intervention.[14] Kārlis also offered his thoughts about what he called "tolerance projects" more generally (see Introduction, chapters 3). Namely, he expressed concern that "tolerance projects" did not address questions that were of concern to the Latvian cultural nation, but rather engaged superficial issues, such as politically correct speech and conduct. He attributed this to the fact that "tolerance projects" simply demanded that Latvians align their conduct with the rest of Europe and did not pay attention to the historically specific conditions that shaped the post-Soviet present in Latvia. He emphasized that the situation in Latvia is different than elsewhere in Europe: "In Europe, nobody has lived for fifty years with strangers in forced togetherness and nobody has undergone such demographic changes in this way." He thus invoked what many consider to be one of the most injurious aspects of Soviet rule, namely the radical remaking of the Latvian state's population through the deportations of local residents and the in-migration of a large labor force from other parts of the former Soviet Union, mostly the Soviet Socialist Republics of Russia, Ukraine, and Belorussia. Given the effects of Soviet policies and practices—namely, the fact that 29.6 percent of Latvia's residents are now Russians or Russian speakers—Kārlis argued that Latvians simply couldn't afford to open their doors to everyone if they want to ensure the existence of the Latvian state and the nation.[15] The nation and the state were intricately linked in Kārlis's statement—the existence of the state was under threat if there was no Latvian nation and the Latvian nation was under threat if the state did not ensure its existence.

Most people who are not ardent supporters of right-wing nationalist politics would mark Kārlis's concerns as reactionary and nationalistic. Yet, such concerns were not solely a product of Kārlis's or Latvians' inherent nationalist sensibilities, though they were undoubtedly shaped by local histories. Importantly, his concerns were also grounded in state-based thinking associated with modern political forms that included, but were not limited to nationalist regimes. For example, his concerns pertained to the threat that migration might pose to the vital forces of the "state people" (Arendt 1979). However, the threat of migration in relation to a base population is not a concern unique to cultural nationalists. Such a concern is widespread in European nation-states regardless of the conception of the nation prevalent in each. As discussed earlier, liberal political virtues themselves can be appropriated as constitutive of the nation and therefore become basis for exclusion. Kārlis argued that certain exclusionary practices were merited, because the threshold of openness had been reached. In his view, compensatory measures were necessary to ensure the coherence of the Latvian nation and the viability of the Latvian state. Similarly, on other occasions during my fieldwork people attempted to calculate the appropriate threshold for when the "state people" would become threatened in their national territory. For example, a Latvian language expert suggested that the threshold is crossed when the percentage of the titular population in its national territory falls below 75 percent (Veisbergs 2008). In order for such statements to make sense, the public must not only value cultural belonging, but also be versed in modern statecraft and techniques of power. Thus, Kārlis did not simply police the borders of the nation out of ideological conviction or passionate attachment to the past, but also invited an argument in the register in which modern statecraft operates.

Kārlis's statement also illustrated that the state restored after the collapse of the Soviet Union in 1991 reentered the international arena as a national state with a minority problem. Similar to the interwar years, tensions between the state, the nation, and a plurality of residents were part of statecraft, yet who was to be a minority and how they were expected to act had changed. If the interwar state negotiated relations between Latvians, Baltic Germans, Jews, and Russian Old Believer and Orthodox minorities, the renewed state's minority politics pertained to Russians and Russian speakers that, as David Laitin (1998) remarks, were "beached" once the borders of their country—the former Soviet Union—receded. Thus, in addition to being a feature of modern statecraft, the "minority problem" of post-Soviet Latvia was also a legacy of Soviet rule insofar as one of the defining features of Soviet rule in Latvia was a substantial alteration of the makeup of the population as a result of large-scale population transfers, which entailed the deportation of Latvians and other ethnically marked individuals and an in-migration of significant numbers of predominantly Russian-speaking Soviet citizens of various ethnic backgrounds. However, the Soviet legacy was not only numerical. The minority framework was new to many of post-Soviet Latvia's residents. To take it up meant remaking one's ethical and political orientations and one's sense of self. This suggests—and I pursue this argument in the sections that follow—that the Soviet project of making a multiethnic Soviet people had tangible, if unexpected, effects, especially in national republics such as Latvia.

The Soviet Nationalities Policy, Soviet People, and the Post-Soviet Minority Category

Within liberal democratic contexts, the minority category enables claims-making vis-à-vis the state as the arbiter of majority/minority relations. The assumption is that minorities are at risk of being discriminated by majorities and therefore require protection. In the European Union, minority rights can be claimed as collective cultural rights vis-à-vis the Framework Convention for the Protection of National Minorities (to which I return further in the chapter) and vis-à-vis antidiscrimination legislation that protects individuals of minority background from differential treatment, or group-based antidiscrimination legislation, such as hate speech laws, which strive to prevent demonization of ethnically, racially, or religiously marked groups in public space. While the minority category is therefore a useful political tool, it does not necessarily overlap with the sense of self of those who take it up for political or other reasons. Moreover, even majorities sometimes do not recognize themselves as majorities, or at least, as the kind of majorities that threaten minorities. This was certainly the case in post-Soviet Latvia.

In the early post-Soviet years, the mainstream Latvian public (and some even to this day) did not think that Russian speakers—or simply Russians, as most Latvians referred to all those who used Russian as their primary language—constituted a minority (see chapter 5 for a discussion of naming). Instead, many suggested that it was Latvians who were the minority in need of protection, because of the way Russians conducted themselves in public space. To illustrate the "nonminority conduct" of Russians, many Latvians, especially those of the older generation who had lived through most of the Soviet period, pointed out that most Russians did not know or speak Latvian, that Russians continued to feel entitled to conduct public and political life in Russian, as they had during the Soviet period, and that Russians openly disrespected the Latvian language and its speakers. It was very common to hear indignant accusations in mid-to-late 1980s that "Soviet Russians have lived here for more than forty years and don't speak a word of Latvian." Moreover, Latvians were convinced that Russians not only did not speak Latvian, but also disrespected it. For example, while looking for something entirely different in a 1956 archive of the Central Committee of the Latvian Communist Party, I found a letter from a resident of Jūrmala to the editorial office of the Latvian language newspaper *Cīņa* (the Struggle), which contained a complaint that people in management and public service positions do not speak Latvian. The resident reports phoning the Dubulti wood-processing facility and inquiring in Latvian about obtaining wood for the winter and receiving the following response in Russian:

"Chto vy po-sobac'hi, govorite po-russki!" ("Why do you speak the dogs' language, speak Russian").[16]

Whether accurate or not, such stories were told and retold during the late Soviet and early post-Soviet years to argue for the need for compensatory politics.[17] In addition to blaming Russians for lack of civility, Latvians also criticized themselves for too readily switching to Russian if it was easier for their conversation partner to converse in Russian. This was attributed to the Latvians' "serf mentality," that is, adaptability for the purposes of survival amidst changing political regimes.[18] As a result, Latvians on occasion also became targets of the state's efforts to promote the use of Latvian in public space. For example, in 2008, the State Language Center launched a campaign titled *Runāsim latviski!* (Let's speak Latvian), which targeted mostly Latvians who switch to Russian in everyday encounters. One of the television advertisements produced by the State Language Center shows a woman in a button shop speaking in broken Russian with the seller who is having equal trouble with Russian. Both women struggle for a while until they realize that they could also use Latvian, which is their first language.[19]

Thus, along with the "700 years of German rule" narrative discussed in the previous chapter, the story of Russian disrespect toward Latvians and the Latvian language profoundly shaped the post-Soviet national imaginary. From this perspective, asking Latvians to take on responsibility for ensuring the protection of the "Russian-speaking minority" was thought to misrecognize the historically shaped power relations between the two categories of difference and their traces in the present. Simply put, many Latvians thought of Latvia's Russians as the foot soldiers and heirs of Russian chauvinism masquerading as Soviet socialism.

Many Russians and Russian speakers also did not recognize themselves in the minority category. Some thought that the Latvian state's minority politics wanted to make them into ethnographic subjects—gather them all "under the samovar," as one of my interlocutors put it. Whereas during the Soviet period titular nations were indeed gathered under their respective samovars, that is, encouraged, even required, to live national difference ethnographically, Russians never did that (see also Slezkine 1994). Instead, post-1930s Soviet nationalities policy emphasized the pan-humanist aspects of Russianness, which included both Pushkin and Soviet socialism. Thus when post-Soviet Latvia's minority politics seemed to want to transform a civilization into a tribe, many Russians were puzzled, even offended. Others thought that Latvia should indeed be a binational state and that becoming a minority amounted to giving in to the idea of the national state. Others yet thought that the minority category was part and parcel of identity politics, which they rejected. For example, Alexandre Beliaev (2014) describes the dilemmas faced by youth activists associated with political parties commonly perceived as "Russian parties." These youths wished to build coalitions rather than make identity claims. Yet, in order to be able to practice politics as a vocation, they relied on an electorate that voted for Russian parties and thus had to engage in identity politics.

All in all, the liberal minority framework did not sit well with Latvians and Russian speakers alike. Both had to learn to inhabit their respective slots when Latvia was restored as a national state with a minority problem. Latvians, however, were more prepared than the Russian speakers. Despite feeling insecure about their majority position, being the interwar "state people" and a Soviet "titular nation" had prepared Latvians for linking ethnicity with political nationhood. For post-Soviet Russian speakers, however, learning to inhabit the minority slot meant one or more of the following: (1) learning to inhabit Russianness as parochial ethnicity rather than Sovietness or civilization; (2) learning to inhabit non-Russian ethnicity—such as Ukrainian or Belorussian—publicly rather than treating it as a formal ascription in the passport that does not bear on public conduct, as was common during the Soviet period (Malakhov and Osipov 2006); (3) or refusing the minority framework altogether. To put it another way, there was no sociological reality of minority/majority relations. Coming to inhabit these categories was and continues to be part of becoming European, which entails reorienting ethical and political dispositions and disciplining conduct.

The predicament faced by Russian speakers in Latvia suggests that the late Soviet project of creating a multiethnic yet Russian-speaking Soviet people had partly succeeded (see also Aktürk 2012). From about 1950s onward, identification with Soviet people was supposed to replace national identification as the diverse peoples of the Soviet Union forged a path toward a socialist future. This was known as the path of *rastsvet-sblizhenie-sliianie* (flourishing-drawing together—merging), whereby socioeconomic and political development of nationalities would eventually lead to their disappearance altogether (Aktürk 2012). As historians Yuri Slezkine (1994) and Francine Hirsch (2005) have shown, the 1920s and 1930s were characterized by an excessive focus on non-Russian nation-building throughout the Soviet Union in order to diffuse the animosity many "nationals" felt toward pre-Soviet Russian imperialism, as well as to deepen the reach of socialism, for which native forms were thought to be most effective. As a result, multiple ethno-territorial units were created almost overnight. As Slezkine argues, "Soviet federalism combined ethnicity with territory and—at least for the first twenty years—guaranteed the cultural rights of various diasporas" (1994, 417). Each ethnic unit needed an institutional infrastructure to become a nation, such as their own schools, libraries, and party cells. In many cases, this meant that the Soviet state codified previously only spoken languages (Hirsch 2005). Moreover, nationalities within ethno-territorial units—for example, Estonians in Siberia—were provided with books and newspapers in order to make sure that socialism was available in the native language (Slezkine 1994, 421). For the same reason, there were multiple minority schools in Abkhaz-speaking Abkhazia, itself part of Georgia in the 1920s (Slezkine 1994, 430).

When Latvia was incorporated into the Soviet Union in 1940 (and then again in 1945), the nation-building fervor had subsided. Around 1934, Stalin had announced that backwardness was conquered and that the socialist future had arrived (Slezkine 1994). The Soviet government proceeded to decrease the number of national units in order to cut back on resources, but did not question the prevalent conception of national republics as circumscribed spaces where ethnic, territorial, and linguistic markers bind people together into autonomous units (Hirsch 2005). In fact, those ethnic groups with republics and bureaucracies were told to redouble their efforts, while their conationals outside the bounds of the republic were left to their own devices (Slezkine 1994, 445–446; see also Malakhov and Osipov 2006, 509). For Latvia, the relaxation of indigenization of socialism meant that while Soviet socialism did come in a national form insofar as Latvians had their own administrative and political unit, the content was increasingly Soviet or Russian. As reported by Michael Loader, in Khrushchev-era party politics in Latvia, most party activities in secretariats and in workplaces took place in Russian despite the large constituency that spoke Latvian; technical literature was published in Russian; and Russians, Ukrainians, and Belorussians who came to work and reside in Latvia after World War II were reluctant to learn Latvian (2015, 120).

This created resistance and divisions within the Latvian Communist Party. In the 1950s, a fraction of "national communists," led by Eduards Berklavs, were concerned that postwar party politics diverged from Lenin's policy to indigenize socialism. The national communists worried that "if Latvian were relegated to the status of [a] rural and cultural language, not only would it adversely affect Latvian identity, but it would also make Latvians second-class citizens in their own republic," thus attesting to the significance of the ethno-territorial formula throughout the Soviet period (Loader 2015, 121). The national communists in Latvia tried to prevent Russification by limiting migration to Latvia, especially to Riga, by passing resolutions that reinforced the demand that local party cadres should know both Latvian and Russian languages in order to deliver socialism in Latvian (Loader 2015). Both measures resulted in open discontent among Russian-speaking cadres, as some of them considered their time in Latvia temporary, while others considered that the era of cultivating national difference was over and that the party language was now Russian (Loader 2015, 131). What would have been viewed as anti-imperial indigenization in the 1920s and early 1930s was seen as anti-Soviet bourgeois nationalism in the 1950s (Loader 2015, 180).

As a result of divisions within the Latvian Communist Party, the national communists were crushed and residency and language policies reversed, favoring Russians and Russian-Latvians (individuals who were formally ethnically Latvian, but were born in Russia and often did not speak Latvian) in leadership positions. The 1962 Party Program reasserted the voluntary principle of language learning, thus reinforcing the role of Russian as the common medium of communication and preventing any further attempts to implement policies that would require local cadres to be bilingual (Loader 2015, 325). As reflected in a 1972 protest letter of "seventeen Latvian communists," which was smuggled out of Latvia and sent to Western communist parties critical of Soviet policies, this intensified the Russification of Latvians and non-Russian nationalities residing in Latvia.[20] The letter pointed out that at the time of writing only 18 percent of Latvia's communists were Latvians, and that only 17 percent of party secretaries were Latvians (Berklavs 1998, 200). Moreover, according to Loader, the 1970s census indicates that "26 years after the re-establishment of Soviet power, just 18 percent of all Russians in Latvia spoke Latvian, as opposed to the 47.2 percent of Latvians who spoke Russian" (2015, 128). The letter contained a detailed account of formal and informal practices of Russification, such as exclusion of local names from public spaces, publishing literature mainly in Russian, disproportionate Russian language teaching in schools, and many more. The "seventeen Latvian communists" expressed concern that Latvia could be dissolved as a territorial unit, as had happened to Karelia, which had been incorporated into the Russian Federation due to the low percentage of the native population (the letter also mentioned Kazakhstan, where the native population was at 30 percent; see Loader 2015, 298; Berklavs 1998). The letter claimed that Latvians now made up only 57 percent of the total population, and that this was a result of massive and unnecessary industrialization and militarization, accompanied by migration (Berklavs 1998, 201). Contrary to Lenin's policies, the seventeen Latvian communists argued, the party openly practiced Russian chauvinism rather than indigenization (Berklavs 1998, 198).

To be sure, ethnic identification remained important to the Soviet state in the form of inscription of ethnicity in the passport, as well as standardized public performances of national difference (Adams 2010, Aktürk 2011, Hirsch 2005, Slezkine 1994,). In the late Soviet period, however, ethnicity became a rather formal inscription in the passport, which could be easily forgotten in lieu of a more Sovietlike mode of being. This was especially so for the multiethnic Soviet people residing in national republics, who did not have a sense of themselves as national minorities. The seventeen Latvian communists pointed this out as yet another instance of Russification: "Russians have everything in all republics, titular nationalities in their republics have something, but the others have nothing" (Berklavs 1998, 204).[21] However, the Russian speakers, "Russified minorities" among them, did not necessarily feel that way during the last decades of the Soviet Union. Despite the widespread assumption that a Soviet people was more of an ideological ruse than reality and that the Soviet state created nations rather than destroyed them, the Soviet state did create conditions for the emergence of a Soviet people, especially in national republics such as Latvia. The Soviet people were held together by a specifically Soviet sociality, that is, by social bonds, which emphasized multiethnic solidarity on the basis of the Russian language and common experience of socialism. Some of the people who identified as Soviet were surprised—or at least claimed to be so—when they encountered nationalism. One former self-identified Soviet person who had grown up in Soviet Latvia speaking Russian, but had learned Latvian and become a civil servant responsible for national minority politics of the Latvian state, narrated her experience of Sovietness and ethnicity as follows:

> What I knew for certain was that I belonged more to the Russian speakers rather than Latvians. Latvians were the only ethnic group that existed; the rest of us were non-Latvians and together we were all Soviet people (*padomju tauta*). My mother was upset that I am not, that I do not have inside me this sense of belonging to Ukrainians. She was a very ardent Ukrainian, and she was distraught that I was not a carrier of language, nothing. She gave me a lot of knowledge about Ukrainian culture; I know a lot. More than I know about Belorussians and so forth. My father was a Soviet person; he did not care where he came from; the main thing for him was to know his place in society. He was a construction worker, worked in the administration, was an organizer. But there were people for whom ethnic identity was so important that they were willing to break the law. It was the Jews with whom I was friends, because my first husband was a Jewish musician and he introduced me to a circle of musicians. That is when I first found out about Judaism, about the Jewish tradition, about Zionism (philosophically speaking). It was in 1973. It was a shock for me; I had never thought that a people would preserve their ethnic foundation so strongly while at the same time being afraid from those around them. . . . I understood that there were people who had not lost their identity. Small nationalities or discriminated nationalities preserved this identity—when there is pressure, there is resistance. I had a Tatar acquaintance, producer of documentary films. He was an *inteligentnyi* (educated, cultured) man

without any Tatarisms [*sic*], but he was deeply upset about the deportation of Tatars from Crimea. It was important for him. Armenians—it was very, very, very deep in them . . . they were grateful to the Russians for saving them from the Turks, but they longed for Ararat. It was strange for me that each group had its own painful issue. My concern, as a Soviet person, was the number of victims during the war [World War II], also the 1930s. I cared about that, but I did not separate out issues that were of concern to specific ethnic groups. . . . It was through relations with these people that I understood that ethnic identity is not a light issue.

The civil servant narrated her awakening to the importance of ethnicity as a long-term process, which reached culmination during Latvian independence struggles. Of course, one cannot be certain when the distinction between "Soviet persons" and people for whom ethnicity was important emerged for her in this form. In Latvian public and political life, the collective subject of Soviet people became most visible precisely after the collapse of the Soviet Union when a good number of people did not recognize themselves in the nationalized public life. It is the presence of this collective Soviet subject with its associated political and ethical orientations that created a challenge for the Latvian government's attempts to organize and order the population with the help of categories friendly to the national state, such as "national minorities."

Minorities and Migrants

In the late 1980s and throughout the 1990s, Russian-speaking residents became the target of the Latvian state's "reawakening efforts" aimed to recruit national minority subjects out of Soviet people. This was a frustrating process for the Latvian state and the Latvian public, because of the perceived success of Russification. As explained by Nils Muižnieks, the former Latvian special tasks minister for the integration of society and the current Council of Europe's human rights commissioner:

What shocked most people [ethnic Latvians] over the course of the first few years [after independence] was that ethnicity was not so important for many people and that language [Russian] was the key thing. People were a little surprised about a lack of demand for minority education and languages other than Russian, except with the countrywide exception of the Poles. They were hoping for what Latvians would consider to be Ukrainian or Belorussian "awakening," but the

Ukrainians and Belorussians did not oblige. They were too asleep. (Muižnieks in Silova 2006, 54)

While the Latvian state faced a historically specific challenge with regard to Soviet people, it was not the only European state to sort its residents into national minorities and unruly subjects who threaten to unsettle the nation and the polity. In postcolonial Europe, distinctions are continuously made between domestic difference—that is, national minorities, such as Danes in Germany—and foreign difference, that is immigrants, such as Turks in Germany.[22] The category of "immigrant" is widely used to designate people who may have been born in Europe, but who are not considered to be historically of Europe, thereby carrying the label "immigrant" through generations.

The distinction between these categories of difference and the differentiated rights attached to them can be traced in the Framework Convention for the Protection of National Minorities launched by the Council of Europe in the early 1990s, largely to deal with "the minority problem" in postcommunist states (Kymlicka 2007). By signing and ratifying the Framework Convention, European states were expected to promote "full and effective equality of persons belonging to minorities in all areas of economic, social, political, public and cultural life together with conditions that will allow them to express, preserve and develop their culture, language and traditions."[23] Contrary to the Article 27 of the UN's International Covenant on Civil and Political Rights, which pertains to "ethnic, religious, and linguistic minorities," the Framework Convention stipulates the rights of "national minorities," typically defined as "historically settled minorities living on or near what they view as their national homeland" (Kymlicka 2007, 593). The Framework Convention does not include a clear definition of "national minorities," instead leaving it up to the signatories to do so in good conscience. As a result, most European states have adopted restrictive definitions of national minorities who can claim rights within the framework of the convention, thus effectively distinguishing between historical minorities and newcomers (Council of Europe 2013). As Will Kymlicka has noted, "Most European countries have explicitly stated that immigrant groups are not national minorities and some have also excluded Roma from the category on the grounds that they are a non-territorial minority" (2007, 593). Such restrictive definitions are being increasingly contested, but the original intention to distinguish between minorities and migrants is reflected in the way that signatory states have defined national minorities.

When Latvia ratified the convention in 2005, ten years after signing it in 1995, it did so by stipulating that national minorities are citizens of Latvia who belong to a culturally distinct community that has historically—that is, at least in three generations—resided in Latvia and wishes to cultivate its culture and language. This effectively established World War II as the cutoff point, for most of those former Soviet citizens who came to reside in Latvia after the World War II were not citizens and could trace their residence in Latvia to, at most, two generations. However, the definition attached to the convention also includes a supplement, which states that "persons who are not citizens of Latvia or any other country [thus specifically referring to Latvia's noncitizens], but who permanently and legally reside in Latvia and do not belong to national minorities in the sense of the Convention, can avail themselves to the rights stipulated in the Convention if they identify with a national minority and if the law does not stipulate exceptions."[24] This meant that noncitizen Russian speakers could benefit from state support for the cultural life of national minorities with which they identified. They were rewarded for good minority conduct. At the same time, they were exempted from the rights stipulated in articles 10 and 11, namely from the right to use their language in public and private communication, as well as from the right to write their names in their own language. Latvia resolved this disjuncture between the convention and national politics by adding a supplementary clause that these particular articles will be implemented in a way that does not counter the Constitution of the Republic of Latvia and the Latvian Language Law (Council of Europe 2013).

It took Latvia ten years to ratify the treaty precisely because politicians and stakeholders could not agree on how to define national minorities. The problem with the legal definition of minorities was largely due to the fact that Latvia's Russian-speaking residents presented a challenge in terms of distinguishing between domestic difference, that is, national minorities, and foreign difference, that is immigrants. Given the various waves of migration, the Russian-speaking population consisted of people variously positioned in relation to the national state and thus national minority status could not be mapped onto ethnic criteria. While Russians as an ethnic group were a historical minority in Latvia, namely, they had resided in Latvia for generations, there were also Russians that did not count as a national minority, because they came during the Soviet period and did not have a relationship with the original body of citizenry. Not only that, in the eyes of the Latvian state, they could not be trusted to conduct themselves as proper national minority subjects. At the same time, there was huge political risk associated with denying cultural rights to the large number of Soviet-era Russian speakers who themselves were rapidly learning to lay claims against the state in the language of national minorities. Moreover, there were those who did consider a national way of life important, and alienating them by denying them minority rights would have worked against the purposes of the national state. All in all, the Latvian state adopted a definition that carefully wove conduct into the legal framework. The definition essentially said that all those who resided in Latvia at the time it gained independence from the Soviet Union, identified with the national state, and conducted themselves accordingly could benefit from the rights granted to national minorities.

Similar to other European states, the category of "migrant" marked difference that could not be incorporated into the nation, neither in majority nor national minority status. Here too, however, it was conduct that mattered and not necessarily one's ethnicity or even migratory routes. To put it another way, the category of the migrant emerged in popular and political discourse as an ethical juxtaposition to that of a proper national subject, whether majority or minority. If a *proper national subject* exhibited appreciation of belonging to a cultural community, cared for its history, and strove for its political and/or cultural self-determination, *a migrant* was thought to not care about cultural belonging, the past, or national self-determination. In the Latvian popular imaginary, migrant conduct was epitomized by the civil servant quoted at length above when she described her father as "someone who did not care where he came from, as long as he knew his place in socialist society." While in her view this was positive insofar as her father did not sort people by their background, in the view of many Latvians, the fact that her father did not care about where he came from rendered him incapable of establishing a respectful relationship with the place in which he had arrived, namely Latvia.

Dominant understandings of the category of migrant as an ethical category also shaped a poster exhibit prepared by the Ministry of Foreign Affairs in 2005 with the aim to explain Latvia's historical dilemmas to the European Parliament (MFA 2005). In many conversations I had during my fieldwork, politicians and laypeople alike emphasized that the international community simply did not understand the historically specific contours of the minority question in Latvia and thus kept making unreasonable demands on the Latvian state to include all former Soviet subjects in the body of citizenry without asking them to abide by criteria such as speaking the Latvian language and knowing Latvian history. The exhibit was one of the ways in which the Latvian government attempted to explain the effects of the Soviet nationalities policy, which, they argued, necessitated a particular course for minority politics in Latvia.

Through chronologically arranged images, the poster exhibit tells the story of the flourishing of national minorities in cultural and political life during the first independent Latvian state from 1918 until 1940. The poster of the interwar years focuses on accomplished Jewish, Baltic German, and Russian politicians and civil servants. The impression it aims to give is one of the active participation of minorities—and their recognition—in the public and political life of the Latvian state.

FIGURE 1. Minority policy of the Republic of Latvia in the period between the world wars. From the exhibit *National Minorities in Latvia: Then and Now*. Ministry of Foreign Affairs, 2005.

Selectively skipping over the authoritarian rule of Kārlis Ulmanis (1934–40), characterized by the closure of minority schools and intensive nationalization of the state, the exhibit turns to the Soviet period.

It is here that the category of migrants appears to illustrate the ethically and civilizationally inferior conduct of those who came to reside in Latvia during the Soviet period. Their conduct was thought to be ethically inferior insofar as they moved en masse in search of a better life, thus exhibiting lack of loyalty with

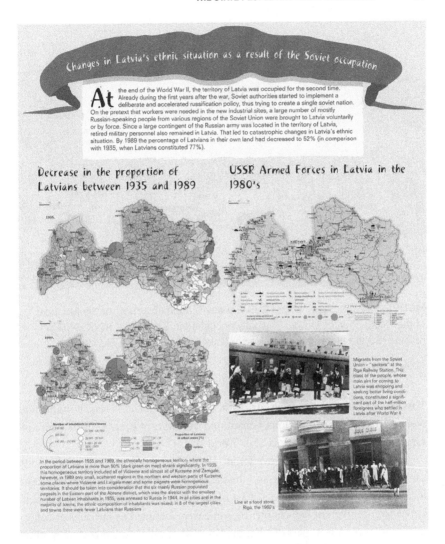

FIGURE 2. Changes in Latvia's ethnic situation as a result of the Soviet occupation. From the exhibit *National Minorities in Latvia: Then and Now.* Ministry of Foreign Affairs, 2005.

regard to the places they came from.[25] And their conduct was thought to be civilizationally inferior insofar as they unabashedly stormed Latvia's shops (see figure 4). Unlike the distinguished minority intellectuals and politicians of the interwar years, Soviet period images depict women standing by a recently arrived train in the Riga train station (see figure 3). Their cloth bags, which lent them the name *meshochniki* (sackers in Russian), are on the ground next to them. The narrative explains: "Migrants from the Soviet Union—"sackers" at the Riga Railway Station.

FIGURE 3. "Sackers" at the Riga Railway Station. Courtesy of the Museum of the Occupation of Latvia. Originally published in Egils Jarls, *Rīga 1955–56: rusiāde* (Copenhagen: Latviešu Nacionālais fonds Skandināvijā, 1957).

This category of people, whose main aim for coming to Latvia was shopping and seeking better living conditions, constituted a significant part of the half-million foreigners who settled in Latvia after World War II."

While people arrived from different places during the Soviet period, many came from Ukraine, Belorussia, and Russia. Some were sent by Moscow to become local party cadres, some came as part of Soviet military units and remained in Latvia after retirement (see chapter 6), some were recruited by factories or collective farms and came as part of what the Soviet state called "organized migration," and some others arrived on their own and presented the problem of "chaotic migration" to the Soviet state and also to Latvia's national communists, especially in Riga (Loader 2015, Riekstiņš 2004). Yet, it was important for the purposes of the exhibit to highlight the difference between national subjects (minority and majority alike) and migrants, that is, between nationally and economically oriented modes of life. While the former affirmed the constitutive relationship between individuals, place, and culture at the foundation of the Latvian national state, the latter was thought to be inferior and threatening, because it did not recognize the significance of this relationship.

The exhibit organizers expected the distinction between national minorities and migrants to resonate in Europe, even if both categories were somewhat

FIGURE 4. "Line at the food store, Rīga, the 1960s." Courtesy of the Museum of the Occupation of Latvia. Originally published in Egils Jarls, *Rīga 1955-56: rusiāde* (Copenhagen: Latviešu Nacionālais fonds Skandināvijā, 1957).

differently deployed in Latvia. The distinction between minorities and migrants was supposed to invoke the distinction between domestic and foreign difference widely familiar in Europe. This distinction, as I have been arguing all along, rested on conduct more than on legal status. To illustrate this further, I now turn to the case of Vladimir—a member of a minority cultural association who accompanied the aforementioned exhibit to Brussels.

Exemplary National Minority Subject

Vladimir was one of many minority subjects I encountered in my work with the Secretariat for the Special Tasks Minister for the Integration of Society, a state institution implementing the National Program for the Promotion of Tolerance, but also the National Program for Support of National Minorities. I have chosen to focus on Vladimir's case because he was an exceptionally successful national minority subject. Vladimir was a Belorussian artist who claimed that it was precisely Latvians' strong national consciousness (*nacionālā apziņa*) that inspired him to begin to cultivate his national consciousness back in the 1950s. Until then, he had been a Russian-speaking Soviet citizen with the only ethnic marker being the inscription of ethnicity in his passport. I met with Vladimir in a dark basement studio filled with his paintings and clippings of newspaper articles about his art, all of which emphasized his extraordinary sympathy with and respect for Latvian culture and his pride in being Belorussian. While Vladimir was a citizen of Latvia and spoke some Latvian, he apologetically told me that he felt much more comfortable speaking Russian, and we continued in Russian. Vladimir told me that he had arrived in Riga as a young man in the 1950s speaking only Russian. After becoming friends with Latvians at the university, all of whom actively practiced their nationality by speaking Latvian, he began to think about why he, ethnically marked as a Belorussian, spoke only Russian. Soon thereafter Vladimir started reading about Belorussian history and learning the Belorussian language. He started to organize Belorussian artists and intellectuals who frequented his place together with Latvian artists and intellectuals. All found solidarity not only in artistic endeavors, but also in their orientation toward a virtuous life understood as a life of cultural belonging.

Plugged into these circles of intellectuals, Vladimir was on the frontlines when the Latvian independence movement began in the late 1980s. As part of the movement, known as "the third awakening," minorities were invited to "awaken" along with Latvians from the slumber of deethnicization and/or Russification imposed by the Soviet state.[26] In 1988, Latvia's Popular Front organized the first People's Forum where minority representatives were invited to come and express their grievances toward the Soviet state and to collectively think about the ways in which they would like to cultivate their collective identities within the framework of a national Latvian state. Vladimir was an exemplary national minority subject from the perspective of the state not only because he recognized himself as Belorussian in lieu of belonging to the generic category of Russian speakers, but also because it was Latvians who had inspired his "awakening." While he was not part of the Latvian cultural nation, the fact that he exhibited national consciousness by practicing his Belorussian-ness meant that he was cut of the same cloth, as it were. The state recognized this by sponsoring Vladimir's trip to Brussels to accompany the exhibit on the flourishing life of national minorities in Latvia.

After his "awakening," Vladimir continued to be a proponent of the Latvian state's national minority politics. During our interview, he spoke poorly of those he saw as lacking proper national consciousness. He marked them by the derogatory term *sovki* (a word playing on a combination of 'Soviet' and the Russian word for "dustpan"). In Vladimir's view, *sovki* were guided by economic considerations, similar to the "sackers" depicted in the exhibit; that is, material well-being was more important to them than cultural belonging. In contrast, Vladimir spoke of himself as having national consciousness and therefore as living in accordance with ethically more palatable understandings of the good life.

If Vladimir's case points to the importance of ethical-political conduct in filling the national minority slot, the Russian Tatar women to whom I turn next illustrate the ambiguities of the project of recruiting national minority subjects out of the former Soviet people.

"We Are Not Russians, We Are Svoi," or Soviet Ways of Being Ethnic

The Tatar Cultural Association of Latvia was established in 1988. The organization claimed to be the heir of a similar interwar association, though much of its membership had arrived in Latvia during the Soviet period, including the founder of the organization, who was a former Soviet military officer. The organization was both cultural and religious, as most of its members attended religious services at the nearby makeshift mosque. This meant that women and men often congregated separately. For reasons of access outside formal interview settings, I spent more time with the women. Some of the women had come to Latvia as wives of Soviet military officers, while others had come as workers on construction sites or factories. They had not known each other during the Soviet period, though most of them had lived in Riga for quite a while. They had all ended up together because some of the women had responded to an ad placed in the paper by the founder of the association in the late 1980s, while others had found the association by meeting someone of Tatar origin in a dentist's office, for example. On the premises of the association, as well as in the mosque, they were learning and relearning how to be culturally Tatar and religiously Muslim. They learned Tatar folk songs with the help of a karaoke machine sent from Kazan. And they learned how to pray properly, because, as one of the regular mosque attendees, who was a recent convert and thus saw herself as a proper Muslim, put it, "They are ethnic Muslims, they don't know how to pray." But most of all, they seemed to enjoy the sociality that their togetherness afforded, the sociality of being both ethnic and Soviet.

On my first visit, Taina, who was the informal leader of the group, told me her version of Tatar history in relation to the Russian Empire. She wanted to counter perceptions of Tatars as related to Mongolians. Backed by other women in the room, she emphasized that "we are Bulgars"—a seminomadic people of Turkic descent who lived to the north of the Caucasus and in the Volga River region and are said to have given rise to the Bulgarian Empire. "It was Ivan Grozny," Taina claimed, "who named these people Tatars." The women insisted, however, that "Tatar" is a denigrating term. Instead, they explained, "we call each other

svoi chelovek." The women had rediscovered their shared belonging to a historically constituted cultural and religious community in post-Soviet Latvia, but it
also meant grappling with the negative Soviet-era stereotypes attached to the
word that marked their shared heritage. With the help of the term *svoi*, which
in the straightforward sense means "one of ours," the women were able to think
of themselves as a collectivity without having to use the denigrating term *Tatar*.

It was not so surprising, then, that Taina's story emphasized belonging to an
ancient, cultured, and racially distinct civilization that was superior to Russians.
For example, the women explained how Russians would call Tatars black or yel-
low, but, they argued, "we are like Bulgars—light, blue-eyed." "The Bulgar state
[Bulgarian Empire, seventh to eleventh centuries CE]," Taina continued, "was
very developed and civilized." When other women joined in, they claimed that
their everyday practices were also superior to those of Russians. "Tatars usually
do not drink, while Russians drink a lot, though it is becoming more difficult to
distinguish one from the other since now everybody drinks in the countryside,"
said one woman. Another one added: "But one can still differentiate on the basis
of cleanliness. If Tatar women are clean, decorate their homes with flowers, take
their shoes off in the house and wash the floor with brushes, Russian women do
not take care of themselves, wear boots in the house, and their farm animals are
all over the place inside the house." The third one chimed in: "We are great cooks,
whereas the Russians only made cabbage. Sour cabbage and dirty floors, that's
how we remember them." Seamlessly moving between a distant and mythologized past and a more recent, but therefore no less mythologized past of Russian/
Tatar cohabitation in Kazan and in the surrounding areas, the women construed
themselves as belonging to a wrongfully denigrated historical, cultural, and religious community.

But the Russian-language term *svoi* was not only another term for marking
ethnic belonging. As pointed out by Alexei Yurchak (2005), during late Soviet
socialism svoi marked *understanding* rather than belonging (see also Dzenovska
2014). Yurchak describes svoi as a sociality characterized by an ethics of responsibility that connected people as fellow travelers across lines of power. For example, svoi would understand that it is necessary to go to the party meeting, so
as not to get colleagues into trouble. That is, svoi shared tacit understandings
of power-laden situations and knew how to behave accordingly. As put by Yurchak, svoi designated "a kind of sociality that differed from those represented in
authoritative discourse as 'the Soviet people,' 'Soviet toilers,' and so forth" (Yurchak 2005, 103). When the Tatar women insisted that they refer to each other
as svoi chelovek, they carried some of the Soviet-era Russian sense of svoi—as
an understanding-based sociality—into their post-Soviet identifications. It was
not necessarily always clear whether the women who gathered under the roof

of the Tatar Cultural Association were held together by awakened nationality, by the shared experience of being Soviet people in a national republic, or both. When I entered their gathering space on one of my last visits, singing along to the karaoke machine had given way to an aggravated discussion. One woman said: "They all think we are occupiers!" As it turned out, the night before several of the women had watched news on a Moscow-based TV station. The news broadcast had included a report on beggars in the streets of Moscow. The appearance of beggars on city streets was a distinctly post-Soviet phenomenon both in Moscow and in Riga. In the early post-Soviet years in particular, there were a lot of elderly people among street beggars, as they could not survive on their meager pensions. The women were visibly irritated about the economic and social changes that had sent so many old people begging into the street. Despite the fact that news pertained to Moscow, the women seemed deeply and personally affected by the broadcast. The beggars depicted on the streets of Moscow were not necessarily of Tatar or Central Asian origin, and the women certainly did not live in Moscow. But they took this phenomenon to stand for post-Soviet expulsions more generally—for expulsions from the labor market, from homes, from the nation, and even the polity (as in the case of Latvia's noncitizens) (Sassen 2014). They identified with the victims of these expulsions—in this case beggars in the streets of Moscow—via their own experiences. In the process, they conjured up nostalgia for a particularly Soviet sociality. "It was not like this before," they exclaimed, "but now nobody cares about you." One woman said that she had spent all her life working on construction sites, building houses for Latvians. "We were a good team," she said, "there were different people there, different nationalities. Nobody cared. I spoke to my husband in Russian. I did not care. But now? Now we are all occupiers!"

Commentary on the dire post-Soviet socioeconomic situation transformed into a commentary on their marginalization in the public and political life of contemporary Latvia. Even though they fit into the institutional framework of "national minorities" insofar as they belonged to a minority cultural association and engaged in cultural practices, the women felt the loss of a sociality that had allowed them to live public lives without cultural affiliation. The women recalled times when they felt a sense of personal worth, companionship, and pleasure in society. They were able to reproduce some semblance of companionship within the confines of the association, which they had come to see as a space of svoi, but they felt alienated from society. The public certainly did not recognize their personal worth, and they did not recognize themselves in addresses to the public. Instead, some of them felt interpellated by the designation "occupiers," which radical nationalist organizations and parts of the Latvian public used to refer not only to the Soviet state, but also to Soviet era "migrants." While they could collectively inhabit the subject position of national minorities, individually they were not "good citizens" (Anderson 2013), as most of them did not speak Latvian. In fact, many of them were not Latvia's citizens at all. Thus, legally they did not qualify for minority status as stipulated by the Framework Convention for the Protection of National Minorities, but insofar as they behaved like national minority subjects, they could benefit from the rights granted to national minorities. Their Soviet way of being ethnic had provided them with enough ethnicity to recognize themselves as svoi and therefore to be able to identify with a minority and conduct themselves as one. At the same time, unlike Vladimir, they did not fully embrace aspirations for cultural self-determination. The cultural association, created as a response to the Latvian state's efforts to "awaken" Russified ethnics, had provided the women with the possibility of being svoi, of being ethnic vis-à-vis a Soviet type of sociality. They lamented the loss of this sociality in the public space and reproduced it within the confines of their cultural association. Somewhat ethnic, but certainly not national, these women most forcefully inhabited a Soviet sociality that constituted a limit to the national minority subjectivity, interpellating them in crucial moments as occupiers (Althusser 2001). On the one hand, they responded to the encouragement of the Latvian state by ethnicizing themselves; on the other, they opposed that state by contrasting positively marked Soviet internationalism with negatively marked Latvian ethnicization. However, this disjuncture was not visible when the women appeared in public space singing Tatar songs.

Disciplining Unruly Subjects

From the perspective of the state, both Vladimir and the Tatar women complied with the state's vision of how collective ethnic difference should be lived publicly. However, as individuals outside the national minority slot, they were subject to the Latvian state's integration policies, namely policies that attempted to bring Russians and Russian speakers into Latvia's public and political life through the Latvian language.[27] Insofar as neither Vladimir nor the Tatar women spoke Latvian, they could be penalized by the state. The Latvian State Language Law stipulates that individuals occupying certain professions (ranging from a butcher to a parliamentary deputy) are required to know and use the Latvian language to the extent that is necessary for fulfilling their duties. This is regulated by a complex grid of language proficiency levels, which correspond to particular professions. Thus, for example, manual laborers, such as a house cleaner and a shepherd, are required to have the lowest qualification (A1), which would enable them to comply with "basic work safety." Bus drivers and postal workers are required to have mid-level qualification (B1) in order to be able to serve the public. And professionals of all sorts are required to have the highest-level qualification (C1–C2).[28]

Whereas the national communists' attempts to regulate language skills with policy measures in the 1950s failed, this controversial, contested, and much disliked piece of legislation is quite effective, especially as it is boosted by an extensive disciplinary apparatus. Namely, the Latvian government established the State Language Center to oversee the implementation of the law. The State Language Center employs language inspectors who enforce the law by going on random visits to workplaces according to a monthly plan or on the basis of citizens' complaints, which range from not being served in Latvian in a store to noticing signs that are only in English (Dzenovska 2017). While the Latvian State Language Law has been criticized and contested on the basis of arguments that it inflicts unnecessary violence on an ageing population, it is also unsettling for the individuals who fulfill the functions of language inspectors. The disciplinary state apparatus is alienating for its objects and subjects alike, as the following episode indicates.

On a July morning in 2008, I met two language inspectors to accompany them on a visit to a public transportation authority (the company) to check its employees' Latvian language proficiency.[29] Many of the company's employees were Russian speakers fifty to sixty years of age or older. The inspectors had visited the company back in November 2007, at which point they had determined that many employee's language proficiency levels did not correspond to those required for their profession. As a result of that first visit, the company had begun to provide Latvian language training courses for its employees.

As we sat on the bus, our conversation turned to the skills and dispositions required to do the job of a language inspector. Anna, who had worked as a language inspector for several years, said: "The job is not great. It is stressful and does not pay much, but we do it because we are people of the idea (*idejas cilvēki*)." Raita, who had been working as a language inspector for a little over a year, nodded her head in agreement as Anna elaborated how one needs to be psychologically strong and tolerant to do the job of a language inspector: "You need to be able to stay calm and polite even if everything inside is boiling. If you lose your calm, that is a trump on their [that is, their subjects'] side." It seemed they were preparing for a hard day ahead, and they were right.

When we arrived, the personnel director of the company escorted us to a large hall with a long table placed in the middle. The inspectors took their seats on one side of the table, placing chairs in front of them for their subjects to sit on. A line of summoned employees was already forming outside. One of the first to come in was a man I will call Vadim. He sat down in front of Raita. Reports from the previous visit indicated that Vadim did not have the right language proficiency level for being a bus driver. "Can you try to speak Latvian?" Raita asked Vadim in Latvian.

Vadim slouched back in his chair and did not rush to answer. After a while he said, in Russian: "Eto po rabote, ia ponimaiu" (this is about work, I understand). The personnel director—who was still in the room—intervened by saying that Vadim has been attending language courses held on the premises of the company for the last three months and that he does understand the questions.

Vadim tried to explain, in Latvian: "All is clear . . . there is no time. I work every day. [switches to Russian] I was not born here, I was born in Siberia. Worked at the radar [a Soviet military radar that was located in Skrunda], there was no language environment there. Now I work here for ten years. There were no conditions for learning. I will retire in July. I do not have any problems at work." Unsatisfied with Vadim's performance, Raita proceeded to write out a penalty protocol.

In the meantime, at the other end of the table, Anna was interviewing a man who said he did very badly in all languages at school and that he could not write at all, even in Russian. Somewhat surprised, Anna whispered to me in Latvian: "The man cannot write. How can he take the language test?" At a loss of what else to say, she instructed the man to study. Once the man left, Anna turned to me again and said that she felt very sorry for him: "I even want to cry."

Next, a woman who had recently passed her language exam brought along all of her study materials and proudly began to decline verbs in order to show what she had learned. Anna told her that she was very pleased to see her progress. The scene was unsettling. The state's disciplinary apparatus, embodied in this moment by the language inspectors, made people into submissive, anxious, and eager subjects. At the same time, the language inspectors also experienced this scene as individuals. For example, they shared with me their sense of hopelessness in relation to the insurmountable task of "getting all these people to speak Latvian." Caught between personal and professional commitment to a linguistically Latvian public space and the near-impossibility of their task, the language inspectors in our conversations never reflected on the scene of inspection itself, though evidently they were often deeply affected by it. Thus, throughout the day, Anna kept revisiting her interview with the man who could not write, and reiterating that she felt very, very sorry for him. But it never occurred to her to help this man navigate the bureaucracy and perhaps get an exemption from the written test. Instead, during a break, Anna told me that after busy days—days when you have to write many penalty protocols—"you feel such repulsion towards life that you cannot regain your composure the whole evening." Feeling repulsion was Anna's sacrifice for the nation. Regardless of the feeling of repulsion, Anna and Raita both remained "people of the idea."

Having realized that the language inspectors were inflicting penalties, the men and women in the line outside were becoming increasingly agitated. Their voices were becoming louder and, as the door opened for someone to come in or out, the language inspectors were also becoming aware of the increasingly tense atmosphere. Raita noted in a nervous jest: "We will get beat up when we leave." Half-jokingly, the inspectors discussed how they need to get home with honor (*ar godu mājās jātiek*). But with many people still out in the hallway, the day was far from over. A man now sitting across from Raita aggressively asserted that if he gets fired from this job he would and could find another job as a janitor. After a brief and tense exchange, the man left the room clinching his fists and screaming in Russian: "Suka tam sidit!" (The bitch just sits there!"). Raita complained about falling blood sugar levels and asked the personnel director to bring her some candy. In the meantime, Anna was having a tense conversation with a man named Kolya:

> ANNA (in Russian): Each state has its requirements. In our state, one needs to know the language.
> KOLYA (in Russian): You cannot punish me twice. What do you want from me?
> ANNA (in Russian): I want you to learn the language.
> KOLYA (in Russian): What does it do for anyone?
> ANNA (in Latvian): Why such an attitude?
> KOLYA (in Latvian): Like you with us, we with you. [*Switches to Russian*]. Do we get shot after the third penalty? I will walk out of here and resign. Will not even finish my shift.
> RAITA (interjecting in Russ.): Oh, you are so important!
> KOLYA (in Russian): I live where I want. I do not need to study. I have lived here for thirty years and will live for thirty more. I will not remain without work. What can the state do? I will earn my money one way or another.
> ANNA (in Latvian): He sits here and mocks us. He is not conscientious [*viņam nav godaprāta*].
> KOLYA (in Russian): Let's stop this mockery. Let's do it humanely (*po chelovecheski*).
> ANNA (in Russian): You are mocking us. You think that the world will stop turning without you.

In addition to being a scene where the state asserted its disciplinary power, the scene of inspection was shaped by conflicting perspectives about the past and the present, which led to mutual accusations of disrespect. Whereas the language inspectors were suggesting that Kolya mocked them by refusing to acknowledge that learning Latvian is not only an act of compliance, but also respect, Kolya suggested that the whole scene was a mockery because of the state's disciplinary power and asked for the encounter to occur in a different modality—*po chelovecheski.* While literally meaning "humanely," the term *po chelovecheski* also suggests a recognizably Soviet form of humanism: not an overarching set of abstract humanist principles enforced by the state, but rather a kind of informal and humane sociality within which individuals relate to each other as fellow travelers regardless of the formal requirements of the situation they face.

What unfolded on the premises of the company that day was an episode in an extended struggle for recognition of the ways in which the Soviet past placed demands on the Latvian present. If the inspectors considered that the Russian speakers were obliged to conscientiously learn the Latvian language out of respect for the Latvian nation and state and therefore the law, the inspectees considered that their long-term residence and labor in Latvia, as well as a historically shaped humane sociality, should override Latvians' sense of injury, which animated the state's Language Law and was at this moment inhabited by the language inspectors. All parties involved were aware that the nature of the encounter exceeded the relationship between law and its subjects and pertained to the relationship between two historical communities—"like you with us, we with you."

The sense of belonging to a nation that had suffered from Soviet-Russian domination and the conviction that language politics was the main terrain of struggle for undoing the effects of this domination motivated the inspectors to do the job despite occasionally feeling sympathy toward their subjects of inspection, as well as a general nausea about the job itself. But these strong affective responses did not—at least not on this occasion (see chapter 6)—make them question the work they were doing. The sympathy that Anna and Raita felt toward particular individuals did not make them see their inspectees as equals, as individuals who were not only nervous or angry, but also just like them were both complicit with and victimized by history. The way that Anna and Raita experienced sympathy was not separable from the historically shaped subject positions they inhabited. Their personal sentiments were entangled with a collective sense of identity that shaped the way they experienced the world. Their way of being human was to be Latvian. At the same time, Anna and Raita were also agents of the state on a mission to fulfill their tasks as language inspectors. There was a law—the Language Law—and they were supposed to make sure that the law was being observed. They did not heed Kolya's appeal to connect as people aside from being subjects of law. The scene was thus shaped as much by statism as by nationalism. And it is precisely this articulation between statism and nationalism that created what seemed to be an insurmountable wall between Anna and Raita, on the one hand, and Kolya, Vadim, and everybody else in the line, on the other. If during the Soviet period, Kolya, Anna, and Raita may have been able to connect po chelovecheski over and against Soviet state bureaucracy without necessarily sharing political ideals, now when the state was firmly articulated with the nation, they did not seem to have resources available for such a connection. Instead, what emerged were instances of repulsion, compassion, anger, and tiredness, neither of which seemed to be able to transform into the kind of understanding or solidarity that might lead to change.

Between Soviet History and the European Present

Latvian public and political life can be characterized by a tension between anger and tiredness with regard to the continued salience of ethno-politics practiced by all political forces and a continuously reproduced sense of existential threat on the part of Latvians that has been exacerbated even more by recent events in Ukraine and Russia. In such conditions, the affective states of compassion, repulsion, anger, or tiredness are not transformed into political alternatives, but rather reinforce the tensions that have been constitutive of the Latvian state since its formation.

The liberal politics of inclusion that is often advocated as a solution fails to appreciate that the problem only partially lies in the fact that the Latvian state has come to rely on a narrow articulation of the state and the cultural nation of Latvians. Liberal politics of inclusion is limited insofar as it fails to appreciate that expanding the conception of the nation and the borders of the polity are not only acts of inclusion, but also acts of exclusion insofar as both still entail categorizing people and sorting them into those who are in and those who are out. Citizenship is by definition an exclusionary formation. There is no such a thing as "becoming everyone" (Papadopoulos and Tsianos 2013). Given the Soviet history and the fact that the contemporary nation-state system still requires nations for there to be states, the Latvian state and Latvians as its "state people" refused those lessons in political liberalism that they thought were threatening to the existence of the nation and thus the very foundations of the state. Rather than an aberration or a failure, the Latvian case thus brings into sharp focus the foundational tensions of the modern political order.

Tolerance arrived in this contested terrain between the Soviet past and the European present as Latvia was preparing to join the European Union and European political institutions more broadly. As I show in the chapters that follow, tolerance was not a term that was used to govern relations between Latvians and Russians, which were most often discussed within the framework of integration. Rather, tolerance was a term that was used to designate a specifically liberal political virtue in relation to new categories of difference—for example, refugees or African Latvians. Moreover, tolerance as a liberal political virtue came hand in hand with the problem of intolerance that suddenly appeared to be a pervasive feature of Latvian society across the Latvian/Russian divide. Some of the "tolerance workers" even remarked how the appearance of "new others" could unite the ethnically divided Latvian society insofar as neither Latvians nor Russians were particularly welcoming of new residents or receptive to the imperative to welcome them through the tropes of openness and tolerance. In the next chapter, therefore, I turn to analysis of how tolerance came to Latvia and what this contested process adds to the understanding of the paradox of Europeanness.

KNOWING SUBJECTS AND PARTIAL UNDERSTANDINGS

Diagnosis of Intolerance and Other
Knowledge Practices after Socialism

For many of the tolerance workers who formed a loosely connected and partly institutionalized network in the process of devising the National Program for the Promotion of Tolerance (hereafter the program), embracing tolerance as a political virtue meant becoming European. However, what tolerance actually meant was less clear. Laimonis, a Latvian academic, an established authority on ethnic relations and nationalism, and a member of the group of experts assembled to develop the program, told me that "tolerance connotes the meeting of two different types of people where each comes with their own values, worldview, with their historical memory and consciousness, but each feels absolutely sovereign in these spheres. They simply sincerely and patiently establish human relations with each other." By referring to "two different types of people" with different "historical memory and consciousness" that remain "absolutely sovereign," Laimonis was referring to the tensions between Latvians and Russians in Latvian public and political space. He thus placed tolerance in the historically specific context of Latvia as a virtue that might help Latvians and Russians to craft respectful relations with each other. Elena, a Russian academic and also a member of the expert group, thought that tolerance always meant a positive attitude. She was definitely for it, but how far did one have to go? "Does it also mean accepting the other's position, embracing it as my own?" she asked. "But how can I accept everyone and everything? Will I not lose myself in the process?"[1]

These and other conversations indicated that even as tolerance workers shared an understanding that there was a problem of intolerance in Latvia, they did not necessarily agree on the precise contours of the problem, its scale, the required interventions, or the nature of the desired outcome. The network was held together not by agreement, but by an institutional framework, as well as affects, arguments, and practices that, taken together, constituted the problem-space of intolerance. If tolerance workers struggled with interpreting tolerance even as they consolidated and institutionalized the problem of intolerance, so did their audiences. The liberal politics of difference and the associated virtue of tolerance were not necessarily recognizable to Latvian- and Russian-speaking publics. Many people did not link tolerance with identity or the politically recognized categories of difference outlined in the program. In countless seminars and discussions on tolerance held as part of program activities, participants insisted that it does not matter to them who people are, but rather what they do. They also thought that tolerance (iecietība) was already part of everyday life; that to live was to continuously negotiate with others, that is, to be tolerant, until such negotiation was no longer possible, because a threshold of tolerance had been reached. One teacher gave the following example: "My threshold of tolerance is reached when a driver of a mikriņš (a public transportation van) starts smoking and all passengers are quiet." Another said that her tolerance is disturbed when a child with a big backpack gets on a bus and is being pushed around.

In discussions among experts, as well as between experts and their audiences, who or what was to be tolerated and by whom was far from clear. Was it particular individuals or groups that were to be tolerated? Or, was it the things that people did? If the latter, then why would one be more concerned about things done by ethnically different people rather than by mean people? Moreover, were both Latvians and Russian speakers to be tolerant toward each other and their common others? Or, were Latvians as "state people" the main subjects of tolerance with everyone else being objects of tolerance (Arendt 1979, Brown 2006)? This confusion gestured toward competing understandings of tolerance that structured not only social and political life in Latvia but also scholarly debates about tolerance in Western political theory (Locke 2007 [1689], McClure 1990, Mendus 1989, Rawls 1997, Walzer 1997). Most significantly, this confusion indicated a shift that had occurred in understandings of tolerance as a moral and political virtue during the course of the twentieth century, namely a shift from tolerating difference of thought, opinion, or practice to tolerating difference of identity or belonging (Brown 2006, McClure 1990). It is precisely the latter form of tolerance—tolerance of persons for who they are or what groups they belong to—that was worked into the National Program for the Promotion of Tolerance insofar as it identified objects of tolerance vis-à-vis categories of difference, such as race, religion, and ethnicity. Moreover, people's tolerance came to be measured by their willingness to put up with or accept the presence of others. Thus the program document justified the need for tolerance promotion on the basis of a survey conducted among Latvia's residents, which, among other things, asked whether people would be willing to live next door to variously defined "others" (e.g., Muslims, Africans, homosexuals, refugees, Jews, Roma, etc.) and/or allow such "others" to enter and reside in Latvia (BSZI 2004).

Once it became publicly known that the Special Tasks Secretariat for the Integration of Society would implement a National Program for the Promotion of Tolerance, the Russian language press referred to its offices as *Dom Terpimosti* (House of Tolerance)—a term used to denote brothels in postrevolutionary France and in Russia, thus mocking the hierarchies that the public virtue of tolerance entails. In turn, drawing on common understandings of tolerance as a social virtue that requires putting up with things that one does not necessarily find agreeable, many Latvians protested the transposition of the social virtue of tolerance into the political domain. If social life could not but be a life of negotiation and compromise, of putting up with disagreeable practices that were nevertheless not consequential for one's ability to go on with life, political life, especially that of the nation, was not to be a life of compromise, but rather of self-determination. As self-identified members of the cultural nation of Latvians and as formal members of the Latvian polity, many of those targeted by tolerance promotion efforts argued that Latvians as a nation have been putting up with all kinds of things for centuries (referring here to the domination of Baltic German landlords, Russian imperial administrators, and Soviet socialists), and that it was time to straighten the national backbone (*iztaisnot mugurkaulu*). They thought that, with independence after the collapse of the Soviet Union, Latvians had finally achieved the political right to determine how they were to live and whom they were to live with.

The program did not explicitly depict Latvians as more or less intolerant than Russian speakers, who at the time of research constituted about 29.6 percent of the population (BSZI 2004, chapter 2). However, the research used to support the program did divide research subjects into Latvian and Russian speakers and concluded that Latvians were more negative toward contact with non-Latvian others, which included Russian speakers, while both Latvian and Russian speakers exhibited intolerant attitudes toward minority groups that have not been historically present or publicly visible in Latvia, such as Chinese and Muslims, as well as sexual minorities, the disabled, and HIV patients (BSZI 2004). This, the researchers concluded, was a trend that was echoed in other European countries as well. All in all, in their intolerance, both Latvian and Russian speakers were deemed to be average Europeans. There was, however, one major difference between Latvians and Russian speakers, as well as between Latvians and Western Europeans with liberal sensibilities—namely, Latvians actively refused or were thought unable to recognize the existence of intolerance as a public and political problem. They did not seem to understand that inhabiting the political and moral landscape of Europe required continuous exposure to and reflection on societal problems linked to shameful legacies of the past, such as colonialism and racism. This does not mean that Russian speakers actively accepted tolerance discourses, but rather that Latvians as "state people" were more readily interpellated by criticism of Latvian public and political space. Many Latvians did not think that objecting to an increased presence of ethnically, racially, or religiously different others amounted to intolerance. Rather, they argued that such objections derived from their concern with the survival of a historically embattled nation. They were afraid that openness to difference and immigration would further undermine the existence of the cultural nation of Latvians, already injured by the forced movement of Latvia's residents associated with the establishment of Soviet power after World War II and the movement of Russian-speaking Soviet citizens from other parts of the Soviet Union to live and work in Soviet Latvia due to the Soviet nationalities policies (Riekstiņš 2004, chapter 2; Skultans 2008). Not unlike Elena's comment, those concerned with the survival of the nation worried that they might lose themselves—quantitatively and qualitatively—by embracing difference. They felt that it was the integrity of the nation that required strengthening rather than their and the nation's ability to live with difference.

In turn, it was precisely this stance that tolerance workers took to be the biggest obstacle on Latvia's path to Europeanness. They often described this obstacle as lack of political liberalism. Most of my interlocutors among tolerance workers considered that political liberalism had not taken root in Latvia. A few of them did not particularly like liberalism, but thought that it would enrich the political field, while most considered that the lack of political liberalism in the public imaginary indicated the stunted development of the polity. For most of my interlocutors among tolerance workers, liberalism meant individualism over communalism, the ability to think independently and not feel threatened by different viewpoints and different bodies in the political space of the nation. They thought that difference was never threatening, except when in turned against the virtue of tolerance itself.

In this chapter, I begin to tell the story of what happened when tolerance promotion projects arrived in a polity that had just liberated itself in the name of ethno-national statehood. Paradoxically, tolerance promotion projects invited Latvia's residents to view ethnic, religious, and racial difference as a matter of inconsequential diversity in a state built on consequential ethno-national difference.[2] At the same time, similar to national minority politics, tolerance was a project that focused on educating conduct and attitudes. This meant that it did not necessarily challenge the foundations of the state, at least not openly or immediately. Instead, it strove for cultivation of manners to mitigate for the state's foundational exclusions (Brown 2006). However, the Latvian-speaking public was still reluctant to comply, many rejecting "tolerance projects," like Kārlis in the previous chapter, on the grounds that they were just that—reeducation of manners demanded by Europe. This pushed the tolerance workers to frame the problem of intolerance as, first and foremost, a problem of not recognizing the problem of intolerance.

Thereafter, tolerance workers set out to convince others of the existence of the problem of intolerance. The tolerance workers were unsettled, repulsed, and angry every time they heard or heard about racial slurs, disrespect, or violence directed at minority groups or individuals. They translated their affective unsettlement vis-à-vis the discursive frames—such as that of the problem of intolerance—provided by transnational and institutionalized forms of political liberalism. Subsequently, they circulated accounts of racism or intolerance in society as a way of forming themselves as tolerant subjects and as a way of institutionalizing political liberalism in Latvia.

As a result, knowledge production about racism and intolerance in Latvia primarily consisted of operations of *diagnosis* whereby policymakers, analysts, the media, and NGOs deployed standardized and taken-for-granted categories that circulated in European policy discourse for rendering visible the problem of racism and intolerance. The pronounced "end of history" in Eastern Europe, that is, the widely accepted victory of liberalism over socialism, seems also to have meant the end of attempts to understand the power configurations of the postsocialist present and the multiple and overlapping modes of often-racialized differentiation that they entailed. Public and political life came to be dominated by a diagnostic mode of knowledge production whose critical operation was to identify symptoms that prevented the full achievement of liberal democracy and free-market economy, and thereafter to propose measures for mitigating, alleviating, or otherwise correcting the ailments.

Hostages of Certainty

"Our core problem is the inability to recognize the problem," Signe explained the state of affairs with regard to tolerance promotion efforts in Latvia during a conversation we had in late 2005. Signe was an internationally recognized human rights expert. At the time of our conversation, she was the director of a Latvian nongovernmental organization, a trusted partner of international institutions such as the European Commission against Racism and Intolerance in their efforts to monitor racism and intolerance in European states.[3] A Western-educated political scientist, Signe was born into a Latvian exile family abroad but came to live and work in Latvia after independence. Signe was also a member of the Consultative Council of the National Program for the Promotion of Tolerance and belonged to the network of tolerance workers who may not have always agreed on the precise contours of the problem of intolerance, but who most certainly agreed that tolerance promotion efforts had to start by making the public recognize the problem.[4]

When Signe and I talked in late 2005, the National Program for the Promotion of Tolerance had already been approved by the Latvian Cabinet of Ministers and funded with the help of the European Commission. For many tolerance workers, cabinet approval of the program in 2004 with the stated goal of promoting tolerance toward racial, ethnic, and religious minorities was an achievement in itself, a culmination of an arduous struggle to place tolerance on the policy agenda. However, Signe found it lacking. She pointed out that the title of the program emphasized the *promotion of tolerance* rather than a *fight against intolerance*. For her, this was paradigmatic of the most serious problem faced by the Latvian society in the context of the global fight against racism and intolerance. She said:

> We, as an organization [the human rights organization she represented], try to objectively point to problems, but many people think of us as traitors. They say: how can you say such things in front of foreigners and talk about our problems? The politicians think that everything is imposed. They are motivated by a desire to pretend that they are better than they are, to show the West that we already are a democracy.... The Durban [conference against racism in 2001] slogan is "against intolerance," and we could not even accept that, because we cannot admit that it [intolerance] exists here.

The title of the draft program had, in fact, included the phrase "against intolerance." The draft program document drew its legitimacy and borrowed its language from a long list of international documents, including the UN Declaration of Human Rights, the UN Declaration on the Elimination of Racial Discrimination, a number of EU directives against racial discrimination, recommendations of the European Commission against Racism and Intolerance, and others. It was also inspired by the UN World Conference Against Racism, Racial Discrimination, Xenophobia, and Related Intolerance held in Durban, South Africa, in 2001, especially by the preconference preparatory work in which Signe herself was involved. However, during the public discussion process that took place in Riga in March and April 2004, some of those consulted, from academics to civil servants to members of civil society organizations, expressed their dislike for the double-negativity of the title—"against intolerance." Others objected to the privileging of racial, ethnic, and religious minorities and argued that people with disabilities, as well as old people, were also targets of intolerance in Latvia and that therefore the program should focus on promotion of tolerance more broadly. For them, "promotion of tolerance" was not a formulation that obscured the problem, as Signe thought, but one that broadened the field of intervention beyond categories of difference recognized by institutionalized forms of political liberalism. As a result of these debates and in an attempt to push the program through the Cabinet of Ministers, the phrase "against intolerance" was dropped from the title.[5] Signe was not satisfied. In an interview she gave right after the public discussion process, Signe said: "We do not have sufficient scientific basis for defining tolerance. But we need to define groups against which there is intolerance. No person considers themselves intolerant. If there will be no concrete criteria [of intolerance], I can just read the document and conclude that I am tolerant and all is well."[6]

Plugged into international circuits of institutionalized antiracism that were routed through Durban and had a vibrant life in European institutions of governance and activist networks, Signe considered that public recognition of the problem of intolerance—rather than a vague commitment to the general virtue of tolerance—was an important indicator of the public's *political maturity*.[7] She, as well as other tolerance workers, thought that the lack of such a recognition was the root cause of a variety of hurdles on the road to Europe—for example, delays in ratifying the Framework Convention for the Protection of National Minorities (see chapter 2), as well as implementation of various pieces of human rights legislation. From Signe's perspective, politically mature individuals should be able to openly acknowledge the social and political problems that hinder the functioning or development of a liberal democratic society. This would be a sure sign that the society is moving in the right direction. Instead, Latvia's "people and politicians" seemed to think that such acknowledgment would taint Latvia's image in the eyes of the West. Signe saw this as a weakness, as an infantile attempt to project a positive image of oneself to the outside world. However, there is another possible interpretation, namely that, by exhibiting reluctance to publicly acknowledge the problem of intolerance, the politicians and the public implicitly commented on the power hierarchies within which the demand to recognize it was embedded. Perhaps not entirely without reason, they were concerned that the problem of intolerance could add to an archive of lacks and failures that have come to define the post-Soviet Latvian state and people vis-à-vis normative visions of liberal democratic societies.[8]

In order to move the society in the right direction, Signe and other tolerance workers engaged in knowledge work, that is, they commissioned a variety of research reports on the state of things with regard to tolerance, discrimination, and racism. These research reports were products of a more general reorientation of knowledge practices after socialism, which, in the process of striving to produce true knowledge, ended up producing ignorance about the present.

Reorientation of Understandings and Knowledge after Socialism

When the effervescence of independence struggles subsided and state building began, it was widely thought that Latvia's people needed to supplement their will to freedom with new understandings of the world and that Latvia's scholars needed to learn how to produce proper knowledge in lieu of the distorted Marxist-Leninist perspectives that had shaped social sciences to date (cf. Ule 2014). In conditions in which previous sources of both everyday understandings and authoritative knowledge were discredited, Western individuals and institutions emerged as authority figures that helped postsocialist subjects to apprehend the new situation for the purposes of guiding action. The postsocialist reorientation of understandings and knowledge drew on and solidified a discursive juxtaposition between Western and Soviet "mentalities," as well as between Western scientific knowledge and Soviet ideological knowledge.[9] *Rietumnieki* (Westerners), those who hailed from the other side of the Iron Curtain as far as Australia and the United States, including several generations of Latvians who had resided abroad during the Soviet period, became experts of how things were to be done in the new post-Soviet present merely by virtue of having lived in "the free world" (*brīvajā pasaulē*) (cf. Pickles and Smith 2007). Rietumnieki arrived as staff members of development agencies, such as the UN Development Program and the World Bank, as entrepreneurs and investors, as government advisors, as researchers, translators, visitors, and relatives. The Soviet era "imaginary West" had become real through the mere presence of Westerners (Yurchak 2005). Rietumnieki's knowledge of "the West," which ranged from high-level professional skills to everyday knowledge of banking operations to the embodied skills of opening food packaging until recently not available in Latvia, was valued regardless of their political commitments. They knew, for example, that run-down places, such as the island of Ķīpsala across the river from downtown Riga, would become desired waterfront real estate, and so some bought property there when locals still thought of the island as a hotbed of poverty and criminal activity. Whether liberals, conservatives, or leftists, rietumnieki were thought to have the kind of understanding, often referred to as "mentality," that was needed to operate in the "free world" which Latvia had just joined.

Former Soviet citizens, regardless of their education, skill, or life experience, became handicapped, for their understanding of the world was thought to be tainted by Soviet ideology and practice. Even if a person did not associate themselves with the ideology of the Soviet state, their knowledge and skills were still found to be lacking, because they simply had not been exposed to a wide variety of "Western practices," as well as because of the ideological nature of the Soviet education system, which was thought to have discouraged critical thinking and self-initiative (Larson 2011, 2013, see chapter 4). To this day, Latvia's publicists, government officials, and politicians use references to "Soviet mentality" to explain all kinds of ills of the post-Soviet present, including corruption, emigration, intolerance, lack of civic activity, insufficient entrepreneurial skills, people's expectations in relation to the state, and more. In a way, references to the Soviet legacy became a crutch for explaining the present without the need to understand it.[10]

The juxtaposition between the useless or corrupted knowledge of former Soviet citizens and the useful and proper knowledge of Westerners became hegemonic in debates about organizing economic, social, and political life after socialism. There was one domain of life, however, in which Western understandings were not unanimously privileged. And that was ethno-politics. As noted in the previous chapter, Latvia's politicians, government officials, and the majority of the public thought that Westerners, especially various human rights monitoring institutions and European commissioners and their local allies, did not thoroughly understand the effects of the Soviet nationalities policy on the Latvian society. Therefore, they could not see that the history of Soviet/Russian domination in Latvia necessitated compensatory measures in the present, such as restrictive language, minority, and citizenship policies that demanded Latvia's Russian-speaking residents to accept, if not embrace, the new state as a national state. I engage in in-depth analysis of the minority question in post-Soviet Latvia in chapter 2, thus my point here is to simply note that in this particular domain it was the liberal West that was thought to lack in understanding appropriate for guiding action. At the same time, it was precisely the Latvian politicians' and public's insistence on the demands of history on citizenship, language, and minority politics that the liberal West, including local minority and human rights professionals and activists, considered to be the problem hindering development of a liberal democratic society in Latvia. It is this that also prompted Signe to say that "our biggest problem is the inability to recognize the problem."

Meanwhile, in the realm of formal knowledge, social sciences and humanities were largely discredited as ideological projects of the Soviet state—as sciences of Marxism-Leninism (cf. Amsler 2007). As argued by Sarah Amsler in her analysis of knowledge practices in Kyrgyzstan, the collapse of the Soviet Union was also thought of as the liberation of knowledge from power (2007, 5). Sociology, political science, and related disciplines had to rebuild themselves, often by borrowing knowledge practices from Western colleagues. Moreover, as noted by Latvian sociologists Tālis Tisenkopfs (2010), Aivars Tabūns (2010), and Evita Kļave and Brigita Zepa (2010) in a volume dedicated to the development of the discipline of sociology in Latvia, in the 1990s Latvian sociology turned into an applied and empirical science, largely because it needed to survive in post-Soviet market conditions. Tālis Tisenkopfs (2010) writes that the theoretical aspirations that the discipline experienced in the 1980s after having proved its applicability to the Soviet authorities dissipated in the 1990s as Latvian sociologists established firms and began to fulfill the demand for knowledge about social practices and attitudes that could be used for crafting new government programs and policies (see also Creed 2011, 162). Social scientists drew on generic and standardized social sciences methods used across disciplines, such as structured interviews and focus groups, that could produce fast, reproducible, and comparable results.[11] Most, if not all, of this research was funded by donors, such as the Soros Foundation, the UN Development Program, and the European Commission (cf. Amsler 2007), who needed to justify their development initiatives—such as tolerance promotion—on the basis of scientific research.[12] Aivars Tabūns (2010) writes that in the 1990s Latvian sociologists undertook short-term research, often simultaneously working on several projects funded by different agencies that were not thematically related. Tabūns writes that in undertaking both quantitative and qualitative research sociologists used theoretical instruments developed elsewhere and that their methodological strategies could not confront the assumptions of these borrowed theories. For example, Evita Kļave and Brigita Zepa describe how research on ethno-politics, which included questions of racism, xenophobia, and tolerance, used various theoretical framings and explanatory tools borrowed from Western colleagues, such as intergroup connection theories, social identity theories, conflict theories, social distance index, critical discourse analysis, and more (2010, 215). Tabūns argues that as a result of these changes data produced about social processes, practices, and attitudes became comparable to that from other countries and thus were thought to gain in quality (Tabūns 2010, 118).[13] However, it is precisely this comparability that, while increasing the perceived quality of Latvian social sciences in accordance with the standards of Western policy research, hindered development of a deep understanding of the workings of power in the post-Soviet present.

As a result of Western perceptions about the inferiority of scientific research in former socialist contexts, Latvian social scientists were mostly informants and data sources for their Western colleagues, as well as desired, if marginal, partners in various European Union funding schemes (Creed 2011, 5; see Burawoy and

Verdery 1999 for critique). As Gerald Creed and others have noted (e.g., Greenberg 2010, Hann and Dunn 1996), much of research in postsocialist contexts that was conducted by Western scholars focused on "core concepts of Western political economy: democracy, civil society, the market, privatization, rule of law, minority rights, and gender equality; often in concert with the supposed indigenous barriers to these goals: corruption, patriarchy, nationalism, and various socialist legacies" (Creed 2011, 5). "To start our analysis with these foci," Creed argues, "is to establish an already and always ideal image against which the events in Eastern Europe are measured" (Creed 2011, 5). However, as I outline in the Introduction, contrary to postcolonial contexts, Eastern Europe did not have a space of difference—an indigenous space—to which to retreat and from which to mount critiques of the developmentalist and evolutionary thinking that prevailed in both research and policy. Socialism was dead, nationalism was a discredited political platform against which the European Union constructed itself (McDonald 2006), thus Western liberalism emerged as the dominant frame for making sense of and organizing collective life. This contributed to creating conditions of self-validating circularity whereby the "Western model remains unchallenged by the difficulties it encounters, which are always displaced to the lack or failures of the society in transition" (Creed 2011, 6).

Thus, in the post-Soviet present, the comparison carried out in social sciences, but also in public life more broadly, did not simply compare and contrast, but also arranged units of comparison on an evolutionary scale. Comparison was undertaken with the sometimes explicit, sometimes implicit goal of determining how far away the future lay and whether things were proceeding in the right direction. The articulation of Latvia's future as the West's present was visible in most spheres of life, including that of tolerance promotion. Here, the Soviet past was thought to have obfuscated the full range of human difference (not unlike the "lid theories," which argued that socialism kept a lid on ethnic strife which its collapse unleashed; see Martin 2001 for critique, also Hann 1998), whereas the present was thought of as a period of transition when both difference and intolerance had erupted onto the public arena. Tolerance, in turn, represented the liberal democratic future toward which Latvia and Latvians should aspire. For example, one of my interlocutors—the same civil servant who spoke about her "awakening" to her ethnic roots in chapter 2—explained to me:

> You know, there were some gray groups, like homosexuals, who did not exist [in the Soviet Union]. They were not visible. I, for example, I did not have a sense that it [homosexuality] was possible until about tenth grade. It could be said that the potential of intolerance was great, but it was not promoted and was not articulated. And the taboo

was not doubted. Critical thinking was not promoted. . . . Starting with the awakening, people began to problematize things, and one extreme is acceptance and the other is exclusion. Perhaps it is connected with the fact that there was no thinking and therefore there was no tolerance.

This former Soviet person-cum-tolerance worker attributed the lack of the problem of intolerance during the Soviet period to the Soviet state's oppression of difference and lack of critical thinking within the population. On the one hand, there was no difference, difference was invisible, so there was no public intolerance. On the other hand, this invisibility was not problematized, because there was no critical thinking and therefore there were also no conditions for tolerance to emerge as a public virtue opposite to intolerance. Now that intolerance has erupted into public space, because human difference has become visible, there is no other way forward but to become liberal.

At the time of my research, in the mid-2000s, tolerance workers thought that the path was predetermined. For example, during my fieldwork, LGBT activists often lamented that Latvian society was not yet sufficiently democratic, while assuring themselves and others that it will eventually "catch up" with the world's liberal democracies. Thus, one activist born and raised abroad by Latvian émigré parents told me that what is happening in Latvia today very much reminds her of her childhood in the country of her birth: "Whether with regard to emancipation, paternity rights, or security belts in cars, or helmets for bikers, all environmental issues, all these things were not present when I was a child, but they had been implemented by the time I was an adult. And when I read the papers here, I have a déjà vu of sorts. And then I know where all these discussions will end up, with the exception that here it all happens so much faster." On another occasion, in a seminar on intercultural communication for teachers held as part of the activities of the National Program for the Promotion of Tolerance in 2006, a civil servant of the Secretariat of the Special Tasks Minister for the Integration of Society began his address to the participants by noting that whereas Western European countries have reached a level of consensus about the fact that racism is bad and diversity is good, this was still a contentious question in Latvia. "It's an interesting time we live in," he added.

Between the Soviet past and the European future, the former thought of as hindering the arrival of the latter, the present was in a state of permanent transition (Coronil 2011). The present was not visible in this interplay between the past and the future that was characteristic of transition temporality. As Ozra Pupovac has argued, such traffic between the past that has a hold on the future and thus continuously needs to be overcome and a future that is continuously deferred,

thus requiring more intervention, produces profound ignorance about the present. As soon as postsocialism

> is interrogated about its present, about the actuality of its condition,
> the post-socialist consciousness starts playing an endless game of dis-
> placements, constantly shifting the question backwards and forward,
> constantly pointing either to what it no longer is, to its supposed break
> with the past, or to what it is not yet quite, to what it ought to be. This
> misplacement in time reveals an important feature of the historical situ-
> ation that we are facing: its unconsciousness. Between the ideological
> promises of its future and the traumatic encounters with its past, no
> less ideological in their form, post-socialism is a state marked by a stark
> ignorance of its own present (2010, 2).

For much of the 2000s, this deferred future in the name of which transition
unfolded was marked as European. Whether praised or contested, Europe was
the placeholder for the future toward which postsocialist transformations were
moving, thus it was not necessary to think about the present as a unique configuration. Rather, it was a transitional phase. It was known through its distance
from both the socialist past and the European present. This amounted to a certain ignorance about the present. Ignorance, however, was not lack of knowledge or understanding. The space of ignorance delineated by Pupovac was filled
with understandings and knowledge, with knowers and knowing subjects, with
experts who knew what had to be done and who could evaluate the present in
relation to the normative future. Rather than liberating knowledge from power,
then, the reorientation of understandings and knowledge after socialism meant
directing understanding and knowledge along different circuits of authority
shaped by different fields of power. The juxtaposition of the ideological knowledge of socialism with the true or free knowledge of the West that shaped postsocialist transformations obscured these fields of power.

The Solution and Its Problem

The liberal politics of tolerance that came to dominate the governance of difference in European Union member states in the 2000s provided a discursive frame
for making sense of human difference in post-Soviet Latvia vis-à-vis problematic attitudes toward a number of categories of difference, most of which were
not operative in the public domain during the Soviet period. Thus, for example, race erupted onto the public and political agenda through the problem of

racism, whereas same-sex sexuality emerged through the problem homophobia. To be sure, ethnic difference was socially racialized during the Soviet period—for example, in Latvia, people from Caucasus, especially those selling produce in the market, were commonly referred to as *melnie* or *chernye* (blacks). It was not thought of as racism, however, especially since the Soviet state took an explicitly antiracist stance. While the existence of social racism in the Soviet Union is not contested, scholars disagree on the relationship between the Soviet state and racial politics. For example, Eric Weitz (2002) suggests that, despite the explicit antiracist stance, imaginaries of racialized difference shaped the organization of social and political life in the Soviet Union. In response, Francine Hirsch (2002) argues that the Soviet state did not incorporate racial differentiation in statecraft and state practices. She argues that blurring the lines between race and nationality lumps distinctive regimes of difference into one. Alaina Lemon (2002), in turn, calls for attention to race as a discursive practice, which does not require state-based racial politics. On the basis of ethnographic research, Lemon argues that Soviet police could identify people as Gypsies and treat them differently, even as the state did not subscribe to racial politics. At the same time, the mainstream public view in the Soviet Union, including in Latvia, was that race and racism existed elsewhere—in the United States or in the "Third World" (Dzenovska 2010). Thus, for Latvia's residents, the fall of socialism and the subsequent development and implementation of the National Program for the Promotion of Tolerance meant the loss of racial innocence. Some became white, others black; some became tolerant, whereas others were diagnosed as racist or intolerant.

The program defined and measured the extent of the problem in Latvia by referring to research reports of the Latvian Center for Human Rights and Ethnic Studies (now the Latvian Center of Human Rights), monitoring reports of the European Commission Against Racism and Intolerance, as well as specially commissioned research (ĪUMSILS 2004). For example, a report on cultural diversity and tolerance in Latvia commissioned by the Special Tasks Ministry for the Integration of Society in 2003 defined intolerance as a negative attitude "towards people, their lifestyle, their views, interests, feelings, rituals, which is based on stereotypes about people on the basis of their social and ethnic belonging" (ĪUMSILS 2003). It defined racism as "not only negative, but also demeaning attitudes and behavior towards people with different skin color, religion, ethnic belonging, etc. that lead to discriminatory action" (ĪUMSILS 2003). The line of difference between intolerance and racism in this report was drawn along: (1) the difference between conduct and identity, whereby intolerance can manifest toward people's views, rituals, or interests that are linked to group belonging, while racism can manifest toward people on the basis of mere group belonging; and (2) the difference between attitudes and conduct, whereby intolerance amounts to negative attitudes while racism manifests as both demeaning and discriminatory attitudes and conduct. The definitions provided in the report lie somewhere between folk theories of racism described by Jane Hill (2008) that link racism with skin color and institutionalized liberal understandings of racism, which broaden the definition of racism to include negative attitudes and behavior toward a variety of categories of difference. In terms of actions, the program proposed the dissemination of information and awareness raising, but also changes in antidiscrimination legislation. The measure of success was to be opinion poll data, which would indicate that intolerance toward racial, ethnic, and religious difference, as well as toward immigrants and asylum seekers, was decreasing compared to base line data collected in 2004, which indicated that people in Latvia exhibit anti-Semitic stereotypes and prejudice, as well as stereotypes and prejudice toward Roma and Muslims. For example, the 2004 report presented data that showed that 27.2 percent of Latvia's residents did not want to live next door to Roma, 14.5 percent to Muslims, and 5.2 percent to Jews (ĪUMSILS 2004).

While mainly focusing on religion and ethnicity and less prominently on race, the program document also mentioned instances of intolerance toward people with HIV and sexual minorities. The document emphasized, however, that the program does not specifically target intolerance toward these social risk groups.[14] At the same time, it noted that people who exhibit intolerance toward racial, ethnic, or religious difference also tend to be intolerant toward other socially marginalized groups, thus suggesting that working on tolerance promotion toward ethnic and religious difference was likely to indirectly address other forms of intolerance as well. The program document thus defined intolerance as a moral shortcoming of particular individuals or categories of individuals that can be addressed through a reworking of their ethical orientations.

But how was the problem understood by tolerance workers and would-be objects of tolerance, such as representatives of minority groups, in their daily practices? To put it another way, if the policy solution was tolerance promotion, what did the problem look like on the ground? Tolerance workers, some of whom were also would-be objects of tolerance insofar as they identified with one of the categories of difference written into the program, spoke about the problem they faced by sharing examples of instances of prejudice or racism they had heard about or experienced themselves. For example, Michael—an African American man who moved to Latvia with his Latvian wife in the 1990s—often spoke about being stared at on the street. One day in the winter of 2006 Michael explained to me the difference between looking and staring: "Looking is like: I see you, fine. Maybe I like what I see, maybe I don't, but the moment is brief. Staring takes longer. People stare all the time. And I always want to know what they want to mark by staring. Are they saying: I see you, you are dark-skinned, you should know it? But every morning I wake up, I look in the mirror, and I know that I am dark-skinned. Why should I find out from you?" At the time we met, Michael had lived in Latvia for eleven years. He said he had experienced racism all his life, but on arrival in Latvia, had finally decided "not to run from it" and thus became, as he called himself, a "civil rights activist."

The stares were occasionally accompanied by slurs. Most members of the African Latvian Association—an organization that was formed as a support group for Africans living in Latvia and subsequently became involved with tolerance promotion activities—had experienced verbal insults ranging from slurs to suggestions to go home. On a nearly daily basis they and their family members faced what for most of Latvia's residents was a marginal problem, if a problem at all. However, not all of them wanted to talk about it publicly. Some members of the African Latvian Association, several of whom had come to Soviet Latvia or other parts of the Soviet Union as students, did not think that antiracism should be the public face of the organization. A few of them wanted the organization to remain an inward oriented support group. Others wanted it to portray positive images about the countries they came from to the Latvian public. For example, Theo considered that the first step was "to introduce yourself through cultural events and then make demands for rights. Otherwise, people will say: you have not introduced yourself!" Most members of the organization were concerned about misguiding stories about Africans and life in Africa that appeared in the media. For example, on one occasion a couple of members of the organization told me about a newspaper article that, they thought, had perpetuated images of Africa as an uncivilized and backward place by misreading research on child marriage practices and attributing them to the whole continent. They were not primarily concerned about public attitudes, but rather about the circulation of skewed, stereotype-producing, and racialized knowledge, which went unchecked and which tolerance promotion efforts did not address.

In 2005 and 2006, members of the organization were also concerned about physical attacks by isolated individuals or small groups of what they called "skinheads" in the streets of Riga. They tried to convince the police that what the police tended to classify as hooliganism was actually racially motivated hate crime. And they tried to convince the Security Police that these were not just misguided youths, but rather organized groups. They wanted the state to recognize racially motivated crime and to prosecute the perpetrators.[15]

Moreover, the most active among the members of the organization thought that it was their experience of racism that made them qualified to speak about it. This was corroborated by some of the speakers invited as part of conferences or training seminars, especially those hailing from the United States. For example, a retired African American police officer who was invited to lecture at a seminar on hate crime in 2006 explained that his expertise partly comes from personal experience in the United States, from having to enter stores through the back door, from being attacked when attending a zoo in a low-income white neighborhood, and more. Michael agreed. So much so that he questioned those who lacked such experience—or who did not have family members with such experience—for their involvement in tolerance promotion activities or tried to legitimize their involvement through finding a link with experience. For example, when I sought membership in the African Latvian Association, Michael presented me not only as a researcher but also as someone who was partnered with a Mexican American, thus suggesting that my concern with racism is routed through family and not only through scholarly interest or political solidarity.

Michael also considered that racism is a historically specific form of violence that should not be diluted by fitting any and all forms of discriminatory differentiation under the umbrella of racism. For example, Michael became disillusioned with the Special Tasks Minister for the Integration of Society who was responsible for the National Program for Tolerance Promotion, because, in Michael's view, he was broadening the definition of racism to include anti-Semitism and homophobia. Michael thought it lessened the importance of his cause and belittled his experience of the violence of racism when coming of age in the United States. He also thought that the minister was not really in the position to understand this, because he was white. The minister, who shared a US background with Michael as someone who was born to Latvian émigré parents in the United States, had come to know Michael through work, but also through social circles. He was well aware of Michael's views. He thought that Michael perceived the broadening of the definition of racism as a threat to his identity. From the minister's point of view, Michael was too attached to his identification as an African American shaped by racism, which prevented him from broadening his perspective and transcending identity politics in order to become truly liberal. From Michael's point of view, the minister lacked direct experience with racism, which prevented him from truly understanding the problem of racism. As I argue in the next section, it is precisely this partial understanding that enabled the minister to become a properly tolerant subject, and it is experience that prevented Michael from doing the same.

Knowing Subjects, Partial Understandings

The knowledge produced for the purposes of political justification of the National Program for the Promotion of Tolerance constituted "knowledge without knowers" (Barth 2000), that is, it took the form of policy research reports that were disarticulated from the understandings of specific individuals, but that nevertheless posited a particular knowing subject—namely, a liberal subject that oversaw the transition from socialism to liberalism while keeping nationalism at bay. At the same time, everyday tolerance work depended on individual knowers whose understanding of the world included a sense that there was something amiss with how Latvia's residents understood and related to human difference.

Understanding, as argued by Andreas Glaeser (2009, 2014), is not formal or abstract knowledge, but rather the kind of knowledge that informs practice. It is formed not only through cognitive processes, but also through embodied engagement with the world, that is, through affective and intimate relations with people, places, and institutions (Connolly 2005, Glaeser 2009). The formation of such practical understanding crucially depends on validation, that is, on a number of operations through which emerging understandings are confirmed. Glaeser identifies three modes of validation: recognition, direct corroboration, and resonance. Recognition entails validating understandings in relation to other people's understanding, more specifically the understanding of those people whom one trusts. Direct corroboration entails testing one's understanding in the world, that is, acting on the basis of a particular understanding and seeing whether it provides the necessary guidance or whether it fails. And, finally, resonance entails checking whether a particular understanding aligns with one's other values, desires, and understandings, and thus fits within one's larger life world (Glaeser 2009).

The process of validation is a central organizing element in the relationship between people's understandings that are formed and transformed through everyday experience and the political institutions people create and re-create. In other words, understandings inform actions, which form institutions, which, in turn, form and reform understandings. Once institutionalized, however, understandings can become "knowledge without knowers" reproduced along established circuits of authority and thus hindering necessary adjustments in understanding if the situation changes (see also Yurchak 2005).

Tolerance workers' actions were guided by understandings formed through a variety of modes of validation. Some of them, such as Michael from the African Latvian Association or Laila from the Jewish Community Association, claimed experiential knowledge of racism and intolerance. Other tolerance workers, especially those who could not or did not make political claims on the basis of politically recognized categories of difference, explained that they acquired their tolerant sensibilities in the process of socialization and education. Many emphasized that their commitment to tolerance work went beyond their professional duties as civil servants or staff members of research institutions or nongovernmental organizations. Zaiga, a staff member of a donor organization, described tolerance as follows: "Tolerance is a search for balance, an answer to discrimination. It is a logical, functional search for balance. If that were not the case, then I would not be doing the job that I am doing. I need to believe in that which I do." She described the path to her commitment to tolerance work as routed through democratic institutions that enabled her to "breathe the air of democracy": "I got interested in the notion of civic education. And I had the opportunity to spend three months at the University of Indiana. And the air of democracy that I breathed there! I cannot call it otherwise, but the air of democracy." Zaiga, similar to other tolerance workers with liberal sensibilities, thought of intolerance as a natural, if backward, state of affairs—that is, as a natural aversion to everything that is different and therefore strange, yet that could be reworked through education. She even narrated her own past as one of prejudice—for example, toward people with different sexual orientation—which she had learned to overcome through education and contact.

Another activist narrated his path to liberal sensibilities through his experiences growing up as a Latvian in the United States, attending a US university for his Ph.D. in political science, reflecting on Latvian nationalism after his arrival in Latvia, and realizing that "this was going to be a problem that needed to be addressed." He said he had wanted to build "a normal democratic society" in Latvia. Among other projects he undertook in his various professional capacities, he also worked to construct a "usable past"—he cited Timothy Garton Ash—for the purposes of building a liberal tradition in Latvia. For example, he collaborated on a book project that described historical figures of various ethnic backgrounds that represented forms of liberal thought in pre–World War II Latvia.

As these individuals became "tolerance workers" in the context of the National Program for the Promotion of Tolerance and related activities, they continued to form and reform their own understandings about human difference and the way people in Latvia understood and related to it. In the process of forming their own understandings, tolerance workers institutionalized the problem of intolerance in the agendas of government offices, research institutes, and nongovernmental organizations. They also formed themselves as authorities on the matter, though "Europe," including European funding institutions, remained the legitimating authority in the last instance, the beacon of the liberal democratic future toward which Latvia aspired. While these practices of forming and institutionalizing understandings resulted in a self-referential circuit of knowledge production, the process itself was messy, fraught with puzzlement, speculation, misunderstanding, and disagreement.

Michael, the African American man who spoke out about the racializing stares, often suspected those who did not have any direct experience with discrimination, racism, or intolerance, for having ulterior motives for becoming involved in tolerance work, such as remuneration or a political career. In turn, some of the professional tolerance workers expressed dissatisfaction with the partial understandings of the problem exhibited by minority representatives. Throughout the numerous meetings, discussions, and private conversations during the course of my fieldwork, a picture emerged whereby professional tolerance workers—human rights experts, paid NGO employees—tended to think that, for example, some members of the African Latvian Association were on occasion homophobic or at least reluctant to form solidarities with the mainly white middle-class LGBT rights activists in Latvia. They also suspected Jewish community representatives of being intolerant toward other "communities of belief," such as Hare Krishnas, and thought that Russian minority rights activists were on occasion both racist and homophobic. Interestingly, LGBT activists often emerged as the most tolerant and thus the most liberal of minorities measured by their professed willingness to form solidarities with other minority subjects in the struggle to obtain state-based recognition and protection. In turn, tolerance toward LGBT people was often marked as the key indicator of democracy (Fassin 2010; Puar 2011, 2007). As one activist and researcher told me, "Democracy in Latvia is not fairing much better than sexual minorities." And yet, there were occasions when LGBT activists too did not seem to be able to hold a straight liberal line, succumbing to exclusionary interpretations of the nation. For example, LGBT activists' interventions occasionally appealed specifically to the Latvian nation. "We were there too," read the caption of a postcard LGBT activists designed to advertise the 2007 LGBT Friendship Days. On the black-and-white postcard depicting the mass choir of the Latvian Song and Dance Festival—an important cultural event for the cultural nation of Latvians—some figures were marked in rainbow colors. The postcard worked on a number of registers: it suggested that, save for their sexual orientation, gays and lesbians are indistinguishable from the Latvian nation, and it suggested that gays and lesbians are an integral part of the culturally defined people.

Consequently, it was only those who were neither nationalists nor could themselves be objects of intolerance—and thus could not be linked with "single issue" tolerance politics—that emerged as proper subjects of tolerance and inhabited the subject position of the unmarked liberal subject able to establish equivalence between politically recognized categories of difference, as well as exhibit consistency in professing tolerance toward them. As Signe, the director of the Latvian NGO explained to me: "A person who is intolerant towards a particular religious group, is also likely to be racist or xenophobic." Ensuring the opposite consistency, that is, tolerance as a virtue across contexts of difference, meant that some of the tolerance workers themselves—mainly those that identified as minorities—became objects of the critical gaze of the proper tolerant subject, as the case of Laila illustrates.

When we talked in her office, Laila jokingly described herself as a "conference squirrel" (*konferenču vāvere*). There were so many conferences to attend in her capacity as a representative of the Jewish community and a member of the Consultative Council of the National Program for the Promotion of Tolerance that she suggested the conference organizers should pay her, that it was almost a job for her. In her role as a tolerance worker, Laila spent a lot of time addressing a particularly contentious issue, namely, convincing the Latvian public that the Jewish community should be referred to by the term *ebreji* (Hebrews or Jews) rather than *žīdi* (Yids) (see chapter 5). Laila knew very well how Latvia's contemporary Jewish community—mostly hailing from the former Soviet territories, as the pre–World War II Latvian Jewish population no longer existed—perceived the word *žīds*, as well as was familiar with the Latvians' insistence that the word does not mean anything bad in the Latvian language, that the pre–World War II Jewish community used it to refer to themselves, and that therefore its negative connotations come from the Russian language where the word *zhid* was derogatory. However, Laila worked to convince the public that it was worth taking into account what the Jewish community wanted rather than continue insisting on the historical innocence of the word *žīds*, as many Latvians did.

Laila's work addressed issues that were of great importance to the transnational network of tolerance workers. At the same time, Laila readily admitted that she did not understand and even despised the conduct that was expected of her in the international conferences she attended as part of her tolerance work. She chuckled as she recalled a conference where the organizers had called her *uz tepiķa* (literally, on the carpet—an expression used to suggest that one was reprimanded by authority), because she had been "intolerant towards people of another skin color." She explained that during a roundtable discussion some ten people were each given five minutes to say why they were attending the conference. When an "African man from St. Petersburg" had been, as she put it, "lecturing on the history of blacks in Africa" for much longer than the allotted time, she had suggested that he should not lecture now, because otherwise there will be no time for other presentations. According to Laila, this had been the basis for the accusation of racism she later received. She recounted another conference where she was deemed intolerant because she had referred to Latvian Roma as *čigāni*, or gypsies, "because that is how they call themselves," she explained (see chapter 5). Laila thought such an accusation was outrageous, especially coming from "someone in Luxembourg who had no understanding of the Latvian situation." Even though her own work had to do precisely with what language to use to refer to a particular group, Laila did not think of the Jewish and Roma cases as equivalent, mostly because for historical reasons Latvian Roma themselves used the word *čigāni*, whereas the contemporary Jewish community vehemently objected to the word *žīdi*. Laila claimed that "someone from Luxembourg" did not understand the Latvian situation and thus was mistaken when they measured her discourse by standards that established equivalences between categories of difference across time and space. Her rhetoric resembled that of the Latvian politicians and public when they claimed that the West did not understand Latvian history and thus was viewed as yet another instance of "denying the problem" and therefore part of the problem itself. From the perspective of the transnational network of tolerance workers, Laila did not possess valuable local knowledge, but rather exhibited a partial understanding of the liberal politics of tolerance—partial, because, on the one hand, she worked to promote tolerance toward the Jewish community, but on the other hand, seemingly failed to extend her efforts across what liberal tolerance workers thought were equivalent contexts of difference.

Laila found herself disciplined and though she said, "I learned," she also swore that she will no longer go to conferences where "nobody says anything to you in a conversation, because they are afraid to say something wrong. It is those people, the carriers of tolerance from Europe, who are most afraid to say anything." Laila was particularly upset that the conference delegates had not engaged in a conversation with her, but had rather policed her conduct through silence and subsequent disciplining behind closed doors. The silent tolerant subject of international conferences emerged as a disapproving and disciplining subject, as well as a subject that removed itself from a potentially contentious or uncomfortable conversation, whereas Laila depicted herself and other minority subjects in Latvia as individuals willing to engage in a conversation about themselves and their partial understandings.

Whether Laila accurately recounted the reasons she was called *uz tepiķa* and how that took place I cannot know. I also cannot know to what extent Laila's personality played a role in the encounters she described. She did, after all, have quite a flamboyant presence and took pride in saying things that other people may have kept to themselves. However, her reflections do point to the emergence of a hegemonic mode of conduct in international circles of tolerance promotion, conduct that I too experienced in my encounters with tolerance workers. For example, during my first meeting with Daniel, a civil servant working on the implementation of the National Program for the Promotion of Tolerance, he told me about a seminar he had recently organized for schoolteachers with the aim to educate them about the problem of intolerance. During the seminar, Daniel had illustrated what he thought racial intolerance looked like by presenting the teachers with quotes of negative public statements about potential African or Asian migrants who might arrive in Latvia following Latvia's accession to the European

Union. The months leading up to Latvia's accession to the European Union in 2004 had provided ample material to draw on as a variety of accession opponents tried to convince the public that one look at London or other European metropoles struggling with diversity should be enough to cool down the desire to join. For Daniel, these statements were a clear indication of the magnitude of the problem of intolerance. Daniel reported that the teachers had been puzzled that Daniel asked them to reflect on racism, given that there were not many racially marked others in Latvian public space that could become objects of racism, and so they did not take the statements as a cause for concern. Daniel argued that the racialized and racist discourses were nevertheless problematic, because Latvia was not going to remain homogenous for long and that, in any case, such statements signaled attitudes that were not appropriate for citizens of Europe.

"And then," Daniel continued, "a teacher came up to me and said: 'If we, Latvians and Russians, cannot get along as it is, what are we going to do when *all those blacks* start coming?'" After reciting the statement with emphasis on the words "all those blacks," Daniel fell silent and looked at me meaningfully. I, too, was silent. I think I shook my head in agreement or as a mark of attention, but was not exactly sure how to react. I wondered whether Daniel was concerned with the sudden unity between Russians and Latvians against "all those blacks," the designation "all those blacks," the anti-immigrant sentiment, or all of the above. I felt interpellated as someone who should clearly understand that, on the one hand, this statement was outrageous, and that, on the other hand, it marked our—Daniel's and mine—difference in relation to those who uttered it (Althusser 2001). The silence that followed Daniel's recounting of the scene of intolerance worked as a validating technique in the formation of understanding. On the one hand, it conjured up the unmarked, knowing, and properly tolerant subject. On the other hand, it contributed to the formation of tolerance workers as a community of understanding by way of inviting me to join it.

The circulation of similar statements as examples of intolerance was common among tolerance workers. Signe, the human rights activist introduced earlier, pointed out that however difficult the work was, there was a certain advantage to the widespread intolerance in Latvia: "The advantage that we have is that when you get access to people [politicians, for example], they say incredible things; they are not used to being monitored and they don't recognize that they are making problematic statements." This unbridled intolerance—of politicians, teachers, and even minority subjects—provided the necessary data to validate knowledge about the problem of intolerance within the network of tolerance workers. Further work required that people beyond the network of tolerance workers also recognize its existence. And it is here that diagnosis emerged as an important tool of knowledge production. As put by Elena, an academic and a member of the

Consultative Council, "Intelligent people understood that there is a problem in Latvia." "For the rest," she continued, "it is necessary to diagnose the situation. . . . what do we have and what do we need? Society really needs reflection and diagnosis." Nevertheless, even as diagnosis slowly became institutionalized in policy research, the interplay between reflection and diagnostic knowledge production that occurred while tolerance workers were still grappling with the question of why other people did not recognize the problem of intolerance, provides some useful insights. Tolerance workers were right, there was indeed a problem. However, they too quickly localized this problem as a problem of attitudes and as a cultural and psychological ailment of the Latvian society, thus overlooking its enduring transnational and structural qualities (Goldberg 2009).

Diagnosing Attitudes

A meeting of the Consultative Council of the National Program for the Promotion of Tolerance in October 2005 began with a discussion on what more could be done to incite public recognition of the problem of intolerance. For that, members of the public needed to have experiences that would corroborate the existence of the problem. One member of the Consultative Council suggested hiring a camera operator and a journalist or a social scientist to accompany a member of the African Latvian Association on their daily routine and to film and record the kind of reactions and gestures the person received on city streets. In her suggestion, the filming and broadcasting of acts of intolerance would amount to a useful pedagogical exercise through which the public could finally see how dark-skinned persons were treated on the streets of Riga and thus recognize the problem of intolerance. This project never materialized because the rest of the group thought it was too vague and that public shaming of concrete individuals was too risky. Another tolerance worker, a woman working for a large nonprofit foundation, considered conducting an experimental project where a group of people would be exposed to literature, film, and arranged meetings with the "other," while keeping a diary on what, if anything, triggered changes in the way they thought about that person, group, or about themselves in relation to difference more generally. She wanted to find out what kind of situations were able to create *critical insight* that could, in turn, produce a shift in understanding.

Elena, who was an academic and also a member of the Consultative Council, had conducted a small experimental project with her students. In preparation for the annual tolerance day in 2004, Elena asked her students to interview people on the street about tolerance. Elena explained that the purpose of student research was to find out "whether we are really so intolerant that we need a special program." Elena reflected on this project during the Consultative Council meeting and offered insights about what prevents people from recognizing the problem of intolerance. The conclusion Elena and the students had reached was that people did not have negative reactions to tolerance as such, but rather toward the fact that they were asked to think about problems that were not directly related to their everyday life. Elena explained: "Intolerance resides within people, they are not ready to hear others, listen to others, talk with people who think differently, hear people who right now have problems different than theirs." "What are you talking about? My pension is so small!" she provided as an example of the prevalent disposition, which referred to the problem of the below poverty-level pensions that many elderly Latvia's residents received. "Society is not ready for dialogue," she continued.

> Society is not ready not only to accept another position, but to hear and realize that people have different problems. The general disposition is that if this does not pertain to me, I do not want to think about it. Students thus discovered that people simply do not hear [sic] the problem and thus the program may not have positive results. We need to think about technologies. Perhaps we need to implement some activity to bring attention to the problem of intolerance, a social mirror of sorts where we show people their reactions, where we, for example, provoke reactions towards gypsies. We need to record people's faces—can they recognize themselves? Can they see their aggressiveness?

All of these suggestions supported Signe's observation that "our biggest problem is the inability to recognize the problem." Subsequently they located the inability to recognize the problem of intolerance—and intolerance itself—within individuals and assumed that the corrective could consist of "seeing oneself in the mirror" or of critical reflection on oneself. Since most of Latvia's residents did not encounter potential objects of intolerance on a daily basis and thus, in the view of tolerance workers, did not have the possibility to reflect on themselves through these encounters, the tolerance workers thought people needed to be provoked, confronted, and observed. The project of tolerance promotion, therefore, was a project of remaking sensibilities, attitudes, and conduct, which were thought to be lacking either because people had not had enough exposure to difference; were socialized in corrupt settings, such as the Soviet past; or could not rise above the socioeconomic difficulties that affected their daily life. The tolerance promotion project focused on what it saw as problematic attitudes or lack of critical thinking in the present and used textbook explanations and the postsocialist transition narrative to make sense of them. Consider this narrative of the staff member of the Special Tasks Secretariat for the Promotion of Integration of

Society, who was introduced already in chapter 2 as a former Soviet person who discovered the importance of nationality through her Jewish husband:

> If we opened [Soviet] textbooks, they would all have texts about "people's friendship," "kalmik tjebe brat" (Kalmyk is your brother). I will say that xenophobia has existed forever, but it was hidden, and could not be publicly expressed. It was silenced. And the fact that everyday xenophobia is increasing every year concerns me greatly. People have difficult times socioeconomically and they look for someone to blame. Fifteen years are nothing, and we cannot expect that we will get developed democracy in such a time and transformation of society. That is naïve. In difficult times, phobias flourish. People need to find an enemy. It happens now as well. I try to read research on questions of tolerance, and they frighten me. People start hating those who do not yet live here—Chinese, Muslims, blacks.

Her narrative exhibits nearly all of the elements of the post-Soviet knowledge production apparatus that I have outlined so far and that the reader may recognize as a series of established certainties that underlie political and policy discourses. First, it harks back to the Soviet period and the obfuscation of negative attitudes toward difference. It then moves on to argue that now, in the post-Soviet present, the veil of silence has been lifted and xenophobia that has existed forever is exacerbated due to the difficult socioeconomic situation, which causes people to blame the other. Moreover, this inability to cope with socioeconomic difficulties other than through xenophobic scapegoating is a sign of backwardness that democratization should overcome. The fact that "people start hating those who do not even live here yet" is only an indication of the severity of the socioeconomic challenges that post-Soviet transformations present, as well as of the serious challenges for democratic development. What is especially noteworthy in her commentary is that "xenophobia has existed forever." The explanations she deploys—scapegoating and backlash in conditions of socioeconomic difficulties—do not say anything about how it is that xenophobia has existed forever and continues to exist today.[16] Rather it naturalizes it as a human condition that needs to be addressed through civilizational development, that is, through democratization.

As tolerance workers grappled with the refusal or inability of "regular individuals on the street" to "hear about the problems of others," they also institutionalized knowledge production about the problem of intolerance through surveys and policy research reports. In other words, they moved back and forth between trying to come up with ways of getting the intolerant public to recognize its failures and diagnosing the extent of the problem in society. With regard to the latter, they relied on tools provided by European monitoring institutions and transnational activist networks. Over the years, tolerance workers commissioned quite a few surveys and questionnaires to research the problem of intolerance (Austers 2007; Austers et al. 2007; BSZI 2004; Golubeva 2005, 2007; Kruks and Šulmane 2005; Krūmiņa-Koņkova and Tēraudkalns 2007; Makarovs 2006, 2007; Osis and Ose 2006). The research methodology used drew heavily on established European policy research traditions. For example, political scientist and historian Marija Golubeva (e.g., 2005) frequently used Teo van Dijk's popular discourse analysis tools to identify intolerance and racism in public discourse. Using this method, racism could be diagnosed by identifying a number of discursive strategies, such as sentences that began with the phrase "I am not a racist, but . . ." and others (Golubeva 2005, van Dijk 2002). Another political scientist and tolerance activist Viktor Makarov adapted the method of measuring the temperature of society with regard to attitudes toward sexual minorities. The "temperature survey" established a degree scale from 0 to 100 (with 0 being the most negative and 100 the most positive) and asked respondents to choose a number on that scale to express their "evaluation of homosexual people" (Makarovs 2006). The conclusion was that the "average temperature" with regard to homosexual people was 30.15, which was thought to be fairly negative. The purpose of the survey was to get the public to "realize and recognize" the situation "in order to take the necessary steps towards a democratic dialogue and tolerance" (Makarovs 2006).

Makarov's report is explicit about aiming to measure the extent of intolerance as a social and political phenomenon without dwelling on the reasons for various attitudes and connections between them. In other words, the survey is not concerned with how understandings are formed, but focuses instead on expressions of already formed opinions. In that sense, the survey "put a certain version of liberalism into practice," insofar as it focused on individuals' supposedly already formed opinions without paying attention to the context of formation of such an understanding, which would have included the survey situation itself (Glaeser 2009, 397).[17] It did, however, allow for changes in public mood, insofar as it was conducted for at least two years in a row precisely with the aim to see whether any progress had been made with regard to rooting tolerance as a public and political virtue.

Yet another survey, carried out by the public policy center Providus in 2007, aimed to measure levels of intolerance among teachers (Austers et al. 2007). The authors used popular social psychology tools, such as "social dominance orientation" and "right-wing authoritarianism scale" to diagnose the teachers. Whereas "social dominance orientation" measures the extent to which individuals support the hierarchical organization of society with their particular group at the top of the hierarchy, the "right-wing authoritarianism scale" measures such character traits as conventionalism, authoritarian aggressiveness, and submission to authority (Austers et al. 2007, 3). As described in the report, ideal-type "right-wing authoritarians" are uncritical, exclusionist, hateful toward other groups, cowardly, dogmatic, and more. This particular diagnostic exercise rendered intolerance a pathological trait of a particular kind of personality—the nonliberal authoritarian personality. The teachers in the aforementioned survey came out as higher than average authoritarians, and the authors suggested that they probably did not differ in that regard from the rest of society (Austers 2007). The formation of the authoritarian personality in Latvia was traced to both Soviet years and the pre-Soviet independence period, especially the late 1930s when the state was governed by the authoritarian president Kārlis Ulmanis (Matīsa 2007).

These institutionalized antiracism and tolerance promotion initiatives were entangled with the more general remaking of knowledge and understanding that was taking place as part of postsocialist transformations. They became complicit with reproducing ignorance about the present while at the same time producing knowledge about the distance from the imagined democratic future. They drew on the resources of the newly established sociological institutions or policy research centers that were increasingly well-prepared to produce comparative data with the help of standardized methods and interpretive frames. While such surveys may have produced internationally comparable data between states and nationally comparable data between ethnic groups, they did little to probe into the specific articulations of race, racism, and racialization. As lamented by Robert, an active member of the African Latvian Association, "All these surveys tell you is that people do not want to live next door to this or that person, but they don't tell you why." Roberts was not the only one who felt unsatisfied with surveys while at the same time continuing to use them. Signe also invoked this and similar surveys in public seminars to illustrate that people in Latvia "have very negative attitudes towards Africans and Chinese, and do not even want to let Muslims into the country." Yet on a different occasion she told me in a conversation that she does not think this research is any good and does not, in fact, tell anything. And yet, she and others continued to use it.

This critique of knowledge production about racism and intolerance in postsocialist Latvia is not meant to suggest that there was no genuine interest among tolerance workers to understand racism or that there was no racism in Latvia, but rather that the knowledge produced about racism and intolerance in Latvia within the framework of institutionalized political liberalism drew on standardized theories and methods that may have produced comparable data, but that did not further understanding of the postsocialist politics of difference. In his analysis of Stasi knowledge practices in late socialist East Germany, Andreas

Glaeser (2009) identifies a paradox with regard to socialism and knowledge that may be relevant for thinking about knowledge in the context of actually existing post–Cold War liberalism in Latvia: individuals living within socialism, from party officials to laypersons, had insight with regard to the malfunctioning of socialist modalities of organizing life. Some of the best critiques were produced from within the system. However, this insight could not penetrate institutional settings: "The institutional arrangements making up the party state systematically undercut both the deepening of locally produced knowledge and its systematic integration into an overarching analysis of socialism within a larger social world" (Glaeser 2009, xvi). Glaeser's analysis pertains to late socialism but could well be applied to actually existing post–Cold War liberalism insofar as tolerance workers were caught in self-reproducing circuits of knowledge production that reiterated the core understandings at the foundation of the institutions they had established. Critique of these institutions and institutionalized understandings of racism and intolerance was diffused by depicting it as part of the problem that the institutions were meant to address. As Signe said, "Our biggest problem is the inability to recognize the problem."

Lessons for Liberalism?

The confidence of political liberalism that history had indeed ended with the collapse of the Soviet Union created conditions for the emergence of closed circuits of knowledge production that hindered, if not foreclosed, formation of critical insight about postsocialist power configurations. The need to catch up with Europe came to structure all spheres of life, including tolerance work, which was embedded in the logic of overcoming survivals of a known past or problematic present—for example, socialism or nationalism—in order to arrive into an equally known future, that is, liberalism. The need to report to European monitoring institutions, as well as to legitimate policy interventions through research, led to the prevalence of a *diagnostic mode of knowledge production* in public and political life. Rather than generating understanding of whether and how post–Cold War power configurations shaped and reshaped institutionalized and vernacular forms of racism and racialization, diagnostic knowledge practices measured how particular people and places fared in relation to an already defined problem. Similarly, diagnostic knowledge practices aimed to measure the extent of civil society in Latvia rather than generate in-depth understanding of associational activity in concrete places. Or, diagnostic knowledge practices aimed to measure the extent of economic activity in the Latvian countryside rather than generate an in-depth understanding of how people craft their lives in uncertain economic conditions. Diagnostic modes of knowledge production assume prior knowledge of the disease. Whether HIV or a sovereign debt crisis, the disease is already known; it does not have to be explained. The description of symptoms alone is supposed to elicit its recognition on the part of those who are versed in the political and social maladies that haunt society. As in Latvia amongst tolerance workers, the logic of diagnosis is irrelevant, for those who share understandings *know*—implicitly—the link between the symptoms and the disease. Tolerance workers, who knew that there was a problem of intolerance in Latvian society and that their task was to diagnose it, engaged in circulating stories and reiterating statements as both symptoms of the problem of intolerance and as a problem in and of itself. The closed circuit of knowledge production that emerged in the process of reiteration led to a situation whereby tolerance workers did not push for a deeper understanding of the postsocialist politics of difference.

The knowledge practices of tolerance workers standardized discourses on tolerance and contributed to the formation of conditions similar to those of late socialism described by Alexei Yurchak, whereby "it became increasingly more important to participate in the reproduction of the *form* of these ritualized acts of authoritative discourse than to engage with their constative meanings" (2005, 25). In the book in which he elaborates the argument, Yurchak (2005) analyzes how these conditions enabled the formation of various alternative spaces where life unfolded in full view of the state, but did not concern itself with the state at all—people reproduced the standardized discourse as needed, but went on living, thinking, arguing, and hoping in the interstices of the state. However, standardized forms of knowledge and discourse can also produce forms of ignorance that are detrimental to the system. For example, Andreas Glaeser has shown in his meticulously researched work on knowledge practices within the East Germany security forces (Stasi) that the East German Communist Party "aimed at engineering a monolithic intentionality that would bring about socialism as a self-fulfilling prophecy" (2009, xv). The institutionalization of this "monolithic ideology" meant that everyone's daily choices had to be made in line with more general determinations, which prevented secret police officers from allowing the contradictions that they were observing at the street level to be absorbed by the system. Glaeser uses the case of East German socialism to point out the risks associated with self-referential circuits of knowledge production, whether socialist or otherwise.

At the time of writing this book, it seems that political liberalism is in crisis (Boyer 2016, Krastev 2007; also see Epilogue). In the least, there is a significant disjuncture between institutionalized forms of political liberalism and the politics of significant numbers of "ordinary people" who are increasingly voting for illiberal forces across Western and Eastern Europe, as well as in the United States.

My analysis in this chapter suggests that the crisis of liberalism might also be a crisis of understanding insofar as knowledge practices that proliferated in the context of actually existing post–Cold War political liberalism failed to produce insights about post–Cold War power configurations and their effects on a significant numbers of lives. Western liberals seem to agree that the crisis of liberalism is also a crisis of knowledge, but on different grounds. For example, the current historical moment is widely characterized as a moment of "post-truth" or "post-factual" politics, whereby "populist" political actors deny the validity of expert knowledge and govern through confusion. However, this overlooks the fact that it was the knowledge practices of the actually existing forms of post–Cold War political liberalism that may have contributed to the crisis as much, if not more, than populist politics.

BUILDING UP AND TEARING DOWN
Critical Thinking in the Context of
Tolerance Promotion

Tolerance workers, who thought that the biggest problem Latvian society faced with regard to tolerance was its inability to recognize the problem of intolerance (see chapter 3), attributed this problem to widespread lack of critical thinking and general reluctance to engage in critical public reflection. They tended to think of Latvia's residents as a collectively thinking public that needed to be remade into a public of educated liberal citizens prepared and willing to engage in critical public reflection about their past, present, and future, especially with regard to their relations with others. The public's unenlightened condition was frequently attributed to the influence of overlapping and therefore particularly toxic effects of two dogmatic state-supported systems of thought—the Soviet one and the nationalist one. Both were thought to instill and cultivate collectivist loyalties in lieu of individual reflection, and the Soviet state in particular was thought to have hindered people's ability to engage in critical thought, because its education system focused on memorization rather than independent thought (e.g., Burkhalter and Shegebayev 2012; see Reeves 2005 for critique). Insofar as the tolerance workers thought that the Latvian public exhibited traces of such thinking, they deemed it stuck in an immature stage on the developmental scale leading toward a mature and civilized public sphere.

For example, in their analysis of intolerant speech (see chapter 5), communications scholars Sergejs Kruks and Ilze Šulmane (2005) analyzed the culture of public discourse in Latvia and, drawing on Douglas Walton's work, argued that it resembles "quarrel dialogue" where people do not engage each other's arguments, but attack each other's personas. Kruks and Šulmane observed that the "quarrel dialogue" was an especially dominant form of public engagement with regard to Latvian-Russian relations. The main aim of participants was to cultivate in-group solidarity, and no one was prepared to change their position even when confronted with reasonable arguments (Kruks and Šulmane 2005, 66). Kruks and Šulmane juxtaposed this "quarrel dialogue" with "critical discussion," where multiple viewpoints are considered and attempts are made to resolve conflicts between them. While Kruks and Šulmane recognized the value of emotions in arguments, as well as the need to establish identifications, they considered this to be an initial stage of acquainting the opponent with the deep structure of one's worldview, following which the encounter should move onward to a more mature stage where critical discussion is possible. Latvian and Russian-speaking publics, they thought, were stuck in the early stage of identity affirmation, unable to reach the stage of public reason.

In the previous chapter, I introduced the argument that the self-referential and circular knowledge practices of tolerance workers prevented formation of critical insights about postsocialist power configurations. This chapter delves deeper into considering how that came to be by examining how discourses about critical thinking and critical public reflection became part of the civilizational project of tolerance promotion and the standardized repertoire of actually exist-ing post–Cold War political liberalism. With this civilizational project, the liberal mode of critical thinking was evacuated from critical thinking as understood by postsocialist subjects. For example, while rarely anybody in Latvia denied the value of critical thinking, people had considerably different understandings of where and how it manifested, who was engaged in critical thinking, and who was simply adhering to a dominant ideology.[1] People also had different under-standings of what, if anything, critical thinking was supposed to lead to. Toler-ance workers thought that critical thinking—as rational evaluation of multiple points of view and arguments—should help individuals overcome their natural, if backward, fear of the strange that, they thought, fueled intolerance. They also thought that critical thinking would help individuals see through the narrow frame of nationalist ideology and rework their closed and negative sensibilities and dispositions into more open and tolerant ones. To put it another way, from the perspective of tolerance workers, critical thinking was the tool with which to dismantle the limitations that collectivist ideologies, such as nationalism or socialism, placed on people's sense of self and their understanding of the world. It was, after all, the end of history, and critical thinking could not but lead one to embrace the victorious ideology.

Those who disagreed with the tolerance workers claimed that it was they who were engaged in critical thinking insofar as they critically appraised the uneven field of power relations within which Latvia's citizens and residents operated. Tolerance skeptics claimed that they recognized the power dynamics involved in attempts to institutionalize political liberalism, including its tolerance promotion dimension. The way they saw it, tolerance workers advocated replacement of one ideological system with another, and the new system required as much critical distancing as the old one. But it is also precisely because of the particular ways in which the field of power relations was reconfigured after socialism that asserting such critical distance from institutionalized forms of political liberalism risked landing one in the camp of one of the other two competing ideologies—that is, socialism or nationalism—and therefore in the category of the uncritically thinking (Zarycki 2014). In the process, critical thinking became institutionalized as liberalism's civilizational project. It did not have—and perhaps could not have— a place of its own outside the frame of the three competing ideologies.

As I proceed with the discussion of the role of imaginaries about and practices of critical thinking in tolerance work, I find it important to distinguish between public reason, understood as the most advanced form of public engagement based on rational dialogue, from forms of public engagement that I will refer to as embedded reason. Public reason is a normative liberal mode of reasoning that citizens in pluralistic democracies are expected to engage in by justifying their preformulated positions with arguments that are generally acceptable to others (Button 2005, Rawls 1997). According to theorists of public reason, the main foes of public reason are arguments embedded in substantive traditions—for example, religion—that those who do not belong to these substantive traditions cannot accept. As Mark Button has pointed out, it is not that public reason bars arguments supported by substantive traditions. Rather, it demands that such arguments also have to be acceptable to others, as well as defensible by other means, thus effectively rendering the substantive tradition redundant. Public reason is both a discursive requirement of liberal citizenship and "a way of being in which citizens are to understand themselves and to relate to one another" (Button 2005, 263). It allows only those elements of substantive traditions that conform with universal principles of liberal public reason. In that sense, public reason itself might be deemed to be a substantive tradition that obscures its substance by claiming to be procedural—an accusation directed at liberalism often enough.

Embedded reason, in turn, does not leave incompatible elements of substantive traditions outside the conversation, but draws on them as recognizably different resources in the process of constructing arguments and speaking to subjects and their publics (e.g., Bowen 2003, 2005; Larson 2013).[2] Moreover, embedded reason is not limited to rational discourse, but can include affect, which theories of public reason wish to leave aside. Embedded reason, then, is a historically, culturally, and socially embedded way of public engagement, of constituting and arguing about consequential issues, including about what is and what is not an acceptable mode of reasoning.

This distinction between public reason and embedded reason is nicely supported by Mark Button's (2005) reading of Hannah Arendt's work on "spaces of appearance" and political action. Contrary to the Rawlsian demand to leave substantive traditions aside when exercising public reason, Hannah Arendt argues that one's self—formed through substantive traditions—cannot be left behind when appearing to others in public space. Arendt argues that public discourse is a way of self-disclosing and self-constituting through public reasoning. This, Button suggests, is what for Arendt amounts to politics—self-disclosure in conversation with others. Disclosure is at once a constitution of the self insofar as the self appears in its humanity and individuality only through conversation with another. In Arendt's own words, "In acting and speaking, men show who they are, reveal actively their unique personal identities and thus make their appearance in the human world" (in Button 2005, 265). In that sense, the substantive tradition that shapes the self also appears through conversations with another, which makes it hard to know what to leave behind in public encounters, as liberal public reason demands. Moreover, how could respect—as "a regard for the person from [the] distance that the space of the world puts between us" (Arendt in Button 2005, 274)—arise between people who withhold such important things about them as "their faith, their conception of the good, their sense of values and the source of these values" (Button 2005, 274)? Thus, whereas liberals assume that opinions are formed and shaped through tradition, Arendt suggests that they are constituted through discourse. Thoughts are formed through critical publicity, which itself changes from one context to another.

This is to say that appearing in public space as a subject shaped by a collectivist tradition of thought does not preclude critical publicity. Thus, instead of judging the presence or absence of critical thought on the basis of liberal conceptions of public reason, it might be useful to consider different historical instances of critical publicity and the types of critical thinking they enable or foreclose. In the following sections, I suggest that the assumption that there was no critical thinking or critical publicity during the socialist period is not entirely true, as well as that this assumption makes for a narrow understanding of critical thinking in the present. To the extent that tolerance workers and other liberal educators subscribed to the view that there was no critical thinking under socialism, they overlooked the multiplicity and heterogeneity of critical practices of former socialist subjects and obfuscated the historical specificity and ideological underpinnings of their own discourses of "critical thinking" as the special truth-producing instrument of actually existing political liberalism (Foucault 2003c).

Kritika and Critical Thinking

In the 1990s and throughout the 2000s, a wave of liberalization and democratization programs promoting tolerance, rule of law, civil society, as well as critical thinking, swept across the former socialist world (Creed 2011, Hann and
Dunn 1996, Greenberg 2014, Larson 2013). These efforts were financed by various European Union accession mechanisms, as well as bilateral and multilateral
donors. One of the biggest funders of such initiatives was the Soros Foundation,
established by the financier and philanthropist George Soros, who was taken by
the ideas of Karl Popper while at the London School of Economics and subsequently framed the work of his foundation as the "promotion of open society"
(Burkhalter and Shegebayev 2012, Reeves 2005, Soros 2017). For example, in
1998, the Latvian branch of the Soros Foundation launched a series of projects
focusing on critical thinking in education (IAC 2008). The first project, titled
"Reading and Writing for Development of Critical Thinking," was implemented
by the Education Development Center (Izglītības attīstības centrs), which,
among other things, resulted in a research report titled "The Use of the Critical
Thinking Development Approach in Education: Influence and Effectiveness in
Latvia" (IAC 2008).[3] The report defines critical thinking as a form of reasoning
that entails analysis of alternative viewpoints and a well-argued choice between
them, and juxtaposes it to "traditional dogmatic ways of thinking" that simply
assert inherited values and arguments (IAC 2008, 5).

Neither this report nor other critical thinking promotion initiatives across
the former socialist world spent much time proving that postsocialist subjects did not exhibit patterns of thought that could be understood as critical
thinking. Rather, the failure or reluctance to take up forms of liberal public
discourse, as well as themes prevalent in European public sphere, was taken
to be sufficient proof that critical thinking was indeed lacking from the former socialist subjects' repertoires. Such lack was routinely linked with socialist
legacy. For example, in an article on critical thinking and the education system
in Kazakhstan, Nancy Burkhalter and Maganat R. Shegebayev ask: "Can a culture that discourages teacher dissent learn to criticize authority? Can a system
that promotes homogeneity of thought evolve into one that encourages independent thinking? Can teachers who once suffered under a harsh top-down,
authoritarian system learn to collaborate and support one another to teach
reasoned conclusions and in turn teach their students to do the same?" (2012,
58). Yet, it is not necessarily clear that the new pedagogies of critical thinking
promoted by liberal educators in the former socialist world produced superior forms of thought and public reflection. For example, in her analysis of
the education reform in Kyrgyzstan, which also included training teachers in

critical thinking skills, Madeleine Reeves (2005) shows how the teachers criticized conduct that they associated with the form of thought they were now asked to embrace. Reeves describes how her interlocutors criticized postsocialist critical thinking projects as resulting in straightforward—and sometimes unfounded—criticism of authority rather than "sustained, informed analysis" (2005, 14). In other words, if the socialist system protected authority from criticism, some liberalization projects seemed to have simply inverted this relationship by encouraging relentless criticism of authority—and of self—as expression of critical thinking. In both cases, it seems, critical thought remained in the shadows of criticism.

Reeves suggests that understanding the socialist practice of *kritika* is important for understanding how people in the former socialist world perceived the new paradigm of "critical thinking." Reeves suggests that in the Soviet era, kritika had "less to do with exploring disagreement on the basis of plurality of opinion, than [with] exposing positions that were 'officially' (and hence 'objectively') incorrect. The kritika that you give is not expected to be perspectival—i.e. taken to be wrong, inconsistent, logically flawed or problematic 'from my point of view'—but rather wrong 'in and of itself'" (2005, 14; see also Larson 2013). Reeves further describes the legacies of kritika for interpreting state-based efforts to promote critical thinking in postsocialist Kyrgyzstan: "For the legacy of such a conception is that criticism is seen as having only a tenuous relationship to the pursuit of truth, having much more to do with attacking views that are 'politically incorrect' according to the priorities of the day, celebrating 'opinion for opinion's sake,' and riding roughshod over previous scholarly findings, than with informed, engaged and scholarly analysis" (2005, 14).

Kritika, then, was a truth-producing instrument of the Soviet socialist state. During Stalin's rule, kritika in the form of self-criticism was also a tool for working on oneself that could lead to purges (Fitzpatrick 1999, Kharkhordin 1999; see also Larson 2013). However, if one understands critical thinking as rational argumentation in the public arena, then the Soviet Union was also a modern, industrialized state that relied on professional expertise and scientific accomplishments brought about via scholarly debates in formal environments. The most widely cited quotation from Stalin's 1950 article on linguistics was: "It is generally recognized that no science can develop and flourish without a battle of opinions, without freedom of criticism" (Stalin 1950).[4] As in other public matters, Stalin was understood to be the final arbiter of such debates (Yurchak 2005). After his death, political discourse became standardized (Yurchak 2005), whereas the party rarely interfered in specific arguments in particular scientific fields, even as it policed their boundaries. Thus, for example, in the 1980s, despite adhering to the Marxist-Leninist frame, Latvian sociology could develop as a theoretical discipline—a feature that it lost with the onset of postsocialist transition and the need to survive in market conditions (Tisenkopfs 2010, see chapter 3).

Moreover, there was thinking, learning, and arguing that took place in socialist kitchens, basements, *pulciņi* or *kruzhki* (activity clubs), and more. In his analysis of the last Soviet generation in urban Russia, Alexei Yurchak describes such practices as "living *vnye*," that is, as deterritorialized milieus where people lived simultaneously inside and outside the system and, moreover, without much concern for it (2005, 128). It is within these deterritorialized milieus that people read, argued, learned, and discussed. Yurchak describes a literary club attached to the Leningrad Palace of Pioneers where his interlocutors—the last Soviet generation—met to read, discuss, and question Soviet aesthetic canons of literature (2005, 113). Importantly, Yurchak notes, critique was possible provided that the arguments were serious (2005, 135). Other "deterritorialized milieus" included an archeological club whose members went on expeditions, made friends, and argued; boiler rooms where officially and unofficially educated intellectuals sought jobs to give themselves time and space for reading; and cafés, such as Café Saigon, where regulars circulated forbidden or hard to get literature (2005, 139). Yurchak's interlocutors describe the socializing (*obschenie*) that occurred in these places as follows: "We talked about aesthetics, about Tolstoy and Pushkin, about poetry, about Brodsky. . . . We talked a lot, we just talked a lot. We walked around the city and talked about architectural styles, about modernism. We walked around courtyards, climbed around rooftops, and we discussed everything" (Yurchak 2005, 136; see also Larson 2013).

Similarly, in his book *Spirit and System: Media, Intellectuals, and the Dialectic in the Modern German Culture*, Dominic Boyer (2005) describes conversations with former East German journalists in which they reminisced about their attempts to obtain books, how they navigated the constrained state terrain, how some developed a critical take not only on the socialist state, but also the West. As Boyer describes his many fieldwork conversations: "The discussion of the GDR [German Democratic Republic] past inevitably turns to sorting out one's subjectivity from the exterior forces of party and state that exerted so much effort to produce ideal socialist citizens" (2005, 7). What is particularly striking is the former GDR journalists' reflections about how they were part of the system while also being critical of it, which exhibits a certain awareness of how power and subjectification work and sets them apart from Western journalists who tend to think they are outside the system and speak truth to power. In contrast, Boyer's interlocutors referred to the postsocialist world as equally a system, only a functioning one in comparison to the socialist system of a bygone era (Boyer 2005, 7). For Boyer's interlocutors—former GDR journalists—both systems were simultaneously enabling and constraining, both required critical distancing.[5]

It is striking, then, that the liberal critical thinking promotion initiatives did not consider the multiple and heterogeneous contexts of thinking and arguing that proliferated during the socialist period, instead justifying their conviction that there was no critical thinking under socialism by focusing attention solely on the formal socialist education system. They did also invoke the socialist public sphere where critical publicity was indeed configured differently, insofar as politics, political economy, or anything else covered by Marxism-Leninism, were beyond argument, even as they were also understood to be rational traditions of thought. People living under socialism did argue about these things in private, but their arguments did not translate into public criticism. This does not mean, however, that the socialist subject's cognitive patterns lacked a consideration of multiple perspectives and the formation of one's own opinion (Larson 2013, 183). And yet, in postsocialist contexts, absence of particular forms of critical public reflection—ones that criticize power from within a liberal democratic framework—are taken as indicative of the failure of postsocialist subjects to think critically. Moreover, insofar as postsocialist subjects express reservations about actually existing post–Cold War liberalism, a system that claims not to be a system, rather than critically reflect on themselves, they are thought to be mired in the legacies of the past. Thus, for example, a Latvian parliamentary deputy explained to me that Latvia's residents do not trust the government or experts (as various surveys consistently indicate), because of their Soviet mentality (*padomju mentalitāte*), which propels them to distrust power rather than embrace the new form of governance and become its willing subjects. I am not therefore suggesting that the former socialist subjects are in possession of superior critical thinking skills that position them above and beyond all forms of power. Rather, I am suggesting that, contrary to the assumptions of promoters of liberal critical thinking, socialist subjects were not cogs in the machine who merely reproduced the system. They read, thought, and discussed, and it is precisely through reading that they developed critical relationships to power, especially power that claims not to be power. These critical relationships diverged—if the last Soviet generation in Russia read Pushkin and Solzhenitsyn, the last Soviet generation in Latvia read the pre–World War II nationalist canon and Solzhenitsyn, though they may have read Pushkin as well. Again, this did not posit any of them outside power, but rather positioned them differently in postsocialist fields of power. As I show in the following chapter, many Latvians made their own competing truth claims in relation to the Latvian language as the expression of the spirit of the historical community of Latvians. But it is precisely through considering the truth-claims of Latvian nationalism alongside the truth-claims of European liberalism, both claiming critical power in relation to the other, that it becomes possible to get a fuller picture of postsocialist power configurations, as well as to recognize liberalization initiatives as putting forth competing truth-claims rather than emancipating truth from power.

There was one other aspect of the liberal discourses of critical thinking that was particularly unsettling for post-Soviet Latvians. The demand to overcome one's collective attachments through critical thinking seemed to require dismantling the self, whereas many Latvians thought that the self needed to be built up to compensate for the Soviet past, but also to cultivate coherent and confident selfhood in a globalizing world.[6] If Elena in the previous chapter wondered how much acceptance of difference is possible without losing oneself, others wondered whether continuous public self-criticism and reflection on the problem of intolerance would construe Latvians as fundamentally intolerant and racist. These fears manifested in the responses that tolerance workers received when they tried to get people, especially politicians, to talk about the problem of intolerance (see chapter 3). For the politicians and members of the public who were reluctant to recognize the problem of intolerance, public reflection on the problem of intolerance and racism was a form of tearing down rather than building up. They had a point, insofar as embracing such forms of criticism risked confirming what Europe already knew, namely that Eastern Europeans, including Latvians, were mired in nationalism and socialist legacies, as a result of which their arrival in Europe was perpetually deferred. But they also missed the point, insofar as Europe demanded a degree of self-destruction in order to become fully European. Within the prevailing European political and moral landscape, being European meant continuously and critically reflecting on stains in European history, such as colonialism and fascism, and their legacies in the present, such as racism and intolerance. For Latvia and Latvians, as a place and people in Europe, but "not-quite-European," public reflection on past sins and present blemishes seemed to be a double-edged sword that tended to cut in a way that took away rather than granted Europeanness, whether one engaged in critical public reflection or not.

Eugenics and Europeanness

In 2009, German historian Björn Felder published a work on the Soviet and German occupation of Latvia during World War II (Felder 2009), and soon thereafter turned to a more specific field of study in Latvian history, namely late nineteenth- and early twentieth-century physical anthropology and eugenics. Felder placed special emphasis on analyzing the relationship between physical anthropology, the newly developing field of eugenics, and the efforts to nationalize the state during the authoritarian rule of Kārlis Ulmanis from 1934 until 1940. For example, during that time, the Latvian state financed the work of the Institute for Research of National Vitality (Tautas dzīvā spēka pētīšanas institūts), led by the first Latvian physical anthropologist Jēkabs Prīmanis. In a piece published in 2013, Felders suggests that during the 1930s the Latvian state was a racial state. Felder describes a racial state as "a non-democratic state that defined its population in biological terms and followed eugenics as the main agenda" (2013a, 6, 2013b). He argues that the Latvian state during the rule of Ulmanis was a racial state insofar as "the Ulmanis regime was wedded to a *völkisch* biologised nationalism. Following the racial approach of a national self-image, and propaganda and efforts to 'improve' and homogenize the national body, this regime can be described as a racial state" (Felder 2013b, 126). Throughout the rest of the article Felder asserts that the nationalizing project of the Latvian state was underpinned by notions of racial purity and the belief that "the ruling power and the titular nation should have the power to decide on the biological shape of the nation, as well as on the question of who should have the right to procreate" (2013b, 133). The intention was there, Felder suggests, even though minorities were not particularly targeted either by "negative" or "positive" eugenics efforts. It was mainly the "feeble-minded" and "inferior" elements of the Latvian nation that were targeted by the voluntary sterilization program (Felder 2013b, 131–132). Nevertheless, Felder argues, the strong racial ideology of the Latvian state of the late 1930s lent particular potency to ethno-nationalism and xenophobia.

Felder places Latvian physical anthropology and eugenics within the broader European context (2013b, 136). He notes that it was a Swedish scholar by the name of Gustav Backman who founded physical anthropology in Latvia, partly to extend his own research on the "Nordic race." He also notes that most Baltic scholars of physical anthropology and eugenics were trained in Germany and regularly attended various international scientific congresses where they further developed their thinking (Felder 2013a, 5). While recognizing the transnational features of Latvian physical anthropology and eugenics, Felder nevertheless takes a traditionally comparative approach (also referred to as methodological nationalism, Wimmer and Glick Schiller 2002) by spatially and temporally delineating his object of analysis as Latvian physical anthropology and eugenics of the 1930s. This comparative approach demands that the a priori delineated object of study is positioned in relation to others, identifying similarities and differences between them. Thus Felder suggests that Latvian racial anthropology, "with its focus on race, biology and 'genetic improvement' . . . was far from Sweden's model" (2013b, 136). It was closer to the Nazi regime of racial hygiene, Felder argues, "with the exception that there were no mandatory sterilisations and certainly no euthanasia-killings of the mentally ill" (2013b, 136). To put it another way, Latvian racial anthropology and eugenics fell somewhere in between Sweden and Germany on a scale leading from positive to negative eugenics, from bad to very bad racial anthropology.

Overall, there is little room for nuanced discussion of historical tensions and continuities in Felder's work. For example, Felder does not acknowledge tensions between what he describes as racial conceptions of the nation of the Latvian authoritarian regime and the nonracial, even nonethnic, conceptions of citizenship at the foundation of the Latvian state (see chapter 2). Moreover, there is no consideration of continuities between practices of "racial states," as defined by Felder, and contemporary states that may not have forcefully sterilized certain segments of the population to ensure the well-being of the whole, but that are still concerned with what Michel Foucault (2003b) has termed biopolitics, that is, governing the biological well-being of populations (see also Palsson and Lock 2016). For example, Felder overlooks how contemporary social and biological sciences are connected to the scholarly concerns of those he posits as practitioners of eugenics in interwar Latvia, such as Verners Kraulis and Jēkabs Prīmanis. Verners Kraulis's early works are long elaborations of demographic data, birth rates, deaths, rates of reproduction, migration, and so forth (Kraulis 1939a, 1939b; Kuznecovs 2013). His concerns, while put to work in the name of a nationalizing state, do not substantially differ from the concerns of contemporary demographers, such as Pēteris Zvidriņš (2005), with the life of the nation that is not reproducing at a proper rate.

Most important for the purposes of this chapter, however, Felder not only considers the Latvian state a racial state and himself a pioneer in researching it, but posits most Latvian historians that have written or spoken about the topic— Rita Grāvere, Vita Zelče (2006), Aivars Stranga (2008), Vladmirs Kuznecovs (2013), and Andrievs Ezergailis (1996)—as either actively denying the existence of eugenics in Latvia by not recognizing the link between racial anthropology and eugenics, or making it look better than it was (Felder 2013b, 118). Indeed, Kuznecovs (2013) and Zelče (2006) have both argued that that the Latvian version of eugenics was liberal or positive, namely, that it did not forcefully exterminate and sterilize people, but focused on the cultivation of health and well-being while providing sterilization on a voluntary basis (Kuznecovs 2013, Zelče 2006). Rita Grāvere argues that Latvia was not unique with regard to late nineteenth- and early twentieth-century racial anthropology and eugenics, as well as that Latvia's racial sciences were a product of translocal learning practices as much as homegrown ideologies.[7] On this note, of course, Felder agreed. Neither side had gotten their history wrong. What they did disagree about was how to interpret it, where to place Latvia on the scale of bad to worse racial anthropology and eugenics. They also diverged in their views about the political and ethical implications of arguments that Latvia was a racial state versus arguments that the Latvian version of physical anthropology and eugenics was no better or worse than that of other European states.

These arguments are consequential on two accounts. First, how one sees the relationship between transnational connections and nation-state frames matters for understanding racial science and eugenics in late nineteenth and early twentieth centuries and their legacies in the present. It is analytically and politically consequential whether one begins with interconnections or whether one begins with a nation-state frame (Goldberg 2009).[8] Felder's methodological move to bound his object temporally and spatially meant that he set out to study the somewhat predictable contours of Latvian eugenics and did not necessarily contribute much to deepening historical understanding of the contours of European modernity as a relational formation. But it is also here that his research turns political and the second consequential aspect comes into view: namely, delineating racial anthropology and eugenics as matters of national history that demand national accountability in the present is part and parcel of how the European political and moral landscape is governed today.

Felder's justification for undertaking his study of Latvian physical anthropology and eugenics is that nobody else has done it before.[9] As Felder puts it, "While eugenics and bio-politics in Scandinavia and Central Europe have been studied in depth, it is quite astonishing that the Baltics' biopolitics and eugenics remain outside the broader focus of historians. Such studies would contribute fundamentally to a different evaluation of authoritarian regimes, the social debates, and the social and political implications of eugenics projects during the 1930s" (2013a, 6). But which historians is Felder referring to? And, moreover, what does he mean by suggesting that a study of Baltic biopolitics and eugenics would contribute to a "different evaluation of authoritarian regimes"? Does Felder expect historians in general to develop better scholarly understanding of authoritarian regimes or does he expect Latvian historians and Latvians as a political community to work through their problematic history, as other Europeans have done? In a conversation we had about his experience of researching and talking about eugenics in Latvia, Felder pointed out that Germans had begun the process of working through their problematic history about thirty years ago. Felder also argued that in Latvia critical evaluation of historical knowledge is hindered by the prevalence of the Soviet tradition of positivism, which treats history as a collection of facts (Felder 2013a, 5). In doing so, Felder established a consequential difference between Germans and Latvians. This difference did not necessarily lie in whether and how eugenics and racial science were practiced in the past—there, Felder argued, both were quite similar, even if the Latvian state did not engage in forceful sterilization—but in the fact that Germans have critically reflected on their past (and continue to do so), whereas Latvians have not.

It is not my aim here to adjudicate between Björn Felder and Latvian historians. I wish to suggest, however, that their argument was first and foremost political despite each side accusing the other of politicizing science, while claiming true science for themselves. If Felder considered that Latvian historiography was hindered by a positivist tradition cultivated during the Soviet period, some Latvian historians considered that Felder did not actually understand the science whose history he was trying to write and that he was therefore conducting politics rather than writing a history of science.[10] What they were arguing about was how a properly European people should write and relate to their history, especially those moments in history, such as colonialism, eugenics, and the Holocaust, that are commonly recognized as problematic within the political and moral landscape of Europe. Both Felder and his critics rendered racism and racial thinking as constitutive of European modernity. However, they differed in their views of whether the Latvian version required particular attention in the broader European context. Felder thought that it did because Latvians had not yet come around to critically evaluating their relationship to their authoritarian past and its eugenics projects. At the same time, some of Latvia's historians seemed quite reluctant to embrace Felder's suggestion that they should engage not only in research, but also in critical public reflection on the relationship between eugenics, racial anthropology, and the Latvian state. One historian was particularly concerned about Felder's sense of mission in arguing for critical historical knowledge about eugenics and racial anthropology at a moment in which "there were much graver problems to think about." She exclaimed in an interview with me: "Look at what's happening around the world— U.S. imperialism, Israeli colonialism—why focus on us in particular?" What emerged from the argument between Felder and some of the Latvian historians was an unproductive comparison of whose version of eugenics and racial science was worse, thus overlooking how the argument itself was caught up in the distribution of vices and virtues within Europe's political and moral landscape. Felder's call for atonement seemed to fall on deaf ears, leaving him to conclude that critical thinking had not yet made its way into Latvian historiography.

Critical thinking, then, was understood to be in deficit across different spheres of life, from historiography to ordinary people's understandings of themselves in relation to others. For Felder, as for tolerance workers, critical thinking was a crucial tool for cultivating properly European political and ethical dispositions. In turn, some of the tolerance skeptics among my interlocutors thought that intolerance—rather than tolerance—suggested the presence of critical thought.

Intolerance as a Critical Position

As I showed in chapter 3, popular understandings of tolerance differed from those of tolerance workers. If tolerance workers considered that tolerance as a liberal political virtue was achieved through education and countered the natural state of fear or suspicion toward others, some teachers targeted by tolerance promotion efforts thought that tolerance was a social virtue and therefore part of everyone's constitution. Some people may be less virtuous than others and more prone to express anger, but generally tolerance was necessary to navigate the world with its daily challenges. When a virtuous person, a generally good person, became intolerant, it meant that they were provoked to become actively and reflectively engaged with the world. Take the example of Maija, a civil servant at the Ministry of Education who was often delegated to participate in various tolerance promotion events. I spoke with Maija about her stance toward the controversial LGBT Pride parade, which literally erupted into the Latvian public space in 2005 (Dzenovska and Arenas 2012).[11] Maija told me that prior to Pride 2005 she had "a neutral attitude towards homosexuality"—a neutrality that presumably only emerged in retrospect, perhaps even during the course of our conversation. Moreover, Maija specifically emphasized that she had been tolerant, but that the polarized and politicized debates that ensued after Pride 2005 forced her to become intolerant, that is, to take "an active political position":

> The manipulation led to some sort of an active position. Perhaps there are others whose neutral positions turned into active positions. And I started to become angry. I started from a neutral position—let them walk and let the society see that there are such people, but then my tolerance was turned into intolerance. Regardless of whether one has a positive or negative attitude towards Pride, that's an active position. Why are those who support them tolerant and those who don't intolerant? No, both are intolerant. "I go to fight those who think differently"—this is not tolerance.

Maija tried to redefine intolerance from something that can be attributed to individuals who are wrong from the liberal political perspective to something that marks practices through which people engage each other regardless of what they think of, for example, homosexuality or Pride. She tried to pry intolerance apart from the liberal political discourse, which defined it as uncivilized and backward attitudes toward particular forms of difference, and rearticulate it as an active political position. In Maija's rendering, it was not necessarily the Pride parade itself that caused her to become intolerant, but rather the depiction of the opposition to Pride as intolerant and homophobic, while emphasizing support for Pride as a tolerant position. Some of this opposition may indeed have been homophobic, Maija pondered, but some of it may have been a reaction to particular forms of politics, such as the parade. Maija was upset that these distinctions were not made and that everyone was lumped into the same category of intolerant homophobes. Maija added that she was unhappy about such a turn of events. She noted that many other people too felt provoked and thus formulated strong positions, whereas otherwise they might not have cared; that is, they would have remained tolerant. In her narrative, tolerance was not an active political stance, but rather a "passive, relaxed, benignly indifferent [attitude] to difference" (Walzer 1997, 10). Contrary to the activists' claims that Pride parades aimed to promote tolerance by rendering homosexuality publicly visible and by exposing the unreflective discriminatory practices prevalent in society, Maija claimed that Pride parades provoked tolerance, here understood as unreflective indifference, into becoming intolerance, here understood as an active and oppositional political position.

Maija's view provides an interesting perspective with regard to the tolerance workers' call for critical thinking and public reflection. For Maija, the contentious debates that emerged in relation to Pride parades marked a form of public reflection, whereas for tolerance workers this was a clash between critically thinking and tolerant people, on the one hand, and a mob of uncritical homophobes on the other. Whereas tolerance workers thought that critical thinking and public reflection would result in a climate of tolerance, Maija seemed to suggest that the activities of tolerance workers in the sphere of LGBT rights created public reflection, except that this public reflection did not look like the one that tolerance workers expected.

In the midst of heated debates about tolerance in the context of Pride politics, a well-known poet Uldis Bērziņš brought forth a Soviet-era dictionary in which he had found a definition of tolerance. The dictionary defined tolerance as "living without objections" (*bez iebildumiem*). In other words, indifference, lack of objecting to certain presences, identities, or conduct, was thought of as tolerance, whereas taking an active position, whether one of agreement or disagreement, was no longer thought of as tolerance. By way of parallels, it is interesting to note that living without objections is precisely what Jonathan Larson's (2013) interlocutors in Slovakia defined as lack of critical thinking that has historically plagued the Slovak society and continues to present a problem after socialism. For them, too, intolerance meant critical public engagement, whereas from the perspective of tolerance workers, it is tolerance rather than intolerance that is linked with critical thinking. In his book, Jonathan Larson (2013) recounts a bus trip to a small village outside of Bratislava with his new acquaintances. The day was hot and the bus was packed, but the driver demanded that passengers squeeze together even more to take new passengers aboard. Larson's acquaintances—who worked for an NGO promoting civil society—lamented the fact that people put up with the driver's demands rather than refuse to comply and request that the bus company put more buses on the route (2013, 2). Larson provides this as an example of the young Slovaks' frustration with what they saw as lack of critical public engagement with one's environment (lack of critical public thinking). Larson also notes that Slovak intellectuals tend to attribute such mode of life not only to socialist legacy, but also to a submissive mindset cultivated over centuries of living in the shadows of foreign rule. For Latvians too, living without objections conjures up images of submissiveness of long duration, often referred to as a "serf-mentality" that, similar to the Slovak self-narrative, has been cultivated during centuries of foreign rule. From within such a perspective, where living without objections was thought of as lacking the ability to publicly voice critique, tolerance did not necessarily appear as a virtue. Thus many in Latvia did not think of tolerance as *work*, as an actively formulated positive attitude or state of mind toward human diversity, as liberals would have it, but rather as a normal, authentic state of affairs that could be disturbed or provoked, or as a submissive mode of life that should be disturbed and provoked into intolerance as a form of critical public engagement.

Intolerance as critical public engagement could take different forms. It did not necessarily expel affect or substantive traditions from the public realm. The challenge was to negotiate both the issues discussed and the form of discussion itself. For example, many Pride opponents, as well as supporters of LGBT rights, questioned whether Pride parades were the most appropriate political form through which to build such engagement. For tolerance workers, in turn, critical thinking and public reflection were to be guided by reason. The exercise of reason was to ensure predictable outcomes—namely, tolerance—insofar as such an outcome already had been achieved in Western Europe where liberal democracy was mature. In order to achieve this level of maturity, tolerance workers thought that people were to, first, learn to think critically as private persons and, second, engage in public reflection through which they were to contribute to the cultivation of a public climate of tolerance.

Teaching Critical Thinking

One of the main problems that hindered the development of critical thinking and public reflection in the eyes of tolerance promoters was that individuals in Latvia were hostages to a historically shaped collectivist mode of thinking. This mode of thinking was thought to be a product of both Soviet socialism and Latvian nationalism. Many tolerance workers strongly identified with the Latvian polity, as well as the nation, and thus were especially frustrated in thinking about the collective fate of a polity and nation whose members seemingly lacked critical thinking. While on occasion their opponents called them traitors, as Signe noted in chapter 3, they felt themselves to be patriots.

For example, Vita Matīsa (2007), an American-born Latvian political scientist who has spent much of her life in Switzerland, took up this theme in an article published shortly before Latvian Independence Day in 2007. She argued that as a result of a historically formed lack of independent thinking, Latvians tend to exhibit loyalty to power rather than to principles and that this is so regardless of the quality or legitimacy of that power. She suggested that this might be attributed to people's cultivation of survival strategies under various regimes, but in her view, it was also the effect of a historically formed servile attitude. Matīsa further argued that Latvians think that there is power in unity, but not in solitary reflection, therefore they are prone to be brave participants of mass demonstrations, but are not likely to be able to adhere to ethical principles when confronted in private. Matīsa drew on a semiautobiographical novel by Vizma Belševica (2004)—specifically a section titled "State Holiday" ("Valsts svētki")— to illustrate this. In the story, the author's grandmother—clearly in Matīsa's view one of the few individuals who could think critically—yells at a participant of a mass parade commemorating state independence during the authoritarian rule of Kārlis Ulmanis in the 1930s: "Fool! What has God given you? What has Ulmanis? All you have is the result of your own work!" As a result, the author's grandmother has to flee, because the crowd wants to hand her over to the police. "A typical scenario," Matīsa concluded—independent thinking and adherence to intangible principles rather than tangible authorities have always been unpopular and dangerous in Latvia. Rather than the unity loudly advocated by politicians, she further argued, Latvians need to cultivate the ability to cordon themselves of from power (norobežoties no varas) in order to reflect in solitude on their ethical and political principles. This liberal position posited a private space where power did not reach, where reason could be exercised, thus producing an individual capable of engaging in critical public reflection, recognizable as criticism of authority and collectivist loyalties.

It was commonly agreed within the network of tolerance workers that such abilities to think critically—to distance from power and to reflect in solitude— had to be taught in school. And this is precisely what the Soros-supported critical thinking promotion initiatives set out to do. Tolerance workers, however, had to address an audience that was already outside the school system. Thus, they considered other mechanisms through which they could incite adults to think critically, that is, to think for themselves rather than borrow from a discursive repertoire provided by figures of authority. At the same time, tolerance workers also emphasized the need to target what they called "opinion leaders" (*viedokļu līderi*), that is, people who did carry some authority with various segments of the population—for example, intellectuals, artists, politicians—in order to educate the discursive repertoire itself, if that's what people ended up drawing on instead of their own critical capacities.

Inciting critical reflection was a difficult task, according to tolerance workers. It was even more difficult to get people to educate themselves to make the right choices in the process of critical reflection, that is, to choose tolerance rather than intolerance or even to recognize when they were being intolerant. People associated with the network of tolerance workers pondered on many occasions how they could incite critical thinking. Could they use literature, films, or stage encounters with the other that might force people to recognize the other's humanity and thus change their views, that is, transform negative attitudes toward difference into positive ones? In all of their attempts to render visible intolerance, including in the episode I describe in chapter 3 where the tolerance workers wished to film public reactions to a black man on the street, tolerance workers were dismayed at the layers of filtering that would be necessary to get their point across. They understood that it could also backfire since all attempts to come up with public critical thinking teaching scenarios sounded suspiciously like attempts to tell people what to think and to shame them for thinking the wrong thing.[12] For much of my fieldwork, then, tolerance workers stuck to the conventional format of seminars and discussions during which they wished to educate the audience about how to engage in critical public reflection. Similar to Vita Matīsa, they thought that this entailed distancing from collective identities and substantive traditions. Their audiences also thought that critical public reflection required distancing, but not necessarily of the kind imagined by tolerance workers.

Critical Public Reflection and Distancing

During a seminar for teachers held in 2006 under the auspices of the National Program for the Promotion of Tolerance, the topic of discussion was public occurrences of racism. The moderator showed newspaper clippings describing an incident where two Sri Lankan students had been verbally assaulted and physically threatened on the street in Riga near the university they attended. The epithets the assailants—two young women—used did not leave anyone in doubt that the attack was indeed racially motivated, yet some teachers expressed resentment that such incidents were used to suggest that Latvians must collectively and publicly reflect on the problem of racism. Trying to mend the situation by explaining the resentment and suggesting a solution for how to publicly address the problem of racism, one of the seminar participants suggested that Latvians, as members of the titular nation, intimately identify with the public space of the nation-state and thus are personally offended when it is suggested that racism is a problem in Latvia. In other words, Latvians perceive the suggestion that racism is a problem in public space as an accusation directed at the collective virtue (or the lack thereof) of the cultural nation of Latvians.

There are at least two trajectories for tracing how the suggestion that there is a problem of racism in Latvia comes to be seen as a suggestion that Latvians are racists. One derives from the articulation of "state people" as responsible for what occurs in their state's territory and in public space (Arendt 1979, Feldman 2005, Hirsch 2005). The other derives from a historically specific articulation of Latvians as a cultural community with the national public space in Latvia. It complements the first and would not be possible without it. At the same time, the first would remain an abstract statement without attention to the concrete contours of the latter. The teacher did not turn to theories of the state to explain how it is that Latvians felt offended by the suggestion that there needed to be public reflection on the problem of racism, but rather to cultural repertoires. The teacher associated Latvians with public space in part because of a historically specific understanding of the relationship between people and place exemplified by the mythology of *viensēta* (single farmsteads)—a sociospatial arrangement of rural living that tends to be invoked as paradigmatic of a specifically Latvian understanding of the good life and thus as deeply constitutive of Latvian subjectivities. The imaginary of viensēta is mythological insofar as it is no longer and perhaps has never been the prevalent mode of rural life in Latvia (Purs in Schwartz 2006, 44). Yet, it shapes the way many of those who identify with the cultural nation of Latvians think of themselves in relation to space and place. Imaginaries of this sociospatial arrangement get articulated with modern forms of political life, such as the public sphere, and subsequently inform arguments about tolerance and public reflection. Thus, what I am concerned with here is not the selectively derived prevalence of the single farmstead mode of rural living in the imagination of the nation, but rather its role in shaping the public and political subjectivities of Latvians.

Viensētas, or single farmsteads, are thought to distinguish a specifically Latvian way of life from that of their neighbors, especially from Russians who are said to favor a communal type of rural dwellings. Historically, Latvia's single farmsteads were located at a sufficient distance from each other, separated by fields and natural landmarks. They consisted of an ensemble of buildings—for example, living quarters, a granary, a barn, and so forth—with common open spaces between them, and were occupied by a master family (*saimnieki*) and their farmhands. Within the Latvian social imaginary, the farmsteads represent the kind of living where people are in a hierarchical, yet symbiotic and harmonious relationship with nature, work, and each other (Schwartz 2006). Narratives of single farmstead living are central to how Latvians think of themselves in space and place and therefore also in relation to others. On the one hand, narratives of single farmstead living provide guidance for conduct and, on the other hand, they serve to explain conduct. For example, when discussing the results of a survey that included a standardized social distance question about whether the residents of Latvia would want to live next door to variously defined others—for instance, homosexuals, Muslims, Gypsies—participants of the aforementioned teacher seminar argued that Latvians are after all *viensētnieki* (single farmsteaders or homesteaders), and thus they do not want to live next to anyone, not just Muslims or Africans (BSZI 2004, 65). By invoking this paradigmatic mode of living, the participants argued that the responses to this survey should not be read as indicative of a climate of intolerance in Latvia, but that they should rather be considered in light of Latvians' culturally and historically specific way of life. Clearly, it would be grossly misguided to argue that a viensētnieki disposition accounts for the fact that 45 percent of Latvians do not want to live next door to Muslims or that 38 percent of Latvians do not want to live next door to homosexuals, if only because the results are similar for residents who do not identify as Latvian (BSZI 2004, 65). Nevertheless, the repeated invocation of viensēta to explain or guide social practice suggests that it is an important element of the cultural repertoire through which people locate themselves in the world, including in relation to the public space of the polity.

The teacher suggested that there is a constitutive relationship between the discourses about patterns of living and cohabitation that the image of the single farmstead invokes and contemporary conceptions of the relationship between public space and the cultural nation of Latvians. In other words, in the interpretation of this teacher, in Latvia, the modern formation of the public is conceived vis-à-vis the mythology of single farmsteads; this is a powerful social fact that shapes people's sense of self and conduct. Given that within this mythology people and place are seamlessly intertwined, the positive content of the national public space is deeply consequential for many Latvians' sense of self. Subsequently, claims that there is racism within the public space of the nation become inseparable from claims that Latvians are also, in a way, racists.

Having marked this existentially entangled articulation of Latvians and public space, the teacher who attempted to explain why Latvians are so reluctant to publicly talk about racism further suggested that in order to enable a discussion of racism that would not be taken as a personal offense, some sort of distancing was in order. So far, she seemed to agree with tolerance workers, who also thought, as did Vita Matīsa above, that distancing from power and tradition was necessary for critical reflection. However, the teacher argued that Latvians should keep in mind that it is mostly Russians who are aggressive and therefore more prone to commit racist crimes.[13] This move absolved Latvians from the need to question themselves in the process of talking about racism and instead propelled them to ask how to handle the blemish that was in their public space, but not of it. The kind of distancing the teacher proposed entailed the collective *alienation* of the Latvian cultural nation from public space. In her suggestion, Latvians could not seamlessly identify with public space due to the presence of Russians, who were rendered accountable for the presence of racism. While ultimately undesirable, such collective alienation was nevertheless seen as necessary if racism was to be acknowledged as part of the local landscape.

In contrast, tolerance workers suggested that public reflection on racism requires a different type of distancing. Rather than collective alienation of the Latvian cultural nation from polluted public space, they proposed a distancing mechanism that can be thought of in terms of the practice of liberal *abstraction* whereby the self enters public space (and the public sphere) as an individual in a critical and distanced relationship with the community and its past. This meant that Latvians as individuals should distance themselves from too passionate of an attachment to the cultural nation in order to reflect on the problem of racism, which affects them as citizens of a liberal democratic state and not as members of a historical and cultural nation. Such abstraction distinguishes between two publics—one racist and the other antiracist, as well as places the reflecting individual in the latter. Such a maneuver also constitutes the categories of the civic public sphere and a private sphere of belonging that did not necessarily figure as separate spheres in the discourse of the teacher. In the narrative of the teacher, when distancing occurs, it involves the recognition that the approximation of the seamless intertwining between public space and the cultural nation has been interrupted by the presence of those not of the nation. The presence of racism is thus understood as an interruption that is external to the public of the nation.

In conditions where many experience the demand to reflect on racism as existentially unsettling, it is particularly important to ask what work distancing—whether as alienation or as abstraction—performs. Interestingly, both of these discourses—that of the teacher and that of tolerance workers—converge in positing racism as a blemish that can be removed, albeit in different ways, while leaving foundations of either the nation or the state intact. The discourse of alienation of the Latvian cultural nation from public space protects the cultural nation from fragmentation that might result from liberalization. It repositions the nation in relation to public space. The discourse of liberal abstraction reconfigures the individual's relationship with the nation in order to enable critical reflection, yet it retains faith in state-based politics and liberal political culture.

In other words, in one case racism is thought to be a feature of another ethnically conceived population group, whereas in the other case racism is thought to be a feature of bad individuals. Juxtaposing these two forms of distancing obfuscates that both of them carve out spaces or bodies that are not tainted by racism, thus overlooking the ways in which racial thinking might shape the very conception of the nation or the structure of the liberal state. This is precisely what Felder also did, when he focused his critical analysis on the Latvian state during the period of Ulmanis's authoritarian rule while ignoring entirely the fact that most modern states govern populations by sorting them into categories differently distributed across the "make live and let die" spectrum (Foucault 2003b, 254–263). It is therefore questionable whether subjecting the cultural nation of Latvians to liberalization can be the solution to the problem of racism. At the same time, displacing racism onto "the Russians," as the teacher did, also falls short—to say the least—in terms of analysis of racism. What it does help to see, however, is the limits of the juxtaposition between nationalism and liberalism that dominates in arguments about racism in Latvia.

Irony and the Limits of Tolerance

Toward the end of 2006, I agreed to conduct a Latvian language focus group discussion on questions of tolerance for a policy think-tank that aimed to produce research-based policy recommendations to promote tolerance.[14] I was given research questions, yet the discussion was to be open and generative of ideas and examples of "best practice." We began with a round of introductions and a discussion of whether the people present thought of themselves as tolerant or not and why. One of the participants said: "I think of myself as generally tolerant, but then I read Bankovskis's recent article and thought to myself: well, perhaps I am not so tolerant after all." In the context where most invitations to rethink one's self-ascribed virtue of tolerance were met with resentment or resistance, it was intriguing that the participant both marked a shift in the way she thought about herself in relation to tolerance and identified a specific moment that invited reflection and subsequent reevaluation of her previous stance. When I prompted the participant to tell the group more about the article and why it had had such an effect on her, she merely repeated that it had indeed had an effect, but refrained from explaining how it had worked. It seemed the effect was felt more than thought.

Following the discussion, I looked up the article she mentioned. It was published in *Diena*, one of the Latvian language dailies, as a commentary by Pauls Bankovskis (2006b)—a novelist who frequently contributed opinion pieces to

Diena and other media. The article was titled "A Tu Neliecies" (Don't Get into My Face) and could be described as an ironic reflection on collective virtue. Given that the piece is an essay that builds its point in a cumulative manner, as well as that it seemed to have an effect on the participant of the focus group discussion without her providing an analysis of it, I reproduce the essay here at length:

> What are you looking for? Why are you staring? You think you will read this crappy little article, leaf through this little newspaper and will become smarter? That you will be the cool intellectual and the cultured individual? That you will be able to think that you are better than others? I should beat you up, you damn snob. No, I am not aggressive; in fact, I am utterly unfamiliar with aggressiveness. You simply should not provoke me. There is no need to ask for it yourself.
>
> Like those girls in the summertime. Walking the streets nearly naked. You can see their boobs, their belly buttons, even some butt cracks, the pants are so low. But when someone fucks these prostitutes, they complain that they've been raped. But they asked for it themselves! That's probably what they wanted. They should not have been so provocative.
>
> Well, at least it's pleasant to look at the girls. But all those mobs of pensioners, who walk around in the summer with shorts and short-sleeve shirts! They should be shot or at least deported. No, I have nothing against old people in general; let them walk around naked at home. But when they—spotty and varicose—wander around the city center, I cannot stand it. All I want to do is slap them across their face.
>
> . . .
>
> No, but I am generally calm and peace loving; it's just that it drives me crazy from time to time. For example, all those shops in Riga. Everything is so expensive there; no normal person can afford anything! And then they wonder that people steal—they are provoked!
>
> . . .
>
> I am quite tolerant indeed. For example, I have no prejudice against people with different skin color. Only if all those blacks and coloreds did not come to live here. Let them live in their own land. But when I see someone like that on the streets of Riga, I want to show them where their place is. Just don't misunderstand me, I am not a racist; it's just that they ask for it. The same with the Jews. I am not an anti-Semite, but I know that they are to blame for all their misfortunes. They have provoked it all. But I do not have any hatred toward the Jews—I even studied with one of them. The main thing is—don't get into my face! The same with the Russians. I know some of them, so it's not that I don't

know what I am talking about. It's just that they should not be here in Latvia provoking me and talking about their rights.

I don't have any prejudice toward all those gays and lesbians. Let them do what they want in their own circles, but leave me alone. One thing I cannot stand, however, is when I see them on the street. Let's say, two pederasts are walking down the street, holding hands. I want to kick their ass!

Truth be told, I am very tolerant. I just get really mad if I am being provoked all the time. No need to stare at me. Didn't like the article? Go take a nap or eat something, or do something else. I have nothing personal against you, just don't . . . (Bankovskis 2006b)

The object of reflection in this short piece is the speaking subject and its virtue rather than a single act of intolerance. The author traces a particular disposition through various contexts and relationships, beginning with a direct address to the reader and subsequently covering contexts of gender and sexuality, generational differences, ethnicity, and race. What this performative and exaggerated reiteration calls into question is the very existence or possibility of the virtue of tolerance in conditions where most everything seems to be a provocation. What form does the virtue of tolerance take if it only comes into focus through a provocation, which is its negation? But is the commentary really on what the speaking subject thinks of the various categories of difference, or is it rather on the hyperirritability of this person who is constantly feeling provoked by the mere presence of others—be they old and varicose or young and black—in public space? On the one hand, the essay establishes equivalence between provocateurs in relation to the provoked, somewhat resembling the liberal equivalence between categories of difference I discussed in chapter 3. (To remind the reader, the liberal politics of tolerance equates categories of difference—race, religion, ethnicity—and assumes that an intolerant person is likely to be intolerant toward all categories of difference rather than just one.) The intolerant subject lacks the virtue of tolerance because he—and it does seem to be a he in the essay—has not critically evaluated his understanding of difference in relation to public and political life. In the essay above, the author also establishes equivalence between provoking contexts—the speaking subject is provoked by young barely clad girls, by high prices, by old people in shorts, and so forth and so on. These are not, however, politically recognized categories of difference, but rather heterotopic provocations which all irritate the speaker, provoke him out of his "authenticity" (his unprovoked state). The effect is such that the shortcomings of the virtue of the speaker are exposed. The speaker is truly intolerant insofar as he jumps at the first sign of discomfort, whatever it is. It is impossible to tell whether the focus group participant who recognized herself in some aspects of the essay recognized herself as someone who is often irritated or as someone who is often irritated with regard to a particular category of difference.

To put it another way, the object of reflection in the essay is ambiguous—it is a sentiment, an affective state through which the speaking subject relates to public space rather than a particular view about a defined other. The essay also differs from liberal incitement to reflection on another account, namely with regard to "the kind of authority through which a subject comes to recognize the truth about herself, and the relationship she establishes between herself and those who are deemed to hold the truth" (Rose in Mahmood 2005, 30). It is noteworthy that Bankovskis's article contains no explicit reference to authority—such as reason, capacity for critical reflection, European Union directives, civilized Europe, or democracy—through which the reflecting subject would be invited "to recognize the truth about herself." Importantly, the article does not require that the reflecting subject *establish* a relationship between "herself and those who are deemed to hold the truth." Rather, the subject herself already holds the truth. Yet there is a discrepancy between what she thinks the truth to be and what her conduct indicates. This discrepancy, however, is not brought into focus through the kind of distancing that requires the reflecting subject to relocate to some more neutral realm, but rather through an ironic exaggeration of the subject's conduct. Instead of forging an ethical bond as in the case of the circulation of repugnant statements described in chapter 3, the essay conjures up a subject that recognizes herself in both the conduct described and in the reflecting subject. In other words, one could recognize oneself as both the subject and object of reflection, as the participant of the focus group did.

In his work on the legacy of the Romantic tradition, Charles Larmore suggests that Romantics consider that "standing back entirely from our way of life is to basically find ourselves without any guidance, yet they do not contest the necessity or possibility to stand back. They are contesting the easy and absolute notion of standing back—they do not want to let the Enlightenment object off the hook of its own history" (Larmore 1996, 45). Reason, then, as conceived through a Romantic lens, does not mean that we detach ourselves entirely, but rather that we think about how we are to go on with our way of life (Larmore 1996, 58). While the liberal subject claims autonomy and a capacity to choose as instruments of self-reflection (that is, the ability to distance oneself through the application of reason), the Romantic subject relies on irony as a tool entailing a two-mindedness that posits neither radical distancing nor radical identification with a tradition: "If [the] two-mindedness of irony makes it an expression of individuality, it also keeps this sense of self from swelling into a posture of sovereign, unlimited power. Ironic subjectivity, whatever its intimations of the infinite, is essentially a finite subjectivity" (Larmore 1996, 79). I find Larmore's take on Romantic reason useful for thinking about the critical power of embedded reason. From this perspective, Bankovskis's article invites engagement with the self whereby the subject of reflection remains accountable to the historical and cultural context in which he is embedded. It does not call for a radical distancing, but rather asks him to consider whether he actually is what he says he is, whether he possesses the virtues he claims he possesses.

Bankovskis's ironic depiction of the constantly irritated subject who thinks of himself as a victim of constant provocation does not ask whether there is a problem of intolerance in Latvia. And yet, by exaggerating the defensive aggressiveness with which the protagonist of his short essay relates to the world around him—and not just to politically recognized categories of difference—Bankovskis managed, at least in one instance, to incite reflection about the virtue of tolerance regardless of whether it was manifest in relation to someone with different skin color or one's mother-in-law. At the same time, while the semidistant ironic subject is different from the abstract liberal citizen, the "other" against which both define themselves seems to remain the same, that is, an aggressive and irrational subject of intolerance. But, as the concluding section shows, affect is very much part of the liberal subject's repertoire as well. In fact, it is precisely through affect that the threshold of liberal tolerance appears.

Affect and the Limits of Liberal Tolerance

Upon returning to Latvia a year or so after having completed fieldwork, I was invited to participate in a conversation with tolerance workers about what was to be done about the "democratic deficit" in Latvia organized by a nongovernmental organization. As part of this conversation, I mentioned that institutional forms of political liberalism, including antiracism and tolerance promotion initiatives, have been criticized by scholars of postcolonialism, postsocialism, and critical race theory, including anthropologists, for extending standardized models of thought and conduct and in the process overlooking local specificities. By doing so, I wanted to invite a conversation about how institutionalized forms of political liberalism were located in uneven fields of power and the limitations that it entailed.

In order to make the point, I used the example of Gerald Creed's (2011) book *Masquerade and Postsocialism: Ritual and Cultural Dispossession in Bulgaria*. In the book, Creed makes two moves: first, he describes the revival of mumming rituals in rural Bulgaria. These are rituals where village men dress in elaborate costumes and go from house to house demanding food, drink, and money in exchange for invocations of fertility and abundance. These mumming rituals usually involve a recognizable lineup of characters, including transvestite brides and Roma figures. These figures are at once stereotypical and recognized as part of the village social milieu. Second, Creed makes the argument that, contrary to the liberal assumptions that Bulgarian mumming rituals are backward cultural forms that espouse problematic gender and ethnic stereotypes, they could be analyzed as resources for thinking about historically and culturally embedded forms of cohabitation with difference. Creed argues that the hegemony of liberal politics that has emerged in postsocialist Bulgaria and elsewhere in the former socialist world has foreclosed any generative identification of local resources for cohabitation with difference. He also argues that the mumming rituals amount to a form of "differential inclusion" insofar as they depict local social relations that are inclusive despite being othering. For example, Creed suggests that "mumming rituals were not offensive to some Roma precisely because the rituals reference and demonstrate a larger message about the nature of local ethnic relations that are inclusive, despite being discriminatory and derogatory" (Creed 2011, 167). To be sure, Creed cautions against romanticization of such inclusion, because it can morph into "standard categorical racism."

Creed has a point insofar as he suggests that traditional practices should not be taken as shorthand illustrations of backward racism prevalent in Eastern Europe, but rather that they require careful analysis to illuminate both their dangers and possibilities. Creed points to the tension between local-level inclusions and national survey data, which show that 70 percent of Bulgarians have negative attitudes toward Roma. Western models do not notice such tensions but rather gloss over the traditional practices as just another example of the problem, even its denial, thus "creating the homogenous pervasive racism that knows little nuance against which they [the Western models] were originally formulated" (Creed 2011, 197). In other words, "the success of imported models may require the replication of the relations the model was designed to redress, which may actually reformulate existing relations into more antagonistic ones" (Creed 2011, 199). "Imported models" also create the Western knowing subject, who passes judgment on local forms, but remains outside of critical analysis. Creed does not suggest that the relations between Bulgarians and Roma were ideal or needed to be replicated, but he does suggest that local configurations of inclusion/exclusion should not be easily dismissed and replaced by liberal models, but rather used as potential critical resources for rethinking inclusion/exclusion regimes (2011, 200).

In my conversation with tolerance workers, I wanted to communicate Creed's point that institutionalized forms of political liberalism are too quick to identify racism and intolerance in local configurations of inclusion and exclusion, while exempting liberal ones from similar scrutiny. Having introduced the point, that is, having outlined the argument I wanted to make, I proceeded to describe the mumming practices. When I got to describing the Roma figures that participated in the mumming ritual, one of the tolerance workers could no longer bear it. He interrupted me and exclaimed: "Did they also yell 'let's hang the Jews'?" My description of the mumming rituals, including the Roma figures, resembled the stories tolerance workers usually circulated among themselves to form their own ethical understandings and to differentiate them from those of the intolerant majority (see chapter 3). As the disconcerted tolerance worker was listening to my description, it resonated with what he had heard or seen before and thus he reacted affectively. He viscerally recognized the account as just another instance of racism and this recognition prompted a reaction not unlike the one by the constantly irritated individual depicted by Bankovskis. As his interjection demonstrates, he equated the rural villagers' depiction of the Roma with other forms of intolerance. The Bulgarian villager was the ultimate intolerant subject. Taken together with Bankovskis's essay, this episode reveals how the liberal tolerant subject shares with the intolerant one an affective disposition that polices the boundaries of critical discourse.[15] For both, it is affect as much as reason that signals the boundaries of tolerance.

To be fair, the disconcerted tolerance worker could have turned to European history to argue that the inclusive othering depicted in Latvian folk songs and literature did not save Jews during World War II from Latvian complicity with Nazi atrocities. Indeed, racialized inclusion or inclusive othering can transform into politicized violence. This is a standard argument in the repertoire of institutionalized political liberalism, namely that discursive othering sows the seeds for scapegoating and violence (see chapter 5). However, as Hannah Arendt (1979) has argued, it is not the traditional social nationalism of the Eastern European kind—or scapegoating—that led to the most atrocious violence of the twentieth century, but rather complex historical conditions of Jewish integration into European nation-state structures and the international—rather than national— reach of Nazi ideology. This is to say that identifying backward intolerant subjects, whether nationalist or socialist, is not sufficient for eradicating racism and preventing race-based violence.

Exclaiming in protest to my suggestion that the villagers' form of racialized inclusion might be worthy of consideration alongside the liberal form of racialized inclusion, the tolerance worker constituted his own position as one of a knowing subject in the position to diagnose Bulgarian villagers as backward racists in need of tutelage and civilization. With this exclamation he also closed the conversation, and we did not get to discuss the issue further. I had no more resources at my disposal to get his attention back to my initial point, namely that the mumming practices might offer valuable insight with regard to how various forms of racialized inclusions, including liberal ones, operate. For him, racism was firmly lodged in the backward sensibilities of Bulgarians and Latvians, and what was needed in Eastern Europe was more rather than less liberalism. This incident is indicative of the fact that, despite disagreements, resistance, critique, and openings, liberal models have proved largely immune to critique. Historically and socially embedded critiques of liberalism tends to be diffused by depicting it as part of the problem that needs to be addressed. In other words, a historically and culturally embedded critique of liberal politics of tolerance is often read as a denial of the problem of intolerance or racism and thus itself a problem that needs to be tackled.

It is hardly possible to say that in this episode the tolerance worker exhibited critical thinking. If he had, he would have at least allowed for the possibility that his truth could be questioned. In that case, however, he may not have been able to confidently engage in the work that he was doing. When one engages in critical thinking or critique as the ethos of modernity that pushes against the historically constituted limits of thought and conduct, it becomes quite difficult to confidently and continuously assert a coherent ideological position. Like Latvians who thought they needed to build themselves up rather than tear themselves down, the tolerance worker also needed to maintain the coherence of his position, and this required the presence of an easily identifiable intolerant subject, as well as suspension of critical thinking.

5

LANGUAGE SACRED AND LANGUAGE INJURIOUS

Ethical Encounters with the Other

"Latviešu valodā derdzīgu vārdu nav; tādēļ pārņemam tos no citām valodām." (There are no repulsive words in the Latvian language; we take them from other languages)

—Advertisement from the series *Domā, kā runā* (Think How You Speak), Latvian Language Agency, 2008

Language was one of the primary and thus most contested terrains of tolerance work.[1] It is in language that tolerance workers found plentiful examples of intolerance insofar as politicians, civil servants, intellectuals, and members of the general public often uttered words or made statements that tolerance workers deemed intolerant. To tolerance workers, these words and statements illustrated the speakers' problematic dispositions and sensibilities, which ranged from outright racism to mild prejudice to unacceptable ignorance. Tolerance workers often circulated examples of public use of intolerant language as a way to confirm to themselves and to illustrate to others the pervasiveness of the problem of intolerance in the Latvian society (see chapter 3). They drew these examples from their own conversations with members of professional groups they worked with, such as border guards (see chapter 6), from the media, from research reports that deployed discourse analysis and were specifically commissioned for this purpose, as well as from casual everyday encounters and accidentally overheard conversations. This created the sense that intolerance was entrenched in the social fabric. During the height of European Union–funded tolerance work from mid- to late 2000s, the circulation of examples of public use of intolerant language was almost a routine daily practice among tolerance workers. It was often the case that upon meeting another tolerance worker on the street or during a meeting someone would begin by reporting on instances of intolerance in language that they had encountered that day.

The focus on intolerance in language in Latvia resonated with the broader Europewide approach to institutionalize attempts to change public discourse alongside prosecuting hate speech (Bader 2013, Maussen and Grillo 2013). Marcel Maussen and Ralph Grillo argue that the focus on countering intolerant speech in institutions of governance in Europe's liberal democracies emerged in response to the "breakthrough of anti-immigrant parties in the European [parliamentary] elections in 1984 and 1989," which, in turn, followed the intensive and planned immigration in the 1970s (2013, 180). As Maussen and Grillo write, "Given that it was thought xenophobic attitudes risked undermining the integration of immigrants, it seemed plausible to argue that politicians and citizens should show restraint and refrain from speaking in a racist and discriminatory way" (2013, 181). Besides extreme-right groups targeted by hate speech legislation, it was now the general public that also came under scrutiny for its contribution to the social subordination of minority groups and individuals vis-à-vis language. Language was recognized as a site of potential exclusion, thus requiring vigilance and efforts to cultivate inclusion through language. Politicizing language in this way amounted to what Judith Butler, writing about hate speech in the United States, has called the "linguistification of the political field," whereby utterance itself is regarded in inflated and highly efficacious ways, no longer as a representation of power or its verbal epiphenomenon, but as the *modus vivendi* of power itself" (1997, 74). Indeed, tolerance workers in Latvia considered that words not only expressed problematic sensibilities of the speakers, thus revealing them as failing ethical and political subjects, but also performed the social and political exclusion of discursively constructed "others." That is, words did things in addition to expressing pre-existing thoughts and feelings (Austin 1975). Moreover, the intolerant utterances were not only failures of individual subjects, but were also indicative of a general discursive climate of intolerance.

Within the theory of performativity, language precedes the speaking subject insofar as the subject cites rather than invents the discursive repertoire (Butler 1997). The speaking subject is constituted in language and does not have sovereign control over the utterances he or she makes, which can have unexpected effects and be reiterated in new ways (Butler 1997). For example, a racial slur is a racial slur insofar as it is cited by speaking subjects in specific speech acts. In other words, there has to be a socially and discursively constituted context for recognizing an utterance as a racial slur. At the same time, the racial slur can be cited subversively—for example, when it is used by individuals and groups targeted by it to refer to themselves in reaffirming ways. However, in the case of tolerance work in Latvia, there was an additional dimension. The contested language that constituted the individual speaking subject was not only intolerant, but also Latvian. Latvian language speakers and experts often claimed that the words deemed intolerant by tolerance workers were proper Latvian words. This was most evident when tolerance workers criticized the use of words such as *nēģeris* (negro) or *žīds* (yid), which the Latvian-speaking public and Latvian linguists considered to be linguistically correct and historically innocent (that is, not offensive) (see also Gullestad 2005, Hübinette 2012, Hylland Eriksen 2007, Rastas 2012). Insofar as the speakers insisted on these being proper Latvian words, they claimed collective sovereignty for the Latvian language and agency for themselves as its proper stewards. Most Latvians thought that freedom and sovereignty meant that the Latvian nation was free to speak the way it saw fit, and that it was the Latvian language—rather than discursively constructed "others"—that was in need of protection after decades of Russification at the hands of the Soviet state (see chapter 2). Philologist and former director of the Latvian Language Center Dzintra Hirša's statement in an interview in *Latvijas Avīze* is exemplary in this regard: "I do not understand why I, as a Latvian, have to think about integration at all, to integrate someone or integrate myself. I live in my own country. Those who do not know the real history of Latvia, the history that was obscured and skewed until independence, now have the opportunity to acquaint themselves with it. Similarly, there is the choice—to stay or not to stay and live in this country the way it is" (Mūrniece 2005). Moreover, some Latvians blamed the Russian language for tainting proper and benign Latvian-language words, such as *žīds* (e.g., Klimovičs 2013), thus suggesting that the very possibility that these Latvian words were deemed intolerant was itself the result of a history of domination of Latvians by Soviets and of the Latvian language by Russian. It was through the contestation of the use of these words that the Latvian language itself—and not just intolerant speech acts or public discourse—came under scrutiny. In the eyes of the tolerance workers, the speakers' and the experts' insistence on historical innocence of the problematic words amounted to refusal of critical reflection about the Latvian nation's ethical relationship with the "other."

To be sure, there were similar words in the Russian language, such as *negr*, that Russian speakers used and that were deemed unacceptable by tolerance workers. Yet, Russian speakers themselves were on occasion thought to be objects of intolerance—whether as new citizens, noncitizens, migrants, or occupiers (Golubeva 2007), thus their implication in the perpetuation of the problem of intolerance in Latvia, as well as their understanding of it, was rendered as partial (see chapter 3). Moreover, it was the Latvian-speaking public that recognized itself in the discourse about "intolerance in Latvian society" insofar as tolerance promotion efforts were part of a state-based program conducted in Latvian. Despite efforts to establish Latvian as the common public language for Latvia's citizens and residents, its use still largely interpellated Latvians rather than all of Latvia's residents, just as the use of Russian interpellated Russian speakers rather than all of Latvia's residents. Many Latvians thought this to be unfair, because they did not recognize themselves as the intolerant majority and, moreover, equated demands to reflect on intolerance in language to Soviet-style censorship, that is, to external and ideological control of the use of language (see chapter 2). For example, in 2006 a contemporary Latvian writer and publicist Pauls Bankovskis (2006a) reviewed a new edition of *Baltā Grāmata* (The White Book)—a collection of short stories by Jānis Jaunsudrabiņš (2006 [1927]), which depicts childhood in a typical rural setting of single farmsteads. Bankovskis noted that the new edition includes a hundred stories, compared to the ninety published in the censored Soviet edition. Therefore, upon purchasing the book, he first turned to the previously omitted stories to see what the Soviet censorship machinery had considered dangerous. Most of the omitted stories, he concluded, entailed characterizations of particular ethnic groups, such as Jews, and were edited out despite the fact that, "Jaunsudrabiņš writes from the perspective of a child, with kind-hearted curiosity" (Bankovskis 2006a). Bankovskis's article, mockingly titled "Jaunsudrabiņš un ž . . . ," (Jaunsudrabiņš and Y***) therefore marking the problematic word *žīds* by erasing it, criticized contemporary manifestations of political correctness, which demand not using words deemed problematic, by comparing this to the "idiocy" of Soviet censorship. He praised the literary work of Jaunsudrabiņš for providing insight "into the age of innocence when children talked children's talk and everything that came into one's way could be named."

Such power-laden collective and historical dimensions of language use are often overlooked in scholarship on hate speech and intolerant speech, which privileges the individual speaking subject and a legal perspective (Maussen and Grillo 2013, Butler 1997). However, collective subjects and historically shaped power relations are crucial in debates about whether and how language matters in negotiating relations of difference. For example, the infamous Danish cartoon scandal assumed a collective subject—the people—on behalf of whom the editor of *Jyllands-Posten* made the controversial decision to publish cartoons about the Prophet Muhammad, which significant numbers of Denmark's Muslims—and, subsequently, Muslims beyond the borders of Denmark—found offensive (Keane 2009). The editor claimed to have been disturbed by the self-censorship exhibited by Danish publishers who routinely refused to publish visual depictions of Muhammad—a practice forbidden in Islam—and wanted to remind the public about the virtue of free speech by refusing such censorship. Posited as an opposition between secular freedoms and religious sensibilities, the conflict was, however, about competing moral claims of the Danish people and the simultaneously internal and external Muslim "other," as well as about competing semiotic ideologies. As argued by Webb Keane (2009), the liberal virtue of freedom of speech was appropriated as a constitutive feature of Danishness. Freedom of speech thus became a cultural practice of the Danish nation juxtaposed to the cultural practices of Muslims that were not only illiberal, but also failed to grasp the reality by refusing the distinction between a thing and its representation (Keane 2009). Moreover, the conflict became translocal insofar as Muslims and liberals outside Denmark not only observed, but also became actively involved in the conflict, thus demonstrating the impossibility of containing contemporary political and ethical arguments within national boundaries.

The Danish cartoon scandal exhibited dynamics that Thomas Hylland Eriksen (2016) has discussed under the heading of "overheating." Hylland Eriksen argues that the post–Cold War world is characterized by the accelerated interconnectedness of people and places, creating situations where "people are aware of each other in ways that were difficult to imagine only a century ago; they develop some kind of global consciousness and often some kind of global conscience virtually everywhere" (2016, 10). Indeed, moral communities are constituted through ongoing negotiations with proximate and distant others with competing moral claims. At the same time, calls for an ethics of obligation toward another— as, for example, in Judith Butler's (2015) recent work—are difficult to reconcile with the existential concerns of embattled communities (Dzenovska 2016). Thus, when Latvians claimed innocence with regard to using words such as nēģeris and žīds, as I show later in the chapter, they tried to claim autonomy and authenticity that were no longer—and perhaps never had been—possible. And yet, claims of innocence intensified in response to demands coming forth from tolerance workers and minority groups to critically reflect on the use of contested words and images. This suggested that arguments about intolerance in language were also negotiations of power relations that extended beyond the immediate context of intolerance in language.

This chapter shows that arguments about intolerance in language in Latvia were historically emplaced and concerned the reach and limits of ethical obligations toward others in an intensively interconnected and power-laden world. That is, arguments about intolerance in language were arguments about where and how lines were to be drawn for delimiting the moral and political claims of others in relation to the self. At the same time, arguments about intolerance in language were also arguments about the proper relationship between language as a system of signs and social reality. Learning the liberal virtue of tolerance required adapting new language ideologies, ones that viewed words as doing rather than expressing things. But just as language was the most obvious area of tolerance work, it was also the most sacred national attribute thought to have been abused by Soviet nationalities policies and therefore the most contested political issue for the national state. Thus arguments about intolerance in language were also arguments about the proper relationship between language as a cultural practice and the collective subject of the nation (Kruk 2011, Woolard and Schieffeling 1994). While tolerance workers tried to convince Latvians to drop certain words, such as žīds and nēģeris, Latvians resisted by suggesting that the words only appear as injurious from a foreign perspective. Struggles over language use, then, brought into focus the intersection of competing language ideologies, histories, and moral and political claims as Latvians negotiated their road to Europe.

Language and Power

Demands to reflect on intolerance in language in Latvia were based on the assumption that language constructs reality. Moreover, they were based on the assumption that words have the capacity to construct a hierarchical reality, thus giving voice to some subjects while silencing and excluding others. For example, research produced by the public policy center Providus analyzed political discourse for exclusionary statements and argued that by referring to minority groups and individuals as "non-citizens, non-Latvians, new citizens and potential new immigrants," politicians construed them as "others" and excluded them from the space of citizenship and political participation (Golubeva 2007). This and similar reports deployed the well-established and nearly formulaic method of discourse analysis that made diagnosing intolerance seem straightforward and methodologically sound (see chapter 3).

Similarly, research by Sergejs Kruks and Ilze Šulmane (2005), commissioned specifically by the National Program for the Promotion of Tolerance, analyzed Latvian and Russian-language media discourse for instances of intolerance. However, diverging from a straightforward diagnostic exercise, Kruks and Šulmane concluded that negative depictions of specific minorities were not as widespread in the media as expressions of intolerant attitudes toward those with different political opinions, which included opinions about the extent to which variously marked "others" could make legitimate political and moral claims in Latvian public and political space. Thus, for example, Kruks and Šulmane concluded that there were not many depictions of "Africans" [sic] as inferior in the chosen sample, but there were arguments about whether "Africans" constituted a legitimate collective subject in Latvian public and political space. This suggested that, indeed, arguments about intolerance in language were also arguments about the reach of moral and political claims of the "other" in relation to the self.

In the research report, Kruks and Šulmane also took some time to elaborate on how words did things. They argued that the media discourse constructed chains of association, providing people with a discursive repertoire to draw on when making sense of encounters with minority subjects. This, Kruks and Šulmane argued, had tangible effects: "Research on media discourses is not simply academic reflections about the use of language in press. Discourse is social action; use of language leaves traces in real behavior of people—in this case, with regard to group relations" (Kruks and Šulmane 2005, 8). It was evident that the researchers thought that the approach they used—critical discourse analysis based on the analytic of performativity—was new to the Latvian public. Thus, in addition to presenting research results, they set out to educate the reader about how language did things. The need to educate former Soviet subjects about the fact that language did things may seem strange, given their experience of the Soviet state's manipulations of language, which suggested that the Soviet state also thought that language could construct reality and that the state therefore had to control public discourse (Boyer 2003, Yurchak 2005). However, this was precisely the reason why the Latvian public reacted negatively to the tolerance workers' attempts to change language use and public discourse on the basis of claims that language constructed reality. Most of Latvia's residents had experienced Soviet censorship and were accustomed to reading in between the lines of novels, poems, newspaper articles, and speeches for alternative representations of reality. In the post-Soviet context, many of Latvia's residents wished to protect their alternative representations of reality as truth that existed not only beyond Soviet ideology, but beyond ideology as such. If liberally inclined Latvians thought that the collapse of socialism meant liberation of knowledge from Marxist-Leninist ideology and human diversity from state-enforced sameness (see chapters 3 and 4), nationally inclined Latvians thought that the collapse of socialism meant liberation of language from Soviet nationalities policy. In the view of nationally inclined Latvians, once the external influence of the Soviet state was removed, language—language in general, but, most important, Latvian language in particular—could live its historically shaped, but nevertheless authentic and true life. Tolerance workers' demand to recognize that language did morally and politically questionable things in conditions of freedom seemed like yet another attempt to dominate both language and the people.

At the same time, the life of the Latvian language, even in conditions of freedom, required extensive regulation. Indeed, cultivation and regulation of the Latvian language have been central aspects of nation building in various historical periods. Latvian language was understood by nineteenth-century Latvian nation builders and linguists in the Herderian tradition as the expression of a people's soul and creative spirit and as the means for their further cultivation (Bērziņš 2003, Brastiņš 2007, Herder 2002 [1771]; see also Bula 2005, 2000). Yet, due to long periods of foreign domination, it required careful tending and clearing of foreign influences. In the eighteenth century, it was sympathetically inclined

Baltic Germans who began cultivation of Latvian cultural forms in the spirit of national romanticism, which recognized the right of even the smallest ethnic groups (or classes, as the two significantly overlapped in the Baltic context) to cultivate their culture and language (Zelče 2009, 141). Thus, for example, the first newspaper published in Latvian—*Latviešu Avīzes*—was published by a Baltic German Lutheran priest. This cultural work was taken over by Latvian intellectuals during what is known as the "first national awakening" in the 1860s. Many of these intellectuals—such as Krišjānis Valdemārs and Juris Alunāns—were educated and worked in the intellectual centers of the Russian Empire, such as St. Petersburg and Tartu. They came together in the so-called Young Latvians' movement and criticized the work of Baltic Germans in their own periodicals, such as *Mājas Viesis* and *Pēterburgas Avīzes* (published in St. Petersburg). They argued that "even though *Latviešu Avīzes* played a significant role in establishing the tradition of a reading Latvian press . . . a press that is qualitative and useful for Latvians can only be established by Latvians" (Zelče 2009, 27). However, it was precisely a Baltic German—Kārlis Mīlenbahs, who, together with the first Latvian linguist Jānis Endzelīns, developed Latvian linguistics in late nineteenth and early twentieth centuries. He is thought of as one of the "pioneers of Latvian linguistics" and a founder of standardized Latvian (Kļaviņa 2010). For example, he argued for the transliteration of proper nouns in Latvian, which required extensive regulation and remains controversial to this day, especially in relation to Latvia's Russian speakers (Mawhood 2016).

Language policies, aimed at establishing correct terminology, grammatical forms and spellings, as well as regulating the use of language in state institutions, became crucial instruments of the post–World War I Latvian state for the purposes of consolidating a unified nation and institutionalizing a national state (see chapter 2). The University of Latvia, established in 1919 with the purpose of creating an educated Latvian elite, instituted strict Latvian language requirements for its faculty and students (Horts 2004, Stranga 2008). All entering students had to pass a Latvian language examination, and most faculty, with a few exceptions, were given anywhere from three to five years to switch to instruction in Latvian from either Russian or German. At the same time, contrary to the current Language Law adopted in 2000, which stipulates Latvian as the language of public use and minority languages as cultural heritage, the 1935 Language Law stipulated that in municipalities with 50 percent and more minority population, government affairs could be conducted in the minority language with the permission of the minister of the interior.[2]

Late nineteenth- and early twentieth-century Latvian intellectuals labored to develop Latvian literary language on the basis of vernacular language and folk tradition to compensate for Baltic German domination and Russian imperial influence. Late twentieth- and early twenty-first century language stewards labor to cultivate and protect the public life of the Latvian language to compensate for the Soviet past, as well as to protect the Latvian language from too much global influence. On the one hand, this means establishing the dominance of the Latvian language in public space. As Minister of Education Ina Druviete stated in 2005, "It is time, once and for all, to establish a normal language hierarchy in Latvia" (Krauja 2005). "The main task," she continued, "is to preserve a national state and a national public space." On the other hand, this means continued attention to the cultivation and tending of the language itself, including the Latvianization of a rapidly globalizing vocabulary. Both of these tasks are overseen by a network of state institutions, which include the Latvian Language Center established under the auspices of the Ministry of Justice in 1992, the Terminology Commission of the Latvian Academy of Sciences established in 1946, as well as the Latvian Language Commission established under the auspices of the Office of the President in 2002. The Latvian Language Center is responsible for implementing the Language Law, as well as for ensuring translation of European Union legislation in Latvian. The Terminology Commission is charged with the task of developing and updating Latvian language terminology to be used in standardized language. The Latvian Language Commission analyzes language policy and makes policy recommendations. There is also the Latvian Language Institute of the University of Latvia, which conducts historical, linguistic, and sociolinguistic research.

It is noteworthy that the Terminology Commission of the Latvian Academy of Sciences was established in 1946, when, as pointed out by Valentīna Skujiņa (2003), it took over the work of the Latvian Language Terminology and Spelling Commission established in 1919, which also meant inheriting some of its staff members, most notably Jānis Endzelīns (1873–1961)—the most prominent authority on the Latvian language following Kārlis Mīlenbahs. According to Skujiņa (2007), during the Soviet period, the commission's task was to translate Soviet ideology into Latvian. In her brief reflections on the website of the current commission, Skujiņa (2007) describes instances when members of the commission were instructed to develop terminology that "was closer to the Russian language." Skujiņa, who became the secretary of the commission in 1961, also emphasizes that members of the commission managed to resist Russification attempts throughout the Soviet period. After the collapse of the Soviet Union, the narrative goes, the commission returned to its proper work of tending and cultivating the Latvian language with its rich vocabulary and terminology that had been kept up by language stewards in spite of Soviet attempts to Russify it.

However, even in conditions of freedom, the authority of language stewards to determine what counts as Latvian language and how it is to be used is contested. One of the most contested issues has to do with naming persons and groups.

According to state legislation, proper nouns are to be transliterated in Latvian, usually by adding a Latvian ending. This aspect of language use was introduced in the beginning of the twentieth century and subsequently enshrined in legislation. In current conditions of interconnectedness, when more and more foreigners come to reside in Latvia and Latvia's citizens marry foreigners, it has once again become contested. Moreover, it has become a political and legal matter for some of Latvia's Russian speakers, who wish to retain the Russian language rendering of their names. Writing against such objections and defending the transliteration of proper nouns, linguist Juris Baldunčiks writes:

> "It is barbaric to Latvianize proper nouns from other languages," "let's speak and write in a way that is understood in Europe," "the Latvianization of my last name is a violation of my human rights" and similar objections usually come from certain translators and publishers, lecturers of foreign languages, owners of movie houses, foreigners with education in philology that reside in Latvia, and women who have married foreigners, that is, people who have not conducted a single piece of research on the Latvian language and who, it seems, lack real understanding of its uniqueness. . . . It seems there is no good reason to analyze these near-sighted arguments, whose authors have no idea of the chaos they wish to wreak in the Latvian language.[3]

Baldunčiks explains that the internal structure of Latvian is unique and different from other European languages insofar as in Latvian one writes as one speaks and, moreover, most syntactic functions are expressed through declensions, thus endings of words matter. According to Baldunčiks and other Latvian linguists, it is therefore the scientific structure of language, developed by Latvian linguists at the beginning of the twentieth century that determines how proper nouns should be transliterated and how Latvian should be used more generally (Kruk 2011). In Baldunčiks's view, the scientific structure of language should not be questioned on the basis of identity claims.

While arguments about proper nouns in relation to individuals are both interesting and important, what interests me more in the context of this chapter are arguments about how to correctly and ethically refer to individuals via "categories of identification" (Brubaker 1994)—for example, should one refer to Jews as *žīdi* or *ebreji*? Similar to arguments about proper nouns, these arguments also pertain to the proper use of Latvian language. Moreover, they also pertain to authority, namely who has the authority to decide what term should be used—language stewards, the historical community of Latvians, or the individuals referred to by these terms? Most important, however, these arguments reveal a novel aspect in public reasoning about language, that is, the role of an ethical obligation toward proximate and distant others in negotiating language use. To put it another way, arguments about intolerance in language force the nation as a moral community to grapple with ethics and politics and to negotiate proximity and distance in an interconnected world.

History, Proximity, and Ethics: *Žīds*

In April 2009, I attended a lecture by historian Aivars Stranga, the chair of the Department of History, University of Latvia, at Stanford University. The lecture was part of a three-lecture series and was titled "Battles around History: Latvia and Russia." The previous lecture—several days earlier—had been on the topic of Holocaust research in Latvia, which was Stranga's specialization. When I arrived, the lavish Stanford seminar room was filling with a mix of academics and middle-aged and elderly members of the Latvian diaspora, that is, people who had emigrated from Latvia fleeing Soviet power in 1944, or were descendants of someone who did. It was clear that many of the attendees knew each other—they conversed with great familiarity and shared stories about their children's current whereabouts. Personal conversations were intermingled with comments about the lecturer and his topics. A woman in her fifties turned to the man next to her and asked: "What do we say now? Žīds or ebrejs?" The man replied: "Ebrejs, now we say ebrejs. You know ... the last 60 years ..."

In saying so, he suggested that it was because of Soviet occupation that Latvians now had to use the word *ebrejs* when referring to Jews rather than the word *žīds* that was in wide use prior to World War II. Indeed, the Soviet state legislated the use ebrejs instead of žīds with a decree issued by the People's Commissar for Education and dated September 14, 1940 (Ezergailis 1996). With ebrejs being used in official discourse and žīds in private conversations for much of the Soviet period, the word žīds resurfaced in public discourse after the collapse of the Soviet Union. Some understood this as a manifestation of language being liberated from power, while others understood this as the freeing of intolerance and hatred that had been seething under the surface in Soviet Latvia. When tolerance workers, with the backing of Latvia's Jewish Community and by invoking international norms, urged curtailing the use of the word in public discourse, many Latvians perceived this to be an attack on Latvian sovereignty rather than an invitation for an ethical engagement with others in conditions of human plurality (Connolly 2005).

In his analysis of the prevailing language ideologies in Latvia, Sergei Kruk (2011) suggests that Latvian linguists predominantly subscribe to a "historicist linguistic ideology" where language is an expression of a people's spirit formed in specific environmental and historical conditions. Within this ideology, language has a structure, which can be accessed scientifically, and which shapes the people as members of a linguistic community. Individual speakers, therefore, are proxies for the collective subject—the linguistic community—and have no agency of their own in relation to language. If they use the language correctly, as deemed by linguists with the self-ascribed responsibility as language stewards, they are good members of the linguistic community. If they use words incorrectly, they are failing members of the linguistic community. Moreover, the meaning of the word cannot be fundamentally changed if someone uses it in a negative manner. The negativity does not come from the word as a sign or the speaker as its user, but rather from the signified, that is, the people to whom it refers. For example, those arguing for continued use of the word *žīds* often turned to the linguist Jānis Endzelīns as the source of authority for determining how various peoples were to be called in proper Latvian. Evidently, Endzelīns had already expressed his views on this matter in the 1920s, that is, prior to Soviet occupation and to the 1940 decree. Thus, Rasma Grīsle, a former student of Endzelīns, published several articles in the 1990s in which she quoted Endzelīns saying that Jews should be called žīdi and Lithuanians leiši and that changing names will not change the way people are perceived: "The very word *leiši* (similar to the word *žīdi*) cannot be a slur: the sound of the name depends on its carrier" (Grīsle 2005, 75). Endzelīns was thus invoked to argue that it is not advisable to do away with words, because someone uses them negatively. That would amount to impoverishing language.

Many Latvians agreed, not necessarily on the basis of historicist language ideology, but certainly on the basis of their perceptions of the power relations that shaped the Latvian society in the past and the present. Many Latvian speakers shared the view that the word *žīds* was originally a neutral ethnonym, that is, a term used to mark an ethnos (e.g., Mūrniece 2006). Moreover, such claims were accompanied by the suggestion that the injurious nature of the word was derived from the Russian language, namely, that it was the derogatory Russian word *zhid* that tainted the innocent Latvian žīds (Reinsch Campbell 2004). Oddly enough, the question of why this etymologically similar word was injurious in Russian, but not in Latvian was not considered. One would have to assume that since etymology was not to blame, then it must be the social and political life of the term in Russian that attached derogatory connotations to the word *zhid*. John Klier (1982) traces these to the eighteenth century when the Russian Empire annexed Vytebsk and Mogilev, both of which had large Jewish settlements. In a proclamation issued in 1772 to assure the Jewish population of their equal rights to freedom of religion, person, and property, the governor-general of Belorussia used the word *evrei* instead of *zhid* to emphasize the ordinariness of Jews among other population groups (Klier 1982, 3). There was no sharp break in usage, but following this proclamation, the term *zhid* is said to have gradually acquired derogatory connotations (Klier 1982, 3). Such connotations, therefore, emerged as a result of the social and political life of the term in Russian, and according to Russian publicists, this transformation was completed by the consistent association of the word *zhid* with negative stereotypes in Russian literature. Klier (1982) notes that in other languages, such as Ukrainian and Belorussian, etymologically related terms continued to be used as neutral descriptive terms.

This is also the claim made by Latvians who consistently turned to folk songs and early Latvian language literary works to suggest that the etymologically related *žīds* was a neutral and descriptive term that was used to depict social relations between different ethnicities in the Latvian countryside and cities rather than mark Jews negatively (e.g., Klimovičs 2013). They did not attribute much significance to the social dynamics of differentiation that were present in those literary works; they even thought of them as positive. Thus, for example, defenders of the use of the word *žīds* often turned to *Skroderdienas Silmačos*, a favorite play by Rūdolfs Blaumanis about the social life and romantic (mis)encounters in a Latvian farmstead staged annually for midsummer celebrations. There are three Jewish characters in the play—an elderly tradesman, his son, and a seamstress, the son's love interest. The Jewish characters deal with their own relations, which unfold on the premises of the Latvian farmstead, but are not part of the life of the Latvian farmstead. Relations between the traveling Jewish trade and crafts people and the Latvians on the farmstead are friendly, but separate, sometimes a little bit suspicious, perhaps even antagonistic. The Jewish characters are depicted with stereotypical features. They are good at their occupations, but they are also stingy and speak Latvian with a heavy accent. Nevertheless, the head of the farmstead cares for the well-being of everyone—of her servants, as well as of the traveling Jews. Most Latvians do not see anything bad in this depiction of cohabitation or in the use of the word *žīds* in the play. Some of the tolerance workers, however, commented to me that they can barely watch the play, because of the stereotypes and exclusions that the play performs and the lack of perception of these stereotypes and exclusions as problematic by the Latvian audience.

But, more important than the historical configurations of inclusion and exclusion, the Latvian public was thought to overlook the social and political life of the word *žīds* during subsequent historical periods. As argued by Stranga, while eighteenth- and nineteenth-century uses in literature and folk songs might well be described as benign even if othering, at the beginning of the twentieth century the word *žīds* was almost exclusively used with negative connotations, exhibiting a range of economically, racially, and religiously inflected sensibilities (2008, 338). Moreover, in a recent analysis of Nazi propaganda in the 1940s, Kaspars Zellis (2012) shows that the word *žīds* was consistently and purposefully linked with negative and dehumanizing stereotypes, linking Jews to Bolshevism and depicting them as a subhuman threat to the Latvian nation. These associations were extremely powerful. To this day, the word *žīds* is often attached as an ethnic marker to characterize especially ruthless Bolsheviks at the same time as the links to Nazi propaganda are obscured. The effects of this powerful propaganda machinery on the social and political life of the term are generally dismissed in favor of a purist orientation toward original meaning. This is because the Nazi propaganda machinery is perceived as an external force—similar to the Soviet propaganda machinery—that can be removed, revealing the true meaning of the term. The true meaning of the term, established by linguists, reigns above the social use of the term. The historicist ideology of language renders the Latvian language and its speakers innocent.

Moreover, the claims of the Jewish community are, on occasion, delegitimized by linking them with the history of oppression. Thus, if the Russian language was seen to have tainted the neutral Latvian term *žīds*, then the Soviet occupation is blamed for the in-migration of Russian Jews who could not see the subtle distinction between žīds and zhid, and there were few Latvian Jews left to help them see it. This is despite the fact that the debate about the use of the word *žīds* started prior to Soviet occupation, still within the administrative framework of the Russian Empire. For example, the Riga Jewish journal *Evreiskie zapisi,* which was published only for one year in 1881, broached the topic in the context of similar debates in Russia. Historian Aivars Stranga reports that during the first years of independent Latvia, when there existed a parallel socialist government under Pēteris Stučka (1918–20), the Russian-speaking segment of the Jewish community had apparently complained about Latvian nationalism, as manifested through the use of the word *žīds* (2008, 396).[4] Stučka reports that he responded by explaining that the word does not carry negative meaning in the Latvian language. A similar view was expressed by linguists Jānis Endzelīns and Jānis Šmits during a meeting of the Organizational Council of the University of Latvia in 1920, when rector Edgars Felsbergs proposed replacing the word *žīds* with the word *ebrejs* in official university correspondence (Horts 2004, 62–63).[5] Nevertheless the commonly accepted story is that the problem began with the Soviet occupation (e.g., Klimovičs 2013). As put by Andrievs Ezergailis, a diaspora Latvian historian, in his book on the Holocaust in Latvia, "To add to the Latvian-Jewish tension in 1940, the Soviets applied a Russian-language standard that Jews must be referred to as ebrejs in place of the traditional Latvian word žīds. The word *ebrejs* was annoying to the Latvians because it was associated with the Soviet occupation" (1996, 97). This view is supported by Franks Gordons, a Latvian Jew born in 1928, who emigrated to Israel in 1972, but has remained active in public debates in Latvia. In 1998, in an opinion piece for the diaspora paper *Laiks,* Gordons expresses surprise about the "fear from the anger of

Russified 'evrei'?" thus suggesting that continued contestation of the word *žīds* in post-Soviet Latvia has to do with the fact that Latvia's current Jewish population derives largely from Soviet Russia. In other words, the claim is that the injurious capacity of the Latvian language with regard to the word *žīds* was not only itself the result of historical injury inflicted by the Russian language, but also a matter of perception of Russian-speaking Jews.

Arguments about the word *žīds* take place in relation to a history of Latvian, Jewish, and Russian cohabitation in the context of shifting power configurations. Other words contested in arguments about intolerance in language come with different histories. For example, contestation over the use of the word *nēģeris* is linked with political and moral claims of "new others," who bring with them global histories of colonialism and slavery, which Latvians do not feel connected to, even as some Latvians claim colonial heritage for Latvia (see chapter 1). To put it another way, the word *žīds* was part of concrete translocal histories in which Latvians were directly implicated. Debates about the word *nēģeris*—etymologically related to *negro* (Gullestad 2005)—were also translocal. However, Latvians did not feel directly implicated in the global history of colonialism and slavery. Many, therefore, were resentful when asked to broaden their ethical horizons and to position themselves in relation to both this global history and the claims of "the new others" residing in Latvia. The debate about the word *nēģeris*, then, was a debate about the legitimacy of the claims of "new others" and the reach of Latvians' historical and political consciousness and ethical conscience.

Losing Innocence: *Nēģeris*

During one of our frequent conversations, Michael—whom I introduced in the previous chapter—recounted a story about how a mother of a friend had become offended when she heard a televised interview with Michael where he explained that using the word *nēģeris* was racist. The mother of the friend had become quite upset, saying that she has used this word for as long as she can remember without any negative connotations, and that Michael should therefore understand that in the Latvian language the word does not mean anything bad. After relaying her reaction to me, Michael noted: "Well, I do think she is a racist, then." What made her racist in Michael's view was not only the fact that she was using this word, but that she also refused to consider Michael's claim that the word was offensive. The mother of Michael's friend insisted that the word's meaning was local, that is, Latvian, rather than embedded in translocal connections and histories. She also insisted that the word's meaning was external to the communicative situation, which was also an ethical encounter between her and Michael. She claimed meaning through tradition, which, she thought that Michael, as a relative new-comer to Latvia, had to respect. Michael, she thought, was too sensitive and did not have a good grip on the Latvian reality. Though he spoke fluent Latvian, he did not seem to have access to the true meaning of words. As far as the mother of Michael's friend was concerned, making political and moral claims from such a position was an offense in and of itself. Arguing that in using the word *nēģeris* she was simply speaking the Latvian language, she shed culpability. Instead, she claimed agency as an ideal speaking subject who knew the proper meaning of words and reproduced language as a historically shaped, but nevertheless stable system of meaning. But where did the meaning of this word come from? What was the imagery that Latvians drew on when they used it?

In 2006, I was explaining the topic of my research to a small group of people at a friend's birthday party. One of the guests—a Latvian woman working for a liberal think-tank—brought to my attention a children's poem written in 1908 by the seminal Latvian literary and political figure Jānis Rainis. The poem was republished in 2006 in a volume of Rainis's poems for children. She told me that the poem was so blatantly racist that it was impossible for her to show the poem, and thus the whole book, to her children. The poem—all of its six lines—was about encountering *moris* (a moor) in the streets of Riga. It described the colorful livery he wore and was accompanied by an illustration that depicted a dark-skinned man dressed exactly as described in the poem. The poem was titled *Briesmonis* (the Monster). It read:

> Do you know what I saw on the street?
> I met a black African moor!
> He had a hat on this head;
> It was small, round and stood straight up.
> And his coat was long and red,
> He had gloves on his hands as well.[6]

I sought to clarify what exactly bothered my conversation partner. She said she thought the title was not appropriate—"why would you call a black person a monster?" While she allowed the possibility that at the time of writing—in 1908—such a poem would have gone unnoticed, she questioned the judgment of the editor to include the poem in a contemporary reproduction of the book. "With that in mind," she said, "I put the book away on the top shelf and have never read it to my children."

Following this exchange, I located the book and introduced the poem to a group of teachers who had come to a teacher training seminar to discuss toler-ance in the framework of the National Program for the Promotion of Tolerance. I asked them to share their thoughts. The teachers set out to explain the odd title, which, they thought, did not fit the otherwise gentle and friendly tone of the poem. They were of the opinion that the words used in the lines of the poem did not exhibit any explicitly negative intention, and that the sense of wonder in the poem expressed a natural sentiment with regard to the unfamiliar. One teacher speculated that Rainis lived during a time when black people would have commonly been perceived as "frightening others" in Europe, thus she did not find the poem as indicative of particularly unique or noteworthy Latvian sensibilities, but rather as an average product of a historical moment that extended well beyond Latvia. For her, this meant that the poem did not therefore require Latvians to be particularly reflective about their use of language and images.

Interestingly, while the word *nēģeris* was deemed innocent because of its specifically local context of meaning, the imagery conjured up by the poem, in turn, was deemed innocent because of its embeddedness in a historical moment and associated representations that were fundamentally translocal. In the case of the former, the speaker was thought to reproduce a nation's way of speaking and therefore be herself devoid of moral responsibility, whereas in the case of the latter the speaker was thought to reproduce a Europewide discourse, for which she also carried no moral responsibility. Locating the book within common European history, that is, saying that the poem reflected the spirit of the times, enabled the teachers to claim innocence for the author of the poem. Insofar as the author was a subject of his time rather than a subject with historical agency, he was no better or worse than his European compatriots. They did not push this line of thinking further to ask whether that meant that Europe was racist and how they should relate to that. The compromised European history, they thought, should be acknowledged as a context for the writing of the poem, but it did not make active demands on the present, for the times had changed. My friend who brought the poem to my attention, however, thought that it did. As did Michael.

The teachers were distraught. They remembered the 1974 children's book by Zenta Ērgle and Margarita Stāraste, *Ieviņa Āfrikā* (Little Ieva in Africa), in which black children were affectionately called *nēģerēni* (little negroes) and depicted in loincloths and with red lips. As one of the teachers noted, "It was such an endearing little book!" Indeed, how was she to know that the images of Africans used in the book resonated with the images of Africans used in various world fairs deeply embedded in racialized and colonial imaginaries and practices and, moreover, that such representations have been criticized by postcolonial theory for at least the last three decades (Svece 2008, Vuoerala 2009)? Similarly, they did not know that Black Caribbean and African American activists in the United States have linked the word *negro* to the history of colonialism and slavery. As Richard Moore has argued, the term "was born in indignation" (in Nantambu 2007). While signifying the color black in Spanish and Portuguese colonial exploits, the adjective quickly became a noun as European colonialism and slave trade expanded, designating whole people by their skin color, as well as imbuing this designation with an association of inferiority and dehumanization. There have been times in history when the word was endorsed by intellectuals and activists—for example, W. E. B. Du Bois argued that even though it carried negative connotations, it was etymologically better than the word *colored* (Du Bois 1928). Stokely Carmichael (Ture and Hamilton 1992 [1967]) challenged this view in the 1960s, suggesting the word *black* instead, and by 1970s the word *negro* was no longer used. Thereafter, in the 1980s, Jessie Jackson argued for the replacement of *black* with *African-American*, though both seem to be used simultaneously (Martin 1991).[7] Struggles over naming have formed an integral part of transnational black history and of the fight against racism and domination. Even if the "n-word" was at times thought to be preferable to some other word, there was no disagreement that it emerged in the midst of European colonial exploitations entangled with slavery and development of racialized schemes of humanity.

The teachers—and the Latvian public more broadly—did not think they had anything to do with this history of racism and colonialism (see chapter 1). In the stories that Latvians tell about themselves, Latvians never organized world fairs, never exploited colonial subjects or brought them to colonial metropoles, never owned slaves, never took away native land or native children and thus do not have to reflect on colonial history in the same way as, for example, Australians or other colonial-cum-liberal nations or subjects. Further elaborating their claims of innocence, the teachers collectively reminisced about children's stories of *desmit mazi nēģerēni* (ten little negroes), delicious chocolate cakes that used to be called *nēģera buča* (the kiss of a *negro*), and their own childhood associations, all of which were meant to ascertain the benign nature of their imaginaries about black people of African origin that underpinned their use of the word *nēģeris*. Moreover, they argued that their innocent imaginaries were reinforced by Soviet discourses of racialized class oppression, as a result of which they associated the term *nēģeris* with suffering and victimhood not unlike Latvian own suffering under the system of indentured servitude and foreign domination (see chapter 1). This was all to suggest that under no conditions could they ever imagine that the word *nēģeris* was bad. Thus one teacher argued passionately: "I did not know about the [negative connotations of the] word *žīds* for a long time until I heard a rabbi ask people not to use it. But about *čigāni* (gypsies) we did not know and about *nēģeris* also. I did not know. For me, the word *nēģeris* was not derogatory. I learned it today."

But the teachers no longer lived in an isolated world, whether one of innocence or of solidarity with oppressed Africans and African Americans. They had aspired to "return to Europe," which, as it turned out, required living Europe's history as one's own. This included grappling with the history of colonialism and slavery, as well as with the moral and political claims of "new others" in Latvian and European public and political space. Michael extended such claims in the Latvian public space and was, as a result, thought to be too sensitive. However, the newfound mobility that took the teachers or their students beyond the boundaries of home had made the teachers realize that there was another world out there, a world they could not afford to ignore. Thus one teacher recounted how two of her students, who were sisters, had gone to the United Kingdom to visit their mother who worked there.[8] When they had referred to someone as nēģeris in front of their mother, the mother had reprimanded them and told them that "one cannot use such words here." The girls had come back and had asked the teacher why she had not told them that the word nēģeris should not be used in the United Kingdom. The teacher concluded, sheepishly: "It had not occurred to me at all that this might be so. I guess we can talk amongst ourselves like this, but we should probably tell our students that they should not use such words abroad." The teacher had suddenly and expectedly been forced to realize that the world of her students was likely to be larger than hers and that she had not been in the position to prepare her students for it. The concern here was—on the part of the mother, but also the teacher—that the students had failed to behave properly, according to the norms that prevailed outside Latvia. Thus the use of the word nēģeris became a matter of proper conduct abroad. However, the teachers still tried to protect domestic space as "their own," as a space where such norms were subordinated to local ways. Another teacher suggested: "Perhaps we can use this word when talking amongst ourselves, but use other words, when talking with them?"

But how is one to know when one is talking amongst one's own in an intensely interconnected world? In conditions under which Latvians are called on to recognize their connectedness to and ethical obligations toward people and places beyond their immediate surroundings, many claim innocence and autonomy or, at least, try to delineate and preserve an autonomous space where one can be "amongst ourselves." They are, in a way, refusing radical relationality where the self—individual and collective—is formed through an ethical relation with another, as Butler (2015) would have it. For such a relational self, ethical obligation toward another is prior to communitarian solidarity, whether one derived from habitus or asserted as a political position.

Such claims of innocence are not, however, unique to Latvia. They appear in other European contexts as well, especially in Nordic countries, most of which tend to claim innocence not only with regard to the use of the word negro, but also with regard to Europe's colonial history (Dzenovska 2013a, Keskinen et al. 2009, Loftsdóttir and Jensen 2012, Purtschert 2011, see chapter 1). It is well documented that in Nordic contexts there are similar claims that the word negro in its national iterations is a historically innocent part of cultural heritage as exemplified by a long list of literary works, place names, object names, and the like (e.g., Gullestad 2005, Hübinette 2012, Hylland Eriksen 2007, Rasta 2012). Most of the Nordic states also distance themselves from European colonialism, as I have shown in chapter 1, thus separating the political history of colonialism from complicity with colonial trade, exploration, and trafficking in racialized images. Scholars following these debates, such as Marianna Gullestad (2005) and Thomas Hylland Eriksen (2007) in Norway, have both supported Norwegians of African origin in their criticism of the use of the word *neger*, but have also asked whether it is sufficient to focus on specific words—for example, to replace "negro king" in Astrid Lindgren's Pippi Longstocking with "the King of the South Seas" (Hylland Eriksen 2007) or take out the word *negro* from Ottfried Preussler's "Little Witch" (Stikāne 2013)—without a discussion of the deeper logics that underpin them. Thus intervening in the debate, Thomas Hylland Eriksen (2007) argued that discussion about whether or not Astrid Lindgren's heroine's Pippi Longstocking's father should be called "negro king" or "King of the South Seas" overlooks the assumption that the natives cannot govern themselves, "and, accordingly, eagerly install the first visiting white man as their chief" (2007, 5). Naming, thus, is only one aspect of a much broader problem, namely one of the systematic representation of others through a racialized logic of civilizational difference. This colonial logic, as Barnor Hesse (2007) has argued in his article on racialized modernity, continues to be reproduced in the present through a myriad of micropractices that constitute contemporary political landscapes and mechanisms of government, including—or especially—in liberal democratic contexts.

While tracing how the colonial logic informs prevailing political forms is crucial for understanding and, potentially, dismantling the claims of innocence of Latvians and Norwegians, these matters remain outside the scope of tolerance work as part of political liberalism institutionalized in Europe after the fall of socialism. Institutionalized political liberalism is about minority groups fighting for rights in nationally delineated political spaces, about comparing national contexts for their progress with regard to minority rights and the conduct of the majority, and about critical self-reflection of national subjects rather than relationally constituted Europeans. The question of naming, that is, who has the power to name and to constitute a subject in language, remains an important part of the fight against intolerance within the framework of institutionalized political liberalism. It is a tangible measure of individual and collective tolerance. It is no surprise, therefore, that tolerance workers often used precisely this question to illustrate the problem of intolerance in language during a wide variety of seminars and discussions that took place during my fieldwork. Rather than grappling with interconnectedness and proximity and distance in history, politics, and ethics, tolerance promotion efforts focused on claims of minority groups without distinguishing between their different histories and the different histories of their moral and political claims in relation to the majority. In line with institutionalized forms of political liberalism, minority claims were equivalent vis-à-vis the state and the majority. Except that the minority subjects did not always understand or comply with this and thus themselves became targets of educational efforts.

A Scene of Naming

In order to invite reflection on intolerance in language with the hopes of changing linguistic conduct, tolerance workers organized seminars and discussions for target groups—for example, teachers—to which they invited minority representatives for the purpose of sharing their views and experiences. The tolerance workers themselves often served as moderators or were present as the organizers of the event, as was the case during a seminar on multiculturalism organized by the Latvian Language Program Unit for Latvian language teachers working in minority schools in the fall of 2005.[9] The seminar began with a panel discussion. The panel consisted of representatives from minority organizations, in this case the Jewish Association, the African Latvian Association, and a regional Roma association. The discussion was moderated by Daniel, the staff member of the Secretariat for the Integration of Society who appeared in chapter 3, and who worked on the implementation of the National Program for the Promotion of Tolerance. Besides being a civil servant, he was an academic, as well as in a position to claim a minority voice, which he did not do. Rather, he inhabited the public space as a liberal intellectual. Sometimes those who did claim a minority subject position privately criticized him for such a stance, for not speaking out in crucial moments as a minority rather than a concerned liberal. This position, it seems, was important for him, though we never discussed it explicitly. It allowed him to appear as an objectively concerned subject rather than as a personally interested steward of tolerance, including in the following performative scene of naming.

Having introduced members of the panel, Daniel gave the floor to Laila, a member of the Jewish community in Latvia whom I introduced in chapter 3. Laila explained that she likes to know how to call people without offending them. Turning to her fellow panel member from the Roma organization, Laila theatrically stated that she does not know how to call gypsies these days—do they want to be called Roma, and will they be offended if they are called gypsies? She exemplified the importance of this question by recounting an encounter with another one of her fellow panelists—Robert, a representative of the African Latvian Association:

> Robert and I have known each other for years now, and we love each other, and I thought I could do pretty much everything. He is such a tolerant and nice person and he always explains everything. And then one time at some conference, I was talking about something, perhaps telling a joke, I do not remember, and I said the word *nēģeris* and Robert's eyes get big and he tells me that I cannot say that word in front of people. And you know that in Latvian and Russian language the word *nēģeris* is not a bad word, it has no negative connotations. It is rather the word *black* that has negative connotations. He says, I will understand, but my friends will not understand. I was terrified and was afraid to speak from being all shook up.

Laila's narrative engaged the stories Latvians tell themselves about themselves, that is, that the word *nēģeris* does not have negative connotations. Thus, she explained that, historically, it is the word *melnais* ("the black" in Latvian) rather than *nēģeris* that carries negative connotations for both Latvians and Russians. During Soviet times, the word *melnais* (and *chernyi* in Russian) racialized the Roma and people from the Caucasus, while within Latvian folklore, *melns* (black) is the opposite of virtuous. In relation to these historical articulations, the word *nēģeris* seems benign in the Latvian imaginary, Laila argued. She thus established herself as someone who had a grasp of the Latvian reality. Simultaneously, she appealed to her friendship with Robert and therefore construed Robert as a person she respects, which indicates that she was suggesting alternative grounds for legitimizing demands not to use the word *nēģeris*.

Shortly thereafter, Laila received a question from the audience, asking whether the word *žīds* can be used in Latvia without offending the Jews. Her response is noteworthy, again, in its affirmation of the Latvian historical imaginary and justification of the use of the word *ebrejs* instead of *žīds* on the grounds of a particular ethical orientation—respect toward the wishes of someone who is your friend, but also a member of a minority group:

> A very good question. Thank you! First, it is not the word that determines, but the context. And if my beloved man or woman—let's be tolerant here [*laughter in the audience*]—calls me *muļķīte* [little fool], it depends on why this is being said to me—you are a fool, or is it something else. About the word *žīds*. Jewish society has two parts, as it were. One is small, to which I also belong, which thinks that in normal contexts there is not a big problem with this word. But, really, this group is

very small. But the other group, which is larger, considers this word to be bad and does not want to be called in that name. Why is it so? The majority of the Jewish community, unfortunately it has worked out that way, has come here from Russia where this word has not been used since the times of Catherine II when it was forbidden by her decree and had a radically negative meaning. And all Latvians know that very well, but Latvian linguists and cultural specialists seem to have no other problem to solve, especially when we consider that in Internet discussions people announce that they will say the word *žīds* and then add in parenthesis that in Latvian it is a normal word. Why are they justifying themselves? Apparently, the person has a sense that it is not a good word—why do you justify yourself, if you think it is not a bad word? . . . I will say this— the Jewish community has asked numerous times not to call ebreji žīdi. I think if some person turns to you, for example Baiba, and says, please do not call me Baibiņa or Bucītis, or something else, then I think that you would probably not, unless you want to be on bad terms with that person, call her that. Whatever the reason, the Jewish community asks not to call them žīdi. Is it really such a big deal? I do not understand why the Latvian community insists . . . why it has to be insisted that this word be used, if this is not in the context of *dainas* [folk songs], or history books, or something [meaning, outside of social and political contexts]. Of course, what will you do? Throw it out? No. It's good that it is there. But, please, do not call Jews žīdi.

In her reply to the question, Laila pointed to the insistence of the "Latvian linguists and cultural specialists" that the word *žīds* carries no negative meaning as it is part of the Latvian linguistic tradition, as I have outlined above. She wondered about the merits of such insistence in the face of evidence to the contrary in the social life of the word. She suggested that people do have an awareness that the word *žīds* has the potential to injure, though she did not dwell on how the word may have acquired its injurious features. Therefore it is not clear to her, at least rhetorically, why there is such widespread resistance to requests from the Jewish community not to use it. At the same time, Laila conceded that, yes, the word has been historically used and, as a *Latvian Jew*, she understands the importance of this historical usage. The request for change, therefore, was first externalized through an association with Russia, subsequently the Latvian historical tradition and the use of žīds was affirmed, yet given contemporary social conditions, the plea for change was reasserted on the basis of an ethical orientation toward a particular group of people residing in Latvia.

It should be noted that the context of this scene was highly performative. This was not Laila's first time participating in such events. She was, as she said in chapter 3, "a conference squirrel." This was, then, her public position on how the claim was best to be articulated. She was well aware of the prevailing hierarchies of public visibility and she softened the claim by having it come from a Latvian Jew who asked for understanding with regard to the Russian Jew who could not access the truth about the Latvian linguistic community in the way that she could. Given that an agreement on the nature of the word and its proper uses seemed impossible, she appealed to the social fact of coexistence, to "common life grounded in physical proximity" (Butler 2015, 100), as a legitimate basis for the kind of ethical relations that would lead Latvians to refrain from using the word *žīds*.

Inspired by Laila's answer and determined to push the issue further, Daniel, the moderator of the discussion, asked both the Roma representative Aleksandrs and Robert from the African Latvian Association to clarify for the audience how they would like to be called. While Robert satisfied Daniel's request and explained that instead of the derogatory *nēģeris*, he would prefer to be called African, Aleksandrs proceeded to deliver somewhat of a winding answer, which ended inconclusively by him quoting a proverb: "Call us what you will, just don't throw us over the fence." Aleksandrs himself frequently used the word *čigāns* (gypsy), only occasionally replacing it with Roma. It seemed that he was not quite sure what his stance should be, even as it can hardly be denied by anyone that *čigāni* have consistently been depicted if not in explicitly negative, then certainly in othering and exoticized light both within Latvian and Soviet contexts (e.g., Lemon 2000).

Daniel, unsatisfied with Aleksandrs's answer, suggested that the Roma themselves have formulated a concrete position on this in one of their recent publications, therefore he repeatedly asked Aleksandrs to deliver a conclusive answer. "Aleksandr, čigāni vai romi?!" (Aleksandr, gypsies or Roma?!), Daniel impatiently exclaimed. Feeling pressed, Aleksandrs replied: "You know, I will stick to the . . . what we have from May of 2004 when we joined the European Union . . . in Europe, for more than 30 years, these people are called Roma." Contrary to Laila and Robert, Aleksandrs avoided the interpellation as a self-naming subject, which seemed unacceptable to the liberally inclined Daniel, who was determined to make the subaltern speak by naming himself. Aleksandrs's reluctance to definitively choose between gypsies and Roma suggests, perhaps, some differences between how he, on the one hand, and Daniel, Laila, and Robert, on the other hand, perceived the significance of the naming process. The proverb Aleksandrs invoked seemed to suggest that his concern pertained to being able to live without much concern for recognition. In other words, his ability to live a full life did not necessarily depend on the recognition of the state or "the state people," that is Latvians, as manifest in language. He did not necessarily make a connection between the word Latvians used to refer to the Roma, the negative attitudes and stereotypes about Roma in the Latvian society, and the living conditions of the Roma.[10]

In order to push the point further, someone from the audience asked Aleksandrs what nationality is written in his passport, thus turning to the Soviet-era practice of recording nationality in state identification papers, which had been practiced by the post-Soviet Latvian state as well (see chapter 2). Aleksandrs replied that it used to be čigāns (gypsy), but that now the law allows one to leave nationality unstated in one's passport. Aleksandrs's answer, which was, once again, one of avoidance rather than compliance, was accompanied by laughter in the audience, which seemed amused by the fact that Aleksandrs was refusing to be pinned down as a particular subject in language. In contrast to Aleksandrs's refusal to constitute himself as a proper minority subject in language, in Daniel's, Laila's, and Robert's view, the way the Jewish, African, and Roma communities were named—that is, brought into public life—mattered for their public and private lives, as well as for the majority subject's ethical and political dispositions. Moreover, Daniel's, Laila's, and Robert's request for recognition reproduced the liberal democratic state as the arbiter in a struggle for recognition, whereas Aleksandrs, by not rendering himself knowable and nameable, seemed to refuse this role to the state.[11]

Throughout the seminar and the panel discussion, the words that were contested were reiterated over and over again. Laila's citations of the words žīds and nēģeris constituted a subject that, while distancing from them, did not fully sever its relationship with the tradition from which they emerge. She did, after all, claim to be a Latvian Jew who understands the historical deployment of these words, yet who also does not feel fully at home within this context. Her distancing from the problematic words involved mocking and humor rather than the objectifying and pedagogical distancing performed by Daniel who pronounced the words in a voice seemingly freed of affective orientations as if to emphasize that he was not using the words, but rather talking *about* them (see Butler 1997, 38). The teachers, in turn, spoke from a troubled space of innocence, projecting an ambiguous relationship to the words they spoke—they were using them, yet they were also beginning to talk about them.

Ethnical Encounters with Non-Latvians

A week or so after the teacher-training seminar, Daniel and I both took part in a debate about political correctness organized by a nongovernmental organization. The other participants included a journalist, a philosopher, and Aija, the facilitator of the discussion, who was also the director of the NGO that organized the event. Aija opened the discussion by posing the following question: "If you were invited to be part of a state-established commission charged with the task to come up with another word for the currently used *cittautieši* (literally, other peoples) or *nelatvieši* (non-Latvians) [both used to refer to Latvia's Russian speakers], do you think such work would have any meaning?" "Daniel," she continued, "do you like the term *cittautieši*?" Daniel, who usually appeared in public space as a liberal intellectual and civil servant, was himself from a Russian-speaking background, but spoke excellent Latvian and had integrated into state-based public structures. However, in an interview I had with him at the outset of my fieldwork in 2005, Daniel invoked Aesop's fable about the bat, who belonged neither with birds nor beasts, to illustrate his positionality in relation to Latvians and Russian speakers. Daniel replied to Aija's question with the following: "About three years ago, . . . I tried to come up with a word that would be less alienating. I won't say that I came up with anything terribly exciting, but I proposed the term Latvia's Russians (*Latvijas krievi*) that could capture belonging to this land. When I tested it in an online forum, I got very sharp reactions. The majority of online commentators did not like that that their identity would be attached to a state." Aija then turned to Pēteris, a well-known radio journalist, who was born in the United States, but was part of a small group of second-generation diaspora Latvians, who came to live and work in Latvia in the 1990s.

> AIJA: Pēteris, in one of your last comments, you use the terms *nelatvietis* and *cittautietis*.
> PĒTERIS: Because they have become entrenched in Latvian vocabulary.
> AIJA: But the word *negro* was entrenched in American vocabulary.
> PĒTERIS: But only until the moment the blacks said that they do not like it. I do not know Russian and do not read Russian press, but nobody has ever told me that they do not like these words.
> AIJA: I will say honestly that it bothers me terribly. How can a group communicate to another that they find some word offensive?

Aija then admitted that she did not actually think that a state commission was a good way to resolve the use of contested words, but she did think it was important to "find a space for discussing discourse ethics (*diskursa ētiku*)." Pēteris continued:

> With regard to *nelatvietis* and *cittautietis*, I have not heard a good alternative, because peoples do juxtapose themselves to others and politically there is a difference between Latvians and other peoples who live in this country. The term *latvijietis* [a Latvianization of a Russian construct *latviets* that designates state rather than ethnic belonging] sounds

somewhat tortured. Vaira Vīķe Freiberga [the president at the time] has said that all those who live in Latvia are *latvieši* (Latvians). This is not acceptable to Russians, Belorussians, Poles, etc. I think it would be quite torturous to find one word that would communicate that which right now is captured by the unpleasant words *nelatvietis* or *cittautietis*.

For Pēteris, the decision to use one word instead of another was not a matter of what the word means or whether it is linguistically correct, but, rather, whether or not the group thus referred to finds the word acceptable or not. Moreover, it was also about a historically and politically accurate way of capturing of a person's or group's relationship with the state and the majority. Naming, then, was a matter of a respectful encounter with another that also recognized rather than obscured historical and political difference.

Daniel, continuing the discussion of how Russian speakers refer to themselves, pointed out that words can be used in unexpected ways, that naming practices can become part of political commentary. He gave the example of Russian speakers, some of whom, including journalists of two prominent Russian-language publications, such as *Vesti* and *Segodna*, use the word *negr* (a wordplay on Russian for *negro* and *negrazhdanin*, that is, noncitizen) to remark on their subordinate status and political dispossession in Latvia: "They embraced their subordination and identified with it" (see also Platt 2013, 272). Pēteris vehemently objected to this practice: "But they did it with a racist term!" Moreover, Pēteris argued that in equating the situation of Russian speakers to the history of subordination of black people was not accurate, because Russian speakers have never experienced segregation and have never been considered less than human. Daniel and Aija, who was also of Russian speaking background, began to suggest that, well, political dispossession can be viewed as a form of segregation, even dehumanization, but the discussion moved on. Aija brought up the Jewish community as having succeeded in making the argument that the word *ebrejs* should be used instead of *žīds*. Indeed, despite the arguments and objections from linguists and people who insisted on using proper Latvian, ebrejs fairly quickly replaced žīds in mainstream discourse, probably because ebrejs had been in use in formal discourse during the Soviet period, with žīds being used in everyday discourse. After independence, then, the use of žīds did mark a political position rather than being an example of simply "speaking Latvian" and came to mark the speaker more so than the person or group referred to. Indeed, as Pēteris noted, "It is about the level of civilization. . . . a civilized person will never in public discourse use words like *pederasts* [used to refer to homosexuals], žīds, *nigers*, though čigāns [gypsy] is used more often. There is a mean philosophy underlying these terms, and it is a matter of education—not only is it ugly to use such terms, but it is also ugly to hold in your soul the conviction that a person deserves such an ugly naming." Daniel then turned to the previous week's teacher training seminar and told the participants of the discussion how

> we managed to get on stage representatives from the Jewish Association, the Roma Association and Afrolat [the African Latvian Association] and, since several teachers were afraid to address them directly, they were sending us little pieces of paper with questions where they revealed all their . . . [fears and prejudices]. . . . I have these papers, they had questions like: how do I call you not to offend you? And then Laila [the representative of the Jewish Association], said that the first principle for using a particular word is to know how the person or the group wants to be called. If they want to be called *ebrejs* rather than *žīds*, then there is no question about it.

Continuing the thread, Pēteris recalled a conversation he had with a caller on his show: "Some elderly man called and said: Blaumanis [a Latvian writer] used žīds, Ulmanis [Latvian president, 1934–40] used žīds, and I will use žīds. I told him: listen, how would it be if I now decided to call you a monkey? And I don't care what you think of it, I have decided to call you that and I will do it. He thought for a while, and then he said: okay, I will never call them žīds. And that's how the conversation ended. And that's why I say it is a question of education."

There were two claims of historical and political accuracy that appeared in this discussion: one, recognized as legitimate by Pēteris, that a minority group's historical and political difference must be recognized in language; and, another, dismissed by Daniel and Pēteris both, that the majority had a right to claim proper use of historically formed language. The legitimacy of one claim and the illegitimacy of the other were distinguished by the fact that recognized minority status in relation to the state enabled claims of historical and political difference, whereas the majority status in relation to the state made claims of historical and political difference—in this case of majority vis-à-vis language—suspect and, moreover, tools of marginalization and exclusion. Majority language had to become more inclusive, while at the same time minorities, such as Russian speakers, also could not freely use racist terms to mark their own condition of dispossession. Above all of this, however, stood a person's or a group's wish to be referred to one way rather than other. Aldis, the philosopher, qualified:

> I think the question of political correctness is interesting, because it is a tool with the help of which we try to live together. There is no formula, and the only thing we can do is what we are doing now. I say čigāns, but he says, no, I want to be called Roma. Then I say, but I want to call you

čigāns, and then there is a discussion and perhaps it can be changed. And the important thing is that the discussion is about the fact that people can actually do something that is not natural [i.e., that does not come naturally to them]. And political correctness is one such thing, and I see it as an attempt to live together in a civilized manner.

But does the ethics of cohabitation thus established have the force to change mechanisms of subordination? Consider the following. When discussing how to refer to Russian speakers in Latvia, Pēteris said that he does not like the term Russian speakers, because there are other Russian speakers in Latvia besides those who use Russian as their first language of communication.

> AIJA replied: Not acceptable to you, but if it is acceptable to me? You can use it, because I allow you to use it.
>
> PĒTERIS: No, I am not saying that it is unacceptable, but I think it is not logical. We have to consider the state and society in which we live, and between Latvians, and, okay, Russian speakers, there are political differences where one group is largely on one side and the other on the other. If there is no sociopolitical communication, then there are also difficulties with linguistic communication.
>
> ALDIS: But language does not work like that. . . . There are many words we use without thinking about what they actually mean. . . . Let's say Jānis Ozoliņš [literally, the little oak]. How many times do we actually think that his name is related to the oak tree? . . . What I wanted to say is that introducing other words will not actually change the situation. . . . You say *latviets* is a better word, but there is the teacher who will hear Russian, when they hear *latviets*, because there is also the word *latish*, which means ethnic Latvian.
>
> AIJA: The main thing that we have underscored is cooperation, everything begins with cooperation.

The debate that unfolded, then, was about how to name difference that is relationally constituted rather than about how to name a particular group. The group, as argued by Roger Brubaker (1994), was not a sociological reality as much as it was a politically constituted category of identification. Moreover, positions with regard to how to name difference were themselves seen as matters of civilizational difference. Daniels noted: "Contrary to Latvia, in other countries such politicians [who use intolerant language] would be deposed immediately. These are side effects of development and maturation. We have not yet reached the level of politically correct language, but we are already tired of it." For Daniels, politically correct language was a stage on a developmental and civilizational scale. Aldis slightly diverged: "This maturation discourse posits some sort of a hierarchy between mature societies, say England, and .... I would rather emphasize that other countries have gone through certain historical experiences, such as racism, and learned from it. We consider that all this antiracism is imposed by the European Union and what not, and that we do what we want in our country.... Unfortunately, people do not learn from others' mistakes, and we evidently will have to go through some painful experiences." Pēteris, however, was optimistic about the power of law and concluded that "the EU is a liberal establishment and tends to be ahead of member states with regard to discrimination. And whether people like it or not, certain things will have to be done, certain things will be imposed through courts and so forth."

At the end, Aija staged an exercise in which ethical coexistence could be established in language by performing radical voluntarism, namely by asking everyone how they would like to be identified, as if this was solely a matter of identity politics and interpersonal ethics. The participants' willingness to grant everyone the right to name themselves suggested to Aija that "we are all tolerant here." But the larger question remained—what were the spaces for an ethical encounter with the other and how was one to reconcile recognition of difference shaped by historically constituted power relations with an ethical relation to another, itself embedded in fields of power? There seemed to be a tension between interpersonal and intergroup ethics, on the one hand, and overlapping histories of subordination and domination, on the other. For example, what was to take the upper hand: the Jewish request not to be called žīdi or Latvian attempts to clear language from traces of domination that render the word žīdi problematic in the present? Moreover, there was a tension between proximity and distance, both historical and contemporary. If Latvians had no historical experience of cohabitation with black people, what were the grounds for legitimizing their moral and political claims? Was one to go purely on the basis of interpersonal or intergroup ethics in "conditions of unchosen cohabitation" (Butler 2015), or was a history of confrontation and cohabitation necessary in order to ground these claims without them seeming as impositions from the outside? Finally, were civilizational imperatives sufficient for making these claims stick, so to speak? At the time of my fieldwork it seemed, at least to Pēteris, that, indeed, if nothing else, the EU political institutions would help to change discourse ethics through institutionalizing civilizational imperatives. Today, however, it seems that whereas the radical openness and interconnectedness of individual and collective selves might be a historical reality, it is receding as a political reality. The EU might still be a liberal establishment and Europe might still remain a normative trope of civilizational achievement and development, but the polities of EU member states are becoming radically contested political spaces, ones where liberalism, as David

Westbrook (2016) has put it, is at risk of being deposed as the "house ideology." Rather than the end of history, it seems, European polities—and the West more broadly—are seeing the return of history and politics.

Ethics of Interconnectedness

As this and other chapters in the book show (see chapter 6 in particular), the ways in which Latvian lifeworlds are interconnected are changing. It is no longer through imagining the West, as during the Soviet period (Yurchak 2005), that Latvians are encountering it, but via colleagues, visitors, coresidents, family members, tourists, or on occasion, via their own assertions of Westernness. It is no longer about imaginary Africans, as in the poem titled *Briesmonis* or the book about little Ieva in Africa, but about Michael making moral and political claims in Latvian public space. Coexistence with difference has become plural, simultaneously proximate and distant, and multilayered. The model where Latvians lived together—in tension or otherwise—with Russians, Jews and other "historical minorities," as policy documents put it, is now accompanied by everyone grappling with living with "new others"—Western consultants and businessmen, European Union civil servants, dispossessed former colonial subjects, globally marginalized groups, people running from war, and more. The question that looms large is this: How is one to orient in this space ethically and politically, while at the same time maintaining a sense of historical and cultural embeddedness? How far do ethical obligations toward the other reach?

Some of the demands that this new situation of interconnectedness makes are unsettling and may even seem threatening. As Judith Butler puts it in her reflections about ethical obligations in an interconnected world, "Obligations to those who are far away, as well as those who are proximate, cross linguistic and national boundaries and are only possible by virtue of visual or linguistic translations, which include spatial and temporal displacement" (2015, 103). Valuation of displacement as a modality through which to critique and unsettle exclusionary and bounded spaces, communities, and imaginaries is widely embraced in anthropology and in left-liberal scholarship more broadly (Dzenovska and De Genova 2018). But the question still remains: how much displacement is too much? Moreover, what if displacement is perceived not as a fundamental condition of being, a foundational relationality prior to the solidification of sovereign subjects (Butler 2015, Markell 2003), but rather as a form of domination? Is it permissible, from the perspective of this foundational and ethical relationality, to wish to maintain some form of emplacement or coherence of the self? For Butler, the location of the body matters and ethics is only possible through a continuous negotiation of "hereness" and "thereness," of "accepting and negotiating the multilocality and cross temporality of ethical connections we might rightly call global" (2015, 105). In Butler's reflections, the ethical subject is located, that is, historically and culturally embedded. However, this embeddedness is not primary—the ethical subject is in a permanent state of negotiating proximity and distance, of negotiating how to respond to an ethical call that comes from afar via visual or textual images of suffering (Butler means war here). In the case of Latvia, the historically and culturally embedded ethical subject is negotiating how to read and respond to the calls coming from both proximate others with adjacent, if different histories, such as Jews or Russians, and distant others, such as African Americans, with distant histories who call on Latvians to recognize their present interconnectedness. Compared to Felder, who in chapter 4 called on Latvian historians and the Latvian public to repent for their past complicity with racial anthropology and eugenics, these invitations extend beyond policing Europe's moral and political landscape and pertain to concrete forms of present and future cohabitation.

The teachers in this chapter pondered whether it is possible to appear only to "one's own" without being seen by "them." That is, they were asking whether there is a space where the bounded self is prioritized or untouched by the claims of others. Others, such as Michael's friend's mother and some of Latvia's philologists, claimed that Latvians are free to speak Latvian and to use proper words that, according to their communal tradition, are not offensive. Following Butler's interpretation of ethical obligation on the basis of Emmanuel Levinas's and Hannah Arendt's philosophical texts, such an assertion of choice is in itself an ethical response that invokes freedom and sovereignty over ethical appeal (2015, 105). In such instances, that is, when sovereignty and freedom were invoked in response to an ethical appeal of a proximate or distant other, the ethical appeal was understood as complicit with forms of power that threaten the self. For example, the ethical appeal of the other was understood as backed by liberal institutions and forms of globalization that threatened the Latvian self in ways reminiscent of past instances of domination. In Butler's normative rendering of the ethics of relationality, this does not justify a defensive stance. Again, drawing on Levinas and Arendt, Butler argues that an ethical obligation toward the other—or treating the other as a political equal—requires inhabiting precarity, that is, inhabiting the threat without resorting to boundedness and communitarianism (2015, x). More than that, for Butler, resorting to boundedness and communitarianism as a response to a perceived threat is especially dangerous, as the case of Israel indicates, for "state people," that is, a people backed by a state and an army. The challenge that Butler poses to Israelis and Jews supportive of Israel is this: How is one to feel at once vulnerable to destruction by the other and responsible for the other (2015, 109)? For Levinas, whose philosophy of ethics Butler uses despite the fact that Levinas himself did not live up to the radical possibilities that it offers, ethical responsibility—openness to other despite the threat of destruction—precedes ethical responsiveness, that is, the response to the call of the other (Butler 2015, 110). Drawing on this interpretation of ethics, it might be said that Latvian teachers and the public more broadly lack ethical responsibility that could shape the ethical response to the call of the other, whether as a request of the Jewish community to use the word *žīds* instead of *ebrejs* or whether in Michael's call to stop using the word *nēģeris*. Arendt's thought, in Butler's interpretation, leads to a similar conclusion. For Arendt, ethics and politics derives from unchosen cohabitation, that is, men [sic] cannot choose with whom they inhabit the earth and thus this condition of unchosen cohabitation must guide politics and policies. Politics and policies aimed at self-preservation are unjustifiable. In fact, self-preservation can only be achieved through the other, in a relation to the other, for the self is produced through sociality.

Many Latvians thought that the reestablishment of an independent state meant that Latvians as a cultural and historical community had finally arrived at a point when they could choose with whom and how to inhabit the earth. But insofar as they gained such freedom, they also joined an interconnected world, which made particular demands on them. These demands came in the form of liberalization and democratization projects, such as tolerance promotion, and they came in the form of moral and political claims of proximate and distant others. While at the time of my fieldwork the Latvian public was only beginning to grapple with the political and ethical claims of proximate and distant others on them, such claims became particularly audible in the context of Europe's "migrant/refugee crisis." The Somalis, with whom I began this book, were the first "distant others" who generated intensive public and political debates within government structures and the broader society. In the following and concluding chapter of the book, then, I return to the Somalis to reflect on Europe's moral and political landscape through analysis of bordering and migration governance.

REPRESSION AND REDEMPTION
The Tensions of Rebordering Europe

The bus to the foster home that took in the Somalis after they were let go from the detention center was to leave at 10:00 a.m. on a Saturday in August 2006.[1] The foster home was hosting a welcoming event for the Somalis, and the African Latvian Association (ALA) was organizing a bus for Riga-based invitees to attend the event. ALA had befriended the Somalis for several reasons. First, Roberts, one of the leaders of ALA (who appeared in chapter 3), was also a member of the church that was associated with the foster home. Second, the leaders of ALA were actively involved in tolerance promotion and antiracism activism, even as the membership disagreed on whether the organization should engage in anti-racism activism or simply stick with its original purpose, namely the provision of social networking and community support for people of African origin in Latvia. Roberts thought that the organization had to do both, and that the Somali experiences only confirmed this. The Somalis did not know anybody in Latvia, thus they needed community support. And they had already become targets of racism both on the street and in public discourse. For example, after the adults of the group had spent a day in Riga looking for work, Roberts wrote to me saying that they had experienced racist slurs and physically threatening encounters. "It is their reality now," was how he concluded his message.

The bus eventually left at 11:00 a.m. after waiting for latecomers, trips to the bathroom, and last-minute shopping for gifts in the nearby shopping center. The company on the bus was diverse. It included members of the African Latvian Association and their families, a civil servant who worked at the Secretariat of the Special Tasks Minister for the Integration of Society, a girl who had worked for the Red Cross but had become disillusioned with its bureaucracy, a journalist from the *Baltic Times*, a couple of German women affiliated with the church, a staff member of the Human Rights Organization who had worked on the Somalis' cases, and myself.[2] When we got to the foster home, others, who had taken different modes of transportation, were already there—two representatives of the International Organization for Migration, one staff member from the Office of Citizenship and Migration Affairs, another journalist, the director of the local school that the teenage Somalis were to attend, as well as a filmmaker, who would subsequently produce a film about the Somalis entitled *Pirmie* (*They Were the First*).[3]

This event brought together nearly the whole spectrum of actors who were involved in making sense of and dealing with the Somalis' cases. While they were all at the foster home in a festive atmosphere, relations among them were not always smooth, as they tried to make the asylum system operational as professionals, but also as historically embedded individuals with divergent worldviews. It was a learning process for all. As put by Līga Vijupe, a staff member of the Office of Citizenship and Migration Affairs, in the film *They Were the First*, "They were the first to come as a group. We did not know their routes, and it was also the first time we had unaccompanied under-aged asylum seekers." Aija, Robert's girlfriend, who worked with state institutions on integration related matters, agreed: "They were like a litmus test—all the theoretical policy frameworks had to function in practice, and all the gaps and shortcomings were revealed."

One institution that was not represented on this friendly visit was the Latvian State Border Guard. This, however, did not mean that border guards did not visit the foster home. The border guards had been right to think that the Somalis— "seven black people in the streets of Riga"—could not disappear without a trace (see Introduction). The Somalis' arrival at the foster home was noticed by neighbors and soon the local and then the national media dutifully reported on their whereabouts. The border guards, who until then had seemingly forgotten about the Somalis, arrived at the foster home shortly thereafter and much before the welcome event. It was a strange visit by all accounts. Sigita, the "mom" of the foster home, as its inhabitants endearingly called her, described the encounter as intimidating: "It was late evening, and the children told me that there is a car outside. Some man, who turned out to be a border guard from the nearby town, came up to the house and asked me why we keep our cats outside. He said he had come to see whether the Somalis were here. He had gone around to the neighbors, asking about us." When Sigita called the regional State Border Guard office the next day, she was told that it was their task to know who lived in the area, and that the foster home should go on "living peacefully," for they will not be bothered anymore. But that was not true. The foster home had several other contentious and intimidating encounters with border guards. On one visit, an officer from the Department of Asylum of the Riga office of the State Border Guard told Sigita that he "will do anything to get the Somalis out of Latvia." On another occasion, Sigita received a phone call from the children telling her that a border guard—the same one who had paid the first visit—was waiting at the house. When, upon returning home, Sigita asked him the reason for his visit, he replied: "Nothing. Can't I visit young people?" Sigita told him that they are not family friends and that his visits are not welcome. On yet another occasion, the same border guard told Sigita that he knew her passport had expired. "They work with KGB methods," Sigita concluded.

This was not far from the truth, as the border guards did often work with methods they had inherited from the Soviet state, especially in the early 1990s, when Soviet border control laws, regulations, and practices provided the only point of reference for their work. "Procedures were fully taken over from the USSR," said a staff member of the Department of Border Control of the State Border Guard at the Riga Airport, when I interviewed him on the border in 2006. "We only changed the name of the country," he chuckled.[4] But it would be erroneous, if convenient, to assume that the border guards' repressive practices were a survival from the "Soviet times" (*padomju laiki*). As I show in this chapter, such practices were also part of the lessons that the border guards learned in the process of becoming European. It was not merely out of habit that they used methods resembling those of the KGB, but also because they tried to do their job well, and their job was to secure Latvia's and the European Union's external border against what they perceived to be intensifying flows of unwanted people and goods. Controlling the borders of an independent Latvia in the European Union meant learning to navigate the paradox of Europeanness, namely the imperative to profess and institutionalize the values of inclusion and openness while at the same time practicing—and also institutionalizing—exclusion and closure.

Borders are sites par excellence of the paradox of Europeanness insofar as they do not simply foreclose movement, but rather regulate it. They do so in a highly uneven manner, resulting in closure and exclusion for some and openness and inclusion for others (e.g., Cunningham and Heyman 2010, Follis 2012, Kotef 2015, Mezzadra and Neilson 2013, Reeves 2014, Wilson and Donnan 1998). Border control is a mechanism that regulates the balance of inclusion and exclusion on which European nation-states and the European Union depend. This balance has been differently configured in different historical moments—for example, the post–World War II openness to "guest workers" came to an end in the 1970s (Hansen 2003, Mandel 2008), while the 2000s saw the enlargement of the European Union and thus the opening of internal borders to "labor migration" and the closure of external borders to unwanted "economic migrants" (Bacas and Kavanagh 2013, Follis 2012). Throughout, entry was granted to a deserving few, such as "refugees" and "asylum seekers." Inclusion and exclusion in relation to borders thus crucially depends on categorization. It matters greatly whether one is categorized as a citizen, a refugee, an asylum seeker, an economic migrant, or an illegal immigrant. The line between the deserving few and the undeserving many is drawn, redrawn, and hotly contested (Anderson 2013, Cabot 2014, Follis 2012, Ticktin 2011). Latvian border guards participated in this line drawing. They firmly believed that the Somalis were among the undeserving many, that is, economic migrants, but were on the verge of passing as the deserving few, that is, as refugees. By following the Somalis to the foster home after they were let go from the detention center, the State Border Guard refused to give up on getting to the bottom of what they believed to be the Somalis' true categorical belonging.

But it was not just border guards—along with migration officials—who worked to implement the Latvian version of Europe's migration regime. The activities of the State Border Guard were closely monitored by the Human Rights Organization—an NGO implementing various human rights and minority rights monitoring projects. The staff members of the Human Rights Organization saw the Border Guard as one of several "closed institutions" that they had to monitor for human rights abuses. They were convinced that Latvian border guards were falling behind their Western European counterparts with regard to observing human rights norms due to backward attitudes (see also Rosga 2010). By demanding that the border guards supplement their border securitization duties with observing human rights norms and behaving in a civilized manner, the Human Rights Organization performed a crucial role in enacting the paradox of Europeanness on the border. In the process, representatives of both institutions came to see themselves as belonging to opposing camps—border guards thought that the Human Rights Organization's sole purpose was to simply accuse all civil servants of human rights abuses, while representatives of the Human Rights Organization thought that the State Border Guard was populated by unenlightened and prejudiced individuals. It is precisely through this antagonism that they simultaneously enacted the paradox of Europeanness and obscured the tension between values of inclusion and practices of exclusion at the foundation of European polities.[5]

As I argued in the Introduction, the case of the "seven Somalis" embodies the tension between openness and closure that the Latvian society has had to negotiate as part of becoming European. The "seven Somalis" are simultaneously exemplary objects of tolerance and a difference that threatens the Latvian nation, but also European political space at large. Openness is only possible if borders are securitized and movement regulated. In this concluding chapter, therefore, I take the case of the "seven Somalis" as an entry point for analyzing the rebordering of Europe after socialism. I focus on migration governance and the way in which various actors involved in migration governance—borders guards, civil servants, lawyers, and human rights activists—embodied and negotiated the tension between the need for bounded selves and polities and the imperative to profess values of inclusion and openness. I show how the antagonisms that emerged as Latvia's state and nonstate institutions worked to establish borders, devise migration control, and implement the asylum system were shaped by the internal tensions of the project of Europeanization that unfolded in a place where history had not ended and where geopolitics mattered a great deal.

(Re)establishing Borders and Devising Migration Control

The collapse of the Soviet and Eastern European socialisms was followed by intensive rebordering. This included dismantling and establishing borders and border controls, shifts in national imaginaries about borders, and changes in the lives and identities of the people living in borderlands (Bacas and Kavanagh 2013, Berdahl 1999, Follis 2012, Laitin 1998, Lulle 2016, Pelkmans 2006, Reeves 2014). For post-Soviet states, former internal boundaries between Soviet republics became variously demarcated, sometimes ignored and sometimes contested, national borders. For Latvia, the shift was also one from guarding the Soviet Union's external western border to guarding the European Union's external eastern border.

In Latvia, rebordering was crucial for several reasons. First and foremost, agreeing on territorial borders and establishing border controls was an important act of national sovereignty (Chandler 1998, 8; see also Follis 2012, Reeves 2014). While all borders mattered, it was the historically contested border with Russia that mattered most. An attack on the Masļenki border post on the night of June 14, 1940, is widely understood as the first Soviet act of aggression against independent Latvia and thus the beginning of Soviet occupation, even as on the day of its occurrence it was barely noticed due to the national song festival that was taking place at the same time and occupied the hearts and minds of the public and the pages of the local press (Saburova 1955, 39).[6] Reestablishing the Latvian-Russian border as an international border with proper border control, therefore, was not just any sovereign act, but a sovereign act in relation to the successor state of a historically threatening polity.[7] It mattered little to the Latvians that it was the Soviet state who occupied Latvia, while its current neighbor was Russia, as both the Soviet Union and Russia were thought to be Russian and expansionist.

In addition to being a matter of national sovereignty, Latvia's eastern border was also a matter of European and transatlantic security due to Latvia's aspirations to join the European Union and NATO, which were duly fulfilled in 2004 despite some popular doubts.[8] Both NATO and the European Union were concerned with securing their external borders and thus with Latvia's border control capacity, but their concerns were somewhat different. From the NATO perspective, securing the eastern border was about geopolitics, even if in the 1990s and early 2000s most Western politicians did not think that Russia was a serious threat to its neighbors—a situation that has changed considerably since the war with Georgia in 2008 and the annexation of Crimea in 2014. For the European Union, the eastern border was about a different kind of security. It was about securitizing the border against irregular and unauthorized flows of goods and people into Europe (Bigo 2002, De Genova 2011, Huysmans 2006). This was to be done through the alignment of legislation, building of border infrastructure, and strengthening of technological and administrative capacities. As Karolina Follis (2012) has noted in her study of rebordering the Polish-Ukrainian frontier, Poland, as a European Union frontier state, had to reorient its bordering vision from protecting the national territory to protecting all of Europe. This included becoming concerned not only with border control and geopolitics, but also with migration control, which had barely registered on public and political agendas prior to Poland's Europeanization.

The same was not true for Latvia. Despite the fact that Latvia's migration politics amounts to what Ivars Indāns (2012, 91) calls a "bureaucratic regulatory approach," migration has been on Latvia's political agenda since before independence. Given the Soviet history of population movement, Latvia's politicians and the Latvian-speaking public from very early on saw migration control as a matter of national survival (see also chapter 2). For example, the Office of Citizenship and Migration Affairs narrates the history of the institutionalization of migration control as follows:

> Due to free movement of people within the former USSR territory, Latvia has inherited more than half a million incomers and their descendants. Already at the end of the 1950s, the proportion of *cittautieši* [literally, other nationals, but commonly used to designate Russian speakers] in the largest Latvia's cities (Riga, Daugavpils, Rēzekne) exceeded 50%. At the end of the 1980s, with the onset of Awakening (*Atmoda*), Latvian society became increasingly unsatisfied with the continuous inflow of *cittautieši* in Latvia, because these people brought other traditions, other

culture, mentality, and language. Latvia's inhabitants began to feel the need for a determinate migration politics in Latvia, which would ensure control over migration processes.[9]

In a policy-oriented academic publication, Maira Roze (2006), the deputy head of the Office of Citizenship and Migration Affairs, emphasized the unfairness of Soviet-era migration from the perspective of the distribution of resources rather than the ethnic composition of the population:

> Migration politics in Latvia began with the "Law on the Entry and Residence of Foreigners and Stateless Persons in Latvia," which was adopted on July 1, 1992. This law was the beginning of migration politics. The law was shaped by national interests, because Latvia had only recently regained independence from the Soviet Union. There were large factories being built in Latvia [during the Soviet period], and guest workers were invited from other USSR republics. They immediately received housing in newly built apartment buildings. But the locals remained in their old apartments without proper amenities and waited in long lines for new apartments that would not move at all. Of course, it is not possible to hold this against the newcomers, for they were invited to come and help and were promised good living conditions in return. However, it is possible to understand the local inhabitants who became increasingly resentful. Thus the law reflects their desire to put a full stop to the stream of incomers.

Contrary to the desire animating early post-Soviet migration politics, migration control in European Latvia could not be about "putting a full stop" to movement. Migration control in conditions of freedom, that is, in conditions of economic neoliberalization, political liberalization, and integration into Western political and economic structures, meant regulating movement according to shifting and sometimes contradictory political and economic interests and moral imperatives. Some labor migrants were needed (especially as Latvians themselves were emigrating to Western Europe in search for work and a better life (Dzenovska 2018a, 2013b, 2012), most economic migrants were to be kept out, and a small number of individuals who fit the criteria of the 1951 Geneva Convention were to be granted protection as refugees, therefore demonstrating the humane and humanitarian nature of European polities, including in Latvia (Fassin 2005, Ticktin 2011, Vollmer 2016). Moreover, border and migration control had to take place in a civilized manner (Follis 2012, Vollmer 2016). All border crossers, regardless of their status, were to be treated humanely, and everybody's human rights were to be respected. Border control was to be an efficient and pleasant service (Follis 2012, Prokkola 2013, Sparke 2006, Vollmer 2016). Thus, for border control and migration officials, European integration meant learning how to live with the simultaneous demand for securitization and civilization of the border. The public reports of the Latvian State Border Guard demonstrate that they worked on both strengthening and civilizing the border.[10] The State Border Guard took pride in infrastructure development and the joint international missions to combat illegal immigration in which they participated, and they also took pride in the continuous education of their staff. The 2007 public report states that "border guards have learned to become more polite, and the border crossers are receiving pleasant service and attitudes on the border."

All of this was new to the Latvian State Border Guard at the time of my fieldwork. The dynamics of inclusion and exclusion had been organized differently during the Soviet period—movement was much more restricted, and people were prevented from leaving as much, if not more, than from entering. It is not uncommon to hear that during the Soviet period there was "too much inclusion," suggesting that Latvians were included in the Soviet Union against their will, and that inclusion was a form of coercion. Moreover, during the Soviet period, the eastern border had not been much of a border at all, with people living in the borderlands to this day treating it as a symbolic line rather than a material and political border. The public reports published by the Latvian State Border guard include annual statistics on people who accidentally violate the border by going mushrooming or tending the graves of their relatives (see also Lulle 2016). At the same time, Latvia's western and the Soviet Union's external border really was sealed from the inside and the outside. The border zone was declared a "forbidden zone" (*aizliegtā zona*), and only those who lived there or had special permission to visit someone who lived there were allowed to enter. The beaches were harrowed in the evening to make sure that attempts to approach the sea or land would be visible in the sand. Soviet border guards were stationed in strategic villages and, according to the locals, once in a while tested the residents' readiness to report on suspicious activity by releasing fake strangers into the community. Border zones developed their peculiar dynamics, especially with regard to the local residents' relationships with the stationed border guards. Many people who came of age in the forbidden zone told me how they accidentally or purposefully violated the harrowed zone and, as punishment, were sent to peel potatoes or wash dishes at the border guard station. Romances developed between local girls and border guards, which meant that some of them stayed on after their service. A tourist information board in Kolka—a village on the meeting point of the Riga Bay and the Baltic Sea—enfolds these romantic encounters as part of local history.

Most important, however, border and migration control in the Soviet Union had not been about human rights (Chandler 1998). It was also not about human rights in the early post-Soviet years. Several immigration control and asylum officers, with whom I spoke at the Riga office of the Latvian State Border Guard, recalled the chaotic beginning of independent border control as nevertheless a period when they had done a good job of controlling the border and illegal migration, which they saw as their primary task. For example, in 2010, a staff member of the Department of Asylum Control of the Latvian State Border Guard explained to me that, despite—or rather because of—this chaos, "immigration control was successfully devised in the beginning, thus there are very few migrants and asylum seekers in Latvia." The task, as seen by this border guard, was to seal the border to safeguard the integrity of the Latvian nation, but also to show the capacity of the State Border Guard to secure the border. The success of this operation was measured by the visual contours of public space in every street and town. Seeing a Somali on the street, thus, was not only a novelty, but also an indication of the porosity of borders. One of the techniques used by the Immigration Police to prevent this from happening was to enact the border in the territory by approaching people on the street if they looked as though they did not belong.

Subsequently, in the process of EU integration, these practices had to change. Approaching people on the street on the basis of their looks could be deemed discriminatory, though, as one immigration control officer put it, "We could still do it if we wanted to, but our attitudes have changed." Learning to live the paradox of Europeanness, then, meant keeping a variety of mutually reinforcing policing techniques at one's disposal, while having the "good sense" of using those appropriate for a properly European border force. And yet, while immigration control in the territory switched to less obvious techniques and increasingly depended on collaboration with various institutions and reports from the public (Dzenovska 2017), border control officers continued to use racialized techniques of sorting and bordering. As the staff member of the Department of Border Control at the Riga Airport told me in 2006, "Of course, we select those we control on the basis of their looks, but we do not advertise that. We have confidential statistics about the nationalities of people who usually commit crimes. We also use race as criteria. There are human rights that are strictly observed in Europe, but not in Latvia. *It is only possible to control borders if you violate human rights* [my emphasis]. They [in Europe] subordinate control procedures to human rights, we don't—that's Soviet influence."

This official attributed the neglect of human rights in favor of border control to "Soviet influence" at the same time as he recognized that "it is only possible to control borders if you violate human rights." He did not think it was possible to resolve the contradictory demand for civilized securitization of the border, but, rather than pointing to this contradiction, he displaced Europe's constitutive tension onto the Soviet past by attributing the neglect of human rights to Soviet legacy. This is precisely the kind of dynamic that I have been tracing in the book—whether through engagement with colonial imaginaries, minority politics, or border control, arguing that the tension between inclusion and exclusion at the foundation of Europe's polities remains obscured due to spatial and temporal displacement of the negative aspects of exclusion onto marginalized subjects, places, or the past, thus allowing the symbolic glorification of Europe as the pinnacle of humanity. The fact that even the border guard official embraced the discourse of "Soviet legacy" fifteen years after independence and after extensive lessons in Europeanness is an indication of how successful such obscuring tactics have been (see Zarycki 2014).

The contradiction between the need to control borders and the need to observe human rights identified by the border guard official derives from the European present—both liberal and national. For example, some of the border guards were not only state officials, but also members of the Latvian nation (others were citizens, but Russian speakers and thus not necessarily included in the cultural nation). Quite a few of them saw Latvia as an embattled nation, which did not need more foreigners, and therefore were inclined to be more control rather than service oriented. In 2005, a staff member of the Department of Asylum of the State Border Guard rhetorically asked me whether I knew how many Latvians there were in Latvia in relation to the total population. He was emphasizing the point that the Latvian state—as a national state established for the purpose of ensuring the flourishing of the cultural nation of Latvians—faced a unique demographic challenge. He said: "There is no unified model [of immigration control] in Europe. It is a continuous struggle, and we know why we are doing what we are doing."

But it would be erroneous, again, to attribute the subordination of human rights to tight border control solely to Latvian nationalism instead of or in addition to the Soviet past. It was also the result of training received from counterparts in exemplary European liberal democracies. My notes from 2005 onward are full with references to twinning projects, seminars, exchange visits, joint operations, and other activities that the Latvian border guards attended in various European countries or that their European counterparts brought to Latvia. For example, in 2001 the Finnish Border Guard assisted with the development of the Integrated Border Management Strategy, while in 2005 Belgian colleagues delivered training on asylum procedures for the staff of the Border Guard, but also for the staff of the Office of Citizenship and Migration Affairs. The public reports of the Latvian State Border Guard provide a detailed record of these training activities, most of which involved infrastructure development, joint operations in combating illegal migration, and capacity building.[11]

In addition to learning about border control, the Latvian State Border Guard and migration officials at the Office of Citizenship and Migration Affairs also learned about migration control, including the need to distinguish between illegal migrants and genuine refugees—an issue that was preoccupying their European colleagues (see also Cabot 2014, Follis 2012, Khosravi 2010), but also global migration authorities (Mountz 2010).[12] What they learned was not only that these were different categories, but that it was difficult to distinguish between people falling into each of the categories because people tried to abuse the system. Thus, in relation to asylum, the dual imperative to strengthen and civilize the border meant that border guards and migration officials had to implement directives arising from the Common European Asylum System, institutionalize human rights practices (such as providing information and legal assistance to asylum seekers among other things), while also tightening procedures and building capacity in order to distinguish genuine asylum seekers from those trying to abuse the system. At the time of my research, it seemed that, despite formal discourses about human rights coming from European institution and local and international monitoring bodies, Latvian border guards and migration officials were primarily learning from their counterparts about the dangers associated with being too humanitarian or too human rights oriented. At least those were the conclusions that they were making. For example, a staff member of the Office of Citizenship and Migration Affairs told me that on her study visits she learned about the catastrophic situation in Europe where the asylum mechanism is constantly abused. Her European colleagues were tightening asylum procedures to prevent false asylum seekers from gaining right to residence. She was worried that if it took too long to process asylum cases, it would be impossible to deport people because of humanitarian reasons: "Once they have children, the children become integrated, and then deportation is not humane." A staff member of the Department of Asylum of the Latvian State Border Guard explained to me that "it is very difficult to abuse our system, because we have the possibility to detain. If people are able to move freely, this promotes the flow." Even as detention of asylum seekers was contested, and the UNHCR urged states not to detain asylum seekers, Latvian officials thought that the only way to ensure the system against abuse was to use the detention mechanism. They thought that their European counterparts were struggling because they tried to do the impossible—keep people out, while respecting their human rights.

On their study visits, Latvian border guards and migration officials also learned about the trials of integration. From high-level civil servants at the Ministry of Foreign Affairs to mid-level bureaucrats of the Office of Citizenship and Migration Affairs to front-line border guards, many recounted Swedish, British, and French problems with "Somalis that do not work" and "asylum seekers that sit on benefits." "France is an old democracy that observes human rights. Why is there all this talk that they are not giving immigrants jobs? Why doesn't anybody want to talk about how the immigrants do not want to work?," pondered a case worker at the Latvian State Border Guard. "The French colleagues were mistaken," said another border guard. "They thought that these people will come, integrate and work, but they made a mistake. There are some who are French patriots, but very few." It was clear to Latvian border guards and migration officials that in order to avoid the problems that their European colleagues were facing, they had to learn not only from their "best practices" (Follis 2012, 166), but also from their mistakes. And their mistake, as seen by one border guard officer, was to have "let these people in in the first place. Now instead of dealing with them at the border, they have to deal with them within the territory."

Latvian border guards and migration authorities were relieved that Latvia did not have these kinds of problems and thought that the risk was low until the economic situation improved.[13] They were convinced that most of those who ended up as asylum seekers in Latvia—for example, the "seven Somalis"—wanted to go elsewhere and arrived in Latvia by accident. But the border guards also contributed to keeping this risk low by other means. Back in mid-2000s, when I did most of my fieldwork, border guards did not hide the fact that on some occasion they closed their eyes (*pievēra acis*) if they saw "human cargo" on ships or trucks. For example, when I spent twelve hours with border agents at the Riga Airport, I heard multiple accounts of an incident whereby some illegal migrants, possibly would-be asylum seekers, had turned up at the port, but nobody wanted to deal with them. So, when the border guards realized that the ship that carried them was on its way to the United States, the border guards talked the "human cargo" into staying on the ship and "going to America." "Everyone was happy in the end," the border guard telling me the story concluded. Over the course of my fieldwork, I also heard vague references to turning people away at the border, known as "push backs" or, in legal language, refoulement (see Vollmer 2016), but these were mostly alluded to rather than elaborated.

All the while, economic improvement and the associated increase in both living standards and immigration, which was promised, hoped for, and feared by Latvia's political and intellectual elites, remained matters of a distant future, whose arrival, in turn, was a matter of faith rather than certainty (Guyer 2007). Toward the end of my fieldwork, Latvia was gripped by financial crisis. Instead of immigration, Latvia was experiencing outmigration.[14] It was Latvia's residents, including border guards and migration officials, who were seeking work abroad.[15] And so when migration and asylum politics did return to the public and political agenda in 2014, it was not because of an improved economic situation, but because of the intersection of two crises that exposed the lines of power dividing

Europe: one, the financial crisis and the subsequent austerity measures that put enormous pressure on livelihoods in Latvia, Ireland, and across southern Europe (Dzenovska 2018a, Knight 2015), and two, the implosion of Europe's carefully balanced system of inclusion and exclusion into what is known as a "migration" or "refugee crisis." It had not yet happened at the time of my fieldwork between 2005 and 2010, but already back then some of the border guards and migration officials jokingly remarked that all this attention to the asylum system by European authorities must mean that "Europe is preparing us for 'sharing the burden.'" They did not know then that the demand for sharing the burden would become a real test for Latvia's politicians, migration authorities, and the public only a few years later. Back then, in 2005 and 2006, the asylum system and the Latvian public were tested not by millions of refugees attempting to enter Europe by land and sea, many of them dying en route, but by seven Somalis.

"Seven Somalis" and the Antagonisms that Shaped Latvia's Asylum System

Once the Somalis appeared on the doorstep of the Red Cross office in Riga in the summer of 2005 and were subsequently brought to the Riga office of the Latvian State Border Guard, their path through the system revealed many challenges and stumbling blocks. It also invigorated the largely dormant migration governance community insofar as the case provided the opportunity for the inspectors and officers of the Latvian State Border Guard, the civil servants of the Office of Citizenship and Migration Affairs, judges and lawyers, human rights activists and NGO workers, teachers, private individuals, and journalists to establish and negotiate relations with each other as actors in migration governance. Sometimes this led to the strengthening of cooperation, and sometimes it led to the courtroom, as when an officer of the Border Guard sued a staff member of the Human Rights Organization for slander.

The seven Somalis arrived at the offices of the Red Cross in August 2005. They claimed to have come by taxi from a forest where they had spent two days after being dropped off by a smuggler who had promised to take them to Sweden.[16] The Latvian State Border Guard placed all seven individuals in the detention center for illegal immigrants, which was located in a former prison.[17] The Somalis stayed there for almost a year, all through the process of applying for asylum, waiting for decisions, and, subsequently, appealing the initially negative decisions. The Somalis remained in detention despite the fact that asylum seekers—people who have submitted an asylum application and are waiting for a decision—did not have to be detained and could reside in the asylum seeker reception center. The border guards justified detention by referring to the Law on Asylum, which stipulated that asylum seekers may be detained if they don't have identification papers, and, indeed, the Somalis did not have any papers on them.[18] After the initial detention period of six days, further detention—usually for another limited period of time, such as two months—had to be approved by the district administrative court (Djačkova et al. 2011). Thus, the Somalis' cases—and occasionally the Somalis themselves—were taken to the court in Riga every two months to extend the term of detention.

It was in a Riga courtroom that I first encountered them in November 2005. Their asylum application, submitted on August 31, 2005, was still being reviewed, and their identity was not yet formally established, and so the State Border Guard had brought them from the detention center as objects in the State Border Guard's case for detention. I was in the courtroom because I had scheduled an interview with one of the Border Guard officers. He had told me to meet him at the courtroom, from where he was to take me to the Riga office of the State Border Guard. Waiting for the interview, I sat in the courtroom and listened to how an English language interpreter mediated between the judge, one of the Somalis who spoke rudimentary English, and the rest of the asylum speakers who, to the puzzlement of all involved, spoke only Amharic and not Somali. The interpreter took significant liberties translating the Somalis' answers to the judge's questions. Given that their statements, mediated by the poorly English-speaking person in their group, were incomplete and at times not fully comprehensible, the interpreter added what she felt was missing, often, I thought, failing to hit the mark or filling the gaps according to her own understanding of the situation. There was no pretense that anything that the Somalis said could possibly decide their case against detention. Translation was a formality, and the hearing soon ended with the Somalis being put back in the car to the detention center.

Communication between the Somalis and the State Border Guard and migration officials was difficult, to say the least. On some occasions, migration authorities brought in an Amharic-language speaker from Estonia, on others—like that day in the courtroom—they made do with whatever was available, thus undoubtedly violating regulations in addition to stunting communication. Through further breach of regulation, I was able to visit the Somalis in the detention center that day. After the hearing, in the Riga office of the State Boarder Guard, the officer I was to interview received notice that the Somalis' asylum applications had just been rejected. Decisions in hand, he came into the room and asked me if I spoke English. Minutes later we were speeding down the highway to the detention center, some twenty-five kilometers outside of Riga, where the officer wanted me to translate the decision to the Somalis. While at the detention center,

I verbally translated the decisions and gave the Somalis the phone number of the Human Rights Organization.[19]

The asylum applications submitted on August 31, 2005, were denied on the basis of doubts about the truthfulness of the applicants' stories. Decisions on all cases were justified in nearly identical terms—the applicant claimed to be Somali, but did not speak the Somali language, could not name a place of residence before departure, could not elaborate the structure of the clan he or she claimed to belong to, and there was little information to suggest that he or she was personally under threat in Somalia. The applicants' own stories recorded on the lengthy decisions were also all similar. The Somalis told the authorities that they wished to leave Somalia because of its civil war and unstable political and economic situation, that they paid a smuggler to be taken to Sweden, that their trip took four months, that they all met on a ship (with the exception of the three teenagers who traveled as a family), and that they were all cheated and dropped off in the forest in Latvia. They belonged to different clans, but all claimed to be Somali, even as they seemed to have moved and resided in various parts of the Ogaden region in Ethiopia and the borderlands. Two of them claimed to have been born and lived in Somaliland. None of them spoke Somali, only Amharic—the language used in Ethiopia and Eritrea.

It was the language issue that made the border guards and migration officials especially suspicious. While it was possible for a Somali to speak Amharic, it seemed impossible—and was confirmed to be so by various experts—that a Somali would not speak the Somali language. And yet, the asylum seekers insisted on being Somalis. This remained an unresolved puzzle, and the full story of the seven Somalis is obscure to this day. When I asked the group leader—a man in his mid-forties who spoke bare bones English—for permission to look at the case files in hopes of gathering more details about the case, he replied that they do not want to sign the required permission, because they do not want to remind the State Border Guard about themselves, as they may have made some mistakes in the story. Instead, they gave me copies of the final decisions with lengthy supporting documents, as well as twenty pages of text in Amharic from one of the asylum seekers in an attempt to tell his—and presumably some of the group's—story. I sought translation, but several Amharic speakers that I found with difficulty while in Latvia told me the text was unintelligible, and I could not translate the pages while the case was still ongoing. Thus, as the case was ongoing, the story remained inaccessible to all, despite genuine efforts to tell and listen. This case illuminates a central aspect of the asylum system not only in Latvia, but also more generally, namely that it matters little whether an asylum seeker's story is genuinely true or not. What matters is the performance of the story, the perceived credibility of its teller, and the nature of the bureaucracy that encounters it (Khoshravi 2010).

In July 2006, after ten months in detention, while the Somalis were waiting for decisions on repeatedly submitted asylum applications, the court refused to consider the case for extension of detention, because no suitable translation was provided on the day that the Border Guard had once again taken Somalis to the court.[20] Far from usual court practice, this must have been a case of having been assigned the "wrong" judge. And thus, on July 8, 2006, due to the misfortune—or fortune, depending on one's perspective—of being assigned a judge that was not willing to put up with partial communication, the Latvian State Border Guard lost legal grounds for further detention of the Somalis, and they were let go. They were let go without any means for subsistence, shelter, or movement besides an "exit document" issued by the Office of Citizenship and Migration Affairs that contained their photos, the names they had given, and stipulated that they must leave the country by February 27, 2007. The document was widely recognized to be utterly useless even by the authority that issued it, because the Somalis did not have any means to leave the country and, moreover, they would not have been able to enter any other country with a Latvian-issued "exit document." The Somalis thus ended up on the street without any resources or the ability to generate them, except through illegal means. A senior officer working in the detention center commented on the situation:

> They do not have any status, and state institutions do not have any obligations to help them. It is an absurd situation. The decision was taken in a day, and the doors were opened. They took all their belongings and left. I have been walking around, thinking about what will happen to these people. The papers are valid for traveling back to Somalia. It is not clear what would happen on the border with others countries (such as Lithuania or Estonia), because they do not have permission to enter such countries. All they have is a permit to leave Latvia for Somalia. What happens if they are still in the country after February? Did anyone tell them what they could do until then?

The system that had been trudging along, even if in tension with human rights norms monitored by the Human Rights Organization, suddenly descended into chaos. The Ministry of Justice was demanding from the State Border Guard and the Office of Citizenship and Migration Affairs to be informed of the whereabouts of the Somalis. The answer they got was that someone had spotted the Somalis wandering in one of the main parks of Riga. The Border Guard had apparently informed the Office of Citizenship and Migration Affairs over the phone about the decision to release the Somalis' from detention and requested that the office issue the exit documents, which they did, but they failed to coordinate a transfer from the detention center to the asylum seeker reception center. It is unclear whether the Human Rights Organization knew that the Somalis were about to be put out on the street, but they remained on the sidelines watching the descent into chaos, which they saw as an opportunity to point to the gaps in both legislation and practice. The fact that the Somalis could have technically been taken to the asylum seeker reception center, because they were released while their asylum applications were still pending, became a point of contention and a subject of a lengthy letter exchange between the State Human Rights Office— a state institution charged with the responsibility to enforce that government institutions observe human rights, the State Border Guard, and the Ministry of Justice.[21]

The Human Rights Organization also saw this incident as an opportunity to point out that "society is morally corrupt." As reported to me by a staff member of the Human Rights Organization, one of the border guards had said to her that "it remains to be seen what will happen when food will run out in two days," as well as that "the court took a stupid decision, when they could have detained them for the full twenty months as stipulated in the Law on Asylum." The staff member of the Human Rights Organization further commented that "it's good that there is noise now, for it shows how the Border Guard works, as well as what attitudes they have."

According to the Human Rights Office, border guards, like most of the Latvian public, were mired in intolerant attitudes. This was a running theme while the Somalis' cases were being reviewed. For example, during a seminar on LGBT rights—also falling within the terrain of tolerance promotion of the Human Rights Office—Zinta, another staff member of the Human Rights Office, told me about her visit to the detention center where she had gone to help the Somalis with some paperwork. The border guard sitting in the booth by the gate where visitors were registered had muttered under his breath while registering her that he hopes "these negroes (*nēģeri*) will leave soon." Zinta had asked him whether he has had any problems with the Somalis, and he had responded that, no, he has not, but that he has been in England and Ireland for exchange visits and knows that "they [asylum seekers] are all lazy there and engaged with drugs." Zinta had then asked him whether he knows any people with dark skin color personally, to which he had replied that, no, he does not, but he knows the situation. "I told him that if he worked in Ireland or England, he would be fired," Zinta continued. Zinta subsequently reported the border guard to the director of the detention center. According to Zinta's account, the director had felt uncomfortable and promised to tell his staff to keep such views at home. "They do not edit what they are saying! They have no idea!" concluded Zinta. Editing what one was saying was an important part of becoming tolerant and thus civilized, but the unedited speech was also useful for the human rights activists, as it proved the need for their labors and allowed them to form a "community of understanding" (see chapter 3).

Human rights activists generally thought that migration officials—and border guards in particular—were too nationalistic and got away with all kinds of inappropriate behavior. Staff members of the foster home where the Somalis now lived said that the Somalis' stories about their time in detention should be carefully recorded: "They told us that the border guards put them in isolators. The kids were shaking when they saw border guards in uniforms coming down the hill to visit us. We all surrounded the Somalis, protected them, and told them that we will not let them be taken away."[22] The Latvian State Border Guard was not particularly concerned about such accusations. Rather, its staff members, along with staff members of the Office of Citizenship and Migration Affairs, were annoyed by what they thought were unfair accusations and exaggerated monitoring efforts. State Border Guard officers, inspectors, and case workers, as well as some of the migration officials, saw staff members of the Human Rights Organization as overzealous and funding-driven activists who obsessively focused on the human rights of a select few, namely asylum seekers, at the expense other marginalized subjects, such as stateless former Soviet citizens, the poor, and the Latvian nation as a whole.

Staff members of the Latvian State Border Guard and the Office of Citizenship and Migration Affairs repeatedly expressed their views that the human rights organizations were simply out to get them. For example, one staff member of the Office of Citizenship and Migration Affairs told me that "there is utter distrust on the part of the human rights organizations toward state authorities. They accuse the authorities for not letting people write asylum applications. But that's not true. The would-be asylum seekers are well informed and, if they are not writing asylum applications, it's because they are trying to decide which state to submit them to." To illustrate her point, the staff member told me about an Iraqi family who crossed into Latvia from Russia, wanted to go to Sweden, applied for asylum in Latvia, then tried to move on, but were thrown back because of the Dublin regulation:[23] "Thereafter they lived in Latvia for a year, but then went back to Iraq, because they did not want to live in Latvia.[24] The NGO seems to think that all state organizations are bad, whereas all asylum seekers are good."

To bring into sharper focus the unfairness of the situation as they perceived it, the border guards and migration officials also pointed out that the human rights projects funded by the European Union that targeted asylum seekers overlooked other people who were equally in need of care and protection, such as, for example, former Soviet citizens who had failed to take care of paperwork and found themselves to be illegal migrants in the newly independent Latvia. Indeed, when I examined the cases of illegal migrants and former asylum seekers in the offices of the State Border Guard, it was evident that only those who had been asylum seekers at some point had merited the attention of the Human Rights Organization. While the Human Rights Organization in question did have more general projects about "closed institutions," which included monitoring detention conditions of all detainees, the individual cases in which there was express interest by the Human Rights Organization were those of asylum seekers. The organization had a specific project-based mandate to follow this category of people, to be concerned about legal assistance to asylum seekers, to work on ensuring access to asylum on the border, and to fight for alternatives to detention.

Border guards and migration officials thought that this reflected the priorities of the European political agenda, which ignored real needs in concrete locations. Toward the end of my fieldwork, when the economic crisis had ravished livelihoods, their criticism became louder, and they began to include pensioners and even themselves—as underpaid state employees—in the list of those neglected by European-driven human rights agendas. Some went as far as to juxtapose the exaggerated attention to a few asylum seekers to the centuries-long suffering of the Latvian nation. Within fifteen years, the figure of the Soviet migrant (see chapter 2) who received housing upon arrival while Latvians waited in long lines and was therefore the target of the early post-Soviet migration politics, was replaced by the figure of the asylum seeker defended by the European Union institutions at the expense of other neglected subjects and the well-being of the population at large.

Staff members of the Human Rights Organization took such claims to be unreasonable excuses on the part of border guards and migration officials for dragging their feet on the job. "What are these kind people doing in such posts?" they rhetorically asked. The human rights workers thus insisted that the border guards and migration officials must be professionals who do their job, but overlooked the fact that their own idea of professionalism was deeply shaped by an institutionalized form of political liberalism. Thus, their demand was not only about professionalism, but also about politics and the culture of human rights (Riles 2006). To put it another way, accusations of unprofessionalism did not simply juxtapose professionalism to unprofessionalism, but also juxtaposed institutionalized political liberalism to wrong type of politics that was thought to shape the border guards' attitudes and practices. The implicit aim of the Human Rights Organization was not only to encourage border guards and migration officials to distance themselves from cultural and historical embeddedness by becoming professional, but also to subscribe to a particular ideologically infused bureaucratic culture. In the last part of this chapter, then, I turn to a more in-depth consideration of what kind of critiques of the European political landscape emerge from the politically incorrect and unprofessional statements of the border guards and migration officials, as well as from the solidarities they claimed with the Soviet citizens in lieu of asylum seekers.

Understanding *Savējie*

In addition to dealing with would-be migrants, the initial migration control apparatus, which consisted of a Department of Migration Affairs attached to the Cabinet of Ministers and Immigration Police attached to the State Police, also had to deal with those Soviet citizens who remained outside the pale of Latvian citizenship, but continued to reside in Latvia (see chapter 2).[25] David Laitin (1998) has described Russian speakers in post-Soviet Baltics as a "beached diaspora" created by borders receding around them. In addition to being beached, those who failed to write themselves into the bureaucratic structures of the new state—whether as citizens or legal residents—became illegal. For example, with independence in 1991, some of Soviet Latvia's residents turned into Latvia's citizens and others into Latvia's noncitizens (see chapter 2), foreign citizens with residence permits (or illegal migrants, if they failed to extend their residence permits), or undocumented migrants, if they failed to take care of paperwork that would establish their legal status in relation to the Latvian state or any other state. This took place through a series of political decisions and legislative acts, which included the 1991 Supreme Soviet decision "On the Reinstatement of Citizenship Rights and the Basic Principles of Naturalization in the Republic of Latvia," the 1994 Law on Citizenship, the 1994 Russia-Latvia Agreement on Withdrawal of Troops, as well as various Supreme Soviet or Cabinet of Ministers regulations— for example, the regulation adapted in 1991 by the newly established Department of Migration Affairs to stop issuing residence declarations (*pieraksts* or *propiska*) to people coming to Latvia from other Soviet republics. Residence declarations were crucial for establishing right to residence in post-Soviet polities and in some cases, such as in Russia, right to citizenship (Shevel 2012). This regulation was adapted with the clear goal of stopping more Soviet citizens from being able to claim residence rights in Latvia, but was subsequently amended to allow for residence declarations of returning members of the titular nation, that is, of Latvians (EMN 2006).[26]

Among the nontitular residents of post-Soviet Latvia, the personnel of the Soviet Military Naval Fleet and the Border Guard Corps presented the biggest problem for the newly independent state. At the time of independence in 1991, there were about 60,000 Soviet military personnel in Latvia (Jundzis 2014). In

1992, Russia took over the former Soviet military units in the Baltics, and Latvia and Russia began negotiations about withdrawal of what Latvia considered to be occupation troops. As part of these very complex and politically contested negotiations, it was agreed that military personnel who had retired before January 28, 1992 (the date when Russia took over Soviet jurisdiction), could remain in Latvia with their families. As a result, 22,230 military personnel obtained right to residence in Latvia. Together with their families, they formed about 75,000–100,000 of Latvia's Russian-speaking population. Latvia's politicians and political analysts consider that the price for withdrawing the troops was to allow Russia to leave behind the "fifth column" as a deliberate strategy for maintaining long-term influence in the region (Jundzis 2014, 13; see also Pilkington 1998). Since the Russia-Latvia Agreement on Withdrawal of Troops generated widespread discontent in society, the Latvian government added a protocol to the agreement, which stipulated that the Latvian government would encourage voluntary departure of former military personnel and their families. This did not happen, as most did not want to leave, and quite a few—about two thousand—stayed in Latvia illegally. The presence of former military personnel and their families among Latvia's Russian speakers, widely thought to be apologists for the Soviet occupation and to have political leanings toward Russia, contributed to the widespread use of the term *okupants* (occupier) in nationalist circles when referring to all Russian speakers in Latvia, even if military personnel constituted about 13 percent of Latvia's noncitizens in 1995 (735,000, or 29 percent of the population of Latvia at the time) (Šūpule 2014).

Interpretation of the legislative framework pertaining to individual cases of former military personnel and their family members was contested, on occasion going as far as the European Court of Human Rights. For example, Tatyana Slivenko came to Latvia as a child with her father who was a Soviet military officer (Ziemele 2003). Her father retired prior to January 28, 1992, and thus had legal grounds for staying in Latvia, passing this right onto Tatyana. Tatyana, however, married a Soviet military officer who did not demobilize prior to January 28, 1992 and who therefore had to leave Latvia. The Latvian courts decided that the family—Tatyana, her husband, and their daughter—had to leave Latvia despite Tatyana's right to stay vis-à-vis her father. Since Tatyana and her daughter did not leave by the set date, they were placed in the detention center for illegal immigrants. Tatyana took her case to the European Court of Human Rights, which decided the case in her favor.

The cases of other former Soviet citizens that came to the attention of immigration control authorities of the Latvian State Border Guard were not as publicly visible. In fact, they were not noticed at all. They were "social cases," as one Border Guard inspector put it. In some cases, people had been mobile during the Soviet period, and therefore it was difficult to establish where they had resided at the time of independence and whether therefore they had a right to residence in Latvia regardless of their citizenship status. In other cases, people had not moved at all; it was borders that moved around them. They had failed to notice this or did not care enough to do something about it. The public reports of the State Border Guard from 2002—the year that the State Border Guard began to issue annual public reports—until 2005 separate a category of people who had been former Soviet citizens but had "failed to legalize" (*nav legalizējušies*).[27] This category disappeared in 2006 or, rather, was folded into the more general category of "illegal migrants." The number of individuals who had both "failed to legalize" and were caught was not necessarily great—161 in 2002 (out of 394 detained foreigners in total), 216 in 2003 (out of 609 detained foreigners), 302 in 2004 (out of 721 foreigners) and 265 in 2005 (out of 322 foreigners). But they did constitute a significant proportion of detained foreigners and certainly exceeded the number of asylum seekers during those years, which amounted to 30 in 2002, 5 in 2003, 7 in 2004, and 20 in 2005. And even those were mostly submitted by former Soviet citizens and current citizens of Russia, Belarus, Armenia, Tajikistan, Georgia, and Azerbaijan, with the occasional Palestinian or Iraqi among them. The exception was in 2005, when on the account of the "seven Somalis," the numbers jumped up, as did the proportion of "new foreigners" to former Soviet citizens. Altogether, since 1998, when Latvia's asylum system was put into place, 1,768 people have asked for asylum in Latvia, 71 have been recognized as refugees, and 148 have been granted temporary protection.[28] Until 2010, the annual number of asylum seekers was in single or double digits, with 2011 being the first year when the number of applications rose to 105. At the height of "Europe's migration/refugee crisis," the numbers increased to 364 in 2014 and 328 in 2015, and the countries of origin became more diverse, reflecting the composition of people en route to Europe (for comparison, the total number of first-time applications in Germany for 2015 was 442,000).[29]

If the numbers of asylum seekers from outside the former Soviet space were few and their stories for the most part unfamiliar, even unintelligible, this was not the case with the former Soviet citizens who had "failed to legalize." The border guards understood their predicament very well and could imagine how one could end up in such a situation. The inspectors often distinguished between "pure foreigners" and the "illegals" or "bums of Latvian origin" (*Latvijas izcelsmes bomži*), who were detained "because of their own attitude toward life and documents." Several men—and they were mostly men at the time of my fieldwork, who had ended up in detention as illegal immigrants and whose files I reviewed, had been doing military service in Russia in the late 1980s, had married after finishing service, and stayed to live in Russia for several years thereafter. In one case, a man whom I will call Igor was given Russian citizenship without his knowledge, because he had a declared residence (*propiska*) in the District of Vologda in 1992.[30] All those who had declared residence at the time the first Russian citizenship law came into effect, that is, on February 6, 1992, were included in the citizen register and became Russian citizens unless they objected to being Russian citizens within a year from the law's promulgation (Shevel 2012, 121). Igor found out about this during his efforts to legalize himself in Latvia many years later.

Igor was born in Riga in the mid-1960s and lived in Latvia until he was drafted in the military in the late 1980s, which is when he went to Archangelsk. Igor's father was "more Russian," as Igor put it, and from Abrene—a contested territory that belonged to the Latvian region of Latgale prior to 1940 but was annexed to the Russian Soviet Socialist Republic in 1945 and now remains part of Russia's Pskov region. Igor's mother was "more Latvian," but also from Latgale. While in Russia just after military service, Igor got married and lived with his wife in the Vologda region until he came back to Latvia with a Soviet passport in 1993 (his file says that he was registered as living in the Vologda region from November 24, 1990, until January 20, 1994). His wife came along, but they eventually separated, and she returned to Russia. When attempting to take care of paperwork for Latvian citizenship after the Law on Citizenship was passed, Igor had to produce proof of his parents' prewar Latvian citizenship. According to Igor, since his mother's passport was issued in 1940 after the Soviet occupation, it was not valid for that purpose, and so the authorities had asked him to produce proof that his mother had attended school in interwar Latvia. As Igor explained, it proved to be a time-consuming and expensive bureaucratic process, which he could not afford at the time, and so he put the whole thing off. When he tried again some years later, all the civil servants that he had dealt with previously had changed, nobody remembered the case, and he had to start all over again. As part of this second attempt, Igor was asked to produce proof that he did not have Russian citizenship. Thus began a long exchange of letters between Igor, the Embassy of Russia in Latvia, and Russia's Ministry of the Interior, during which he found out that he did, in fact, have Russian citizenship. He now had to refuse his Russian citizenship in order to obtain Latvian citizenship.[31] Refusing Russian citizenship required that he put together a complicated package of documents, and Igor received a five-month residence permit in Latvia to take care of that.

During that period, Igor ended up in prison. Not wanting to go into details, but suggesting a crime of sexual nature, Igor explained: "I was tired of freedom [by which he meant being without papers]. I had become so degraded, so degraded!" When he got out prison, Igor continued to suffer his freedom. When in 2003 police visited his sister's house in a seaside town about a hundred kilometers from Riga because of a drunken incident, the police discovered that Igor did not have any papers and turned him over to the State Border Guard. That's how he ended up in the detention center, where we had our conversation. "For the first time in seventeen years!" Igor exclaimed. "But it's good that I am here. At least I get some help with the papers."

Igor narrated his life without papers as suffering, the kind of suffering that "degraded" him, as he put it. He longed to be a proper legal subject and to change his life.[32] He said that he keeps having the feeling that all he needs is one more paper and then things will fall into place, but things keep going wrong, and his case keeps dragging on. "Now they are talking about deportation," Igor said at the time we talked in 2010. "If they deported me, at least it would be some kind of a change. I am starting to put my hopes on the Russian passport, maybe it's not so bad there. I really liked the Vologda area. What will be, will be. There are laws, after all, something has to be sorted out. But . . . perhaps I am not a [Latvian] citizen after all. The family is tired, everyone has citizenship."

When I later looked at Igor's file, it contained a record of lengthy correspondence between Latvian and Russian citizenship and migration authorities, of Igor changing his mind about refusing Russian citizenship (in moments when paper struggles seemed to be too much and he was willing to have any papers just to have papers), and of a reinvigorated fight for Latvian citizenship (in moments when Igor realized that he has "nothing in Russia," that all his family is in Latvia and that he has nowhere else to go). Formal decisions, too, wavered between deportation orders and permissions to stay on the basis of connections with the current place of residence. At some point, the file indicated that Igor had even submitted an asylum application, evidently in an attempt to try yet another method for sorting out his situation. He retracted the asylum application shortly thereafter. Igor's file ends in January of 2011 with a decision to deport him with prohibition of return for six months.

Other "long-livers" (*ilgdzīvotāji*), as one Border Guard inspector referred to those former Soviet citizens who were on the radar screen of the State Border Guard for a long time, had similar histories of back and forth movement and confusion with papers. Several had been imprisoned and had not paid attention to paperwork while in prison. Some of them had been turned over to the State Border Guard as the prison authorities realized at the end of their sentence that they had no papers. Some others were reported by their former spouses or partners. As one Border Guard inspector stationed in the detention center explained to me, "Some people do not take their citizenship seriously. They are born in one place, then move to another, cannot settle there and move back. They don't understand how things have changed, and they become illegal because of their own fault. They could have taken care of paperwork in Latvia." Moreover, he thought that those who took on Russian citizenship while remaining residents of Latvia "did not do the smart thing. The problems start if they don't have the money to extend the residence permit. They don't realize how big of a problem they have. People also need work permits, and they resolve this by faking documents or working without documents. We have six such people in the detention center right now [2005]. They have been detained within [Latvian] territory. We even have people who speak fluent Latvian, they are basically Latvians, but without papers. There is no project that could help them. Asylum seekers are entitled to things, but they are not."

Most cases involving former Soviet citizens pertained to people who were on the socioeconomic and often criminal margins of the society. They were poor, unemployed, or casually employed individuals, some of them with "prison careers," who fell through the cracks of the system. At the time of my research, they were the most common "clients" of the State Border Guard, as put by a Border Guard inspector. "We provide a social service," the inspector said, "because at least when they are in detention, the state helps with the paperwork. Nobody else cares about these people." Maija, a staff member of the Office of Citizenship and Migration Affairs, said: "The NGOs are interested only in a particular group of people. They are not interested in the former Soviet citizens. They feed on European Union funds. There was a man—he was in the detention center. He was born and grew up in Russia and had a prisoner's career in Latvia. When he was released from the prison, they could not deport him, because he had nothing in Russia. And he did not have any documents from Russia. He still wanders around here, he has nothing."

As the State Border Guard cast its net across the territory in the form of random bus checks, raids, invitations to report, what they found was not undocumented "third country nationals," but rather former Soviet citizens who had fallen through the cracks, who had not realized the full implications of citizenship, and who treated paperwork as a formality that would not have much bearing on their lives. They were wrong. The border guards did not condone it, but they understood how such a situation may have developed. As a senior officer working in the detention center explained to me, "I understand how these people ended up here. Their papers ran out. I know how that can happen. I almost did not get citizenship myself. My grandmother was not properly registered in Latvia after returning from Belorussia in 1932."

The former Soviet citizens—the ones whose situations the border guards claimed to understand—were not only overrun by borders but were also crossing borders in an attempt to "get to Europe." Thus, in January 2010, a man in his early thirties turned himself over to the offices of the State Border Guard in Riga.[33] He allegedly crossed into the European Union at the former boundary between the Soviet republics of Lithuania and Belorussia (now Belarus) a few days previously and continued on to Latvia. His journey began in Georgia and, as he put it, he wanted to go "deeper into Europe," but gave up because of the subzero winter temperatures.

I happened to be in the offices of the State Border Guard talking with the head of the Department of Immigration Control while reading case files of undocumented migrants. Since space was scarce, both of us were present when an inspector interviewed the man from Georgia who called himself Gia. The four of us were later joined by a Georgian language translator who assisted with the interview. Having come of age after the collapse of the Soviet Union, Gia's Russian language skills were rudimentary, while the rest of us spoke Russian comparatively better. The Georgian language translator was also from Georgia, but had moved to Latvia after meeting her Latvian husband in the early 1990s. She spoke Latvian fluently, as did the inspector conducting the interview. He, in turn, was a citizen of Latvia, but his mother tongue was Russian. The head of department and I shared Latvian as our first language. The head of department thus often assumed and suggested that as a fellow Latvian I surely must understand that the historical legacy of large-scale in-migration of Russian speakers during the Soviet times demands rigid immigration controls in the present in order to protect the cultural nation of Latvians from extinction.

Given the historical and political entanglements, the five of us—the man from Georgia, the head of the Department of Immigration Control, the inspector, the translator, and the anthropologist—made up quite a motley crew of post-Soviet subjects. We were all differently positioned in relation to the Latvian nation and the state, as well as in relation to the Soviet past and the European present. Some of us were citizens, while others legal residents or illegal immigrants. Some of us were law enforcement officers, while others lay persons and even law breakers. Nevertheless, as the encounter unfolded, it appeared that, despite the state-based enforcement of differences between us, we were able to connect, share stories, criticize politics, laugh, and even plan alternative routes that Gia could take the next time he tries to go "deeper into Europe."

As I was talking with the head of the department, the inspector and Gia, the man from Georgia, were looking at a map, trying to reconstruct his travels. Gia drew his finger across the map and called out: Kakheti (a region in Georgia), Minsk, Lithuania, Latvia. He had taken a van, a plane, a taxi and then walked eight hours by foot. He did not have a passport; he said it disintegrated while he was walking and he threw it out in the forest. The head of department intervened: "You need a passport, what is the purpose of your trip?" By now the translator had arrived. The inspector asked Gia whether he wanted to apply for asylum to which he responded that, no, he did not. He had heard that one could be imprisoned for a long time as part of the process, and he wanted to return home to his wife and two children. "No, no, I am going home," Gia exclaimed. He said he had just wanted to go through Latvia and get to France for medical treatment, but the cold got to him. Having stopped in Latvia, with no place to go, Gia walked and walked at night to stave off the cold. He had walked so much that he wore out his shoes. He said: "I will go home now, but I will go to Europe again. I cannot get care in Georgia. My father died with Hepatitis C. What's the difference where I die? I will definitely go to Europe." The head of department asked: "And you could not just get a visa?" "Oh, no! That costs too much money," Gia replied and explained that the only way to get a visa was to pay a large sum of money to an intermediary who then liaised with embassy employees to secure a visa. The head of department responded: "Yes. Then it would be more sensible to wait out the winter so as not to lose another pair of shoes." Everyone laughed. The head of department continued more seriously: "I don't know what to suggest. Next time try in the summer. Winter is rough here. If you had come in December when it was even colder, walking would not have helped. Isn't it closer to go through Bulgaria or Romania?" Then the head of department turned to me and said: "It's understandable. We got lucky. If we had a different passport [not an EU passport], we would be doing the same." Having completed the initial interview, the inspector and Gia stepped outside for a cigarette. In the meantime, the translator told the head of department and me about her own bureaucratic nightmares when trying to secure a residence permit in Latvia. We nodded our heads in understanding.

The scene caught me by surprise. Despite it being a scene of deportation, that is, of a power-laden relationship of subordination between border agents and a border crosser, it was also characterized by identification across these power relations. On the one hand, the conversation attempted to elicit all the necessary information to effect a deportation; on the other hand, it conjured up a modality of engagement in which we conversed about what our lives were like vis-à-vis each other and vis-à-vis the migration regimes that shaped them. Gia had turned himself in and faced deportation, but, in a way, he thought of the deportation as a state-provided service that will get him home after he had failed in his attempt to "get to Europe." He therefore was not anxious or fearful, but rather relaxed and cooperative. The translator, while there to enable communication between Gia and border guards, felt compelled to share her own migration story, which criticized the state that the border guards represented. Having done everything by the book, she had still gone through quite an ordeal to finally secure a residence permit in Latvia. The head of department acknowledged that he and I got lucky to have ended up with the kind of passports that allowed us to freely cross the border that Gia was struggling to cross in the cold purportedly in search for medical treatment, but also more broadly for a better life. The head of department was partaking in effecting a deportation—or providing a service, depending on one's perspective—while at the same time acknowledging the geopolitical differences that rendered us lucky while setting Gia on an arduous journey. More than that, he considered whether other routes might be better for getting to Europe, which still marked a promissory space of future possibility even for those—like the head of the department—who were supposedly already in it.

The staff of the Border Guard continuously grappled with the dilemma of controlling the movement or residence of people they considered, in a way, to be *savējie*: that is, people who recognize each other as fellow travelers across lines of power even if one's job is to deport the other.[34] These included the Georgian who had come all the way to Georgia to move "deeper into Europe," former Soviet citizens who became illegal as borders moved around them, and labor migrants from Ukraine or other parts of the former socialist world. When some of the border guards took up the collective discourse of the nation, Latvia's Russian speakers, who were themselves often referred to as "migrants" (chapter 2), were not usually seen as fellow travelers, but on an individual level and at times on the collective level, especially when juxtaposed to "new foreigners," solidarities emerged. "All these former Soviet people," said a Border Guard inspector, "it is difficult to put them in the category of illegal immigrants. They simply did not get lucky. They are kind of *savējie*, and yet they are not [if one goes by national categories]. The same Ukrainian who lives next door, he is *savējais*. Communication, elementary things, it is known to us. We have a chat, no problem."

Sometimes solidarity arose from past socialities, at other times it arose from a sense of shared experiences of socioeconomic and political subordination in the present. The border guards were also underpaid employees who often left their employment to migrate to Ireland or the United Kingdom for better jobs. While the border guards could legally cross the internal EU borders in comparison with Gia who could only cross them illegally, the reasons they may have wanted to cross them were not all that different—all went in pursuit of a livable life. The Border Guard inspectors' conduct in relation to the former Soviet citizens-cum-undocumented migrants entailed an implicit commentary on their own ambiguous status in relation to Europe even as they manned its borders—"we are just like them, except that we got lucky." For the border guards, the fact that "we have the right passports, but they don't" was a matter of historical contingency and global power relations. Thus, throughout the bordering encounter, none of those present questioned the morality of Gia's attempts to change his conditions of life by moving across borders, though the state demanded that we all question their legality.

This understanding of another's attempt to ensure a life for oneself formed connections across lines of power and across the distinction between legal and illegal movement. This understanding was formed on the basis of shared historical experience and critical awareness of global power hierarchies. The border guards understood how the Georgians and the Ukrainians, like themselves, experienced the turmoil of postsocialist transformations and how the situation, which they tried to change by crossing borders, was not entirely of their own making. For example, they thought that it was not because the Georgians or the Ukrainians did not want to work that they crossed borders, but because improving life through work was rendered difficult, if not impossible, in the context of post-Soviet transformations and the associated rise in poverty, corruption, and inequality. The border guards understood that they too could have been in the same situation had they not gotten so lucky as to have the right passports. In that sense, bordering encounters were quite different from the language inspection encounter I described earlier in the book. Even though Anna and Raita—the language inspectors in chapter 2—experienced empathy during the inspection process, they did not translate it into understanding or political action. They could not afford to do so, insofar as the objects of their empathy were not passing through, but staying. Moreover, they were not simply marginalized subjects that had fallen in between the cracks of the legal system, but rather resentful and defiant Russian speakers.

The border guards' and migration officials' discontent with their and the nation's subordinate status sounded backward and prejudiced to the ears of human rights activists. And it was indeed often accompanied by well-rehearsed lines about "lazy asylum seekers" or racist statements, as in the case of the border guard wishing for "the negroes to go home." Latvian border guards and migration officials did not understand the modes of marginalization and webs of hierarchies affecting the lives of asylum seekers and did not extend solidarities to them quite in the same way as they did to the "former Soviets." To make sense of why Somalis and other people from outside the former Soviet space set on the road, the border guards and migration officials relied on the hegemonic narratives, categorizations, and stereotypes reproduced in European public and political life, especially in the professional institutions with which they collaborated and from which they received their lessons in Europeanness. Thus, theirs was not merely individual prejudice that could be eliminated with the help of thorough lessons in political liberalism. Rather, it was a symptom of Europe's struggle to resolve the tension between values of freedom, democracy, and human rights, on the one hand, and racialized exclusions, on the other.

I suggest, therefore, that the encounter between the institutionalized political liberalism of the Human Rights Organization concerned with the rights of asylum seekers and the "unprofessionalism" or "nationalism" of the border guards and migration officials can be read as a symptom of the intersection of multiple sets of hierarchies: one, the hierarchies between deserving and unde-serving subjects that shape the Europewide migration regime; two, the socio-economic inequalities through which various places are integrated into the global economy; and, three, the civilizational and developmental hierarchies that emerged in the context of postsocialist transition and European integra-tion in Latvia. Europe's racialized migration regime with its violent practices of exclusion, often conducted in the name of protecting freedom, democracy, and human rights, has been thoroughly analyzed (e.g., Cabot 2014, Fassin 2005, Fer-nando and Giordano 2016, Giordano 2014, Ticktin 2011). The juxtaposition of migrants or asylum seekers to socioeconomically marginalized subjects at home has also been criticized in literature (e.g., Anderson 2013). But there is an added dimension in the Latvian case, namely the first two hierarchical differentiations take on particular forms in a marginal European space, which is in a subordinate relationship to the "core of Europe," itself empirically elusive, but normatively powerful (e.g., Böröcz 2006, Dzenovska 2018b, Zarycki 2014).

It is because of the intersection of these multiple sets of hierarchies that the border guards' and migration officials' critical commentary on postsocialist power hierarchies went unrecognized. The border guards and migration officials were learning the paradox of Europeanness, namely how to exclude while pro-fessing values of inclusion, and the human rights activists were engaged in a civi-lizational project that obscured this tension by upholding the value of inclusion while displacing exclusion onto not-yet-civilized people and places. There was no publicly available discourse that could criticize this constellation without risking affinities with the nationalist camp or diagnosis of "Soviet mentality" and thus being folded into the hegemonic discursive space as a subject in need of civiliza-tion. Insofar as the human rights activists and tolerance workers interpreted the border guards' and migration officials' attempts to point to other neglected cat-egories of people, including themselves, as inability to overcome a victim mental-ity inherited from the Soviet times, they worked to obscure the power relations that bound the European political landscape after socialism.

Between Repression and Redemption

The institutionalized political liberalism embraced by human rights activists aligned categories of difference or marginality as equivalent units but did not have the tools for critically evaluating the power constellations that resulted in a situ-ation where all were equal, but where some subjects of rights were institutionally privileged over others. For them, the rights of asylum seekers did not depend on whether or not there were other more or less marginalized subjects, such as, for example, former Soviet citizens, underpaid state employees, or the Latvian nation at large. Moreover, their treatment of asylum seekers did not depend on whether or not they understood their specific historical predicament, as was well visible from the fact that the Somalis' story remained obscure to everyone all throughout the case. The human rights activists could not but see the criticism directed at the institutionalized privileging of the rights of some subjects over others as an indication of a partial understanding of Europe's political and moral virtues on the part of border guards and migration officials, but also within the Latvian society at large (see chapter 3). The border guards' and migration officials' critical discourse sounded like an excuse for institutionalized neglect of human rights. As Annelise Riles has argued, human rights rhetoric neglects appeals of the so-called human rights violators "regarding the special social, political or economic context of their specific acts of violation. Human rights rhetoric is effective only to the extent that it negates such contextually derived distinctions—to the extent that it is possible to claim that a human rights violation anywhere is of the same epistemological order and of the same moral, political and legal significance as a human rights violation elsewhere" (2006, 54). My critique here is not of human rights as an ethical framework, one that Samuel Moyn (2010) has termed "the last utopia," but rather of its institutionalized forms that obscure the power hierarchies within which they are embedded—a phenomenon which is common across the human rights landscape, but takes on a specific form in Latvia. Thus, for example, contrary to the critical human rights lawyers and activists described by Riles (2006), who criticize the institutional politics of human rights while at the same time instrumentalizing human rights law in practice, the human rights activists in Latvia—and tolerance workers more broadly—did not have a discursive space from which to criticize their own work, for they felt embattled and saw themselves as standing up against Soviet legacy and virulent nationalism.

In turn, the critical discourses of border guards and migration officials, variously attributed to nationalism or Soviet legacy by the human rights activists, were based on a relational understanding of marginality, that is, on an understanding of institutionally and politically recognized marginality as connected to power hierarchies that shape Latvia's economic and political life after socialism. They pointed out that European migration authorities privileged rights of asylum seekers over those of locally marginalized subjects, such as former Soviet citizens who failed to legalize. They pointed out that "Europe" was preparing them for "sharing the burden," by which they meant that "Europe" was about to dump its own problems onto Latvia, which was only marginally involved in their creation, if at all (see chapter 1). For example, a migration official told me in a casual conversation in 2010 that "they [Belgium and other Western European states] have had colonies, they feel guilty, it is a different situation. That's why they are so open. We do not have anything to do with Africa, our history was the USSR." And they pointed out how Europe's migration regime demanded that they differentiate between border crossers on the basis of political ideologies. For example, a border guard at the Riga airport told me that "our country asks a lot from Russian businessmen, but does not ask anything from the Brits who come here to drink. They are supposedly citizens of the European Union, and you cannot ask anything from them, but a Russian citizen is actually less dangerous than an English person in terms of violating public order [he was referring the frequent cases of British stag party members urinating on Riga's monuments]." At the same time, the awareness of how political ideologies affected their work did not prevent the border guards from embracing other modes of differentiation about which they learned as part of becoming a properly European border force. For example, they did not object to the use of a list of largely African and Middle Eastern countries, whose citizens were to be checked especially thoroughly, if they tried to cross Europe's external border. They had no historical sense of the people hailing from these polities, and thus they readily called them all "terrorists" in their everyday talk.

The encounter between human rights activists and border control and migration authorities, as well as the encounters described in other chapters in the book, bring into focus the limits of critical discourse in postsocialist Europe that I outlined in the Introduction (Zarycki 2014). With left political discourse discredited as playing into the hands of Russia, there are two legitimate political discourses available in the Latvian public space: liberal or nationalist. As a result, the border guards' and migration officials' attempts to point to the intersecting hierarchies of marginality and to the uneven power relations that structure European integration were interpreted by human rights activists as manifestations of backward nationalist thinking inappropriate for modern European subjects or as effects of Soviet mentality. In turn, the human rights activists' attempts to bring attention to the shortcomings of the asylum system in Latvia and to the racism that permeated Europe's migration regime were perceived by the border guards and migration officials as imposed and funding-driven foreign schemes that at best misunderstood the real situation in Latvia and at worst were manifestations of further subordination of Latvia to the European political agenda.

I have argued throughout the book that the "end of history" narrative and the perceived danger of criticism coming from Eastern Europe of political liberalism have obscured the power hierarchies that shape the European present. The resulting impasse has exempted institutionalized political liberalism from criticism and created a seemingly insurmountable gap between the liberal "community of value" and the not-yet-European—for not liberal—postsocialist subjects. Institutionalized forms of political liberalism have not been able to recognize and address the grievances of historically and culturally embedded subjects experiencing alienation and dispossession as a result of postsocialist transformations. Thus tolerance workers and human rights activists interpreted the border guards' and the broader publics' attempts to point out that there were other marginal subjects in Latvia—whether the poor or neglected former Soviets—besides those falling in the categories of difference protected by institutionalized forms of political liberalism, as excuses of an unenlightened public unwilling to become European. At the same time, the border guards, as well as the broader public, considered that those institutionalizing political liberalism in Latvia did not recognize the historical context or the socioeconomic realities that placed different demands on the present. Moreover, it is precisely bordering and migration governance that shows most clearly that the tension between openness and closure is not to be mapped onto a discursive juxtaposition between liberalism and illiberalism and, subsequently, spatially onto Western and Eastern Europe. It is the foundational tension of the political space of Europe. Latvian migration officials and border guards were generally better at learning the repressive elements of Europe's migration regime (that is, securing the border and keeping barbarians at the gate) than embracing the redemptive ones (that is, tolerance and compassion). Or, rather, their compassion was differently directed—just like former European colonial empires police their boundaries to keep out former colonial subjects while at the same time fighting racism and cultivating tolerance toward them, Latvians policed their boundaries to keep out former rulers (who tend to be perceived as barbarians), while also exhibiting feelings of solidarity and compassion toward them. However, becoming European required that they turn their attention to Europe's former colonial subjects as well—both in terms of keeping barbarians at the gate and treating them right. Insofar as they failed to do so, they were deemed to lack in Europeanness.

Epilogue

LIBERALISM ON THE FENCE

In September 2015, Latvia announced a plan to build a 2.7-meter-high fence along especially vulnerable sections of its 276-kilometer-long border with Russia, amounting to 90 kilometers of fence altogether. The building of the fence was to commence as soon as possible and be completed in 2019. It would cost about 17 million euros. The State Border Guard described this project as "arranging the border zone" (*robežjoslas sakārtošana*) for the dual purpose of facilitating the work of border guards and stemming the flow of illegal migrants across Latvia's and European Union's external border. According to the State Border Guard, the fence was one component of an elaborate border infrastructure, the building of which was approved long before it was publicly announced in 2015, around the same time that the conflict between Russia and Ukraine created security concerns and the "migration/refugee crisis" unsettled the European political landscape.

Latvia's residents, especially those in border regions, were divided about the fence, some welcoming it and urging the state to build an even higher and stronger one, others considering it a useless spectacle and waste of money. As soon as the first sections of the fence were completed in April 2016, construction experts criticized the fence as too flimsy. A founding board member of a Latvian company called "Fence Factory" commented on national television that the fence can be easily cut and that the State Border Guard authority should have selected a more durable panel fence. He compared the Latvian fence negatively to the Hungarian "anti-immigrant fence," which was made of thicker and better wire.

207

He knew, because his company had provided materials for the Hungarian fence (Kļavis 2015). The State Border Guard responded that their purpose was not to build an impenetrable barrier. Walking along the first completed sections of the fence, a State Border Guard official explained to a television crew that the fence is meant to slow down unprepared border crossers, such as the fifteen Vietnamese citizens who were arrested trying to cross the border in September 2015, the month that the construction of the fence was announced.[1]

Even as the Latvian officials emphasized that the fence was part of regular border infrastructure, domestic and international publics connected it with Europe-wide efforts to stem migration. Fences—most, if not all, initiated in 2015—were going up between Hungary and Serbia, Austria and Slovenia, Bulgaria and Turkey, Greece and Turkey, Greece and Macedonia, and Norway and Russia. Spanish enclaves of Melilla and Ceuta have been enclosed by fences for more than two decades. Moreover, border checkpoints were being reintroduced on internal borders of the European Union between Denmark and Sweden, and France and Italy, as country after country claimed their right to secure themselves against the influx of unwanted migrants or refugees. The Latvian fence, too, was interpreted in this context, even as the border between Russia and Latvia—or that between Latvia and Belarus—can hardly be considered a hot-spot of illegal border crossings. In 2015, 476 people were detained trying to illegally cross "the green border" and, in 2016, 376.[2] According to the State Border Guard authority, these border crossers were mostly Vietnamese, Indian, and Russian citizens, aided by Russian citizens of Chechen background. Even as the Latvian State Border Guard tried to distance itself from fences, such as the one built on the Hungarian border, the Latvian fence could not help but be perceived as part of a Europewide securitization of borders in response to a widespread sense that Europe was being overrun by unruly mobile bodies and that Europe's carefully crafted configuration of exclusive inclusion was in danger.

At the same time, Latvian officials were well aware of the possibility that the fence could also be perceived as an attempt to symbolically distance Latvia from Russia. Even though large segments of the Latvian public were likely to welcome such distancing, Latvia's politicians and State Border Guard officials downplayed this interpretation of the fence. In September 2015, Minister of Interior Rihards Kozlovskis emphasized that the fence is not meant as a "wall of China" between Latvia and Russia.[3] However, when viewed together with the fence being built on the border between Estonia and Russia, as well as the fence planned on the border between the Russian enclave of Kaliningrad and Lithuania, it is tempting to link these fences to increasing tensions between Russia and the West. Thus, when the BBC reported on the Estonian decision to build a fence in August 2015, it described the fence as a response to the tensions between Russia and Ukraine.[4]

Indeed, that's how the fence was perceived on the Russian side as well. Konstantin Kosachev, the deputy head of the Russian parliament's Foreign Affairs Committee, pointed out that there are no significant flows of migration across the Estonian border with Russia, and that the purpose of the fence is therefore ideological, namely to depict Russia as Europe's enemy.

Western and Russian media outlets were quick to spin the story of Baltic fences as being about geopolitical tensions rather than migration. For example, the *Business Insider* reporter Jeremy Bender (2015) argued that despite emphasizing migration flows, the Latvian decision to build a fence on the Russian border echoes Estonian concerns about Russian provocations.[5] And when Lithuania announced in early 2017 that it, too, was building a fence on its border with the Russian region of Kaliningrad, there was no pretense about the fence's political and ideological dimensions.[6] As reported by the BBC, Lithuanian authorities explicitly referred to Russian "provocations" as justification for the fence. They used the example of the 2015 incident on the Estonian border where an Estonian security official was kidnapped by Russia. Lithuanian newspapers, as well as the Russian media outlet *Russia Today*, cited the Lithuanian minister of interior as saying that "the fence is like a sign that [Lithuania] views the neighboring country as a potential aggressor."[7] In response to the Lithuanian announcement, the interim governor of the Kaliningrad region Anton Alikhanov offered to supply Lithuanians with bricks from the Kaliningrad brick factory.

As I write this epilogue, media reports indicate that the Latvian State Border Guard has finished constructing the first twenty-three kilometers of the fence along the border between Russia and Latvia. Moreover, the State Border Guard has announced plans to build another fence along the border between Latvia and Belarus. This fervor of fence building looks like reassertion of a territorial nation-state that takes place shortly after the decline of the nation-state was announced at the height of globalization in the 1990s. Moreover, it is a global phenomenon extending beyond Europe—there are walls and fences between Israel and Palestine, the United States and Mexico, South Africa and Zimbabwe, Saudi Arabia and Yemen, Uzbekistan and Kyrgyzstan, and Uzbekistan and Turkmenistan (Brown 2010). Wendy Brown (2010) interprets such fence building as spectacular acts of states that are, on the one hand, losing political sovereignty to capitalism and religion, and on the other hand, trying to erect barriers against what they perceive to be uncontrollable and chaotic flows of goods and people. The actual or imagined war is no longer between sovereign entities, but between particular people living in particular places and a variety of unruly and mobile entities. For many proponents of political liberalism in Europe, such fencing of Europe, as well as of other Western liberal democracies, accompanied by the rise of right-wing "populism," Brexit, and the election of Donald Trump as president of the United States, suggests that liberalism is in crisis.

It is noteworthy that the crisis of liberalism is unfolding simultaneously with the spread of fears about Russia in Western liberal democracies. Thought to have been on a path to a liberal future like other former socialist states throughout the 1990s, Russia in the last decade or so has reemerged as the liberal West's nemesis. Whereas Russian elites claim that Russia is a sovereign democracy, Western elites consider that Russia has not only retreated to being an illiberal democracy, but also works to undermine and threaten "the international liberal order," as Joe Biden put it during the 2017 World Economic Forum in Davos (see also Shekhovtsov 2016).[8]

In Latvia, the fear is existential. It is not only about the international political order but also about the very existence of an independent Latvian state and the continuity of the nation. For most Latvians and for a growing public in the West, the annexation of Crimea in 2014 and the ongoing war in Eastern Ukraine serve as tangible examples of what might happen in Latvia. Given the perception that Russia poses a threat not only to its neighbors, but also to the world's liberal democracies, Latvians and their neighbors in Estonia and Lithuania have gained a willing audience in the West. BBC, for example, produced a show called *Inside the War Room* that entertained the scenario of British politicians and intelligence officers facing the decision of whether to intervene in the Baltics as Russia succeeds in mobilizing Latvia's Russian speakers in the southeastern region of Latgale to demand the region's secession. When I watched the episode, I was struck by the blurring of reality and fiction that it entailed, especially since that is precisely the feature thought to characterize Russia's "post-truth" politics (e.g., Pomerantsev 2015). Moreover, I expected Latvian audiences to object on the grounds that such blurring of reality and fiction not only entertains possible scenarios but actively produces them. And I expected at least some Latvian audiences to object to the depiction of Latvia's Russian speakers as gullible, disloyal, and easily manipulated. There were some who voiced such concerns, but, overall, mainstream publics discussed whether or not the depiction of British decision-making process instilled confidence that Western nations and military alliances would protect Baltic nations in the event of Russian aggression. More than that, this scenario reinforced what the Latvians thought they already knew about their Russian-speaking compatriots and the direction of their loyalties. Latvia's Russian speakers thus remained merely pawns in this game. But Latvians, too, were merely pawns in this game—something that the Latvians knew only too well and thus were trying to discern how best to navigate its shifting terrain. Latvians engaged in collective tactics of survival by aligning with the liberal West. Some claimed this alliance to be a necessary evil, while others conceived of it as an expression of democratic maturity.

Thus while Europe's border fences seem to suggest further securitization of Europe against migration, the Latvian fragment of the European fence has the added dimension of symbolizing the hardening border between Russia and the West. Whereas the "migrant/refugee crisis" was very much shaped by Europe's inclusion/exclusion paradox that I have been describing in this book, fencing off from Russia is entirely about exclusion. Moreover, whereas, in the context of Europe's "migrant/refugee crisis" Latvia along with the rest of Eastern Europe was depicted as failing to mitigate Europe's repressive migration regime with redemptive features, such as tolerance and acceptance of refugees, fencing off from Russia has no immediate moral drawbacks. Instead, it propels Latvia into the vanguard of Europe's defense. On the one hand, Latvians—along with Estonians and Lithuanians—can feel vindicated. They always thought that Russia could not be trusted, that the end of history was a ruse. This is their claim to significance in the post–Cold War world. For example, in a conference on the Baltics that I attended at University College London in the spring of 2016, one Estonian panelist claimed to be an expert on Russia for as long as he has lived and this by mere virtue of having been born in Russia's proximity. In turn, Edward Lucas, the regional editor for the *Economist*, urged the audience "to listen to the Balts, because they know." On the other hand, this has created uncanny alliances. Instead of aligning with the defenders of a European way of life, Latvians, nationalists and liberals alike, are veering toward an alliance with Europe's liberals, for it is they who turn out to be the best ally in Latvian attempts to seek protection in the event of aggression from Russia. European nationalists, in turn, who would have been natural allies for a small state and people trying to survive in the midst of a globalizing world, are too friendly with Russia and thus not particularly helpful. Geopolitics makes for unexpected bedfellows.

But what exactly is the relationship between the crisis of liberalism and the rising fear of Russia? It seems that the exceedingly strong focus on Russia as the new old threat to liberalism risks obfuscating the fact that the actually existing post–Cold War political liberalism—and the "international liberal order" more broadly—did fail on a number of counts, and that these failures cannot necessarily be explained by turning to Russia. As Ivan Krastev has argued, the presence of illiberalism in Central Eastern Europe is not a manifestation of a crisis of democratization (that is, a failure to convert Eastern European unbelievers), but rather a crisis of liberal democracy (that is, a crisis of faith) (2016, 38). More precisely, liberal policies have failed to deliver economic prosperity and social justice, as well as to provide a satisfactory answer to the question of how Latvians—and other people concerned with their ways of life—are to live with strangers without losing themselves.

The crisis of liberalism is not the only crisis in recent years. Most notably, Latvia, along with much of the Western world, experienced severe financial crisis in 2008, which shook the foundations of neoliberalism as the prevalent economic ideology. As argued by Philip Mirowski (2011), the 2008 financial crisis unsettled established economic wisdoms insofar as few economists, neoliberal or not, were able to either predict the crisis or explain it once it had happened. However, Mirowski points out that, despite the ground shaking beneath their feet, neoliberals came out of the crisis stronger than ever. Mirowski explains this by arguing that neoliberal thought, as conceived and institutionalized by a core of neoliberal ideologues gathered in the Mont Pelerin Society and distributed through a myriad of associated institutions and networks, was modeled on the faith in markets as near-natural regulators of contradictions and crises. Mirowski suggests that the neoliberals in various academic and nonacademic posts promoted confusion about the crisis, emphasized that individuals are not in the position to know and understand economic processes, as Friedrich Hayek suggested (Guyer 2007), and posited the market as the only long-term mechanism able to know the crisis, as it were, and thus to resolve it (2011, 81). This, alongside the embeddedness of neoliberal thought in everyday practices, achieved through decades of making individuals into neoliberal subjects, made neoliberal thought and thus also neoliberals in positions of power resilient in the face of crisis.

If neoliberalism came out of the crisis stronger than ever, this was not the case with the previous large-scale ideological crisis, namely that of "actually existing socialism" in late 1980s. Soviet and Eastern European socialisms collapsed. Unlike neoliberalism, Soviet socialism did not seem to have an internal mechanism for resolving crisis. After the death of Stalin as the arbiter of ideological battles, socialist ideology took the form of standardized public discourse where "what mattered was not literal meaning, but rather the reproduction of precise structural forms of discourse" (Yurchak 2005, 14). Soviet citizens participated in reproducing the standardized discourse and socialist rituals, but otherwise led heterogeneous lives within and in between state structures. They believed some socialist ideals, but not necessarily their institutionalized forms. They were not interested in opposing the state and seemed oddly prepared for capitalism, when it arrived (Yurchak 2005). Even though there were attempts to save Soviet socialist thought in Russia—for example, by reviving Lenin as socialism's sacred center and arguing that Stalin and the party had corrupted Lenin's ideas (Yurchak 2015), these did not prove successful in strengthening or even reviving socialist thought and institutions in the face of crisis.

I found similar standardization of discourse in the context of tolerance promotion in Latvia (see chapter 3). However, contrary to Soviet socialists, European liberals—more specifically, the tolerance workers—believed in the institutions and the discourses they were reproducing. Somewhat ironically, given their conviction that former socialist subjects lacked critical thinking insofar as they were reluctant to embrace political liberalism, it turned out to be European liberals who failed to develop critical understandings of postsocialist power configurations (see chapter 4). In the case of Soviet socialism, "system's collapse had been unimaginable before it began, [but] . . . appeared unsurprising when it happened" (Yurchak 2005, 1). In the case of European liberalism, the system's collapse had also seemed unimaginable—it was, after all, the "end of history." But contrary to their former socialist counterparts, European liberals were unsettled and surprised when liberalism appeared to be in serious risk of being deposed as the "house ideology" of Western liberal democracies (Westbrook 2016). How did political liberalism end up in this situation? Could it be that the end of the Cold War was for European liberalism what Stalin's death was for Soviet socialism?

The current fear about Russia certainly gestures in that direction. With the end of the Cold War, liberalism lost its telos, that is, winning the battle against the "unfree world." Once the enemy was conquered, thus positing liberalism as the victorious ideology, conditions similar to late Soviet socialism developed. Liberal discourses became self-reproducing, perpetually fighting not an external enemy as during the Cold War, but the traces of enemy within—for example, socialist mentality among Latvians. With the external source of legitimacy gone, political liberalism fared worse than economic liberalism. Whereas the market became internalized as the source of neoliberalism's ideological authority, being itself part of the ideology and at the same time the authoritative voice on how to resolve internal contradictions and crises, political liberalism, similar to socialism, did not have such a mechanism. While socialism claimed and needed a positive ideology and a sacred center, liberalism denied the existence of an internal sacred center and was therefore in need of an enemy. One needing God, the other the Devil, they were both similar to each other and different from neoliberalism, which needs neither center nor enemy, neither God nor Devil, and relies on the market as a perfect self-functioning system.

When crisis came in the form of political liberalism's inability to address the grievances produced by the combination of neoliberalism and identity politics, political liberalism externalized the threat in the form of Russia, thus returning to a geopolitical power standoff that existed prior to liberalism's victory. Suggestions that a new Cold War is underway are most likely inaccurate, if only because of massive shifts in the relationship between technology and power. There is talk of hybrid warfare, of invisible enemies, and of "little green men" that are more dangerous than the Russian military. It is striking, then, that it is a fence that captures the imagination as a symbolic bulwark against the imagined Russian threat. In that sense, the fence does more for liberalism than for defense. This is to say that the actually existing liberalism's response to the crisis has been to put liberalism, if not back behind, then certainly on the fence.

Notes

INTRODUCTION: PARADOX OF EUROPEANNESS

1. According to the 1951 Geneva Convention on Refugees, a refugee is "a person who is outside his or her country of nationality or habitual residence; has a well-founded fear of being persecuted because of his or her race, religion, nationality, membership of a particular social group or political opinion; and is unable or unwilling to avail him—or herself—of the protection of that country, or to return there, for fear of persecution." http://www.unhcr.org/4ec262df9.html

2. I use quotation marks here to mark the fact that the nature of the crisis is highly contested. Some arguments pertain to the categorical distinction between migrants and refugees, while others suggest that the crisis is of Europe itself, or that it is no crisis at all.

3. http://migration.iom.int/europe/. See also "Europe at a Crossroads" (nearfutures online.org) for a thorough consideration of the issue.

4. For examples, see Gressel 2015, Gross 2015, Hockenos 2015, Komorovskis 2015, Krastev 2015, Lyman 2015, Roland 2015, Rupnik 2015, Sabet-Parry and Ritter 2015, Simecka and Tallis 2015. It should be noted that there were also less noticed counterprotests, counterarguments, and counteractions, arguing for the need to extend help, as well as pointing to the obligation toward other European Union member states to share the burden. These did not get picked up by the media.

5. The title of the broadcast was "Who Will Be the Last One to Dance Sirtaki?" The show is available here in Latvian: http://ltv.lsm.lv/lv/raksts/08.07.2015-sastregumstunda.-krize-griekija.-kurs-dejos-sirtaki-pedejais.id52470/.

6. http://financenet.tvnet.lv/viedokli/567005grieki_varetu_pamacities_no_latviesiem_dazas_noderigas_lietas.

7. The special tasks of the minister and his secretariat included development and implementation of policy initiatives supporting Latvia's minorities, ranging from cultivating the cultural life of national minorities to devising programs that targeted the socially marginalized. As of 2004, it also included the promotion of tolerance. Many integration-related tasks have now been placed with the Ministry of Culture, but in 2005 the secretariat was still a separate institution headed by a minister who was a member of the government.

8. In 2012, Nils Muižnieks was elected for a six-year term as the Council of Europe's third commissioner for human rights.

9. See a related argument by Mayanthi Fernando in relation to France, where laïcéte is "fragmentary and inchoate," which necessitates that "the secular formation called France must continually reconstitute itself as a cohesive entity, redrawing its boundaries and regulating its subjects" (2014, 12).

10. David Theo Goldberg (2008) calls this "racial Europeanization."

11. In March 2016, the European Union and Turkey reached an agreement whereby illegal migrants entering Europe from Turkey would be sent back. In exchange, the European Union promised to resettle Syrian refugees from Turkey (one refugee for one returned illegal migrant), to grant Turkey significant sums of money, and to return to talks about Turkey's accession to the European Union.

12. http://www.bbc.co.uk/news/world-europe-35218921.

13. http://www.independent.co.uk/news/people/refugee-crisis-sweden-deputy-prime-minister-cries-as-she-announces-u-turn-on-asylum-policy-a6749531.html.

14. Following European Union enlargement in 2004, many citizens of the new member states moved to live and work in older member states, especially those, such as the United Kingdom, Ireland, and Sweden, that did not institute a seven-year transitional ban on freedom of labor movement. Many UK citizens consider that the migration flow was too large.

15. http://www.tvnet.lv/zinas/latvija/584842-mucenieku_iedzivotaji_vestule_straujumai_pauz_bazas_par_begliem_sava_ciema.

16. Although, as Scott has also recently argued, the "global conditions of possibility of any postcolonial socialism" were in decline already prior to the collapse of "Second World" socialisms (Scott 2014). Scott suggests that the emergent "end of history," as it later came to be known, was already evident in the failure of the Grenada revolution in the early 1980s (2014, 4).

17. There is an emerging tradition in anthropology that goes against the grain. See, for example, Creed 2011, Greenberg 2014, Larson 2013.

18. There have been some shifts in this regard once the figure of the "Eastern European migrant" erupted in Europe's political space. See Fox et al. 2012.

1. PRIDE AND SHAME

1. Those few scholars who have written about the duchy's colonial endeavors and their treatment in Latvian historiography and popular imagination largely draw on published historical sources in Latvian and German rather than new archival work, thus there is a lot of overlap in terms of the historical details included in the articles. I, too, draw on these sources.

2. Personal communication, April 2010.

3. The island of Tobago features in Daniel Defoe's Robinson Crusoe as the "Island of Despair" (Jekabson-Lemanis 2000, 28).

4. Karin Jekabson-Lemanis notes that the historical record is confused about when and how exactly the Duke of Courland obtained Tobago. Some suggest that he received rights to Tobago from King James I of England as a christening gift (though he still would have had to colonize it), while Jekabson-Lemanis argues that this cannot be, since the island was granted to the Duke of Courland by Charles I in 1639 (2000, 31).

5. In a conversation held at Barnard College, Miriam Ticktin, Paola Bachetta, and Ruth Marshall began their conversation about French colonialism, immigration, and violence by discussing President Sarkozy's 2007 address to African youth at the University of Anta Diop in Senegal where, according to the conversation participants, "he was recapitulating Hegel's ideas about Africa, suggesting that there is no historical time in Africa, that Africans still measure time through nature and that they need to be brought into history with a capital H" (2007, 1). I thank the University of California, Irvine Humanities Research Institute's Residential Research Group, "Imperial Legacies, Postsocialist Contexts," especially Fatima El-Tayeb, for bringing the transcript of this conversation to our collective attention.

6. See Kwon (2010) for the argument that there never was a conflict called *the* Cold War, and that "the bipolarized human community of the twentieth century experienced political bifurcation in radically different ways across societies—ways that cannot be forced into a single coherent conceptual whole" (2010, 6).

7. He diverged from other strands of Latvian socialism, such as *Jaunā Strāva* (New Current), which were more traditionally Marxist (Ijabs 2012).

8. Drawing on Alisdair MacIntyre, Talal Asad develops the notion of tradition as a dynamic argument of long duration about the goods that constitute it (Asad in MacIntyre 1984, Scott 2006; also Mahmood 2005, Pandian 2008).

9. The name Young Latvians was first used by a German priest, G. Braše, who upon reading a collection of poems by one of the intellectuals associated with the movement identified him as an insurgent. Initially, the name was used in a derogatory sense, but its connotations changed once the Young Latvians themselves embraced it (Zaķe 2007b).

10. Many intellectuals, entrepreneurs, politicians, and civil servants left Latvia as refugees in 1944 as the Soviet forces were approaching. Many feared deportations and purges that had already taken place after Soviet occupation in 1940. After spending years in Displaced Persons camps in Germany, these refugees ended up in the United Kingdom, the United States, Canada, Australia, and elsewhere (e.g., Zaķe 2010).

11. Courlanders had named the island St. Andrew's Island. The British later renamed it James Island.

12. Jānis said that the Latvian flag was already there, but I have not been able to confirm this.

13. It should be noted here that while Gambian political rhetoric emphasizes suffering inflicted by European slave trade, it completely overlooks the issue of internal slavery, which continued in Gambia well after the British abolished slavery in the early nineteenth century (Bellagamba 2005).

14. As Gyan Prakash has argued with regard to the codification of Hinduism as a religion in postcolonial India, Western dominance was imperative for constituting Hinduism as a national religion (2000, 289–290). See also Chatterjee 1986.

15. The historical aspects of indentured servitude, as well as the relations between Latvian serfs and their Baltic German owners are described in Strods (1987), as well as in Merķelis (2005 [1797]).

16. Drawing on Johannes Fabian's notion of "denial of coevalness," Jószef Böröcz writes of similar phenomena as "denial of connectedness" (Böröcz 2006, 126).

17. Both the Polish and Latvian cases illustrate that the formation of cultural nations in Eastern Europe did not depend on political structures supporting them. See Verdery (1994) on the specificity of nations and nationalism in Eastern Europe.

18. Gyan Prakash has argued that the impossibility of "the history of the subaltern as a full-blooded subject-agent" does not mean that subaltern histories cannot be written (2000, 287). Subaltern histories do not require that the subaltern's position be entirely outside power. Rather, "subaltern knowledges and subjects register their presence by acting upon the dominant discourse, by forcing it into contradictions, by making it speak in tongues" (Prakash 2000, 293). Prakash defines subalternity as "an abstraction used in order to identify the intractability that surfaces inside the dominant system—it signifies that which the dominant discourse cannot appropriate completely, and otherness that resists containment" (2000, 288). Thus, instead of thinking of subalternity as a category attached to concrete historical communities, Prakash thinks of subalternity as a relationally produced moment of unsettlement.

19. I borrow the distinction between legibility and intelligibility from Anita Starosta who uses this distinction as an analytical tool to engage with Eastern Europe in her work. Starosta explained this distinction in a session of the University of California Humanities Research Institute's Residential Research Group, "Imperial Legacies, Postsocialist Contexts," that took place in the fall of 2012. See also Morris (2010) on subalternity and legibility, as well as Chatterjee (2011).

2. THE STATE PEOPLE AND THEIR MINORITIES

1. The text of the preamble can be found here: http://www.saeima.lv/en/news/saeima-news/22361-saeima-expands-the-*constitution*-with-a-preamble.

2. This manifests, for example, in the mapping of the old distinction between "civic" and "ethnic" nationalism onto Western and Eastern Europe respectively. Rogers Brubaker notes that within scholarly circles the distinction between civic and ethnic

nationalism is increasingly recognized as political in addition to being analytical and that therefore it has become unacceptable to map it onto whole states or geographic regions. Brubaker suggests that it has become more common to argue that elements of both civic and ethnic—and thus good and bad—nationalism are articulated together in practice (2004, 136).

3. Marǵeris Vestermanis, personal communication, 2006. See also Goldmanis 2008.

4. The leader of the Russian party For Human Rights in a United Latvia, Tatyana Zhdanok, also expressed such a view in an interview with me in 2006.

5. In its current instantiation, the Law on Citizenship stipulates that children born in the territory of Latvia after August 21, 1991, are registered as citizens on the basis of an application submitted by one of the parents or after fifteen years of age on the basis of his/her own application.

6. http://www.mfa.gov.lv/arpolitika/sabiedribas-integracija-latvija/pilsoniba-latvija/pilsonibas-likums.

7. During the Soviet period, current-day Belarus was known as the Soviet Socialist Republic of Belorussia. In 1991, the Soviet Socialist Republic of Belorussia was renamed as the Republic of Belarus, thus also Belorussians became Belarusians. Since in this chapter I refer to the Soviet-era polity and people, I will use the terms "Belorussia" and "Belorussians." See also Malakhov and Osipov (2006) for a discussion of the disjuncture between ethnic identification and language use.

8. See Aktürk (2012, 2010) for a discussion of how discourses of sovetskii narod (Soviet nation) shifted throughout the second half of the twentieth century and why attempts to remove ethnicity from passports failed.

9. Drawing on Soviet terminology, I use the term *national* rather than *ethnic*. Within Soviet and post-Soviet usage, the term *national* implies the historically formed sense of collective life of an ethnos supported by an institutional framework, such as educational institutions and so forth. In contrast, the term *ethnic* could be used to describe a group, which may or may not think of itself as a collective subject (Hirsch 2005).

10. See Mahmood Mamdani's (2004) discussion of "bad Muslim" and "good Muslim," as well as Olga Procevska's (2013) article on how to be a good Russian.

11. Jennifer Jackson-Preece traces minority relations to seventeenth- and eighteenth-century Europe when religious minorities clashed with the ecclesiastical loyalties of the sovereigns, thus violating the *cuius regio eius religio* principle at the foundation of the international political order in Europe at the time (1997, 75). Shifts in the international political order in the nineteenth century—namely, the rise of nationalism, which culminated in the solidification of the nation-state as its basic unit after World War I—led to the emergence of language and culture as criteria for identifying difference within sovereign territories. Consequently, after World War I, the minority category came to be articulated with ethnicity (Arendt 2008, Jackson-Preece 1997). It is as a result of this development that it is possible to speak of a Russian minority in Latvia today or of a Hungarian minority in Romania.

12. Saba Mahmood (2012, 2016) has engaged these questions from the geopolitical perspective in relation to Egypt's Coptic minority.

13. It should be noted that the Soviet government did not provide more support for minorities than the authoritarian government of Ulmanis, for it closed down the remaining minority schools and proceeded to cultivate two "categories of difference" in Soviet Latvia—Latvians as the titular nationality and a Russian-speaking Soviet people.

14. See chapter 5 for a more elaborate discussion on injurious language and chapter 3 for a discussion of tolerance.

15. In 1935 Latvians made up 75.5 percent of the population. At the end of the Soviet rule in 1989, Latvians comprised 52 percent of the population (Riekstiņš 2004).

16. LVA, Fund Nr. 101, Description Nr. 19, Case Nr.108.

17. The language of instruction in schools has been a highly contested issue during the last decade. The Ministry of Education has attempted a school reform whereby the percentage of subjects taught in Latvian in Russian-language schools is to be gradually increased. This reform generated considerable resentment and resistance. See Silova (2006) for a more elaborate discussion.

18. The following occurrence described by Imants Ziedonis in his book *Kurzemīte* (1979) is exemplary of such survival skills: in this travels through Kurzeme—the northwest region of Latvia—Ziedonis visited many old rural homes. In one such home, he encountered an elderly woman and asked her whether there were any old magazines or books in the attic, since the old homes often carried such forgotten treasures. In response, the woman said: "Old magazines? In the fire! Here we had army after army come through. Never could understand which books were good and which were bad. All were burnt, by one army or another. At the end, we burned [them] ourselves. So as not to have problems [nepatikšanas]" (1979, 40).

19. See www.valoda.lv.

20. See Berklavs (1998) for the full text of the letter, as well as for a description of how the letter was produced, transported out of Latvia, and disseminated in the West.

21. It should be noted that in his memoirs published in 1998, Eduards Berklavs feels compelled to justify why this letter was written from within the frame of communism and addressed to communist parties abroad. The post-Soviet period demanded absolute distancing from the Communist Party and any socialist ideology. Thus, far from a national hero, Berklavs had to explain his actions (Berklavs 1998, 216)

22. By referring to Europe as postcolonial I aim to mark that problem-space of European public and political life, which is profoundly shaped by the history of (post)colonialism. In other words, I do not refer here to a Europe after colonialism, but rather to a Europe that is actively addressing questions that have to do with postcolonial histories—for example, questions of immigration, citizenship, and racism (Huggan and Law 2009; see also Chari and Verdery 2009).

23. See http://www.coe.int/en/web/minorities/fcnm-factsheet.

24. The state had been implementing minority support programs prior to the ratification of the convention. These programs did not identify minorities on the basis of legal definitions, but rather granted funds to minority cultural organizations for organizing various educational and cultural events. Membership in these organizations and thus the ability to benefit from funding was based on identification rather than legal status. The state thus merely enshrined this principle in law and enabled individuals to be minority subjects in practice without being such legally.

25. The question of whether and how migration amounted to an ethically inferior behavior surfaced forcefully in another context, namely the intensive Latvian out-migration following accession to the European Union in 2004 and the 2008 financial crisis (Dzenovska 2012, 2013b, 2018a).

26. The period between 1850 and 1890, when Young Latvians embarked on nation-building efforts is thought of as the first awakening; the years leading up to the establishment of the Latvian state in 1918 as the second awakening.

27. There were various integration programs implemented by the Latvian state with the assistance from foreign donors and the European Union. These remain outside the scope of this chapter, but more information can be obtained here: http://www.sif.gov.lv/index.php?lang=en.

28. See relevant government regulations: http://likumi.lv/doc.php?id=194735.

29 Fragments of this section were previously published in a Latvian-language article in the internet journal Satori.lv. See Dzenovska 2013c.

3. KNOWING SUBJECTS AND PARTIAL UNDERSTANDINGS

1. See Michael Walzer's (1997) five stages of toleration, ranging from passive putting up with to active acceptance of another's position or difference.

2. Kirstie McClure (1990) distinguishes between diversity and difference. Diversity pertains to coexistence of autonomous and equal entities, whereas difference pertains to entities or formation that are in a hierarchical and consequential relationship to each other: "Something that makes a difference by according priority to one alternative by specifying something peculiar to it necessarily marks its others with the absence or insufficiency of this characteristic, and hence simultaneously and by definition deprivileges its alternatives" (McClure 1990, 373).

3. See ECRI country reports here: http://www.coe.int/t/dghl/monitoring/ecri/activities/countrybycountry_en.asp.

4. See Mark Goodale's (2009) *Surrendering to Utopia: An Anthropology of Human Rights* for a take on "transnational human rights networks."

5. This discussion took place in 2004 when the first version of the program was discussed and approved. The 2004 version of the program did identify groups that suffered most from intolerance and those were "racial, religious, and ethnic minorities." In 2006, the secretariat changed the program to include sexual minorities. In 2008, following pressure from religious organizations, the sentence listing groups was taken out altogether. The program for 2009–13 is a general document promoting social tolerance without articulating it with specific groups (ĪUMSILS 2004, 2008).

6. I am not citing this interview, because "Signe" is a pseudonym.

7. See chapter 4 on critical reflection. See also Jonathan Larson's (2013) recent book *Critical Thinking in Slovakia After Socialism* in which he argues that particular manifestations of critical thinking were thought as necessary for integration in Europe. See Alana Lentin (2004) on institutional antiracism.

8. This liberal political logic, whereby some political actors, often associated or associating themselves with "the West" broadly conceived, position themselves as politically mature and assume the role of overseeing the maturation of others, is familiar from colonial and postcolonial contexts (Cowan 2007, Hesse 2007, Mehta 1999, Mignolo 2007, Mill 2007 [1859], Quijano 2007). Despite the telos assumed by it, this logic fixed the colonized in place. The colonized subjects could never quite reach full maturation; their similarity, as argued by Homi Bhabha (1984) in his article on colonial mimicry, was always an impossibility. In the post–Cold War period, the difference posited by the liberal political logic in colonial contexts came to be seen as cultural, as exemplified in Samuel Huntington's "clash of civilization" thesis (Brown 2006, Huntington 1996, Mamdani 2004). Wendy Brown has pointed out that "the culturalization of conflict or difference discursively depoliticizes both, while also organizing the players in a particular fashion, one that makes possible that odd, but familiar move within liberalism: though "culture" is what non-liberal peoples are imagined to be ruled and ordered by, liberal peoples are considered to *have* culture or cultures" (2006, 150). While the problem of intolerance in Latvia was not necessarily—or, rather, not exclusively—rendered as a problem of culture, the encounter between Signe and the "people and politicians" who wanted "to pretend that they are better than they are" was shaped by a similar logic. The "people and politicians" may have refused to recognize the problem of intolerance. But they did recognize, it seems, that they may not quite have the possibility afforded to Western liberal democracies to contain the problem of intolerance (or of racism or nationalism) as a problem

of the margins of society that does not taint the society as a whole. They were concerned that instead of *having* the problem of intolerance they were going *to be had* by the problem of intolerance, that the problem of intolerance may fix them in place at the same time as it demanded continuous self-improvement.

9. "Mentality" is a term widely used in Latvian sociological discourse to speak of culturally specific collective worldviews acquired in the processes of socialization that inform action (e.g., Beitnere 2011). Derived from Levy Bruhl's work on "primitive mentality" and widely utilized in Soviet social sciences, it has also become a popular term in Latvia and other former socialist contexts. Both in sociology and in popular discourse it is deployed to explain why people act the way they do. References to mentality often work as shorthand explanations, a way to psychologize and naturalize complex social phenomena. Even if, when asked, sociologists will stress that collective mentality is formed through socialization and historical sedimentation, the way the term appears both in public and political discourse is often as a marker of the essential traits of particular collectivities and thus borders on racialization.

10. The juxtaposition between invalid Soviet knowledge and valid Western knowledge overlooks how former Soviet citizens developed skills that were useful in navigating the post-Soviet terrain. For example, Alexei Yurchak has argued that contrary to the assumption that Soviet citizens "were not supposed to be good at inventing and running businesses, because they were raised in society where private business was non-existent," they actually were surprisingly good at it. Yurchak argues that many people from the "late Soviet generation," such as Komsomol secretaries, acquired entrepreneurial skills and knowledge not despite the Soviet system, but because of it (Yurchak 2005, 278). They operated as entrepreneurs in the field of ideological production and acquired skills, such as switching between officialized and personalized relations with the state, which were useful for operating businesses in the post-Soviet period and contributed to the emergence of specifically post-Soviet business practices (Yurchak 2005, 280). From the Western perspective, these were often deemed corrupt, thus rendering post-Soviet entrepreneurs subject to a Western civilizational project.

11. I experienced this in 2005 when three months after I had began my ethnographic work people demanded results and wanted to know my conclusions about racism and intolerance in Latvia. Many did not think long-term ethnographic research was any good, because it could not produce applicable results in a short time period.

12. From 1996 until 2000 I worked for the UN Development Program in Latvia and commissioned some of this research myself. I became disillusioned with the development industry in 2000 and returned to an academic career in anthropology.

13. It is noteworthy that the 1990s and the first half of the 2000s were characterized by research on human development, social integration, and intolerance, whereas more recent research overwhelmingly focuses on national identity. This is due to shifts in funding sources from international donors to national scientific bodies, which have set national identity as the primary research area in the humanities and social sciences (see Dzenovska 2012 for critique).

14. Sexual minorities were not formally included as a beneficiary of the program because the issue was too controversial at the time. The minister thought that the program would not be approved by the Cabinet of Ministers if sexual minorities were explicitly mentioned. Subsequently, LGBT rights organizations did partake in the work of tolerance promotion and collaborated with the Special Tasks Minister for the Integration of Society. This was especially so in 2006 and 2007 when Pride parades became a public controversy (see Dzenovska and Arenas 2012).

15. For more on right-wing extremism in Latvia, see Muižnieks (2005). See also Wodak et al. 2013.

16. In her book *The Violence of Victimhood*, Dianne Enns discusses Hannah Arendt's critique that Jews "did not take the birth and growth of anti-Semitism seriously enough. Instead, they proffered 'hasty explanations,' attributing anti-Semitism to rampant nationalism and xenophobia" (2012, 91). Enns, drawing on Arendt's *Origins of Totalitarianism*, points to the "scapegoat theory" as being especially problematic, as it overlooks how "modern terror" forms in long duration and crucially depends on "mass consent" which gets mobilized in employment of state terror. Similarly, naturalizing xenophobia as something that always has existed and needs to be overcome through education overlooks how xenophobia is made as part of modern forms of government.

17. Glaeser critiques liberal theory for assuming that actors already have opinions and thus for not paying attention to the contingencies through which political understandings are actually formed: "Rather than having to form understandings of various degrees of certainty and thus actionability through conversations, experiences and action, actors are assumed to always already have a well-formed understanding (opinion)" (2009, 394). Glaeser argues that "typically, liberalism fails to problematize the formation of understandings as such; it is blind to the contingent processes that generate and actualize them in more stable institutional form, thus sidestepping questions of political epistemology. . . . Liberalism is never to be genuinely puzzled by human beings" (2009, 394). Glaeser argues that understandings are not natural and essential products of individual reason, but derived, at least in the case of East German dissidents, from "emotive, kinesthetic, and prereflexive discursive understandings, on common experiences and stories about them. The political became more transparent to them only by thinking and emotionally working through experiences in community with others" (2009, 395). The solitary reflecting liberal subject as the source of understanding is a falsity; the formation of understanding is a social process that entails validation through networks of authority; the thoughts and responses of those we consider authorities matter (though not necessarily in the sense of state authority) (Glaeser 2009, 177).

4. BUILDING UP AND TEARING DOWN

1. Here and elsewhere I use ideology to refer to systems of thought, such as liberalism, nationalism, and socialism, that are at once discursive and material and that make truth-claims about the world. In that sense, they resemble Michel Foucault's (2002) "discursive formations," but I find this concept too broad for my purposes. My use, then, is closer to that of Louis Althusser's (2001) "ideology," as well as Antonio Gramsci's (1971) "hegemony."

2. See William Connolly's *Pluralism* for the argument that "avoidance of the problem of evil in faith often involves acceptance of some risk to the stability of your own identity" (2005, 31). He calls for a "generous ethos of engagement between multiple faiths whose participants inevitably bring pieces and chunks of it with them into the public realm" (2005, 31).

3. See Larson (2013) for a discussion of similar initiatives in Slovakia.

4. I thank Yuri Slezkine for pointing this out to me.

5. Svetlana Peshkova (2014), in turn, describes Islamic learning and debates that unfolded in the interstices of the Soviet atheist state in Uzbekistan. Peshkova challenges the assumption that the Soviet education system cultivated only memorization. Drawing on Oleg Kharkhordin's (1999) work, as well as Russian-language sources, Peshkova argues that since the Soviet education system was supposed to produce Soviet individuals willing to enact socialist ethics, Soviet educators did attempt to teach critical reading skills to their students (2014, 86).

6. In this, Latvians' desires converged with neoliberal forms of governmentality that make individuals who succeed by building their confidence rather than pushing

against the limits of their historically constituted selves. As demonstrated by Tomas Matza in his analysis of psychology training programs for children in Russia, they were taught emotional intelligence and affective management for the purpose of offering students a competitive advantage in a capitalist economy (Matza 2012, 807). Similarly, as argued by Jonathan Larson in the afterword to the Slovak language edition of his book on critical thinking in Slovakia after socialism (Larson 2013), teaching students critical thinking in US educational institutions makes not only liberal, but also neoliberal subjects out of them. Drawing on Bonnie Urcioli's work, Larson concludes that "in recent years, US higher education's rhetoric of 'critical thinking' aims increasingly at educating a skilled person for self-advancement through work rather than a more ethically oriented person grounded in cultural traditions of broader humanistic inquiry."

7. Personal communication, 2010.

8. David Theo Goldberg (2009) calls for relational analysis of racism as a simultaneously local and translocal formation. For Goldberg (2008), analyzing racism within national frames is part of "racial Europeanization" whereby racism is written out of the common European past and present and depicted as a feature of marginal people and places.

9. This is why I have selected the case of eugenics—rather than the Holocaust—for the purposes of this chapter. Memories of the Holocaust and its place in contemporary Latvian public and political discourse remain contested, but the Holocaust is much more researched and discussed than racial anthropology and eugenics. Rarely anybody in Latvia would deny the gravity of the Holocaust as a stain in European history, though some would question the distribution of guilt and responsibility. There is not a similar debate about racial anthropology and eugenics, though there are links between eugenics, Nazism, and the Holocaust, as well as between racial anthropology, eugenics, and European colonialism (Bashford and Levine 2010).

10. Marina Mogilner (2013) described in her recent work on racial anthropology in Russia that Russian anthropologists were also critical of her attempt to study race science. Objections to critical sociological or historical investigation of particular fields of science by its practitioners is not all together atypical. A similar dynamic can most certainly be observed in the argument I am describing here. However, this argument is also caught up in a complex power articulation between subjects and objects of critical reflection.

11. The first Pride parade in 2005 was organized by two eighteen-year olds who did not have much experience with LGBT politics, but who had garnered international support for an impromptu Pride parade in Latvia. The Pride parade was so controversial that it triggered more serious political mobilization of LGBT people in Latvia, as well as placed Pride itself as one of the central elements of LGBT activism in Latvia. See Dzenovska and Arenas 2012.

12. While the tolerance workers did not pursue such projects, in the fall of 2013 Latvian television did air a show called "Operation Burka" as part of their *Forbidden Tactics* series. In anticipation of increased immigration as Latvia arrives at "Europeanness," they sent a woman dressed in a burka to rent an apartment, to get a job and to do shopping, aiming to expose intolerance in the Latvian society. It should be noted that there are very few women that wear burkas in Latvia, the Latvian Muslim population of about ten thousand consists largely of former Soviet citizens from historically Muslim areas of Russia, though there are also Muslims from other parts of the world, including converts. Thus the figures used in the experiment were stereotypically construed as foreign Muslims. One part of the experiment placed a woman in a burka in a line in a supermarket and sent a provocateur to follow her. The provocateur stood

in the line behind her and addressed other customers, asking whether they were afraid of the woman in the burka. When the young man addressed replied that he was not, the provocateur said that he was indeed afraid of such women dressed all in black. The episode desperately tried to construe the problem it had set out to address. This is not to say that there is no anti-immigrant or anti-Muslim sentiment in Latvia, but rather that it is much more complex than assumed by the "tolerance workers" behind this show.

13. As it later turned out, it was a Latvian girl from a "good family" that was the main perpetrator in the discussed incident.

14. As a result of this research, the Soros Foundation published a lengthy report, "Research-Based Strategies for Tolerance Promotion" (Osis and Ose 2006).

15. See Fernando (2014) for a discussion of the moral limits of liberal discourse.

5. LANGUAGE SACRED AND LANGUAGE INJURIOUS

1. In 2008, the Latvian Language Agency, an institution established under the Ministry of Education and Science for the purpose of "enhancing the status and promoting sustainable development of the Latvian language," launched a campaign to bring public attention to the everyday use of the Latvian language. As part of the campaign, the Latvian Language Agency produced eight videos about the everyday use of language, which aimed to promote the correct use of language. The videos can be seen here: http://www.valoda.lv/TV_klipi_Doma_ka_runa_/Page-1.

2. Language Law, 1935. http://www.vvk.lv/index.php?sadala=135&id=166.

3. This is an undated internet publication: http://www.letonika.lv/article.aspx?id=personvardi.

4. After proclamation of Latvian independence on November 18, 1918, Soviet Russia supported the establishment of a temporary Soviet government in Latvia that functioned in parallel to the government of independent Latvia for the two years of "freedom struggles" that ended with the signing of the Latvia-Russia peace treaty in 1920.

5. It should be noted that historian John Klier (1982) describes an especially resonant debate with regard to the use of the word zhid between Ukrainian and Russian intellectuals, which occurred in the 1880s. A student had written to a Ukrainian language publication, asking to discontinue the use of the word zhid, because the Jewish community found it offensive. The publication responded by saying that the word does not have any negative connotations in the Ukrainian language, and the editors used folklore to substantiate their claims. The editors of the Ukrainian publication were supported by a Russian Jewish journal, which expressed the view that the meaning of the word is contextual and shifting [presumably referring here also to different linguistic contexts] and that one therefore cannot demand that Ukrainians stop using it: "Even in Russian one can't always take the term zhid to be insulting: the term zhid is more popular and the term evrey is more official, and he who uses the first term from habit, as a custom from childhood, should not be ordered to change it because it offends us" (Klier 1982, 11). It is interesting to note that the contextual and shifting meaning of the word serves here to argue for its continued use, rather than, say, bolster claims that the word can and does have negative connotations and that its use therefore should be discontinued.

6. Author's translation.

7. See Ben Martin's (1991) "From Negro to Black to African American: The Power of Names and Naming" for a more extensive analysis.

8. Following European Union accession, but even more before that, significant numbers of Latvia's residents began to migrate for work, mostly to the United Kingdom, Ireland, and Sweden, because these three European Union member states did not institute

temporary labor market protections after Eastern European states joined in 2004 (see Dzenovska 2013b, 2012). In the early stages, many families were split, as one or both parents went first to settle while leaving children with grandparents.

9. The Latvian Language Program Unit is an institution established through a joint effort of the Latvian government and foreign donors for the purposes of implementation of the National Program for Latvian Language Learning. Their objective is to develop methodology for teaching Latvian as a second language, and to train teachers to teach Latvian as a second language in minority schools. The Latvian Language Program Unit is also a member of the working group of the National Program for the Promotion of Tolerance launched by the Special Tasks Ministry for Integration of Society in 2004. The seminar on multiculturalism took place under the auspices of this program and was moderated by a staff member of the Ministry of Integration.

10. The Special Tasks Ministry for Integration of Society has also launched a program for the integration of the Roma, which targets various Roma communities through education and employment campaigns. The program was subject to a great deal of argument among various Roma elders and the ministry, as some of the elders resisted the state's efforts to make Roma life intelligible and transparent to the state. See the webpage of the Ministry of Culture for more information on Roma integration: http://www.km.gov.lv/lv/ministrija/romi.html.

11. Patchen Markell has argued that the "multiculturalist project creates incentives for people to frame claims about justice as claims for recognition on behalf of identifiable groups. That mode of address, after all, furthers the state's project of rendering the social world 'legible' and governable: to appeal to the state for the recognition of one's own identity—to present oneself as knowable—is already to offer the state the reciprocal recognition of its sovereignty that it demands" (2003, 31).

6. REPRESSION AND REDEMPTION

1. I will refer to this foster home as "foster home," though its identity is hard to conceal, given the publicity that the case received.

2. I refer to the human rights organization as Human Rights Organization, which is not its proper name.

3. An English version of the film can be seen here: http://elmmedia.lv/lv/2015/11/19/pirmie-2013/.

4. This was not the first time in Latvian history when previous military formations lent a helping hand to new ones—for example, some of the commanders of the Latvian Navy in the interwar period were former officers of the Russian Imperial Navy (Saburova 1955, 38).

5. See Samuel Moyn's (2010) work on human rights in history, where he points out that, contrary to rights of man realized through the state, human rights has emerged as a counterpoint to the state. I argue here that this juxtaposition resembles what Timothy Mitchel (1991) has called "the state effect," namely it is a distinction that is itself produced through statecraft.

6. Saburova writes in an article for *Russian Review* in 1955: "Early in June 1940, the Baltic Foreign Ministers held urgent consultations among themselves and made several flights to Moscow to confer with the Kremlin. The press reported these flights and conferences in vague and restrained terms. The population was unworried, being engrossed in preparations for the annual choral festival to be held in Dunaburg. This festival, in which giant choruses attired in national costumes participated, was scheduled for Saturday, June 15. The absence on this occasion of the president, Dr. Ulmanis, who usually opened such celebrations, was explained by an indisposition. The Sunday papers of June 16 were filled with descriptions of the festival and pictures of the participants. Few people

probably paid any attention to a short small-print item in the Russian paper *Segodnia*, which read approximately as follows: "This morning at the village of Maslenki on the Soviet-Latvian border a skirmish occurred, and shots were fired. Several Latvian frontier guards have been taken prisoner, as well as a young village shepherd. The incident is being investigated" (1955, 38–39).

7. This was not so easy, however, as Russia and Latvia could not agree on a border treaty until 2007 due to different historical interpretations of Latvia's incorporation in the Soviet Union. Russia insisted that Latvia joined voluntarily, whereas Latvia insisted that it was occupied. A border treaty was finally signed when Latvia no longer claimed the territory annexed by the Russian Soviet Republic in 1945, which included Maslenki.

8. In the referendum on joining the European Union, 67 percent of the electorate voted for joining the European Union, while 32.3 percent voted against.

9. See here: http://www.pmlp.gov.lv/sakums/par-pmlp/vesture.html.

10. Follis (2012) argues that on the Polish-Ukrainian frontier "civilized" meant "modernized," that is, adhering to the norms and principles of Western European institutions. I would add that "civilized" also entails a moralizing dimension, that is, to be civilized means to adhere to ethical and political norms of Western liberal democracy. Follis emphasizes another sense of civilization that is pertinent in her work, namely the Polish border guards' sense that the Polish-Ukrainian border was also the frontier of civilization in the sense of dividing two cultural groupings. This was not necessarily felt by Latvian border guards. More so than a civilizational boundary, it was a geopolitical and ideological one.

11. After accession to the European Union in 2004, the reports show that the Latvian State Border Guard became involved in a dual process of learning from the West, while conveying their experience and expertise to the East. The Border Guard was involved in missions in Moldova and Georgia (see also Follis 2012, 152). In fact, they developed a close relationship with Georgian counterparts, who sought their expertise precisely because they had undergone the transition from a Soviet to a European style of bordering.

12. Mountz argues that "during the 1990s, public discourse about refugees shifted from themes of humanitarianism, diplomacy, and the protection of human rights to security, criminality, and the abuse of 'generous' asylum programs" (2010, 96).

13. For example, from 1998 until 2010, the end of my fieldwork, Latvia had received 367 asylum applications.

14. In a somewhat ironic turn of events, Latvia's citizens who have migrated to work in the United Kingdom are received with much the same discourse as was used to justify early migration controls of former Soviet citizens (Dzenovska in Green 2016).

15. Several of the people involved in the Somali case, which I discuss in this chapter, now live and work abroad.

16. This did not necessarily make them economic migrants rather than asylum seekers for, as Mountz (2010) has argued, more and more individuals displaced for political reasons also use smugglers, as states that do accept refugees intensify enforcement and are more difficult to reach (2010, 5).

17. In 2011, the detention center was moved to another location.

18. As noted in a report issued by the Latvian Center for Human Rights (Djačkova et al. 2011), Latvian legislation does not stipulate that other alternatives must be sought before detention. It does stipulate that undocumented individuals must be detained, and therefore most asylum seekers are detained, as most travel without documents. This, the authors of the report conclude, is against international norms.

19. When I later spoke with the director of the Human Rights Organization, she reprimanded me for aiding the State Border Guard in transgressing regulations. According

to the Law on Asylum, the decisions should have been delivered in certified translation and in writing. From that moment, the Somalis would have had seven days to appeal the decision. With my verbal translation, the director claimed, I had allowed the Border Guard to start the clock immediately, which gave the Human Rights Organization less time to organize the appeal.

20. The Border Guard allegedly tried to appeal one of the cases, as one of the Somalis spoke some English, but the court was not convinced.

21. The Human Rights Organization was an NGO, whereas the State Human Rights Office was the seat of the Ombudsman, and its mandate was stipulated by law. The State Human Rights Office got involved at this point, because there was a concrete incident to investigate, and they had the authority to demand human rights compliance from government institutions.

22. Treatment of detainees continues to be a problem. In a report commissioned by the Center for Disease Prevention and Control, anthropologists argue that the detainees of the Daugavpils Illegal Immigrant Detention Facility lack systematic health care and are traumatized by discriminatory and outright violent attitudes (Putnina et al. 2015). The report describes cases where border guards deliberately offend detainees—for example, threatening a Muslim male by saying: "I will go and search your wife, if you don't tell me where she hides the money" in an attempt to take account of the belongings of the illegal migrants.

23. The Dublin regulation stipulates that, within Europe, asylum seekers are returned to the country where they originally submitted their application if they attempt to move before their case has been decided.

24. Reports from migration authorities, as well as conversations with volunteers who work with refugees, indicate that most of the asylum seekers who were resettled to Latvia as part of the European Union's attempt to deal with the "migration/refugee crisis" and granted refugee status, have left the country for Germany. See, for example: http://www.delfi.lv/news/national/politics/latviju-pametusi-gandriz-visi-parvietosanas-programma-atvestie-begli.d?id=47872439.

25. The Department of Migration Affairs later became the Office of Citizenship and Migration Affairs, and the Immigration Police was incorporated into the Latvian State Border Guard in 2002 as its Department of Immigration Control.

26. See here: http://likumi.lv/doc.php?id=65436.

27. See here: http://www.rs.gov.lv/index.php?top=0&id=904. The State Border Guard started issuing public annual reports in 2002.

28. Temporary protection, or *alternatīvais statuss*, means that an asylum seeker is granted protection for a fixed period of time. At the end of this period, the case is reviewed to see whether their situation may have improved, or whether they require continued protection.

29. See here: http://www.pmlp.gov.lv/sakums/statistika/patveruma-mekletaji.html; and here: http://ec.europa.eu/eurostat/statistics-explained/index.php/Asylum_statistics#Asylum_applicants.

30. See Shevel (2012) for a discussion of the how Russia's citizenship policy worked in law and in practice.

31. While Latvia does in principle recognize dual citizenship now, it does not recognize dual citizenship with Russia.

32. See Jansen (2015), Cabot (2014), and Gordillo (2006) for discussion of desire for the state and of papers.

33. This episode has been previously described and analyzed at length in an article published in *Social Anthropology* (Dzenovska 2014). It is reproduced here with the journal's permission.

34. Yurchak (2005) interprets the Russian notion of *svoi* as pertaining to people who were not necessarily friends, but who understood each other's predicament in relation to power and who made sure not to get each other in trouble.

EPILOGUE

1. http://skaties.lv/zinas/latvija/foto-un-video-ka-top-zogs-uz-latvijas-krievijas-robezas/.

2. http://www.tvnet.lv/zinas/kriminalzinas/650643-galvenie_cilveku_kontrabandisti_uz_latvijas_robezas_ir_krievijas_pilsoni.

3. http://www.delfi.lv/news/national/politics/uz-latvijas-krievijas-robezas-plano-izveidot-zogu-vismaz-90-kilometru-garuma.d?id=46601395.

4. http://www.bbc.co.uk/news/world-europe-34085926.

5. http://uk.businessinsider.com/latvia-border-fence-russia-2015-12?r=US&IR=T.

6. The *Washington Post* and *EU Observer* reported that Lithuania fears a new Russian invasion and is thus building a fence (Noack 2017).

7. https://www.rt.com/news/373829-lithuania-russia-wall-brick/ See also http://lzinios.lt/lzinios/Gimtasis-krastas/nuo-kaliningrado-srities-atsitversime-tvora/237048.

8. http://uk.reuters.com/article/us-davos-meeting-biden-idUKKBN15217E.

References

Adams, Laura. 2010. *The Spectacular State: Culture and National Identity in Uzbekistan.* Durham, NC: Duke University Press.

Aktürk, Sener. 2012. *Regimes of Ethnicity and Nationhood in Germany, Russia, and Turkey.* Cambridge: Cambridge University Press.

———. 2011. "Regimes of Ethnicity: Comparative Analysis of Germany, the Soviet Union/Post-Soviet Russia, and Turkey." *World Politics* 63(1): 115–164. Accessed July 15, 2014. doi: 10.1017/S0043887110000304.

———. 2010. "Passport Identification and Nation-Building in Post-Soviet Russia." *Post-Soviet Affairs* 26(4): 214–241. Accessed November 15, 2014. doi: 10.2747/1060-586X.26.4.314.

Althusser, Louis. 2001. *Lenin and Philosophy and Other Essays.* New York: Monthly Review Press.

Amsler, Sarah. 2007. *The Politics of Knowledge in Central Asia: Science between Marx and the Market.* London: Routledge.

Anderson, Bridget. 2013. *Us and Them: The Dangerous Politics of Immigration Control.* Oxford: Oxford University Press.

Andersons, Edgars. 1970a. *Tur plīvoja Kurzemes karogi.* New York: Grāmatu Draugs.

———. 1970b. *Senie Kurzemnieki Amerikā un Tobago kolonizācija.* Stockholm: Daugava.

Arel, Dominique. 2001. "Fixing Ethnicity in Identity Documents: The Rise and Fall of Passport Nationality in Russia." Working Paper, The National Council for Eurasian and East European Research.

Arenas, Ivan. 2006. "Oversight/site: Modernity and Its Rem(a)inders." In *Modernism and Modernity in the Mediterranean World*, edited by Luca Somigli and Domenico Pietropaolo, 131–150. Toronto: Legas.

Arendt, Hannah. 2008. *The Jewish Writings.* New York: Schocken.

———. 1979. *The Origins of Totalitarianism.* New York: A Harvest/HBJ Book.

Austers, Ivars. 2007. "Par toleranci nerunājiet." *Politika.lv,* November 13. Accessed June 15, 2009. http://politika.lv/article/par-toleranci-nerunajiet.

Austers, Ivars, Marija Golubeva, and Ieva Strode. 2007. "Skolotāju tolerances barometrs." *Politika.lv,* November 15. Accessed February 10, 2009. http://www.providus.lv/public/27125.html.

Austin, John L. 1975 [1962]. *How to Do Things with Words. Second Edition*, edited by J. O. Urmson and Marina Sbisá. Cambridge, MA: Harvard University Press.

Bacas, Jutta Lauth, and William Kavanagh. 2013. *Border Encounters: Asymmetry and Proximity at Europe's Frontier.* Oxford: Berghahn Books.

Bader, Veit. 2013. "Free Speech or Non-discrimination as Trump? Reflections on Contextualized Reasonable Balancing and Its Limits." *Journal of Ethnic and Migration Studies* 40(2): 320–338. Accessed on July 15, 2015. doi: 10.1080/1369183X.2013.851478.

Baldunčiks, Juris. n.d. "Citvalodu īpašvārdu atveide latviešu valodā." *Letonika.* Accessed February 15, 2017. http://www.letonika.lv/article.aspx?id=personvardi.

Baltijas Sociālo Zinātņu Institūts [BSZI]. 2004. *Etniskā Tolerance un Latvijas Sabiedrības Integrācija.* Riga: Baltijas Sociālo Zinātņu Institūts.

Bankovskis, Pauls. 2006a. "Jaunsudrabiņš un ž***." *Diena,* January 28.
———. 2006b. "A tu neliecies." *Kultūras Diena,* July 28.
Barth, Frederik. 2000. "An Anthropology of Knowledge." *Current Anthropology* 43(1): 1–18. Accessed February 3, 2006. doi: 10.1086/324131.
Bashford, Alison, and Philippa Levine, eds. 2010. *The Oxford Handbook of the History of Eugenics.* Oxford: Oxford University Press.
Beitnere, Dagmāra. 2011. "Par viensētniekuu mentalitāti un solidaritātes apziņu." *Par Likumu un Valsti,* March 23. Accessed June 10, 2012. http://m.lvportals.lv/visi/viedokli/227570-par-viensetnieku-mentalitati-un-solidaritates-apzinu/.
Beliaev, Alexandre. 2014. *Following Politics: Russian Youth Activism in Post-Socialist Latvia.* Ph.D. diss., University of California, Berkeley.
Bellagamba, Alice. 2005. "Slavery and Emancipation in the Colonial Archives: British Officials, Slave-owners and Slaves in the Protectorate of the Gambia (1890ca–1936)." *Canadian Journal of African Studies* 39(1): 5–41. Accessed June 10, 2011. https://www.jstor.org/stable/25067449.
Belševica, Vizma. 2004. *Bille. Triloģija.* Riga: Atēna.
Bender, Jeremy. 2015. "A Nation Bordering Russia Is Building a Fence along a Third of Its Border." *Business Insider,* December 16. Accessed March 20, 2017. http://uk.businessinsider.com/latvia-border-fence-russia-2015-12?r=US&IR=T.
Bennett, Jane. 2001. *The Enchantment of Modern Life: Attachments, Crossings, and Ethics.* Princeton: Princeton University Press.
Berdahl, Daphne. 1999. *Where the World Ended: Re-Unification and Identity in the German Borderland.* Berkeley: University of California Press.
Berkis, Aleksandrs. 1960. *The Reign of Duke James in Courland, 1638–1682.* Lincoln: Vaidava.
Berklavs, Eduards. 1998. *Zināt un neaizmirst.* Riga: Preses Nams.
Bērziņš, Jānis. 2003 [1932]. "Par mūsu tautas dziesmu kā vēstures avotu izlietošanu." In *Latvieši: XX gadsimta 20.-30. gadu autoru rakstu krājums,* edited by Helēna Grīnberga and Muntis Auns, 25–40. Riga: Valerija Belokoņa Izdevniecība.
Bhabha, Homi. 1984. "Of Mimicry and Man: The Ambivalence of Colonial Discourse." *October* 28 (Spring 1984): 125–133. Accessed April 15, 2010. doi: 10.2307/778467
Bigo, Didier. 2002. "Security and Immigration: Toward a Critique of the Use of Governmentality of Unease." *Alternatives* 27(2002): 63–92. Accessed March 3, 2012. doi: 10.1177/03043754020270S105.
Blese, Ernests. 2003 [1932]. "Latviešu literārā valoda." In *Latvieši: XX gadsimta 20.-30. gadu autoru rakstu krājums,* edited by Helēna Grīnberga and Muntis Auns, 68–90. Riga: Valerija Belokoņa Izdevniecība.
Bockman, Johanna. 2011. *Markets in the Name of Socialism: The Left-Wing Origins of Neoliberalism.* Stanford: Stanford University Press.
Böröcz, Jószef. 2006. "Goodness is Elsewhere: The Rule of European Difference." *Comparative Studies in Society and History* 48(1): 110–137. Accessed July 15, 2006. http://www.jstor.org/stable/3879330.
Böröcz Jószef, and Melinda Kovács, eds. 2001. *Empire's New Clothes: Unveiling EU Enlargement.* Central Europe Review e-books. http://aei.pitt.edu/144/.
Bowen, John R. 2005. *Why the French Don't Like Headscarves: Islam, the State and Public Space.* Princeton: Princeton University Press.
———. 2003. *Islam, Law, and Inequality in Indonesia: An Anthropology of Public Reasoning.* Cambridge: Cambridge University Press.

Boyer, Dominic. 2016. "Crisis of Liberalism." Hot Spots, *Cultural Anthropology* website, October 27. Accessed November 1, 2016. https://culanth.org/fieldsights/989-crisis-of-liberalism.

——. 2005. *Spirit and System: Media, Intellectuals, and the Dialectic in Modern German Culture.* Chicago: University of Chicago Press.

——. 2003. "Censorship as a Vocation: The Institutions, Practices, and Cultural Logic of Media Control in the German Democratic Republic." *Comparative Studies in Society and History* 45(3): 511–545. Accessed November 15, 2010. doi: 10.1017/S0010417503000240.

Brastiņš, Ernests. 2007 [1931]. *Latvija, viņas dzīve un kultūra.* Riga: Atēna.

Brown, Wendy. 2010. *Walled States, Waning Sovereignty.* Cambridge: MIT Press.

——. 2006. *Regulating Aversion: Tolerance in the Age of Identity and Empire.* Princeton: Princeton University Press.

Brubaker, Rogers. 2004. *Ethnicity Without Groups.* Cambridge: Harvard University Press.

Brubaker, Rogers, Margit Feischmidt, Jon Fox, and Liana Grancea. 2006. *Nationalist Politics and Everyday Ethnicity in a Transylvanian Town.* Princeton: Princeton University Press.

Buck-Morss, Susan. 2009. *Hegel, Haiti, and Universal History.* Pittsburgh: University of Pittsburgh Press.

——. 2000. *Dreamworld and Catastrophe: The Passing of Mass Utopia in East and West.* Cambridge: MIT Press.

Bula, Dace. 2005. "Johans Gotfrīds Herders un tautas dzejas interpretācijas Latvijā." In *Herders Rīgā*, edited by Elijs Godiņš, Elijs and Ilze Ščegoļihina, Pp. 12–19. Riga: The Museum of History and Shipping.

——. 2000. *Dziedātājtauta:* Folklora un Nacionālā Ideoloģija. Riga: Zinātne.

Burawoy, Michal, and Katherine Verdery, eds. 1999. "Introduction." In *Uncertain Transition: Ethnographies of Change in a Postsocialist World,* 1–18. Latham, MD: Rowman & Littlefield.

Burkhalter, Nancy, and Maganat R. Shegebayev. 2012. "Critical Thinking as Culture: Teaching Post-Soviet Teachers in Kazakhstan." *International Review of Education* 58: 55–72. Accessed March 1, 2017. doi: 10.1007/s11159-012-9285-5.

Butler, Judith. 2015. *Notes Toward a Performative Theory of Assembly.* Cambridge: Harvard University Press.

——. 1997. *Excitable Speech: A Politics of the Performative.* New York: Routledge.

Button, Mark. 2005. "Arendt, Rawls, and Public Reason." *Social Theory and Practice* 31(2): 257–280. Accessed March 15, 2013. doi: 10.5840/soctheorpract200531211.

Cabot, Heath. 2014. *On the Doorstep of Europe: Asylum and Citizenship in Greece.* Pittsburgh: University of Pennsylvania Press.

Chakrabarty, Dipesh. 2000. *Provincializing Europe: Postcolonial Thought and Historical Difference.* Princeton: Princeton University Press.

Chandler, Andrea. 1998. *Institutions of Isolation: Border Controls in the Soviet Union and Its Successor States, 1917–1993.* Buffalo: McGill-Queens University Press.

Chari, Sharad, and Katherine Verdery. 2009. "Thinking between the Posts: Postcolonialism, Postsocialism, and Ethnography after the Cold War." *Comparative Studies in Society and History* 51(1): 6–34. Accessed March 15, 2010. doi: 10.1017/S0010417509000024.

Chatterjee, Partha. 2011. "Reflecting on 30 Years after Subaltern Studies: Conversations with Prof. Profs. Gyanendra Pandey and Partha Chatterjee." Interview conducted by Richard McGrail. *Cultural Anthropology.* http://www.culanth.org/?q=node/469.

——. 1986. *Nationalist Thought and the Colonial World: A Derivative Discourse.* London: Zed Books.

Chernetsky, Vitali. 2003. "Postcolonialism, Russia and Ukraine." *Ulbandus* 7: 32–62.

Clifford, James. 1994. *"Diaspora."* Cultural Anthropology 9(3): 302–338. Accessed May 2, 2013. http://www.jstor.org/stable/656365.

Collier, Stephen J. 2011. *The Post-Soviet Social: Neoliberalism, Social Modernity, Biopolitics.* Princeton University Press.

Collier, Stephen, Alex Cooley, Bruce Grant, Harriet Muray, Marc Nichanian, Gaytri Chakravorty Spivak, and Alexander Etkind. 2003. "Empire, Union, Center, Satellite: A Questionnaire." *Ulbandus* 7: 5–25.

Connolly, William. 2005. *Pluralism.* Durham, NC: Duke University Press.

Coronil, Fernando. 2011. "The Future in Question: History and Utopia in Latin America (1989–2010)" In *Business as Usual: The Roots of the Global Financial Meltdown,* edited by Carig Calhoun and Georgi Derlugian, 231–264. New York: New York University Press and Social Science Research Council.

Council of Europe. 2013. *Framework Convention for the Protection of National Minorities. Collected Texts.* 7th ed. Brussels: Council of Europe.

Cowan, Jane. 2007. "The Supervised State." *Identities* 14(5): 545–578. Accessed June 15, 2013. doi: 10.1080/10702890701662573.

Creed, Gerald. 2011. *Masquerade and Postsocialism: Ritual and Cultural Dispossession in Bulgaria.* Bloomington: Indiana University Press.

Cunningham, Hilary, and Josiah Heyman. 2010. "Introduction: Mobilities and Enclosures at Borders." *Identities: Global Studies in Culture and Power* 11(3): 289–302. Accessed September 15, 2016. doi: 10.1080/10702890490493509.

De Genova, Nicholas. 2016. "The 'European' Question: Migration, Race, and Postcoloniality in Europe." *Social Text* 34(3): 75–102. Accessed March 15, 2017. doi: 10.1215/01642472-3607588.

——. 2011. "The Spectacle of Terror, The Spectacle of Security." In *Accumulating Insecurity: Violence and Dispossession in the Making of Everyday Life,* edited by Shelly Feldman, Charles Geisler and Gayatri A. Menon, 141–165. Atlanta: University of Georgia Press.

Djačkova, Svetlana, Džena Andersone & Kristīne Laganovska. 2011. *Patvēruma meklētāju aizturēšana un aizturēšanas alternatīvas Latvijā.* Rāga: Latvijas Cilvēktiesību centrs.

Dribins, Leo. 1997. *Nacionālais jautājums Latvijā, 1850–1940: historiogrāfisks apskats.* Riga: Mācību apgāds.

Du Bois, W.E.B. 1928. "The Name 'Negro,'" *Crisis* (March): 96–97. Accessed August 10, 2016. http://www.virginia.edu/woodson/courses/aas102%20(spring%2001)/articles/names/dubois.htm.

Dunn, Elizabeth. 2004. *Privatizing Poland: Baby Food, Big Business, and the Remaking of Labor.* Ithaca: Cornell University Press.

Dzenovska, Dace. 2018a. "Emptiness and Its Futures: Staying and Leaving as Tactics of Life in Latvia." Forthcoming in *Focaal: Journal of Global and Historical Anthropology.*

——. 2018b. "'Latvians Do Not Understand the Greek People': Crisis, Endurance, and Europeanness." In *Messy Europe: Whiteness and Crisis in Postcolonial World,* edited by Kristín Loftsdóttir, Brigitte Hipfl, and Andrea Smith. Forthcoming with Berghahn Books.

——. 2017. "'We Want to Hear from You': Reporting as Bordering in the Political Space of Europe." In *The Borders of "Europe": Autonomy of Migration, Tactics of Bordering,* edited by Nicholas De Genova, 283–298. Durham, NC: Duke University Press.

——. 2016. "Eastern Europe, the Moral Subject of the Migration/Refugee Crisis, and Political Futures." *Near Future Online 1: Europe at a Crossroads*, March 2016. http://nearfuturesonline.org/eastern-europe-the-moral-subject-of-the-migrationrefugee-crisis-and-political-futures/.

——. 2014. "Bordering Encounters, Sociality, and Distribution of the Ability to Lead a Normal Life." *Social Anthropology* 22(3): 271–287. Accessed January 14, 2015. doi: 10.1111/1469-8676.12075.

——. 2013a. "Historical Agency and the Coloniality of Power in Postsocialist Europe." *Anthropological Theory* 13(4): 394–416. Accessed February 15, 2014. doi: 10.1177/1463499613502185.

——. 2013b. "The Great Departure: Rethinking National(ist) Common Sense." *Journal of Ethnic and Migration Studies* 39(2): 201–218. Accessed January 15, 2014. doi: 10.1080/1369183X.2013.723254.

——. 2013c. "Valstnācijas slogs." *Satori.lv*. Accessed January 15, 2015. Available here: http://www.satori.lv/article/valstsnacijas-slogs.

——. 2012. *Aizbraukšana un tukšums Latvijas laukos: Starp zudušām un iespējamām nākotnēm*. Riga: Biznesa apgāds Turība.

——. 2010. "Public Reason and the Limits of Liberal Anti-Racism in Latvia." *Ethnos* 75(4): 425–454. Accessed March 20, 2012. doi: 10.1080/00141844.2010.535125.

Dzenovska, Dace, and Ivan Arenas. 2012. "Don't Fence Me In: Barricade Sociality and Political Struggles in Mexico and Latvia." *Comparative Studies in Society and History* 54(3): 644–678. Accessed January 15, 2013. doi: 10.1017/S0010417512000266.

Dzenovska, Dace, and Nicholas De Genova. 2018. "Desire for the Political After the Cold War." Forthcoming in *Focaal: Journal of Global and Historical Anthropology*.

Edgar, Adrienne Lynn. 2004. *Tribal Nation: The Making of Soviet Turkmenistan*. Princeton: Princeton University Press.

Edgar, Adrienne, Sonja Luehrmann, Sergey Abashin, and Elena Gapova. 2008. "Roundtable 'Sub Altera Species': A View at Postcolonial Paradigm from Inside Russian/Soviet History." *Ab Imperio: Studies of New Imperial History and Nationalism in the Post-Soviet Space* 2/2008: 88–89.

El-Tayeb, Fatima. 2011. *European Others: Queering Ethnicity in Postnational Europe*. Minneapolis: University of Minnesota Press.

Enns, Diane. 2012. *The Violence of Victimhood*. University Park: Pennsylvania State University Press.

Ērgle, Zenta, and Margarita Stāraste. 1974. *Ieviņa Āfrikā*. Riga: Liesma.

European Migration Network (EMN). 2006. *Atgriešana*. Riga: European Migration Network.

Evans-Pritchard, Ambrose. 2014. "Hungary Is Becoming the Biggest Reason Why We May Have to Leave the EU." *The Telegraph*, http://blogs.telegraph.co.uk/finance/ambroseevans-pritchard/100026981/hungary-is-becoming-the-biggest-reason-why-we-may-have-to-leave-the-eu/.

Ezergailis, Andrew. 1996. *The Holocaust in Latvia: The Missing Centre*. Riga: Historical Institute in Latvia in association with the US Holocaust Memorial Museum.

Fanon, Frantz. 1967. *Black Skin, White Masks*. New York: Grove Press.

Fassin, Eric. 2010. "National Identities and Transnational Intimacies: Sexual Democracy and the Politics of Immigration in Europe." *Public Culture* 22(3): 507–529. Accessed October 10, 2014. doi: 10.1215/08992363-2010-007.

Fassin, Didier. 2005. "Compassion and Repression: The Moral Economy of Immigration Policies in France." *Cultural Anthropology* 20(3): 362–387. Accessed October 10, 2014. doi: 10.1525/can.2005.20.3.362.

Felder, Björn. 2013a. "Introduction: Eugenics, Sterilization, and the Racial State: The Baltic States and Russia and the Global Eugenics Movement." In *Baltic Eugenics: Bio-politics, Race and Nation in Interwar Estonia, Latvia and Lithuania, 1918–1940.* Edited by Björn M. Felder and Paul J. Weindling, 6–31. Amsterdam: Rodopi.

———. 2013b. "'God Forgives—but Nature Never Will'—Racial Identity, Racial Anthropology, and Eugenics in Latvia, 1918–1940." In *Baltic Eugenics: Bio-politics, Race, and Nation in Interwar Estonia, Latvia, and Lithuania, 1918–194,* edited by Björn M. Felder and Paul J. Weindling, 115–146. Amsterdam: Rodopi.

———. 2009. *Lettland im Zweiten Weltkrieg. Zwischen sowjetischen und deutschen Besatzen 1940 -1946.* Paderbonr: Verlag Ferdinant Schöning.

Feldman, Gregory. 2005. "Culture, State, and Society in Europe: The Case of Citizenship and Integration Policy in Estonia." *American Ethnologist* 32(4): 676–694. Accessed November 10, 2008. doi: 10.1525/ae.2005.32.4.676.

Fernando, Mayanthi. 2014. *The Republic Unsettled: Muslim French and the Contradictions of Secularism.* Durham, NC: Duke University Press.

Fernando, Mayanthi, and Cristiana Giordano. 2016. "Refugees and the Crisis of Europe." Hot Spots, *Cultural Anthropology* website, June 28, 2016. https://culanth.org/fieldsights/911-refugees-and-the-crisis-of-europe.

Ferreira Da Silva, Denise. 2007. *Towards A Global Idea of Race.* Minneapolis: University of Minnesota Press.

Fikes, Kesha. 2009. *Managing African Portugal: The Citizen-Migrant Distinction.* Durham, NC: Duke University Press.

Fitzpatrick, Sheila. 1999. *Everyday Stalinism. Ordinary Life in Extraordinary Times: Soviet Russia in the 1930s.* Oxford: Oxford University Press.

Follis, Karolina S. 2012. *Building Fortress Europe: The Polish-Ukrainian Frontier.* Pittsburgh: University of Pennsylvania Press.

Foucault, Michel. 2003a. "Governmentality." In *The Essential Foucault, Selections from Essential Works of Foucault, 1954–1984,* edited by Paul Rabinow and Nicholas Rose, 229–245. New York: The New Press.

———. 2003b. *Society Must Be Defended: Lectures at the College de France, 1975–1976.* Translated by David Macey. New York: Picador.

———. 2003c. "Truth and Power." In *The Essential Foucault, Selections from Essential Works of Foucault, 1954–1984,* edited by Paul Rabinow and Nicholas Rose, 300–318. New York: The New Press.

———. 2002. *The Archaeology of Knowledge.* Translated by A. M. Sheridan Smith. London: Routledge.

———. 1980. "Two Lectures." In *Power/Knowledge: Selected Interviews and Other Writings 1972–1977,* edited by Colin Gordon, 78–108. New York: Pantheon.

Fox, Jon E., Laura Morosanu, and Ezster Szilassy. 2012. "The Racialization of the New European Migration to the UK." *Sociology* 46(4): 680–695. Accessed December, 2012. doi: 10.1177/0038038511425558.

Fukuyama, Francis. 1989. "The End of History." *National Interest* (summer): 1–27.

Funk, Nanette. 2004. "Feminist Critiques of Liberalism: Can They Travel East? Their Relevance in Eastern and Central Europe and the Former Soviet Union." *Signs: Journal of Women in Culture and Society* 29(3): 695–726. Accessed March 15, 2007. doi: 10.1086/381105.

Fur, Gunlog. 2015. "Colonial Fantasies—American Indians, Indigenous Peoples and a Swedish Discourse of Innocence." *Identities* 18(1): 11–33. Accessed September 16, 2016. doi: 10.1080/14608944.2016.1095489.

Gille, Zsuzsa. 2010. "Is There a Global Postsocialist Condition?" *Global Society* 24(1): 9–30. Accessed March 2, 2010. doi: 10.1080/13600820903431953.

Gilroy, Paul. 1993. *The Black Atlantic: Modernity and Double Consciousness.* Boston: Harvard University Press.

Giordano, Cristiana. 2014. *Migrants in Translation: Caring and the Logics of Difference in Contemporary Italy.* Berkeley: University of California Press.

Glaeser, Andreas. 2014. "Hermeneutic Institutionalism: Towards a New Synthesis." *Qualitative Sociology* 37: 207–241. Accessed November 25, 2016. doi: 10.1007/s11133-014-9272-1.

———. 2009. *Political Epistemics: The Secret Police, the Opposition, and the End of East German Socialism.* Chicago: University of Chicago Press.

Goldberg, David Theo. 2009. "Racial Comparisons, Relational Racisms: Some Thoughts on Method." *Ethnic and Racial Studies* 32(7): 1271–1282. Accessed July 3, 2012. doi: 10-1080/01419870902999233.

———. 2008. *The Threat of Race: Reflections on Racial Neoliberalism.* Wiley-Blackwell.

Goldmanis, Māris. 2008. *Latvijas ebreju minoritātes attēlojums parlamentārisma posma satīriskajā presē, 1920–1934.* Website of the Center for Judaic Studies, University of Latvia. Accessed March 26, 2017. http://www.lu.lv/jsc/pilsetas/kultura-un-tradicijas/sat-prese/.

Golubeva, Marija. 2007. "Nav mūsējie. Izslēdzam!" *Politika.lv,* July 10. Accessed July 11, 2007. http://politika.lv/article/nav-musejie-izsledzam.

———. 2005. "Neiecietība un izslēdzošie diskursi sabiedrībā." *Politika.lv.*

Goodale, Marc. 2009. *Surrendering Utopia: An Anthropology of Human Rights.* Palo Alto: Stanford University Press.

Gordillo, Gaston. 2006. "The Crucible of Citizenship: ID-paper Fetishism in the Argentinian Chaco." *American Ethnologist* 33(2): 162–176. Accessed October 10, 2014. doi: 10.1525/ae.2006.33.2.162.

Gordons, Franks. 1998. "Kāpēc gan vārds 'žīds' būtu izskaužams?" *Laiks,* November 7.

Gramsci, Antonio. 1971. *Selections from the Prison Notebooks.* New York: International Publishers.

Grāvere, Rita. n.d. *Antropoloģijas vēsture Latvijā.* Unpublished manuscript.

Green, Sarah, ed. 2016. "Brexit Referendum: First Reactions from Anthropology." *Social Anthropology* 24(4): 478–502. Accessed August 17, 2016. doi: 10.1111/1469-8676.12331.

Greenberg, Jessica. 2014. *After the Revolution: Youth, Democracy, and the Politics of Disappointment.* Palo Alto: Stanford University Press.

———. 2010. "'There Is Nothing Anyone Can Do About It': Participation, Apathy, and 'Successful' Democratic Transition in Postsocialist Serbia." *Slavic Review* 69(1): 41–64. Accessed April 10, 2012. http://www.jstor.org/stable/25621728.

Gressel, Gustav. 2015. "Understanding Eastern European Attitudes on Refugees." *European Council on Foreign Relations.* September 11. Accessed November 1, 2015. http://www.ecfr.eu/article/commentary_understanding_eastern_european_attitudes_on_refugees4019.

Grīsle, Rasma. 2005. *Spēkildze: Populārzinātnisku rakstu izlase.* Riga: Rīgas Latviešu biedrība.

Gross, Jan T. 2015. "Eastern Europe's Crisis of Shame." *Project Syndicate,* September 16. Accessed November 1, 2015. https://www.project-syndicate.org/commentary/eastern-europe-refugee-crisis-xenophobia-by-jan-gross-2015-09.

Guha, Ranajit. 1988. "The Prose of Counterinsurgency." In *Selected Subaltern Studies,* edited by Ranajit Guha and Gyatri Chakravorty Spivak, 45–88. Oxford: Oxford University Press.

Gullestad, Marianne. 2005. "Normalising Racial Boundaries: The Norwegian Dispute about the Word Neger." *Social Anthropology* 13(1): 27–46. Accessed January 10, 2008. doi: 10.1111/j.1469-8676.2005.tb00118.x.

Guyer, Jane. 2007. "Prophecy and the Near Future: Thoughts on Macroeconomic, Evangelical, and Punctuated Time." *American Ethnologist* 34(3): 409–421. Accessed February 3, 2009. doi: 10.1525/1e.2007.34.3.409.

Hage, Ghassan. 2015. *Alter-Politics: Critical Anthropology and the Radical Imagination.* Melbourne: Melbourne University Press.

Halawa, Mateusz. 2015. "In New Warsaw." *Cultural Studies* 29(5–6): 707–732. Accessed August 3, 2016. doi: 10/1080/09502386.2015.1017141.

Hann, Chris. 1998. "Postsocialist Nationalism: Rediscovering the Past in Southeast Poland." *Slavic Review* 57(4): 840–863. Accessed September 3, 2005. doi: 10.2307/2501049.

Hann, Chris, and Elizabeth Dunn, eds. 1996. *Civil Society: Challenging Western Models.* London: Routledge.

Hanovs, Deniss, and Valdis Tēraudkalns. 2011. *Laiks, telpa, vadonis: autoritārisma kultūra Latvijā 1934–1940.* Riga: Apgāds Zinātne.

Hansen, Randall. 2003. "Migration to Europe since 1945: Its History and Its Lesson." *Political Quarterly* 74(1): 25–38. Accessed November 3, 2016. doi: 10.1111/ j.1467-923X.2003.00579.x.

Harvey, David. 2010. *The Enigma of Capital and the Crisis of Capitalism.* Oxford: University of Oxford Press.

Herder, Johann Gottfried. 2002 [1771]. "Treatise on the Origin of Language." In *Herder: Philosophical Writings,* edited by Michael Forster, 65–166. Cambridge: Cambridge University Press.

Hesse, Barnor. 2007. "Racialized Modernity: An Analytics of White Mythologies." *Ethnic and Racial Studies* 30(4): 643–663. Accessed December 2, 2010. doi: 10.1080/01419870701356064.

Hill, Jane. 2008. *The Everyday Language of White Racism.* Hoboken, NJ: Wiley-Blackwell.

Hirsch, Francine. 2005. *Empire of Nations: Ethnographic Knowledge and the Making of the Soviet Union.* Ithaca: Cornell University Press.

——. 2002. "Race without the Practice of Racial Politics." *Slavic Review* 61(1): 30–43. Accessed September 15, 2008. doi: 10.2307/2696979.

Hochschild, Arlie Russell. 2017. *Strangers in Their Own Land: Anger and Mourning on the American Right.* New York: The New Press.

Hockenos, Paul. 2015. "The Stunning Hypocrisy of Mitteleuropa." *Foreign Policy,* September 12. Accessed November 15, 2015. http://foreignpolicy.com/2015/ 09/10/the-stunning-hypocrisy-of-mitteleuropa-refugees-poland-hungary-czech-republic/.

Hoffman, Lisa, Monica DeHart, and Stephen J. Collier. 2006. "Notes on the Anthropology of Neoliberalism." *Anthropology News* 47(6): 9–10.

Hong Kyungwon, Grace, and Roderick A. Ferguson. 2011. *Strange Affinities: The Gender and Sexual Politics of Comparative Racialization.* Minneapolis: University of Minnesota Press.

Horts, Pērs Bolīns. 2004. "'Svešie elementi': Latvijas Universitātes latviešu un ebreju studentu demarkācija un konflikts (1919–1940)." *Latvijas Arhīvi* 2004(4): 34. Accessed July 15, 2009. http://www.arhivi.lv/index.php?1&207&view=articles-of-topic&top_id=78.

Hübinette, Tobias. 2012. "'Words that Wound': Swedish Whiteness and Its Inability to Accommodate Minority Experience." In *Whiteness and Postcolonialism in the*

Nordic Region, edited by Kristín Loftsdóttir and Lars Jansen, 43–55. Farnham, UK: Ashgate Press.

Huggan, Graham. 2008. "Perspectives on Postcolonial Europe." *Journal of Postcolonial Writing* 44(3): 241–249. Accessed July 2, 2009. doi: 10.1080/17449850802230251.

Huggan, Graham, and Ian Law. 2009. *Racism: Postcolonialism Europe*. Liverpool: Liverpool University Press.

Huntington, Samuel. 1996. *The Clash of Civilizations and the Remaking of World Order*. New York: Touchstone.

Huysmans, Jef. 2006. *The Politics of Insecurity: Fear, Migration, and Asylum in the EU*. London: Routledge.

Hylland Eriksen, Thomas. 2016. *Overheating: An Anthropology of Accelerated Change*. Chicago: University of Chicago Press.

——. 2007. "On Negro Kings and Hottentots." Accessed April 3, 2014. http://hyllanderiksen.net/Hottentots.html

Ijabs, Ivars. 2016. "After the Referendum: Militant Democracy and Nation-Building in Latvia." *East European Politics and Societies and Cultures* 30(2): 288-314. Accessed July 15, 2017. doi: 10.1177/0888325415593630.

——. 2014. "Another Baltic Postcolonialism: Young Latvians, Baltic Germans, and the Emergence of Latvian National Movement." *Journal of Baltic Studies* 42(1): 88–107. Accessed January 15, 2015. doi: 10.1080/00905992.2013.823391.

——. 2012. "Break Out of Russia: Miķelis Valters and the National Issue in Early Latvian Socialism." *Journal of Baltic Studies* 43(4): 437–458. Accessed January 15, 2015. doi: 10.1080/01629778.2012.687901.

——. 2009. "Republikas vārdā." *Politika.lv*, November 17. Accessed January 15, 2015. http://politika.lv/article/republikas-varda

Indāns, Ivars. 2012. *Starptautiskās migrācijas procesi un Latvijas politika pēc pievienošanās ES*. Ph.D. diss., University of Latvia.

ĪUMSILS. 2008. *National Program for the Promotion of Tolerance, 2009–2013*. Riga: ĪUMSILS.

——. 2004. *National Program for the Promotion of Tolerance, 2004–2008*. Riga: ĪUMSILS. Accessed September 10, 2006. http://www.integracija.gov.lv/?id=276&top=43&sa=214.

——. 2003. *Kultūru daudzveidība un iecietība*. Riga: ĪUMSILS.

Izglītības attīstības centrs (IAC). 2008. *Kritiskās domāšanas attīstīšanas pieejas izmantošana izglītības sistēmā—ietekme un efektivitāte Latvijā*. Riga: IAC.

Jackson-Preece, Jennifer. 1997. "Minority Rights in Europe: From Westphalia to Helsinki." *Review of International Studies* 23: 75–92.

Jacobsen, Christine M. 2018. "The (In)egalitarian Dynamics of Gender Equality and Homotolerance in Contemporary Norway." In *Egalitarianism in Scandinavia: Historical and Contemporary Perspectives*, edited by Synnøve Bendixsen, Mary Bente Bringslid, and Halvard Vike, 313–336. London: Palgrave Macmillan.

Jakovļeva, Mārīte. 2010. "Veltījums Kurzemes literatūras un mākslas biedrībai." *Latvijas Arhīvi* 2010(2): 300–302.

Jansen, Stef. 2015. *Yearnings in the Meantime: 'Normal Lives' and the State in a Sarajevo Apartment Complex*. New York: Berghahn Books.

Jaunsudrabiņš, Jānis. 2006 [1927]. *Baltā grāmata*. Riga: Valters un Rapa.

Jekabson-Lemanis, Karin. 2000. "Balts in the Caribbean: The Duchy of Courland's Attempts to Colonize Tobago Island, 1638–1654." *Journal of Baltic Studies* 46(2): 25–44. Accessed February 3, 2017. http://jstor.org/stable/40654122.

Jirgens, Karl E. 2006. "Fusions of Discourse: Postcolonial/Postmodern Horizons in Baltic Culture." In *Baltic Postcolonialism*, edited by Violeta Kelertas, 45–82. Amsterdam: Rodopi.

Jundzis, Talavs. 2014. "Krievijas karaspeka izvesana no Latvijas 1992–1994: diplomatiska uzvara vai politiska piekapsanas?" *Latvijas Zinatnu Akademijas Vestis* 3(4): 4–23.

Juškevičs, Jānis. 1931. *Hercoga Jēkaba laikmets Kurzemē*. Riga: Valsts papīru spiestuve.

Keane, Webb. 2009. "Freedom and Blasphemy: On Indonesian Press Bans and Danish Cartoons." *Public Culture* 21(1): 47–76. Accessed February 2, 2010. doi: 10.1215/08992363-2008-021.

Kelertas, Violeta. 2006. "Introduction: Baltic Postcolonialism and Its Critics." In *Baltic Postcolonialism*, edited by Violeta Kelertas, 1–9. Amsterdam: Rodopi.

Keskinen, Suvi, Salla Tuori, Sari Irni, and Diana Mulinari. 2009. *Complying with Colonialism: Gender, Race and Ethnicity in the Nordic Region*. Farnham, UK: Ashgate Press.

Khalid, Adeeb. 2007. "The Soviet Union as an Imperial Formation: A View from Central Asia." In *Imperial Formations*, edited by Ann Laura Stoler, Carole McGranahan, and Peter C. Perdue, 113–140. Santa Fe: School for Advanced Research Press.

Kharkhordin, Oleg. 1999. *The Collective and the Individual in Russia: A Study of Practices*. Berkeley: University of California Press.

Khosravi, Shahram. 2010. *"Illegal" Traveller: An Auto-Ethnography of Borders*. London: Palgrave Macmillan.

Kideckel, David. 2009. "Citizenship Discourse, Globalization, and Protest: A Postsocialist-Postcolonial Comparison." *Anthropology of East Europe Review* 27(2): 117–133.

Kingsley, Patrick. 2015. "Sweden Calls on Army to Help Manage the Refugee Crisis." *The Guardian*, November 10. Accessed November 15, 2015. http://www.theguardian.com/world/2015/nov/10/sweden-calls-on-army-to-help-manage-refugee-crisis.

Kļave, Evita, and Brigita Zepa. 2010. "Etniskā integrācija Latvijā—pētnieciskais diskurss." *Socioloģija Latvijā*, edited by Tālis Tisenkopfs, 201–219. Riga: LU Akadēmiskais apgāds.

Kļaviņa, Sarma. 2010. "Par Kārļa Mīlenbaha zinātnisko mantojumu." *Latvijas Zinātņu Akadēmijas Vēstis*. Accessed July 15, 2012. http://www.lza.lv/LZA_VestisA/65_1-2/1_Letonika%20klavina.pdf.

Kļavis, Aivars. 2015. "Simtiem kilometru žoga." *IR*, November 25. Accessed March 20, 2017. http://www.irlv.lv/2015/11/25/simtiem-kilometru-zoga.

Klier, John. 1982. "'Zhid': Biography of a Russian Epithet." *Slavonic and East European Review* 60(1):1–15. Accessed January 24, 2010. http://www.jstor.org/stable/4208429.

Klimovičs, Roberts. 2013. "Bez 'deividsonmorāles'—par faktiem, žīdiem un ebrejiem." *Focus.lv*, Available: http://www.focus.lv/latvija/sabiedriba/bez-deividsonmorales-par-faktiem-zidiem-un-ebrejiem.

Knight, Daniel. 2015. *History, Time, and Economic Crisis in Central Greece*. London: Palgrave Macmillan.

Kohn, Hans. 2008 [1944]. *The Idea of Nationalism: A Study in Its Origins and Background*. Piscataway, NJ: Transaction Publishers.

Komorovskis, Broņislavs. 2015. "Cilvēcības vārdā." *Ir*, September 18. Accessed November 15, 2015. http://www.irir.lv/2015/9/18/cilvecibas-varda.

Koslofsky, Craig, and Robert Zaugg. 2016. "Ship's Surgeon Johann Peter Oettinger: A Hinterland in the Atlantic Slave Trade." In *Slavery Hinterland: Atlantic Slave*

Trade and Continental Europe, 1680–1850, edited by Felix Brahm and Eve Rosenhaft, 25–44. Woodbridge, UK: Boydell Press.

Kotef, Hagar. 2015. *Movement and the Ordering of Freedom: On Liberal Governances of Mobility*. Durham, NC: Duke University Press.

Krastev, Ivan. 2016. "What's Wrong with East-Central Europe? Liberalism's Failure to Deliver." *Journal of Democracy* 27(1): 35–39.

———. 2015. "Eastern Europe's Compassion Deficit." *New York Times*, September 8. Accessed November 10, 2015. http://www.nytimes.com/2015/09/09/opinion/eastern-europes-compassion-deficit-refugees-migrants.html?_r=0.

———. 2007. "The Strange Death of the Liberal Consensus." *Journal of Democracy* 18(4): 56–63.

Krauja, Vita. 2005. "Ierēdņa izaicinošā patvaļa." *Latvijas Avīze*, August 24.

Kraulis, Verners. 1939a. "Par iedzimto plānprātību Latvijā." *Tautas dzīvā spēka pētīšanas institūta raksti*: 42–72. Riga: Tautas labklājības ministrija.

———. 1939b. "Tautība un gara slimības." *Tautas dzīvā spēka pētīšanas institūta raksti*: 73–79. Riga: Tautas labklājības ministrija.

Kruk, Sergei. 2011. "Evicting the Speaking Subject: A Critique of Latvian Concepts of Language." *Journal of Baltic Studies* 42(4): 447–463.

Kruks, Sergejs, and Ilze Šulmane. 2005. *Neiecietības izpausmes un iecietības veicināšana medijos*. Riga: ĪUMSILS.

Krūmiņa-Koņkova, Solveiga, and Valdis Tēraudkalns. 2007. *Reliģiskā dažādība Latvijā: Stratēģijas iecietības veicināšanai*. Riga: Klints.

Kuznecovs, Vladmirs. 2013. "Latvian Psychiatry and Medical Legislation of the 1930s and the German Sterilisation Law." In *Baltic Eugenics: Bio-politics, Race and Nation in Interwar Estonia, Latvia and Lithuania, 1918–1940*, edited by Björn M. Felde and Paul J. Weindling, 147–167. Amsterdam: Rodopi.

Kwon, Heonik. 2010. *The Other Cold War*. New York: Columbia University Press.

Kymlicka, Will. 2007. "Multicultural Odysseys." *Ethnopolitics* 6(4): 585–597. Accessed March 20, 2017. doi: 10.1080/17449050701659789.

———. 1996. *Multicultural Citizenship: A Liberal Theory of Minority Rights*. Oxford: Clarendon Press.

Kymlicka, Will, and Magda Opalski, eds. 2002. *Can Liberal Pluralism Be Exported? Western Political Theory and Ethnic Relations in Eastern Europe*. Oxford: Oxford University Press.

Laitin, David. 1998. *Identity in Formation: The Russian Speaking Populations in the Near Abroad*. Ithaca: Cornell University Press.

Larmore, Charles. 1996. *The Romantic Legacy*. New York: Columbia University Press

Larson, Jonathan. 2013. *Critical Thinking in Slovakia after Socialism*. Rochester, NY: University of Rochester Press.

———. 2011. "Circulation of Critical Thinking." *Commentary in Anthropology News* 52(2): 7.

Lazarus, Neil. 2012. "Spectres Haunting: Postcommunism and Postcolonialism." *Journal of Postcolonial Writing* 48(2): 117–129. Accessed July 2, 2012. doi: 10.1080/17449855.2012.658243.

Lemon, Alaina. 2002. "Without a "Concept"? Race as a Discursive Practice." *Slavic Review* 61(1): 54–61. Accessed March 4, 2005. doi: 10.2307/2696981.

———. 2000. *Between Two Fires: Gypsy Performance and Romani Memory from Pushkin to Postsocialism*. Durham, NC: Duke University Press.

Lentin, Alana. 2004. *Racism and Anti-racism in Europe*. London: Pluto Press.

Levitt, Peggy. 2015. *Artifacts and Allegiances: How Museums Put the Nation and the World on Display*. Berkeley: University of California Press.

Linebaugh, Peter, and Mark Rediker. 2000. *The Many-Headed Hydra: Sailors, Slaves, and Commoners, and the Hidden History of the Revolutionary Atlantic.* Boston: Beacon Press.

Loader, Michael. 2015. *The Thaw in Soviet Latvia: Nationalities Politics, 1953–1959.* Ph.D. diss., King's College, London.

Locke, John. 2007 [1689]. *A Letter Concerning Toleration.* Minneapolis, MN: Filiquarian Publishing.

Loftsdóttir, Kristín, and Lars Jensen. 2012. *Whiteness and Postcolonialism in the Nordic Region.* Farnham, UK: Ashgate Press.

Lopes Marques, Joao. 2009. "Tobacco? No, Tobago!" *Baltic Times,* March 25.

Lulle, Aija. 2016. "Revitalising Border: Memory, Mobility and Materiality in a Latvian-Russian Border Region." *Culture Unbound* 8: 44–62. Accessed February 2, 2017. http://www.cultureunbound.ep.liu.se/v8/a05/cu16v8a05.pdf.

Lüthi, Barbara, Franceska Falk, and Patricia Purtschert. 2015. "Colonialism without Colonies: Examining Blank Spaces in Colonial Studies." *Identities* 18(1): 1–9. Accessed March 3, 2016. doi: 10.1080/14608944.2016.1107178.

Lyman, Rick. 2015. "Eastern Block's Resistance to Refugees Highlights Europe's Cultural and Political Divisions." *New York Times,* September 12. Accessed November 5, 2015. http://www.nytimes.com/2015/09/13/world/europe/eastern-europe-migrant-refugee-crisis.html.

MacIntyre. Alasdair. 1984. *After Virtue: A Study in Moral Theory.* Notre Dame: University of Notre Dame Press.

Mahmood, Saba. 2016. *Religious Difference in a Secular Age: A Minority Report.* Princeton: Princeton University Press.

——. 2012. "Religious Freedom, the Minority Question, and Geopolitics in the Middle East." *Comparative Studies in Society and History* 54(2): 418–446. Accessed July 5, 2013. doi: 10.1017/S0010417512000096.

——. 2009. "Religious Reason and Secular Affect: An Incommensurable Divide?" *Critical Inquiry* 35: 836–862. Accessed January 10, 2010. doi: 10.1086/599592.

——. 2005. *Politics of Piety: The Islamic Revival and the Feminist Subject.* Princeton: Princeton University Press.

Makarovs, Viktors. 2007. *Latvijas iedzīvotāju attieksme pret seksuālajām minoritātēm: gada tendences.* Riga: Dialogi.lv.

——. 2006. *Latvijas iedzīvotāju attieksme pret seksuālajām minoritātēm: Dimensijas un "temperature."* Riga: Dialogi.lv and the Soros Foundation Latvia.

Malakhov, Vladimir, and Alexander Osipov. 2006. "The Category of 'Minorities' in the Russian Federation: A Reflection on Uses and Misuses." In *International Obligations and National Debates: Minorities around the Baltic Sea,* edited by Sia Akermark Spiliopoulou, Leena Huss, Stefan Oeter, and Alastair Walker, 497–544. Mariehamn: Aland Peace Research Institute.

Mamdani, Mahmood. 2004. *Good Muslim, Bad Muslim: America, the Cold War and the Roots of Terror.* Harmony.

Mandel, Ruth. 2008. *Cosmopolitan Anxieties: Turkish Challenges to Citizenship and Belonging in Germany.* Durham, NC: Duke University Press.

Markell, Patchen. 2003. *Bound by Recognition.* Princeton: Princeton University Press.

Martin, Ben. 1991. "From Negro to Black to African American: The Power of Names and Naming." *Political Science Quarterly* 106(1): 83–107. Accessed August 10, 2016. doi: 10.2307/2152175.

Martin, Terry. 2001. *The Affirmative Action Empire: Nations and Nationalism in the Soviet Union, 1923–1939.* Ithaca: Cornell University Press.

Massad, Joseph A. 2007. *Desiring Arabs.* Chicago: University of Chicago Press.

Matīsa, Vita. 2007. "Vientuļais patriotisms." In *Diena*, November 16.

Mattiesen, Otto. 1940. *Die Kolonial- und Überseepolitik der kurländischen Herzöge im 17. und 18. Jahrhundert.* Stuttgart: Kolhammer.

Matusevich, Maxim. 2007. "Probing the Limits of Internationalism: African Students Confront Soviet Ritual." *Anthropology of East Europe Review* 27(2): 1–21.

Matza, Tomas. 2012. "'Good Individualism'? Psychology, Ethics and Neoliberalism in Postsocialist Russia." *American Ethnologist* 39(4): 804–818. Accessed January 15, 2015. doi: 10.1111/j.1548-1425.2012.01396.x.

Maussen, Marcel, and Ralph Grillo. 2013. "Regulation of Speech in Multicultural Societies: Introduction." *Journal of Ethnic and Migration Studies* 40(2): 174–193. Accessed August 2, 2016. doi: 10.1080/1369183X.2013.851470.

Mawhood, William. 2016. "Why You Will Almost Definitely Have to Change Your Name When Speaking Latvian." *Deep Baltic*, September 23. Accessed January 3, 2017. https://deepbaltic.com/2016/09/23/why-you-will-almost-definitely-have-to-change-your-name-when-speaking-latvian/.

McClure, Kirstie. 1990. "Difference, Diversity, and the Limits of Toleration." *Political Theory* 18(3): 361–391. Accessed March 15, 2005. http://www.jstor.org/stable/191593.

McDonald, Maryon. 2006. "Neo-Nationalism in Europe: Occupying the Available Space." In *Neo-nationalism in Europe and Beyond: Anthropological Perspectives*, edited by Andreas Gingrich and Marcus Banks, 218–236. New York: Berghahn.

M'charek, Amade, Katharina Schramm, and David Skinner. 2013. "Topologies of Race: Doing Territory, Population and Identity in Europe." *Science, Technology, and Human Values* 39(4): 1–20.

Mehta, Uday. 1999. *Liberalism and Empire: A Study in the Nineteenth-Century British Liberal Thought.* Chicago: Chicago University Press.

Mendus, Susan. 1989. *Toleration and the Limits of Liberalism.* London: Palgrave Macmillan.

Merķelis, Garlībs. 2005 [1797]. *Latvieši.* Riga: Zvaigzne ABC.

Merritt, Harry C. 2010. "The Colony of the Colonized: The Duchy of Courland's Tobago Colony and Contemporary Latvian National Identity." *Nationalities Papers* 38(4): 491–508. Accessed December 2, 2012. doi: 10.1080/00905992.2010.482131.

Mezzadra, Sandro, and Brett Neilsen. 2013. *Border as Method, Or the Multiplication of Labor.* Durham, NC: Duke University Press.

Mignolo, Walter. 2007. "Introduction." *Cultural Studies* 21(2/3): 151–167. Accessed March 10, 2010. doi: 10.1080/09502380601162498.

Mill, John Stuart. 2007 [1859]. *On Liberty.* Woodbridge, NJ: J. W. Parker.

Ministry of Foreign Affairs of the Republic of Latvia (MFA). 2005. *National Minorities in Latvia: Then and Now.* Riga: MFA.

Mirbahs, Otto. 2010 [1899]. *Vēstules par Kurzemes hercogu Jēkabu.* Translated by Elza Stērste. Jelgava: Allunans.

Mirowski, Philip. 2011. *Never Let a Serious Crisis Go To Waste: How Neoliberalism Survived the Financial Meltdown.* London: Verso Books.

Mitchell, Timothy. 1991. "The Limits of the State: Beyond Statist Approaches and Their Critics." *American Political Science Review* 85(1): 77–96. Accessed February 2, 2005. doi: 10.2307/1962879.

Mogilner, Marina. 2013. *Homo Imperii: A History of Physical Anthropology in Russia.* Lincoln: University of Nebraska Press.

Morgensen, Scott Lauria. 2011. *Spaces between Us: Queer Settler Colonialism and Indigenous Decolonization.* Minneapolis: University of Minnesota Press.

Morris, Rosalind C. 2010. "Introduction." In *Can the Subaltern Speak? In Reflections on the History of an Idea*, 1–20. New York: Columbia University Press.

Mountz, Alison. 2010. *Seeking Asylum: Human Smuggling and Bureaucracy at the Border*. Minneapolis: University of Minnesota Press.

Moyn, Samuel. 2010. *The Last Utopia: Human Rights in History*. Cambridge: Harvard University Press.

Muižnieks, Nils. 2005. "Latvia." In *Racist Extremism in Central and Eastern Europe*, edited by Cas Mudde, 101–128. London: Routledge.

Mūrniece, Ināra. 2006. "Starp vārda brīvību un naida kurināšanu."*Latvijas Avīze*, October 11.

——. 2005. "Intervija ar Dzintru Hiršu." *Latvijas Avīze*, November 24, 2005. Accessed December 10, 2009. http://apollo.tvnet.lv/zinas/par-meliem-kas-vieno-latviesus-un-krievus/320182.

Nantambu, Kwame. 2007. "Origin of Terms 'Negro' and Africa." Trinicenter.com.

Noack, Rick. 2017. "Lithuania Fears a Russian Invasion. Now, It Wants to Build a Border Fence." *The Washington Post*, January 17. Accessed March 20, 2017. https://www.washingtonpost.com/news/worldviews/wp/2017/01/17/lithuania-fears-a-russian-invasion-now-it-wants-to-build-a-border-fence/?utm_term=.914fc9a94d16.

Northrop, Douglas. 2004. *Veiled Empire: Gender and Power in Stalinist Central Asia*. Ithaca: Cornell University Press.

Ortner, Sherry. 2016. "Dark Anthropology and Its Others: Theory since the Eighties." *HAU: Journal of Ethnographic Theory* 6(1): 47–73. Accessed January 10, 2017. https://www.haujournal.org/index.php/hau/article/view/hau6.1.004.

Osis, Juris, and Liesma Ose. 2006. *Pētījumos balstītas stratēģijas tolerances veicināšanai*. Riga: Dialogi.vl and Soros Foundation Latvia.

Pabriks, Artis. 2003. *In Defiance of Fate: Ethnic Structure, Inequality, and Governance of the Public Sector in Latvia*. UNRISD.

Palsson, Gisli, and Margaret Lock. 2016. *Can Science Resolve the Nature/Nurture Debate?* Cambridge: Polity Press.

Pandian, Anand. 2008. "Tradition in Fragments: Inherited Forms and Fractures in the Ethics in South India." *American Ethnologist* 35(3): 466–480. Accessed May 25, 2009. doi: 10.1111/j.1548.2008.00048.x.

Papadopoulos, Dimitris, and Vassilis Tsianos. 2013. "After Citizenship: Autonomy of Migration, Organisational Ontology and Mobile Commons." *Citizenship Studies* 17(2): 178–196. Accessed January 15, 2014. doi: 10.1080/13621025.2013.780736.

Partridge, Damani. 2012. *Hypersexuality and Headscarves: Race, Sex, and Citizenship in the New Germany*. Bloomington: Indiana University Press.

Pelkmans, Mathijs. 2006. *Defending the Border: Identity, Religion and Modernity in the Republic of Georgia*. Ithaca: Cornell University Press.

Peshkova, Svetlana. 2014. "Teaching Islam at a Home School: Muslim Women and Critical Thinking in Uzbekistan." *Central Asian Survey* 33(1): 80–94. Accessed January 10, 2017. doi: 10.1080/02634937.2014.889869.

Pickles, John, and Adrian Smith. 2007. "Post-Socialism and the Politics of Knowledge Production." In *Politics and Practice in Economic Geography*, edited by Adam Tickell, Eric Sheppard, Jamie Peck, and Trevor Barnes, 151–162. Thousand Oaks, CA: Sage Publications.

Pilkington, Hilary. 1998. *Migration, Displacement, and Identity in Post-Soviet Russia*. Abingdon, UK: Psychology Press.

Plakans, Andrejs. 1999. "Looking Backward: The Eighteenth and Nineteenth Centuries in Inter-War Latvian Historiography." *Journal of Baltic Studies* 30(4): 293–306. Accessed July 3, 2008. http://www.jstor.org/stable/43212342.

Platt, Kevin M. F. 2015. "Lyric Cosmopolitanism in a Postsocialist Borderland." *Common Knowledge* 21(2): 305–326. Accessed November 15, 2016. doi: 10.1215/0961754X-2872391.

——. 2013. "Eccentric Orbit: Mapping Russian Culture in the Near Abroad." In *Empire De/Centered: New Spatial Histories of Russia*, edited by Sanna Turoma and Maxim Waldstein, 271–296. Farnham, UK: Ashgate.

Pomerantsev, Peter. 2015. *Nothing Is True and Everything Is Possible: The Surreal Heart of the New Russia*. London: Public Affairs.

Povinelli, Elizabeth. 2002. *The Cunning of Recognition: Indigenous Alterities and the Making of Australian Multiculturalism*. Durham, NC: Duke University Press.

Prakash, Gyan. 2000. "The Impossibility of Subaltern History." *Nepantla: Views From South* 1(2): 287–294.

Pred, Allan. 2000. *Even in Sweden: Racisms, Racialized Spaces, and The Popular Geographical Imagination*. Berkeley: University of California Press.

Procevska, Olga. 2013. "Labā krieva uzvedības kodekss." *Satori.lv*. Accessed March 2, 2014. http://www.satori.lv/raksts/5476/Laba_krieva_uzvedibas_kodekss.

Prokkola, Eeva-Kaisa. 2013. "Technologies of Border Management: Performances and Calculation of Finnish/Schengen Border Security." *Geopolitics* 18(1): 77–94. Accessed November 2, 2016. doi: 10.1080/14650045.2012.685791.

Puar, Jasbir. 2011. "Citation and Censorship. The Politics of Talking about the Sexual Politics of Israel." *Feminist Legal Studies* 19: 133–142. Accessed May 2, 2012. doi: 10.1007/s10691-011-9176-3.

——. 2007. *Terrorist Assemblages: Homonationalism in Queer Times*. Durham, NC: Duke University Press.

Pupovac, Ozren. 2010. "Present Perfect, or the Time of Post-Socialism." *Eurozine*. Accessed February 3, 2012. http://www.eurozine.com/articles/2010-05-12-pupovac-en.html.

Purs, Aldis. 2002. "The Price of Free Lunches: Making the Interwar Latvian in the Frontier." *Global Review of Ethnopolitics* 1(4): 60–73. Accessed March 13, 2007. doi: 10.1080/14718800208405113.

Purtschert, Patricia. 2015. "Aviation Skills, Manly Adventures and Imperial Tears: The Dhaulagiri Expedition and Switzerland's Techno-Colonialism." *Identities* 18(1): 53–56. Accessed January 10, 2016. doi: 10.1080/14608944.2016.1095492.

——. 2011. "Chewing on Post-Colonial Switzerland. Redigesting What Has Not Yet Been Swallowed, Part II." In *Chewing the Scenery*. edited by Andrea Thal, 95–100, 121–126, and 149–154. 2nd ed. Zurich: Swiss Federal Office of Culture.

Putnina, Aivita, Signe Mezinska, Kristians Zalans, and Arturs Poksans. 2015. *Patvēruma meklētāju uzņemšanā iesaistīto speciālistu un brīvprātīgo pieredze darbā ar patvēruma meklētājiem un garīgas veselības problēmu risināšana*. Riga: Slimību profilakses un kontroles centrs.

Quijano, Anibal. 2007. "Coloniality and Modernity/Rationality." *Cultural Studies* 21(2/3): 167–178. Accessed April 2, 2009. doi: 10.1080/09502380601164353.

Račevskis, Kārlis. 2002. "Towards a Postcolonial Perspective on the Baltic States." *Journal of Baltic Studies* 23(1). Accessed March 15, 2007. doi: 10.1080/01629770100000201.

Rainis, Jānis. 2006 [1908]. *Prieki Visās Gadskārtās*. Riga: Jāņa Rozes Apgāds.

Rastas, Anna. 2012. "Reading History through Finnish Exceptionalism." In *Whiteness and Postcolonialism in the Nordic Region*, edited by Kristín Loftsdóttir and Lars Jansen, 89–104. Farnham, UK: Ashgate Press.

Rawls, John. 1997. "The Idea of Public Reason Revisited." *University of Chicago Law Review* 64(3): 765–807. Accessed September 20, 2012. http://chicagounbound. uchicago.edu/cgi/viewcontent.cgi?article=5633&context=uclrev

Reeves, Madeleine. 2014. *Border Work: Spatial Lives of the State in Central Asia*. Ithaca: Cornell University Press.

——. 2005. "Of Credits, *Kontrakty*, and Critical Thinking: Encountering "Market Reforms" in Kyrgyzstani Higher Education." *European Educational Research Journal* 4(1): 5–21.

Reinsch Campbell, Anette. 2004. "Latvian Jewish Relations and Images of 'Them': Literature, Historical Consciousness and Questions of Guilt and Shame." *Baltic Sea Area Studies: Northern Dimensions of Europe*. Working papers edited by Berndt Hennigsne, Vol. 11.

Riekstiņš, Jānis, ed. 2004. *Migranti Latvijā. 1944–1989. Dokumenti*. Riga: Latvijas Valsts Arhīvi.

Riles, Annelise. 2006. "Anthropology, Human Rights, and Legal Knowledge: Culture in the Iron Cage." *American Anthropologist* 108(1): 52–65. Accessed November 4, 2016. http://www.jstor.org/stable/3804731.

Rogers, Douglas. 2010. "Postsocialisms Unbound." *Slavic Review* 69(1): 1–15. Accessed March 2, 2013. doi: 10.1017/S0037677900016673.

Roland, Gerard. 2015. "Why the Rift between Eastern and Western Europe on the Refugee Crisis?" *The Berkeley Blog*, September 9. Accessed November 4, 2015. http://blogs.berkeley.edu/2015/09/09/why-the-rift-between-eastern-and-western-europe-on-the-refugee-crisis-2/.

Rosga, AnnJanette. 2010. "The Bosnian Police, Multi-Ethnic Democracy and the Race of 'European Civilization.'" *Ethnic and Racial Studies* 33(4): 675–695. Accessed July 2, 2016. doi: 10.1080/01419870903362602.

Roze, Maira. 2006. "Migracijas politika Latvija." *Latvija Eiropas Savieniba* 2006(1): 10–12.

Rupnik, Jacques. 2015. "The Other Europe." *Eurozine*, September 16. Accessed November 10, 2015. http://www.eurozine.com/articles/2015-09-11-rupnik-en.html

Sabet-Parry, Rayyan, and Karl Ritter. 2015. "Scant Sympathy for Refugees in Europe's Ex-Communist East." *Business Insider*, September 11. Accessed November 15, 2015. http://www.businessinsider.com/ap-scant-sympathy-for-refugees-in-europes-ex-communist-east-2015-9?IR=T.

Saburova, Irina. 1955. "The Soviet Occupation of the Baltic States." *Russian Review* 14(1): 36–49.

Sahadeo, Jeff. 2007. "Druzhba Narodov or Second-Class Citizenship? Soviet Asian Migrants in a Post-Colonial world." *Central Asian Survey* 26(4): 559–579. Accessed June 27, 2014. doi: 10/1080/02634930802018463.

Said, Edward. 1978. *Orientalism*. London: Penguin.

Sassen, Saskia. 2014. *Expulsions: Brutality and Complexity in the Global Economy*. Cambridge, MA: Harvard University Press.

Schwartz, Katrina. 2006. *Nature and National Identity after Communism: Globalizing the Ethnoscape*. Pittsburgh: University of Pittsburgh Press.

Scott, David. 2014. *Omens of Adversity: Tragedy, Time, Memory, Justice*. Durham, NC: Duke University Press.

——. 2006. "The Tragic Sensibility of Talal Asad." In *Powers of the Secular Modern: Talal Asad and His Interlocutors*, edited by David Scott and Charles Hirschkind, 134–153. Stanford: Stanford University Press.

——. 2004. *Conscripts of Modernity: The Tragedy of Colonial Enlightenment*. Durham, NC: Duke University Press.

——. 2000. "Toleration and Historical Traditions of Difference." In *Community, Gender, and Violence*, edited by Partha Chatterjee and Pradeep Jeganathan, 283–304. New York: Columbia University Press.

——. 1999. *Refashioning Futures: Criticism after Postcoloniality*. Princeton: Princeton University Press.

Shekhovtsov, Anton. 2016. *Is Transition Reversible? The Case of Central Europe*. London: Legatum Institute.

Shevel, Oxana. 2012. "The Politics of Citizenship Policy in Post-Soviet Russia." *Post-Soviet Affairs* 28(1): 111–147.

Silova, Iveta. 2006. *From the Sites of Occupation to Symbols of Multiculturalism: Reconceptualizing Minority Education in Post-Soviet Latvia*. Greenwich, CT: Information Age Publishing.

Simecka, Michal, and Benjamin Tallis. 2015. "Fighting the Wrong Battle: A Crisis of Liberal Democracy, not Migration." *OpenDemocracy*, September 16. Accessed November 15, 2015. https://www.opendemocracy.net/can-europe-make-it/michal-simecka-benjamin-tallis/fighting-wrong-battle-central-europe's-crisis-is-o.

Skujiņa, Valentīna. 2007. "Latvijas Zinātņu akadēmijas Terminoloģijas komisija sešos gadu Desmitos." *LZA Vēstis*, March 24. Accessed January 3, 2017. http://termini.lza.lv/article.php?id=204.

——. 2003. "Terminoloģijas darbs Latvijā." *Terminoloģijas jaunumi*, October 21. Accessed January 5, 2017, http://termini.lza.lv/article.php?id=150.

Skultans, Vieda. 2008. *Empathy and Healing: Essays in Medical and Narrative Anthropology*. Oxford: Berghan Books.

Slezkine, Yuri. 2006. *The Jewish Century*. Princeton: Princeton University Press.

——. 1994. "The USSR as a Communal Apartment, or How a Socialist State Promoted Ethnic Particularism." *Slavic Review* 53(2): 414–452. Accessed October 17, 2007. doi: 10.2307/2501300.

Sooman, Imbi, Jesma McFarlane, Valdis Teraudkalns, and Stefan Donecker. 2013. "From the Port of Ventspils to Great Courland Bay: The Couronian Colony of Tobago in Past and Present." *Journal of Baltic Studies* 44(4): 503–526. Accessed September 4, 2016. doi: 10.1080/01629778.2013.835464.

Soros, George. 2017. "These Times Are Not Business as Usual. Wishing You the Best in a Troubled World." *Business Insider*, January 24. Accessed January 27, 2017. http://uk.businessinsider.com/george-soros-essay-on-trump-defending-an-open-society-2017-1?r=US&IR=T.

Sparke, Matthew. 2006. "A Neoliberal Nexus: Citizenship, Security, and the Future on the Border." *Political Geography* 25(2): 151–180. Accessed November 5, 2015. 10.1016/j.polgeo.2005.10.002.

Spekke, Arnolds. 2000. *Latvijas vesture*. Riga: Jumava.

Spivak, Gayatri Chakravorty. 1988. "Can the Subaltern Speak?" In *Marxism and the Interpretation of Culture*, edited by C. Nelson and Lawrence Grossberg, 271–313. London: Palgrave Macmillan.

Stalin, Joseph V. 1950. *Marxism and Problems of Linguistics*. Accessed March 19, 2017. https://www.marxists.org/reference/archive/stalin/works/1950/jun/20.htm.

Stikāne, Ilze. 2013. "'Ka tik kas nenotiek!' jeb cenzūra bērnu grāmatās." *Satori.lv*. Accessed October 2, 2015. http://www.satori.lv/article/ka-tik-kas-nenotiek-jeb-cenzura-bernu-gramatas.

Stoler, Ann Laura. 2002. *Carnal Knowledge and Imperial Power: Race and the Intimate in Colonial Rule*. Berkeley: University of California Press.

Stranga, Aivars. 2008. *Ebreji Baltijā: No ienākšanas pirmsākumiem līdz holokaustam. 14. gadsimts—1945. Gads*. Riga: Latvijas Vēsture.

Strods, Heinrihs. 1987. *Kurzemes kroņa zemes un zemnieki, 1795–1861*. Riga: Zinātne.

Šūpule, Inese. 2014. "Nepilsoņi Latvijā: nostiprinājusies vai izzūdoša tradīcija?" *Providus.lv*, May 28. Accessed on 2 July 2016. http://providus.lv/article/nepilsoni-latvija-nostiprinajusies-vai-izzudosa-tradicija.

Svece, Artis. 2008. "Ieviņa Āfrikā [Little Ieva in Africa]." *SestDiena*, May 17.

Tabūns, Aivars. 2010. "Socioloģija Latvijā: 20. Gadsimts" In *Socioloģija Latvijā*, edited by Tālis Tisenkopfs, 81–124. Riga: LU Akadēmiskais apgāds.

Tadiar, Neferti. 2011. "Remaindered Life of Citizen-Man, Medium of Democracy." *Southeast Asian Studies* 49(3): 464–495. Accessed May 2, 2013. https://barnard.edu/sites/default/files/remainderedlifepublished.pdf.

Tamir, Yael. 1995. *Liberal Nationalism*. Princeton: Princeton University Press.

Ticktin, Miriam. 2011. *Casualties of Care: Immigration and the Politics of Humanitarianism in France*. Berkeley: University of California Press.

Ticktin, Miriam, Paolo Bachetta, and Ruth Marshall. 2007. "A Transnational Conversation on French Colonialism, Violence, Immigration, and Sovereignty." The Scholar and Feminist Conference XXXII, "Fashioning Citizenship: Gender and Immigration," held on March 24, 2007 at Barnard College. http://sfonline.barnard.edu/immigration/conversation_01.htm.

Tisenkopfs, Tālis, ed. 2010. *Socioloģija Latvijā*. Riga: LU Akadēmiskais apgāds.

Tlostanova, Madina V., and Walter Mignolo. 2012. *Learning to Unlearn: Decolonial Reflections from Eurasia and the Americas*. Columbus: Ohio University Press.

Ture, Kwame, and Charles Hamilton. 1992 [1967]. *Black Power: The Politics of Liberation in America*. New York: Vintage Books.

Ule, Mirjana. 2014. "The Reconstruction of Sociology in Eastern Europe—Expectations and Dilemmas." *Sociology Mind* 2014(4): 264–271. Accessed July 3, 2016. doi: 10.4236/sm.2014.44027.

Urena, Lenny A. 2010. *The Stakes of Empire: Colonial Fantasies, Civilizing Agendas, and Biopolitics in the Prussian-Polish Provinces (1840–1914)*. Ph.D. diss., University of Michigan.

van Dijk, Teun A. 2002. "Denying Racism: Elite Discourse and Racism." In *Race Critical Theories*, edited by Philomena Essed and David Theo Goldberg, 307–324. Malden: Blackwell Publishers.

Veisbergs, Andrejs. 2008. "Valodas politikas viļņos." *Diena*, May 14.

Verdery, Katherine. 1994. "Beyond the Nation in Eastern Europe." *Social Text* 38 (spring): 1–19. Accessed January 30, 2013. doi: 10.2307/466501.

Vollmer, Bastian. 2016. "New Narratives from the EU External Border—Humane Refoulement?" *Geopolitics* 21(3): 717–741.

Vuorela, Ulla. 2009. "Colonial Complicity." In *Complying with Colonialism: Gender, Race and Ethnicity in the Nordic Region*, edited by Suvi Keskinen, Salla Tuori, Sari Irni, and Diana Mulinari, 19–34. Farnham, UK: Ashgate Press.

Walzer, Michael. 1997. *On Toleration*. New Haven: Yale University Press.

Warner, Michael. 2005. *Publics and Counterpublics*. Zed Books.

Weeks, Theodore. 2013. "Religious Tolerance in the Russian Empire's Northwest Provinces." *Kritika: Explorations in Russian and Eurasian History* 14(4): 876–884. Accessed May 14, 2014. doi: 10.1353/kri.2013.0051.

Weitz, Eric D. 2008. "From the Vienna to the Paris System: International Politics and the Entangled Histories of Human Rights, Forced Deportations, and Civilizing Missions." *American Historical Review* 2008 (December): 1313–1343. Accessed May 2, 2009. http://www.jstor.org/stable/30223443.

——. 2002. "Racial Politics without the Concept of Race." *Slavic Review* 61(1): 1–29. Accessed November 3, 2007. doi: 10.2307/2696978.

Westbrook, David A. 2016. "Losing Our Manners: The Current Crisis and Possible Durability of Liberal Discourse." *Hot Spots, Cultural Anthropology* website, October 27. Accessed November 15, 2016. https://culanth.org/fieldsights/980-losing-our-manners-the-current-crisis-and-possible-durability-of-liberal-discourse

Wilson, Thomas W., and Hastings Donnan. 1998. *Border Identities: Nation and State at International Frontiers*. Cambridge: Cambridge University Press.

Wimmer, A., and Glick Schiller, N. 2002 "Methodological Nationalism and Beyond: Nation-State Building, Migration, and the Social Sciences." *Global Networks* 2(4): 301–334. Accessed March 3, 2004. http://www.jstor.org/stable/30037750.

Wodak, Ruth, Majid KhosraviNik, and Brigitte Mral. 2013. *Right-Wing Populism in Europe: Politics and Discourse*. London: Bloomsbury.

Woolard, Kathryn, and Bambi Schieffelin. 1994. "Language Ideology." *Annual Review of Anthropology* 23: 55–82.

Yurchak, Alexei. 2015. "Bodies of Lenin: The Hidden Science of Communist Sovereignty." *Representations* 129(1): 116–157. Accessed June 15, 2016. doi: 10.1525/rep.2015.129.1.116.

——. 2005. *Everything Was Forever Until It Was No More: The Last Soviet Generation*. Princeton: Princeton University Press.

Zakaria, Fareed. 1997. "The Rise of Illiberal Democracy." *Foreign Affairs* 76(6): 22–43.

Zake, Ieva. 2010. *American Latvians: Politics of a Refugee Community*. Piscataway, NJ: Transaction Publishers.

——. 2007a. "Nationalism and Statism in Latvia: The Past and Current Trends." Unpublished article. Accessed July 15, 2008. http://users.rowan.edu/~zake/papers/index.html.

——. 2007b. "Inventing Culture and Nation: Intellectuals and the Early Latvian Nationalism." *National Identities* 9(4): 307–329. Accessed July 15, 2008. doi: 10.1080/14608940701737359.

——. 2013. "Laiks, telpa, vadonis: Autoritārisma kultūra Latvijā, 1934–1940." Hanovs, Deniss & Teraudkalns, Valdis. *Journal of Baltic Studies* 44(2): 275–278. Accessed June 15, 2015. doi: 10.1080/01629778.2013.793450

Zalsters, Artūrs Eižens. 2002. *Hercoga Jēkaba burinieki*. Riga: Izdevniecība AGB.

Zarycki, Tomasz. 2014. *Ideologies of Eastness in Central and Eastern Europe*. London: Routledge.

Zelče, Vita. 2009. *Latviešu Avīžniecība: Laikraksti savā laikmetā un sabiedrībā. 1822–1865*. Riga: Zinātne.

——. 2006. "Vara, zinātne, veselība un cilvēki: Eigēnika Latvijā 20. gs. 30. Gados." *Latvijas Arhīvi* 3: 94–137.

——. 2000. "Dažas tendences Baltijas pētniecībā rietumos 20. Gadsimta noslēgumā." *Latvijas Arhīvi* 3: 105–124.

Zellis, Kaspars. 2012. *Ilūziju un baiļu mašinērija. Propaganda nacistu okupētajā Latvijā: vara, mediji un sabiedrība (1941–1945)*. Riga: Mansards.

Ziedonis, Imants. 1979. *Kurzemīte*. Riga: Liesma.

Ziemele, Inese. 2003. "Slivenko pret Latviju." *Providus.lv*, November 1. Accessed on July 5, 2016. http://providus.lv/article/slivenko-pret-latviju.

Zvidriņš, Pēteris. 2005. "Demogrāfiskā situācija šodien un rīt." *Zinātniski pētnieciskie raksti* 3(4). Riga: Zinātne.

Index

Pages numbers followed by f or n indicate figures or notes

Abdi (Latvian of African descent), 27–29
"African American," used in United States, 158
African Latvian Association (ALA), 7, 27, 96–98, 100, 104, 108, 161–62, 164
Somalis and, 174–75
Aija (facilitator), 165–70, 175
Aktürk, Sener, 45
Aldis (philosopher), 168
Aleksandrs (Roma representative), 164–65
Alikhanov, Anton, 209
Alunāns, Juris, 32
Amsler, Sarah, 89–90
Andersons, Edgars, 33–34, 36–38
Anna (language inspector), 75–79, 202
Antiethnic regimes, 45, 47
Anti-Semitism, tolerance promotion and, 97
Anthropology
displacement and, 171–172
physical anthropology, 120–124
tolerance and, 11
Arendt, Hannah, 115, 139, 172–73
Asad (Somali), 1
Ash, Timothy Garton, 99
Atlantic slave trade, 20, 23, 37–40
"A Tu Neliecies" (Don't Get into My Face) (Bankovskis), 133–34, 136–37
Australia, 18, 39–40, 88, 158
Awakenings
first awakening, 148, 219n27
national awakening, 29–30, 32, 62, 148
third awakening, 70

Backman, Gustav, 121
Baldunčiks, Juris, 150
Baltā Grāmata (The White Book) (Bankovskis), 144
Baltic German historiography, 29–34, 148
Bankovskis, Pauls, 133–34, 136–37, 139, 144
Barons, Krišjānis, 32
Belorussia/Belarus, 62–63, 69–70, 152–53, 208–209, 218n8
Bērziņš, Uldis, 126
Beliaev, Alexandre, 57–58

Bels, Alberts, 35–36
Belševica, Vizma, 128
Bender, Jeremy, 209
Berķis, Alexander, 33, 34 (Aleksandrs Berķis)
Berklavs, Eduards, 59
Bielenstein, August, 29
"Black," used in United States, 158
Blaumanis, Rudolfs, 153, 168
Border tensions, 10, 174–206
fences and, 207–14
liberal and nationalist discourse and, 203–6
post-Soviet residents and, 193–203
reestablishing borders and managing migration, 178–86
racial profiling and, 182
Seven Somalis and asylum process, 186–93
see also State Border Guard, Latvian
Bockman, Johanna, 15
Böröcz, József, 23, 43
Boyer, Dominic, 118
Brīvzemnieks, Fricis, 32
Briesmonis (The Monster) (Rainis), 156–57
Brown, Wendy, 209
Brubaker, Rogers, 49, 169
Buck-Morss, Susan, 36, 37
Burkhalter, Nancy, 116
Butler, Judith, 142, 145, 159, 171–73
Button, Mark, 114, 115

Čigāni, Latvians and use of, 158, 164, 165, 167
Carmichael, Stokely, 158
Césaire, Aimé, 23
Chari, Sharad, 26
Chatterjee, Partha, 43
Chernyi, used in Russia, 162
Cilvēki laivās (People in Boats) (Bels), 35–36
Citizenship
defined by exclusion, 79
former Soviet citizens and, 26, 46, 50, 64–65, 71, 89, 106, 191–92, 194–98, 201–204, 206
1994 Law of Citizenship, 46
non-citizens, 146
Cittautieši (other peoples), 166–71

Clifford, James, 37
Collier, Stephen, viii
Colonialism, contemporary moral and
    political landscape of, 8, 19–43
    Atlantic slave trade's history and, 20, 23,
        37–38
    compartmentalization of colonialism in
        Europe, 40
    Latvia's pride in history and aspirations of
        Europeanness, 19–24
    postcolonial and postsocialist theories and,
        24–29
    self-confidence and simultaneous
        identification with and distancing from,
        38–43
    struggle for history and, 29–34
"Colonialism without colonies," 38–39
"Colony of the Colonized: the Duchy
    of Courland's Tobago Colony and
    Contemporary Latvian National Identity,
    The" (Merritt), 21
"Colored," used in United States, 158
Common European Asylum System, 184
"Communities of value," 45, 47, 205
Courland, Duchy of, 19–21, 31–37, 40–41
Creed, Gerald, 91, 137–39
Critical publicity, 115, 119
Critical thinking, and tolerance promotion, 89,
    92, 105, 112–40
    affect and limits of liberal tolerance, 137–40
    eugenics and Europeanness, 120–24
    intolerance and, 125–27
    irony and limits of tolerance, 133–37
    kritika and, 116–20
    public reflection and types of distancing,
        114–15, 118, 128–33, 138
    teaching of, 127–29

Daniel (civil servant), 102–103, 161–70
Danish cartoon scandal, 144–45
De Genova, Nicholas, 22–23
DeHart, Monica, viii
"Deterritorialized milieus," 118
Diagnostic mode of knowledge production,
    tolerance promotion and, 85–88, 109–10
Dialogi (NGO), 54
Diena (Bankovskis), 133–34
Differential inclusion, 138
Di Mullen expedition, 33
Displacement, language and, 171
Distancing
    from colonial history, 29, 38–43
    critical thinking and, 114–15, 118, 128–33, 136

Druviete, Ina, 149
Du Bois, W. E. B., 158
Dunsdorfs, Edgards, 33

Ērgle, Zenta, 157
Eastern Europe, limits of critical discourse
    and, 15–18
Ebrejs, Latvians and use of, 151, 152, 154–55,
    162, 163, 167–68, 173
Education, critical thinking and, 116, 127–29
Embedded reason, 137
    distinguished from public reason, 114–15
End of history narrative, vii, 15, 18, 85, 113,
    171, 205, 211, 213
Endzelīns, Jānis, 148, 149, 152, 154
Eriksen, Thomas Hylland, 145, 160
Ethnicity
    Latvians and nationhood, 58, 95, 135
    regimes of, 45–48
    Soviet policies and, 46, 58, 60–61, 69, 74
    see also Migrants/refugees
"Ethno-symbolist theory," 22
Eugenics, and Europeanness, 120–24
European Commission Against Racism and
    Intolerance, 6, 85, 86, 94
European Court of Human Rights, 194
Europeanness
    becoming European and, x, 3, 7, 10–12, 16,
        23, 43, 58, 81, 176–77, 206
    catching up with Europe, 10–11, 109
    complicities of Europeanness, 39–40, 42–43
    as civilizational aspiration, 21–24, 27, 29, 31,
        74, 91, 99, 158–59, 179
    exclusions and inclusion and, 1–18, 50, 79,
        138–39, 153, 176–77, 181, 183, 186, 203
    Latvia's pride and aspirations and, 19–24
    liberal Europe, ix, 11–13, 15, 17, 41–42
    liberalism linked with and tolerance in
        Latvia, 84–85
    logics of difference and, 10–15
    paradox of, 7–12, 50, 176–77, 182, 203
European Union, 12, 27, 56, 91, 93, 116, 136,
    141, 198–99
    borders and migration and, 3–5, 179–86
    Latvia and, vii–ix, 6, 79, 103, 149, 164, 170,
        176–79, 191–92, 207
Evreiskie zapisi (journal), 154
Ezergailis, Andrievs, 122, 154

Falk, Francesca, 38–39
Felder, Björn, 120–24, 133, 172
Felsbergs, Edgars, 154
Fences, at borders, 207–14

Fikes, Kesha, 39
Financial crisis of 2008–10, vii
    Latvian responsibility versus Greek debt, 4–5
    migrants and, 185–86, 212
Follis, Karolina, 179
Foucault, Michel, 122
Framework Convention for the Protection of
    National Minorities, 48, 56, 63, 74, 87
France
    as antiethnic state, 45
    migration/refugee crisis and, 13, 185
Freiberga, Vaira Vīķe, 167
Funk, Nanette, 17

Gambia, 20, 27–28, 33–36, 40, 42
Gapova, Elena, 24–25, 81, 84, 103–5, 120
Geneva Convention, refugees and, 180
German Democratic Republic (GDR), 118
German Romanticism, 32
Germany
    as monoethnic state, 45
    as national state, 44
Gia (Georgian citizen), 199–201
Gille, Zsuzsa, 25
Gilroy, Paul, 37
Glaeser, Andreas, 98, 108–9, 110
Golubeva, Marija, 107
Gordons, Frank, 154–55
Grāvere, Rita, 122
Greece, sovereign debt crisis in, 4–5, 12
Grīsle, Rasma, 152
Grillo, Ralph, 142
"Groupism," 49
Gullestad, Marianne, 39, 160

Haley, Alex, 34
Hall, Stuart, 25
Hayek, Friedrich, 212
Hill, Jane, 95
Hirša, Dzintra, 143
Hirsch, Francine, 58, 94
History
    Baltic-German historiography, 29–30
    counterhistory tactics, 32–33
    historical agency, 31, 36–38, 143, 152,
        156–57
    Latvian historiography, 22, 31, 124
    place in history and, 36
    struggle for, 29–34
    see also Colonialism; Courland, Duchy of
Hoffman, Lisa, viii
Holbrook, Richard, 15
Holocaust in Latvia (Ezergailis), 154

Homophobia, 18, 94, 97, 100, 125–26
Human Rights Organization, state boarder
    guards and, 175, 177, 186, 188, 189–92, 202

Ieviņa Āfrikā (Little Ieva in Africa) (Ērgle and
    Stāraste), 157
Igor (citizenship seeker), 195–97
Ijabs, Ivars, 31, 51
"Illiberal democracies," 15, 210
Indans, Ivars, 179
Inese (local Latvian), 19, 21
Inga (filmmaker), 35, 36
Innocence
    claims of, 39, 145
    historical, linguistic, 101, 143, 152, 154–61
    racial, 94
Inside the War Room (BBC), 210
Institute for Research of National Vitality, 121
Interconnectedness, language and ethics of,
    171–73
International Covenant on Civil and Political
    Rights, of UN, 63
International Helsinki Federation for Human
    Rights, 6
Intolerance, as critical position, 125–27
Irony, limits of tolerance and, 133–37
Israel, 18, 44, 172–73

Jānis (Latvian living in California), 34–36
Jackson, Jesse, 158
Jacobsen, Christine, 47
Jaunsudrabiņš, Jānis, 144
Jesse, Barnor, 160
Jewish Community Association, 7, 98, 137–38,
    161, 168
Jews, Latvian citizenship and, 45–46
Jyllands-Posten, 144–45

Kārlis (news managing director), 54–55
Keane, Webb, 144–45
Ketler, Duke Jacob, 19–20, 21, 23, 27, 33, 36,
    40, 42
Khrushchev, Nikita, 47
Kļave, Evita, 90
Klier, John, 152
Knowledge production
    diagnostic mode of, 85–88, 109–10
    partial knowledge, 100
    understanding and, 97–104
Kolya (language testee), 75–79
Kosachev, Konstantin, 209
Koslofsky, Craig, 20
Kozlovskis, Rihards, 208

Krastev, Ivan, viii, 211
Kraulis, Verners, 122
Kritika, critical thinking and, 116–20
Krodznieks, Jānis, 29, 36
Kronvalds, Atis, 32
Kruks, Sergejs, 112–13, 146–47
Kuļikovskis, Gundars, 5
Kruk, Sergei (Sergejs Kruks), 151–52
Kuznecovs, Vladmirs, 122
Kwon, Heonik, 25
Kymlicka, Will, 63

Labor migrants, 180, 201
Laila (conference attendee), 98, 101–2, 161–65, 168
Laiks (diaspora paper), 154–55
Laitin, David, 55, 193
Language, and ethical encounters with Other,
    9–10, 141–73, 188
  ethics of interconnectedness, 171–73
  injurious language, 10, 146, 152, 163
  intolerance in, 142–43
  historicist linguistic ideology, 151–52, 154
language ideologies, 145–146, 151
  naming and tolerance seminars, 161–65
  non-Latvians and ethics, 165–71
  power and, 146–51, 152, 154–55, 170
  use of *čigāni*, 158, 164, 165, 167
  use of *chernyi*, 162
  use of *ebrejs*, 151, 152, 154–55, 162, 163,
    167–68, 173
  use of *leiši*, 152
  use of *melnais*, 162
  use of *nēģeris*, 143, 145, 146, 155–61, 162,
    165, 173
  use of *negr*, 167
  use of *zhid*, 152–53, 154
  use of *žīds*, 143–46, 150–55, 158, 162–64,
    165, 167–68, 173
  Seven Somalis and asylum process, 188
Language inspectors, 75–78, 202
Larmore, Charles, 136–37
Larson, Jonathan, 126–27
Latvia
  border fence with Russia and, 207–14
  loss of independence to Soviet Union, 34
  migration/refugee crisis of 2015 and, 3
  national awakening of, 29–30, 32, 62, 148
  as national state, 44
  proclaimed independent state, 30, 51
  as racial state, 121–23
Latvian Center for Human Rights and Ethnic
    Studies (now Latvian Center for Human
    Rights), 94

Latvian Institute, 21
Latvian Institute of History, 30
Latvian language
  discipline and required use of, 74–79
  Russian-speaking residents without
    knowledge of, 56–62
Latvian State Language Center, 143, 149
Latvian Language Commission, 149
Latvian Language Terminology and Spelling
    Commission, 149
Latvian State Language Law, 50, 64, 74–75, 78,
    148–49
Latviešu Avīzes (newspaper), 148
Latvijas krievi (Latvian Russians), 166–67
Law of Citizenship (1994), 46
Law on Asylum, 187
"Law on the Entry and Residence of Foreigners
    and Stateless Persons in Latvia" (2002), 180
Lazarus, Neil, 25
League of Nations, 52
Leiši, Latvians and use of, 152
Lemon, Alaina, 94
Lenin, Vladimir, 212
Levinas, Emmanuel, 172–73
LGBT organizations, 7, 92, 100, 125–27, 190
Liberalism
  actually existing, viii–ix, 8, 9, 12, 109, 111,
    113, 115, 119, 211, 214
  crisis of political liberalism, 207–14
  illiberalism, viii–x, 13, 15, 110, 145, 206
  as immune from critique, 140
  lessons in political liberalism, x, 3–12, 23, 42,
    50, 79, 109–11
  liberal democracy, viii, x, 7, 15, 17, 38–40, 47
  liberal/illiberal nationalism, 45
  post–Cold War political, vii, viii–ix, 6, 8, 12,
    53, 109, 111, 112, 119, 211
Liberal legal theory, Valters and, 31–32
Lindgren, Astrid, 160
Linebaugh, Peter, 37
Loader, Michael, 59–60
Lopes Marques, João, 19, 21, 22
Lucas, Edward, 211
Lüthi, Barbara, 38–39

Mājas Viesis, 148
Māris (expedition member), 28–29
Maija (civil servant), 125–26, 198
Makarov, Viktor, 107
*Masquerade and Postsocialism: Ritual and
    Cultural Dispossession in Bulgaria*
    (Creed), 137–39
Matīsa, Vita, 128, 129, 131

INDEX 253

Mattiesen, Otto von, 33–34
Maussen, Marcel, 142
Melnais, Latvians and use of, 162
Merritt, Harry C., 21–22, 23, 24
Mīlenbahs, Kārlis, 148
Michael (African American living in Latvia),
	95–99, 155–57, 159, 171–73
Mignolo, Walter, 27
Migrants/refugees, 3–4, 6, 12, 13–15, 54–55
	argument of "too many," 13–15
	control of migration, 179–81
	crisis of, ix–x, 3–4, 6, 12–14, 173, 186, 195,
		207, 211
	national minorities distinguished from,
		62–69, 66f, 67f
	political liberalism and, 207–14
	Soviet migration and, 180–81, 192
Milenbahs, Karlis, 149
Military personnel (Soviet), remaining in
	Latvia without citizenship, 193–94
Minorities, Latvian self-perception and, 56–62
Mirowski, Philip, vii, 212
Monoethnic regimes, 45
Moore, Richard, 157–58
Morgensen, Scott Lauria, 18
Moyn, Samuel, 204
Muižnieks, Nils, 6, 62–63
Multiethnic regimes, 45
Muslims, 11, 18, 47, 71, 83, 95, 108, 131,
	144–45

Naming, language and tolerance seminars,
	161–65, 167
Narodnichestvo (Russian populism), Valters
	and, 31–32
National minorities, migrants distinguished
	from, 62–69, 66f, 67f
National Program for Support of National
	Minorities, 69
National Program for the Promotion of
	Tolerance, 6–7, 69, 81–83, 86, 92, 94,
	97–99, 101, 102, 129, 146, 156, 161
	Consultative Council of, 104
	See also Tolerance promotion
National state, with minority problem, 8–9,
	44–80
	exemplary national minority subjects, 69–71
	history of Soviet socialism and national
		state development, 50, 51–55
	Latvian language and, 74–79
	nationalities, minorities, and Latvian self-
		perceptions, 56–62, 66f, 67f
	national awakening, 29–30, 32, 62, 148

national minorities and migrants
	distinguished, 62–69
national state and political liberalism, 44–46,
	79–80
	Russian-speaking residents and conduct
		expectations, 48–50
	Russian-speaking residents disenfranchised,
		46–47
	"state people," 52–55, 58, 79, 82, 84, 130,
		164–65, 172
	statism and nationalism, 51–55
	svoi chelovek and, 71–74
	tensions between Soviet history and
		European present, 79–80
NATO, ix, 179
Nēģeris, Latvians and use of, 143, 145, 146,
	155–61, 162, 165, 173
"Negro," used in United States, 157–60
Nelatvieši (non-Latvians), 166–71
Neoliberalism, viii
	financial crisis of 2008–10 and Latvian
		responsibility versus Greek debt, 4–5
Negr, Latvians and use of, 167
Non-Latvians, language and ethical encounters
	with, 165–71
Nonliberal authoritarian personality, 108
Norway, 39, 47, 159–60

Office of Citizenship and Migration Affairs,
	178, 179–80, 183–86, 198
"On the Reinstatement of Citizenship Rights
	and the Basic Principles of Naturalization
	in the Republic of Latvia" (1991), 193
Orbán, Victor, 13

Palme, Olaf, 44
Pēterburgas Avīzes, 148
Pēteris (Lativan TV producer), 35, 36, 40,
	166–70
Pētersone, Baiba, 48
Performativity, theory of, 135, 142–43, 147,
	161, 164
Pirmie (They Were the First) (film), 175
Plakans, Andrejs, 30
Poland, 3, 15, 19, 41
Political correctness, language and non-
	Latvians, 165–71
Popper, Karl, 116
Popular Front (*Tautas fronte*), 48, 49, 70
Populist political actors, crisis of liberalism
	and, 110–11
Portugal, 39, 157
Positivism, 123–24

Postsocialist theory, Latvia and postcolonial theory, 24–29
Povinelli, Elizabeth, 18, 39–40
Preussler, Ottfried, 160
Prīmanis, Jēkabs, 121, 122
Proper nouns, Latvianizing of, 149–50
Providus (public policy center), 146
Puar, Jasbir, 18
Public reason, distinguished from embedded reason, 114–15
Pupovac, Ozra, 92–93
Purs, Aldis, 52
Purtschert, Patricia, 38–39

"Quarrel dialogue," 112–13

Račevskis, Kārlis, 35–36
Racial hygiene. *See* Eugenics, and Europeanness
Racial state, Latvia as, 121–23
Racism
    partial understanding of and tolerance promotion, 93–97
    use of nēģeris and, 158
Rainis, Jānis, 156–57
Raita (language inspector), 75–79, 202
Rastsvet-sblizhenie-sliianie (flourishing-drawing together), 58
Reason, conceived through Romantic lens, 136–37
Rediker, Mark, 37
Reeves, Madeleine, 116
Regimes of ethnicity/regimes of value, 45–48
Reiris, Jānis, 5
Rietumnieki (Westerners), 88
Riga Latvian Association (*Rīgas Latviešu biedrība*), 32
Riles, Annelise, 204
Rimšēvics, Ilmārs, 5
Robert (of African Latvian Association), 108, 162–65, 174–75
Roma, 7, 63, 95, 101–2, 138–39, 161–62
    language terminology for, 162–65
Roots (Haley), 34
Roze, Maira, 180
Rule of colonial difference, 43
Rule of European difference, 43
Runāsim latviski! (Let's speak Latvian) campaign, 57
Russia, Latvian border with, 178, 207–14. *See also* Soviet Union
Russia-Latvia Agreement on Withdrawal of Troops (1994), 193, 194

Russian-speaking residents, without knowledge of Latvian language, 56–62
Russia Today, 209
Russification, 48, 59–62, 70, 143, 149

"Sackers," 67–68, 68f, 69f
Savējie (people who recognize each other as fellow travelers), 201
Scott, David, 16
Segodna (publication), 167
Self-perceptions, of Latvians, 56–62
"Seven Somalis," 1–2, 174–78, 185, 195, 204
    Latvian asylum system and, 186–93
Shegebayev, Maganat R., 116
Sigita (foster home "mom"), 175–76
Signe (political scientist), 85–88, 89, 100, 103, 105, 108, 109, 128
Silova, Iveta, 49
Skepticism, about tolerance, 114, 124
Skroderdienas Silmačos (Blaumanis), 153
Skujiņa, Valentīna, 149
Slezkine, Yuri, 58
Slivenko, Tatyana, 194
Smith, Anthony D., 22
Šmits, Janis, 154
Socialism, supposed lack of critical thinking under, 115–20
Sociology, in postsocialist Latvia, 90–91
Somalis. *See* "Seven Somalis"
Soros, George, 116, 128
Soros Foundation, 90, 116
Soviet citizens, as illegal migrants after end of Cold War, 191–203
Soviet socialism, national-state development and, 50, 51–55, 56–62
Soviet Union
    border and migration control and, 181–83
    border guard methods of, 175–76
    Latvian citizenship and former residents of, 26, 46, 50, 64–65, 71, 89, 106, 191–92, 194–98, 201–204
    Latvia and, 22, 24, 26, 28
    Latvian language and, 143–44, 147, 149, 151, 154
    as multiethnic regime, 45
    socialism and national state development, 50, 51–55
    Soviet mentality, 89, 119, 203, 205
    Soviet nationalities policy, 10, 48, 53, 57, 65, 84,, 89, 145, 147
    Soviet people, 8, 46–47, 50, 55–63
    see also Russia
Spekke, Arnolds, 33

Spirit and System: Media, Intellectuals, and the Dialectic in the Modern German Culture (Boyer), 118
Stāraste, Margarita, 157
Stalin, Josef, 59, 117, 212
State Border Guard, Latvian, 1, 175–78, 181–99, 207–9
"State Holiday" (Belševica), 128
Stranga, Aivars, 122, 151, 153, 154
Stučka, Pēteris, 154
Substantive traditions, public reason and, 114–15, 127, 129
Šulmane, Ilze, 112–13, 146–47
Svoi chelovek, 71–74
Sweden
    migration/refugee crisis of 2015 and, 13–14
    as national state, 44
Switzerland, 39

Tabūns, Aivars, 90
Tatar Cultural Association, 71, 73
Tatar women (svoi), 71–74
Teachers, tolerance promotion and, 107–8
Tisenkopfs, Tālis, 90
Tlostanova, Madina, 28–29
Tobago (musical), 21
Tobago Island. *See* Courland, Duchy of
Tolerance promotion, 81–111
    affect and limits of, 137–140
    comparisons made in evolutionary scale, 91
    competing understandings of tolerance, 81–83, 99
    diagnostic mode of knowledge production and, 85–88, 109–10
    Kārlis on, 54
    lack of recognition of intolerance, 97–104
    Latvian concerns about social virtue and future of nation, 83–84
    liberalism linked with Europeanness, 84–85
    liberal virtue designation and, 79–80
    postsocialist reorientation of understandings and knowledge, 88–93
    racism and partial understanding of intolerance, 93–97
    skepticism about, 114, 124
    for teachers, 161–65
    use of term, 7–8
    see also Critical thinking, and tolerance promotion; Language, and ethical encounters with Other
Tolerance workers, 27, 80
    demographics of, 6–7
    See also Tolerance promotion

Trump, Donald, 210
Turkey
    as antiethnic state, 45
    migration/refugee crisis of 2015 and, 12
Tur plīvoja Kurzemes karogi (Andersons), 33

Ulmanis, Kārlis, 30, 52–53, 66, 108, 120, 128, 133
UN Declaration of Human Rights, 86
UN Declaration on the Elimination of Racial Discrimination,, 86
UN Development Program, 90
United States
    African Americans and, 157–60
    Native Americans and, 18
Urena, Lenny A., 41

Vārna, Jākobs Pētersens, 33
Vadim (non-Latvian speaker), 75–76, 78
Vaidere, Inese, 5
Valdemārs, Krišjānis, 32, 148
Valters, Miķelis, 31–32
Van Dijk, Teo, 107
Verdery, Katherine, 26
Vesti (publication), 167
Viensētas (single farmsteads), 130–31
Vijupe, Liga, 175
Vladimir (Belorussian artist), 69–71

Walton, Douglas, 112
Weitz, Eric, 94
"West and the Rest," 25–27
Westbrook, David, viii, 170–71

Xenophobia, 90, 106, 121

Yerofeyev, Victor, 27
Young Latvian movement, 32, 148
Yurchak, Alexei, 72, 110, 118

Zālīte, Māra, 21
Zaiga (donor organization staffer), 98–99
Zaķe, Ieva, 51
Zakaria, Fareed, 15
Zaugg, Roberto, 20
Zelče, Vita, 122
Zellis, Kaspars, 153–54
Zhid, Latvians and use of, 152–53, 154
Žīds, Latvians and use of, 143–46, 150–55, 158, 162–64, 165, 167–68, 173
Zinta (human rights employee), 190–91
Zvidriņš, Pēteris, 122

CPSIA information can be obtained
at www.ICGtesting.com
Printed in the USA
FSHW04n0544070318
45163FS